Mill, James, 1773-1836

Analysis of the phenomena
of the human mind

REPRINTS OF ECONOMIC CLASSICS

ANALYSIS OF THE PHENOMENA
OF THE HUMAN MIND

VOLUME I

ANALYSIS

OF THE

PHENOMENA

OF THE

HUMAN MIND

BY

JAMES MILL

SECOND EDITION

[1869]

TWO VOLUMES

VOLUME I

REPRINTS OF ECONOMIC CLASSICS

AUGUSTUS M. KELLEY · PUBLISHERS
NEW YORK · 1967

First Edition 1829

Second Edition, with Notes Illustrative & Critical
by ALEXANDER BAIN, ANDREW FINDLATER & GEORGE
GROTE, *Edited with Additional Notes by*
JOHN STUART MILL, *1869*

(London: Longmans, Green, Reader & Dyer, 1869)

Reprinted 1967 by
AUGUSTUS M. KELLEY · PUBLISHERS

Library of Congress Catalogue Card Number
67 -28292

PRINTED IN THE UNITED STATES OF AMERICA
by SENTRY PRESS, NEW YORK, N. Y. 10019

ANALYSIS

OF THE PHENOMENA OF THE

HUMAN MIND

BY JAMES MILL

WITH NOTES ILLUSTRATIVE AND CRITICAL BY

ALEXANDER BAIN

ANDREW FINDLATER

AND

GEORGE GROTE

EDITED WITH ADDITIONAL NOTES BY

JOHN STUART MILL

IN TWO VOLUMES

VOL. I.

SECOND EDITION

LONDON

LONGMANS, GREEN, READER, AND DYER.

1878

"In order to prepare the way for a just and comprehensive system of Logic, a previous survey of our nature, considered as a great whole, is an indispensable requisite."—*Philosophical Essays* (*Prelim. Dissert.*) p. lxvii. *by Dugald Stewart, Esq.*

"Would not Education be necessarily rendered more systematical and enlightened, if the powers and faculties on which it operates were more scientifically examined, and better understood?"—*Ibid.* p. xlviii.

PREFACE

THE PRESENT EDITION.

IN the study of Nature, either mental or physical, the aim of the scientific enquirer is to diminish as much as possible the catalogue of ultimate truths. When, without doing violence to facts, he is able to bring one phenomenon within the laws of another; when he can shew that a fact or agency, which seemed to be original and distinct, could have been produced by other known facts and agencies, acting according to their own laws; the enquirer who has arrived at this result, considers himself to have made an important advance in the knowledge of nature, and to have brought science, in that department, a step nearer to perfection. Other accessions to science, however important practically, are, in a scientific point of view, mere additions to the materials : this is something done towards perfecting the structure itself.

The manner in which this scientific improvement takes place is by the resolution of phenomena which are special and complex into others more general and simple. Two cases of this sort may be roughly distinguished, though the distinction between them will not be found on accurate examination to be fundamental. In one case it is the order of the phenomena that is analysed and simplified ; in the other it is the phenomena themselves. When the observed facts relating to the weight of terrestrial objects, and those relating to the motion of the heavenly bodies, were found to conform to one and the same law, that of the gravitation of every particle of matter to every other particle with a force varying as the inverse square of the distance, this was an example of the first kind. The order of the phenomena was resolved into a more general law. A great number of the successions which take place in the material world were shewn to be particular cases of a law of causation pervading all Nature. The other class of investigations are those which deal, not with the successions of phenomena, but with the complex phenomena themselves, and disclose to us that the very fact which we are studying is made up of simpler facts : as when the substance Water was found to be an actual compound of two other bodies, hydrogen and oxygen ; substances very unlike itself, but both actually present in every one of its particles. By processes like those employed in this case, all the variety of substances which meet our senses and compose the planet on which we live, have been shewn to be constituted by the intimate union, in a certain number of fixed proportions, of some two or more of sixty or seventy bodies, called Elements or Simple Substances, by which is only meant that they have not hitherto been found capable of further decomposition. This last process is known by the name of chemical analysis : but the first mentioned, of which the Newtonian gene- ralization is the most perfect type, is no less analytical. The difference is, that the one analyses substances into simpler substances ; the other, laws into simpler laws. The one is partly a physical operation ; the other is wholly intellectual.

Both these processes are as largely applicable, and as much required, in the investigation of mental pheno- mena as of material. And in the one case as in the other, the advance of scientific knowledge may be measured by the progress made in resolving complex facts into simpler ones.

The phenomena of the Mind include multitudes of facts, of an extraordinary degree of complexity. By observing them one at a time with sufficient care, it is possible in the mental, as it is in the material world, to obtain empirical generalizations of limited compass, but of great value for practice. When, however, we find it possible to connect many of these detached generalizations together, by discovering the more general laws of which they are cases, and to the operation of which in some particular sets of circumstances they are due, we gain not only a scientific, but a practical advantage ; for we then first learn how far we can rely on the more limited generalizations ; within what conditions their truth is confined ; by what changes of circumstances they would be defeated or modified.

Not only is the order in which the more complex mental phenomena follow or accompany one another, reducible, by an analysis similar in kind to the Newtonian, to a comparatively small number of laws of succession among simpler facts, connected as cause and effect ; but the phenomena themselves can mostly be shewn, by an analysis resembling those of chemistry, to be made up of simpler phenomena.   " In the " mind of man," says Dr. Thomas Brown, in one of his Introductory Lectures, " all is in a state of con- " stant and ever-varying complexity, and a single " sentiment may be the slow result of innumerable " feelings.   There is not a single pleasure, or pain, or " thought, or emotion, that may not, by the influence " of that associating principle which is afterwards to " come under our consideration, be so connected with " other pleasures, or pains, or thoughts, or emotions, " as to form with them, for ever after, an union the " most intimate. The complex, or seemingly complex, " phenomena of thought, which result from the con- " stant operation of this principle of the mind, it is " the labour of the intellectual inquirer to analyse, as

"it is the labour of the chemist to reduce the com-
"pound bodies on which he operates, however close
"and intimate their combination may be, to their
"constituent elements. . . . From the very instant
"of its first existence, the mind is constantly exhibit-
"ing phenomena more and more complex: sensations,
"thoughts, emotions, all mingling together, and
"almost every feeling modifying, in some greater or
"less degree, the feelings that succeed it; and as, in
"chemistry, it often happens that the qualities of
"the separate ingredients of a compound body are
"not recognizable by us in the apparently different
"qualities of the compound itself,—so in this spon-
"taneous chemistry of the mind, the compound senti-
"ment that results from the association of former
"feelings has, in many cases, on first consideration,
"so little resemblance to these constituents of it, as
"formerly existing in their elementary state, that it
"requires the most attentive reflection to separate,
"and evolve distinctly to others, the assemblages
"which even a few years may have produced." It is,
therefore, "scarcely possible to advance even a single
"step, in intellectual physics, without the necessity
"of performing some sort of analysis, by which we
"reduce to simpler elements some complex feeling
"that seems to us virtually to involve them."

These explanations define and characterize the task
which was proposed to himself by the author of the

present treatise, and which he concisely expressed by naming his work an Analysis of the Phenomena of the Human Mind. It is an attempt to reach the simplest elements which by their combination generate the manifold complexity of our mental states, and to assign the laws of those elements, and the elementary laws of their combination, from which laws, the subordinate ones which govern the compound states are consequences and corollaries.

The conception of the problem did not, of course, originate with the author; he merely applied to mental science the idea of scientific inquiry which had been matured by the successful pursuit, for many generations, of the knowledge of external nature. Even in the particular path by which he endeavoured to reach the end, he had eminent precursors. The analytic study of the facts of the human mind began with Aristotle; it was first carried to a considerable height by Hobbes and Locke, who are the real founders of that view of the Mind which regards the greater part of its intellectual structure as having been built up by Experience. These three philosophers have all left their names identified with the great fundamental law of Association of Ideas; yet none of them saw far enough to perceive that it is through this law that Experience operates in moulding our thoughts and forming our thinking powers. Dr. Hartley was the man of genius who first clearly

discerned that this is the key to the explanation of
the more complex mental phenomena, though he, too,
was indebted for the original conjecture to an otherwise forgotten thinker, Mr. Gay. Dr. Hartley's
treatise ("Observations on Man") goes over the whole
field of the mental phenomena, both intellectual and
emotional, and points out the way in which, as he
thinks, sensations, ideas of sensation, and association,
generate and account for the principal complications
of our mental nature. If this doctrine is destined to
be accepted as, in the main, the true theory of the
Mind, to Hartley will always belong the glory of
having originated it. But his book made scarcely any
impression upon the thought of his age. He incum-
bered his theory of Association with a premature
hypothesis respecting the physical mechanism of sensation and thought; and even had he not done so, his
mode of exposition was little calculated to make any
converts but such as were capable of working out the
system for themselves from a few hints. His book is
made up of hints rather than of proofs. It is like the
production of a thinker who has carried his doctrines
so long in his mind without communicating them, that
he has become accustomed to leap over many of the intermediate links necessary for enabling other persons
to reach his conclusions, and who, when at last he sits
down to write, is unable to recover them. It was
another great disadvantage to Hartley's theory, that its

publication so nearly coincided with the commencement
of the reaction against the Experience psychology, pro-
voked by the hardy scepticism of Hume. From these
various causes, though the philosophy of Hartley never
died out, having been kept alive by Priestley, the elder
Darwin, and their pupils, it was generally neglected,
until at length the author of the present work gave
it an importance that it can never again lose. One
distinguished thinker, Dr. Thomas Brown, regarded
some of the mental phenomena from a point of view
similar to Hartley's, and all that he did for psychology was in this direction; but he had read Hartley's
work either very superficially, or not at all: he seems
to have derived nothing from it, and though he made
some successful analyses of mental phenomena by
means of the laws of association, he rejected, or
ignored, the more searching applications of those laws;
resting content, when he arrived at the more difficult
problems, with mere verbal generalizations, such as
his futile explanations by what he termed "relative
suggestion." Brown's psychology was no outcome
of Hartley's; it must be classed as an original but
feebler effort in a somewhat similar direction.

It is to the author of the present volumes that the
honour belongs of being the reviver and second
founder of the Association psychology. Great as is
this merit, it was but one among many services which
he rendered to his generation and to mankind. When

the literary and philosophical history of this century comes to be written as it deserves to be, very few are the names figuring in it to whom as high a place will be awarded as to James Mill. In the vigour and penetration of his intellect he has had few superiors in the history of thought : in the wide compass of the human interests which he cared for and served, he was almost equally remarkable : and the energy and determination of his character, giving effect to as single-minded an ardour for the improvement of mankind and of human life as I believe has ever existed, make his life a memorable example. All his work as a thinker was devoted to the service of mankind, either by the direct improvement of their beliefs and sentiments, or by warring against the various influences which he regarded as obstacles to their progress : and while he put as much conscientious thought and labour into everything he did, as if he had never done anything else, the subjects on which he wrote took as wide a range as if he had written without any labour at all. That the same man should have been the author of the History of India and of the present treatise, is of itself sufficiently significant. The former of those works, which by most men would have been thought a sufficient achievement for a whole literary life, may be said without exaggeration to have been the commencement of rational thinking on the subject of India : and by that, and his subsequent labours as an administrator of Indian interests under the East India Company, he effected a great amount of good, and laid the foundation of much more, to the many millions of Asiatics for whose bad or good government his country is responsible. The same great work is full of far-reaching ideas on the practical interests of the world; and while forming an important chapter in the history and philosophy of civilization (a subject which had not then been so scientifically studied as it has been since) it is one of the most valuable contributions yet made even to the English history of the period it embraces. If, in addition to the History and to the present treatise, all the author's minor writings were collected; the outline treatises on nearly all the great branches of moral and political science which he drew up for the Supplement to the Encyclopædia Britannica, and his countless contributions to many periodical works; although advanced thinkers have outgrown some of his opinions, and include, on many subjects, in their speculations, a wider range of considerations than his, every one would be astonished at the variety of his topics, and the abundance of the knowledge he exhibited respecting them all. One of his minor services was, that he was the first to put together in a compact and systematic form, and in a manner adapted to learners, the principles of Political Economy as renovated by the genius of Ricardo: whose great

work, it may be mentioned by the way, would probably never have seen the light, if his intimate and
attached friend Mr. Mill had not encouraged and
urged him, first to commit to paper his profound
thoughts, and afterwards to send them forth to the
world. Many other cases might be mentioned in
which Mr. Mill's private and personal influence was a
means of doing good, hardly inferior to his public
exertions. Though, like all who value their time for
higher purposes, he went little into what is called
society, he helped, encouraged, and not seldom
prompted, many of the men who were most useful in
their generation : from his obscure privacy he was
during many years of his life the soul of what is now
called the advanced Liberal party; and such was the
effect of his conversation, and of the tone of his character, on those who were within reach of its influence,
that many, then young, who have since made themselves honoured in the world by a valuable career,
look back to their intercourse with him as having had
a considerable share in deciding their course through
life. The most distinguished of them all, Mr. Grote,
has put on record, in a recent publication, his sense
of these obligations, in terms equally honourable to
both. As a converser, Mr. Mill has had few equals ;
as an argumentative converser, in modern times probably none. All his mental resources seemed to be
at his command at any moment, and were then freely

employed in removing difficulties which in his writings
for the public he often did not think it worth while
to notice. To a logical acumen which has always
been acknowledged, he united a clear appreciation of
the practical side of things, for which he did not
always receive credit from those who had no personal
knowledge of him, but which made a deep impression
on those who were acquainted with the official correspondence of the East India Company conducted by
him. The moral qualities which shone in his conversation were, if possible, more valuable to those who
had the privilege of sharing it, than even the intellectual. They were precisely such as young men of
cultivated intellect, with good aspirations but a character not yet thoroughly formed, are likely to derive
most benefit from. A deeply rooted trust in the
general progress of the human race, joined with a
good sense which made him never build unreasonable
or exaggerated hopes on any one event or contingency;
an habitual estimate of men according to their real
worth as sources of good to their fellow-creatures, and
an unaffected contempt for the weaknesses or tempta-
tions that divert them from that object,—making
those with whom he conversed feel how painful it
would be to them to be counted by him among such
backsliders ; a sustained earnestness, in which neither
vanity nor personal ambition had any part, and which
spread from him by a sympathetic 'contagion to those

who had sufficient moral preparation to value and seek the opportunity; this was the mixture of qualities which made his conversation almost unrivalled in its salutary moral effect. He has been accused of asperity, and there was asperity in some few of his writings; but no party spirit, personal rivalry, or wounded *amour-propre* ever stirred it up. Even when he had received direct personal offence, he was the most placable of men. The bitterest and ablest attack ever publicly made on him was that which was the immediate cause of the introduction of Mr. Macaulay into public life. He felt it keenly at the time, but with a quite impersonal feeling, as he would have felt anything that he thought unjustly said against any opinion or cause which was dear to him; and within a very few years afterwards he was on terms of personal friendship with its author, as Lord Macaulay himself, in a very creditable passage of the preface to his collected Essays, has, in feeling terms, commemorated.

At an early period of Mr. Mill's philosophical life, Hartley's work had taken a strong hold of his mind; and in the maturity of his powers he formed and executed the purpose of following up Hartley's leading thought, and completing what that thinker had begun. The result was the present work, which is not only an immense advance on Hartley's in the qualities which facilitate the access of recondite thoughts to minds to which they are new, but attains an elevation far beyond Hartley's in the thoughts themselves. Compared with it, Hartley's is little more than a sketch, though an eminently suggestive one : often rather showing where to seek for the explanation of the more complex mental phenomena, than actually explaining them. The present treatise makes clear, much that Hartley left obscure : it possesses the great secret for clearness, though a secret commonly neglected—it bestows an extra amount of explanation and exemplification on the most elementary parts. It analyses many important mental phenomena which Hartley passed over, and analyses more completely and satisfactorily most of those of which he commenced the analysis. In particular, the author was the first who fully understood and expounded (though the germs of this as of all the rest of the theory are in Hartley) the remarkable case of Inseparable Association: and inasmuch as many of the more difficult analyses of the mental phenomena can only be performed by the aid of that doctrine, much had been left for him to analyse.

I am far from thinking that the more recondite specimens of analysis in this work are always successful, or that the author has not left something to be corrected as well as much to be completed by his successors. The completion has been especially the work of two distinguished thinkers in the present generation, Professor Bain and Mr. Herbert Spencer; in the writings of both of whom, the Association Psychology has reached a still higher development. The former of these has favoured me with his invaluable collaboration in annotating the present work. In the annotations it has been our object not only to illustrate and enforce, but to criticise, where criticism seemed called for. What there is in the work that seems to need correction, arises chiefly from two causes. First, the imperfection of physiological science at the time at which it was written, and the much greater knowledge since acquired of the functions of our nervous organism and their relations with the mental operations. Secondly, an opening was made for some mistakes, and occasional insufficiency of analysis, by a mental quality which the author exhibits not unfrequently in his speculations, though as a practical thinker both on public and on private matters it was quite otherwise ; a certain impatience of detail. The bent of his mind was towards that, in which also his greatest strength lay ; in seizing the larger features of a subject—the commanding laws which govern and connect many phenomena. Having reached these, he sometimes gives himself up to the current of thoughts which those comprehensive laws suggest, not stopping to guard himself carefully in the minutiæ of their application, nor devoting much of his thoughts to anticipating all the objections that

could be made, though the necessity of replying to
some of them might have led him to detect imperfections in his analyses. From this cause (as it appears
to me), he has occasionally gone further in the pursuit
of simplification, and in the reduction of the more
recondite mental phenomena to the more elementary,
than I am able to follow him ; and has left some of
his opinions open to objections, which he has not
afforded the means of answering. When this appeared
to Mr. Bain or myself to be the case, we have made
such attempts as we were able to place the matter in
a clearer light ; and one or other, or both, have supplied what our own investigations or those of others
have provided, towards correcting any shortcomings
in the theory.

Mr. Findlater, of Edinburgh, Editor of Chambers'
Cyclopædia, has kindly communicated, from the
rich stores of his philological knowledge, the cor-
rections required by the somewhat obsolete philology
which the author had borrowed from Horne Tooke.
For the rectification of an erroneous statement respecting the relation of the Aristotelian doctrine of General
Ideas to the Platonic, and for some other contributions
in which historical is combined with philosophical interest, I am indebted to the illustrious historian of
Greece and of the Greek philosophy. Mr. Grote's, Mr.
Bain's and Mr. Findlater's notes are distinguished by
their initials ; my own, as those of the Editor.

The question presented itself, whether the annotations would be most useful, collected at the end of the work, or appended to the chapters or passages to which they more particularly relate. Either plan has its recommendations, but those of the course which I have adopted seemed to me on the whole to preponderate. The reader can, if he thinks fit, (and, if he is a real student, I venture to recommend that he should do so) combine the advantages of both modes, by giving a first careful reading to the book itself, or at all events to every successive chapter of the book, without paying any attention to the annotations. No other mode of proceeding will give perfectly fair play to the author, whose thoughts will in this manner have as full an opportunity of impressing themselves on the mind, without having their consecutiveness broken in upon by any other person's thoughts, as they would have had if simply republished without comment. When the student has done all he can with the author's own exposition—has possessed himself of the ideas, and felt, perhaps, some of the difficulties, he will be in a better position for profiting by any aid that the notes may afford, and will be in less danger of accepting, without due examination, the opinion of the last comer as the best.

CONTENTS

OF

THE FIRST VOLUME.

ANALYSIS

ETC.

INTRODUCTION

"I shall inquire into the original of those ideas, notions, or whatever else you please to call them, which a man observes and is conscious to himself he has in his mind; and the ways whereby the understanding comes to be furnished with them."

Locke, i. 1, 3.

PHILOSOPHICAL inquiries into the human mind have for their main, and ultimate object, the exposition of its more complex phenomena.

It is necessary, however, that the simple should be premised; because they are the elements of which the complex are formed; and because a distinct knowledge of the elements is indispensable to an accurate conception of that which is compounded of them.

The feelings which we have through the external senses are the most simple, at least the most familiar, of the mental phenomena. Hence the propriety of commencing with this class of our feelings.

CHAPTER I.

SENSATION.

" I shall not at present meddle with the physical consideration
of the mind, or trouble myself to examine wherein its essence
consists ; or by what motions of our spirits, or alterations of our
bodies, we come to have any Sensation by our organs, or any
Ideas in our understandings ; and whether those ideas do in
their formation, any or all of them, depend on matter or no.
These are speculations which, however curious and entertaining,
I shall decline, as lying out of my way in the design I am now
upon."—*Locke*, i. 1, 2.

My object, in what I shall say respecting the
phenomena classed under the head of SENSATION, is,
to lead such of my readers as are new to this species
of inquiry to conceive the feelings distinctly. All
men are familiar with them ; but this very familiarity,
as the mind runs easily from one well known object to
another, is a reason why the boundary between them
and other feelings is not always observed. It is
necessary, therefore, that the learner should by
practice acquire the habit of reflecting upon his
Sensations, as a distinct class of feelings ; and should
be hence prepared to mark well the distinction
between them and other states of mind, when he

advances to the analysis of the more mysterious phenomena.

What we commonly mean, when we use the terms Sensation or phenomena of Sensation, are the feelings which we have by the five senses,—SMELL, TASTE, HEARING, TOUCH, and SIGHT. These are the feelings from which we derive our notions of what we denominate the external world;—the things by which we are surrounded : that is, the antecedents of the most interesting consequents, in the whole series of feelings, which constitute our mental train, or existence.

The feelings, however, which belong to the five external Senses are not a full enumeration of the feelings which it seems proper to rank under the head of Sensations, and which must be considered as bearing an important part in those complicated phenomena, which it is our principal business, in this inquiry, to separate into their principal elements, and explain. Of these unnamed, and generally unregarded, Sensations, two principal classes may be distinguished :—first, Those which accompany the action of the several muscles of the body ; and, secondly, Those which have their place in the Alimentary Canal.[1]

---

[1] Important points of Psychology are raised in classifying the senses, and in assigning the order of their exposition. The author justly animadverts on the insufficiency of the common enumeration of the Five Senses, and indicates two grand omissions—the Muscular Sensibilities, and the feelings associated with Digestion.

With regard to the first omission—the Muscular Feelings,—a further advance has been found requisite.   Instead of adding these to the list, as a sixth sense, they are made a genus apart, and put in contrast to the Sensations as commonly understood. They are the feelings of our ACTIVITY, of the Active side of our nature, and are in relation to the Motor or Outcarrying nerves of the body. The Sensations proper, such as Smell and Hearing, are the feelings of our RECEPTIVITY, or Passivity, and arise in connection with the Sentient, or Incarrying nerves. In the exercise of the senses, however, a muscular element is almost always combined. This is conspicuous in Touch, which is most frequently accompanied with movements of the hand, or other parts touched ; it is also the case with Sight, there being six muscles constantly engaged in moving the eye-ball. There is least muscularity in Hearing and Smell, but in neither is it wholly absent. Thus in Hearing, there are certain small muscles for adjusting the tightness of the membrane of the tympanum ; apart from which, there are movements of the head in conjunction with hearing. So in Smell ; the sniffing action with the breath is muscular. Nevertheless, it is easy to separate, in all the senses, the passive and proper sensibility of the sense, (called by Hamilton the *idiopathic* sensibility) from the active accompaniment. We can make experiments upon passive touch, or pure contact ; we can isolate in our consciousness the optical sensibility of the eye ; we can eliminate activity from the ear ; and we can attend to the sensations of smell in their pure passivity.

The best course of proceeding is to deal with Muscularity apart, in the first instance, and to give it the priority in the order of exposition. Chronologically it is an earlier fact of our being ; we move before we feel ; there is an inborn energy of action in the animal system, which goes out, as it were, and meets the objects of sensation. This is one reason of priority. Another is the fact just stated that movement accompanies all the senses, or is a common factor in sensation. To discuss its peculiar sensibility is thus a preparation for treating of the senses.

The importance of drawing a broad line between the active and the passive branches of our primary sensibilities is seen in various applications, but most especially in the problem of

External Perception. The great distinction that this problem
requires us to draw between the external and the internal
sides of our being (so described by an imperfect metaphor)
has its deepest foundation in the distinction between the sense
of expended muscular energy and the feelings that are neither
energy in themselves, nor vary definitely according to our
energies. The qualities of things admitted on all hands to be
qualities of the external (or object) world—called the Primary
Qualities,—Resistance and Extension,—are modes of our
muscular energies ; the qualities that do not of themselves
suggest externality, or objectivity,—the secondary qualities, as
Heat, Colour, &c.—are our passive sensibilities, and do not
contain muscular energy. When these secondary qualities
enter into definite connections with our movements, they are
then referred to the external, or object world. Light and
colour, when varying definitely with our various movements,
as postures and actions, are from that circumstance referred to
the external, or *non-ego ;* without such connections they would
be called internal or subjective states.

The contrasted terms ' Object' and ' Subject' are the least
exceptionable for expressing the fundamental antithesis of
consciousness and of existence. Matter and Mind, External
and Internal, are the popular synonyms, but are less free from
misleading suggestions. Extension is the Object fact by
pre-eminence ; Pleasure and Pain are the most marked phases
of pure Subjectivity. Between the consciousness of extension
and the consciousness of a pleasure there is the broadest line
that can be drawn within the human experience ; the broadest
distinction in the whole universe of being. These then are
the Object and Subject extremes ; and, in the final analysis,
the object extreme appears to be grounded on the feeling of
expended muscular energy.

The second omission alluded to is the Digestive Sensibility,
which ought undoubtedly to be included among sensations,
having all the constituents of a sense ; an object—the food ;
a sensitive organ—the stomach ; and a characteristic form of
sensibility or feeling. The author farther takes notice of

'Sensations of Disorganization, or of the approach to Disorganization, in any part of the body,' which too deserve to be reckoned among mental facts. He might farther have adverted to the acute and depressing feelings of the Lungs, in case of partial suffocation, with the exhilaration attending the relief from such a state, and the change from a close to a fresh atmosphere. Moreover, there are states of purely physical comfort, associated with a vigorous circulation, with healthy innervation, with the proper action of the skin ; and feelings of discomfort and depression from the opposite states. A slight allusion to these various feelings occurs in chapter second towards the close.

These various modes of sensibility seem to be fitly grouped together under the common head of Sensations of Organic Life : their detail being arranged according to the several organs—viz.—the Alimentary Canal, Lungs, Circulation, Nervous System, &c. These would make a sixth Sense properly so called, or a department of passive sensibility.—*B*.

SECTION I.

SMELL.

It is not material to the present purpose in what order we survey the subdivisions of this elementary class of the mental phenomena. It will be convenient to take those first, which can be most easily thought of by themselves ; that is, of which a conception, free from the mixture of any extraneous ingredient, can be most certainly formed. For this reason we begin with SMELL.[2]

---

[2] The order of exposition of the senses is not a matter of indifference. The author, like Condillac, selected Smell to begin with, as being a remarkably simple and characteristic feeling ; he has found another expository advantage in it, by disturbing our routine mode of regarding the intellect as principally made up of sensations of sight. It has a startling effect on the reader, to suggest a mental life consisting wholly of smells and ideas of smell.

There are two principles of arrangement of the senses, each good for its own purpose ; it being understood that the active or muscular sensibility is taken apart from, and prior to, sensation proper.

The first is to take them in the order of Intellectual development. Some of the senses are evidently intellectual in a high degree, as Sight and Hearing, others are intellectual in a much smaller degree, as Smell and Taste. The organic sensations are still less connected with the operations of the intellect. Many of the least intellectual sensations are remarkably intense, as pleasure and pain ; perhaps more so than the intellectually higher class. The organic pains are more unendurable than

In the Smell three things are commonly distinguished. There is the ORGAN, there is the SENSATION,
and there is the antecedent of the Sensation, the ex-

---

the worst pains of hearing or of sight, unless these are
assimilated to the other class, by injury of the organs.

The intellectual superiority of the higher senses shows itself
in two ways, the one strictly in the domain of Intellect, the
other in the domain of Feeling. As regards Intellect, it is
shown in the predominance of the ideas of the higher senses.
Our intellectual or ideal trains, the materials of thought and
knowledge, are made up most of all of ideas of sight, next of
ideas of hearing, to a less degree of ideas of touch or skin
contact, and, least of all, of ideas of stomach and lung sensations
or other organic states. The trains of the scientific man, of
the man of business, and even of the handicraft worker, are
almost entirely made up of ideas of sight and of hearing (with
active or muscular ideas). Our understanding of the order of
nature, our very notion of the material universe, is a vast and
complex scheme of ideas of sight.

The intellectual superiority of the higher senses in the
domain of Feeling is connected with the remembrance or ideal
persistence of pleasures and pains. The pleasures of Digestion
are weakly and ineffectively remembered, in the absence of the
actuality. The pleasures of Smell are remembered better. The
pleasures and pains of Hearing and Sight are remembered best
of any. This gives them a higher value in life; the addition
made to the actual, by the ideal, is, in their case, the greatest
of all. They are said, for this among other reasons, to be
more refined.

The arrangement dictated by the gradation of intellectua-
lity would be as follows :—1. Sensations of Organic Life.
2. Taste. 3. Smell. 4. Touch. 5. Hearing. 6. Sight.

The second principle of arrangement starts with Touch, as
the most simple in its mode of action, and the most diffused in
its operation. Touch consists in mere mechanical pressure on
a sensitive surface; this is the most simple and elementary of

ternal OBJECT, as it is commonly denominated,* to which the Sensation is referred as an effect to its cause.

These three distinguishable particulars are common to all the five Senses. With regard to the ORGAN, which is a physical rather than a mental subject of inquiry, I shall have occasion to say little more than is required to make my reader distinguish, with sufficient accuracy, the part of his body to which the

---

all stimuli. The other senses are regarded as specialised modifications of Touch.

In Hearing, the mode of action is touch or mechanical contact. In the remaining senses, the contact is accompanied with other forces. Taste and Smell involve chemical change, as well as contact. The action of Light on the eye is probably some species of molecular disturbance involving chemical action. This mode of viewing the order and dependence of the senses belongs more especially to the theory of the development of the organic system, which is made prominent in the Psychology of Mr. Herbert Spencer. The arrangement might be variously expressed :—it might be Touch, Hearing, Sight, Taste, Smell, Organic Sensibility ; or Touch, Hearing, Taste, Smell, Organic Sensibility, Sight.—*B.*

* It is necessary here to observe, that I use, throughout this Inquiry, the language most commonly in use. This is attended with its disadvantages ; for on the subject of mind the ordinary language almost always involves more or less of theory, which may or may not appear to me to correspond with the true exposition of the phenomena. The advantages, however, of not departing from familiar terms still appeared to me to preponderate ; and I am willing to hope, that such erroneous suggestions, as are sometimes inseparable from the language I have thought it best upon the whole to employ, will be corrected, without any particular notice, by the analysis which I shall present.—(*Author's Note.*)

separate feelings of his five Senses belong. And with regard to the antecedent of the Sensation, or OBJECT of the Senses, the proper place for explaining what is capable of being known of it is at a subsequent part of this inquiry. My desire at present is, to fix the attention of the reader upon the SENSATION ; that he may mark it as a mental state of a particular kind, distinct from every other feeling of his nature.

The ORGAN of Smell, as every body knows, is situated in the mouth and nostrils, or in the nerves, appropriated to smelling, which are found in the passage between the mouth and nostrils, and in the vicinity of that passage.

Though it appears to be ascertained that the nerves are necessary to sensation, it is by no means ascertained in what way they become necessary. It is a mystery how the nerves, similar in all parts of the body, afford us, in one place, the sensation of sound ; in another, the sensations of light and colours ; in another, those of odours, in another those of flavours, and tastes, and so on.

With respect to the external OBJECT, as it is usually denominated, of this particular sense ; in other words, the antecedent, of which the Sensation Smell is the consequent ; it is, in vulgar apprehension, the visible, tangible object, from which the odour proceeds. Thus, we are said to smell a rose, when we have the sensation derived from the odour of the rose. It is more correct language, however, to say, that we smell the odorous particles which proceed from the visible, tangible object, than that we smell the object itself ; for, if any thing prevents the odorous particles, which the body emits, from reaching the organ of smell, the

sensation is not obtained.   The object of the sense of
smelling then are odorous particles, which only
operate, or produce the sensation, when they reach
the organ of smell.

But what is meant by odorous particles we are still
in ignorance. Something, neither visible nor tangible,
is conveyed, through the air, to the olfactory nerves ;
but of this something we know no more than that it
is the antecedent of that nervous change, or variety of
consciousness, which we denote by the word smell.

Still farther, When we say that the odorous particles, of which we are thus ignorant, reach the nerves
which constitute the organ of smell, we attach hardly
any meaning to the word reach. We know not
whether the particles in question produce their effect,
by contact, or without contact. As the nerves in
every part of the body are covered, we know not how
any external particles can reach them. We know not
whether such particles operate upon the nerves, by
their own, or by any other influence ; the galvanic, for
example, or electrical, influence.

These observations, with regard to the organ of
smell, and the object of smell, are of importance,
chiefly as they show us how imperfect our knowledge
still is of all that is merely corporeal in sensation, and
enable us to fix our attention more exclusively upon
that which alone is material to our subsequent inquiries—that point of consciousness which we deno-
nominate the sensation of smell, the mere feeling,
detached from every thing else.

When we smell a rose, there is a particular feeling,
a particular consciousness, distinct from all others,
which we mean to denote, when we call it the smell

of the rose.   In like manner we speak of the smell of
hay, the smell of turpentine, and the smell of a fox.
We also speak of good smells, and bad smells ; meaning by the one, those which are agreeable to us ; by
the other, those which are offensive.   In all these
cases what we speak of is a point of consciousness, a
thing which we can describe no otherwise than by
calling it a feeling ; a part of that series, that succession, that flow of something, on account of which we
call ourselves living or sensitive creatures.

We can distinguish this feeling, this consciousness,
the sensation of smell, from every other sensation.
Smell and Sound are two very different things ; so are
smell and sight.   The smell of a rose is different from
the colour of the rose ; it is also different from the
smoothness of the rose, or the sensation we have by
touching the rose.

We not only distinguish the sensations of smell
from those of the other senses, but we distinguish the
sensations of smell from one another.   The smell of
a rose is one sensation ; the smell of a violet is another.
The difference we find between one smell and another
is in some cases very great ; between the smell
of a rose, for example, and that of carrion or assafœtida.

The number of distinguishable smells is very great.
Almost every object in nature has a peculiar smell ;
every animal, every plant, and almost every mineral.
Not only have the different classes of objects different
smells, but probably different individuals in the same
class.   The different smells of different individuals are
perceptible, to a certain extent, even by the human
organs, and to a much greater extent by those of the

dog, and other animals, whose sense of smelling is more acute.

We can conceive ourselves, as endowed with smelling, and not enjoying any other faculty. In that case, we should have no idea of objects as seeable, as hearable, as touchable, or tasteable. We should have a train of smells ; the smell at one time of the rose, at another of the violet, at another of carrion, and so on. The successive points of consciousness, composing our sentient being, would be mere smells. Our life would be a train of smells, and nothing more. Smell, and Life, would be two names for the same thing.

The terms which our language supplies, for speaking of this sense, are exceedingly imperfect. It would obviously be desirable to have, at any rate, distinct names for the ORGAN, for the OBJECT, and for the SENSATION ; and that these names should never be confounded. It happens, unfortunately, that the word SMELL is applicable to all the three. That the word smell expresses, both the quality, as we vulgarly say, of the object smelt ; and also the feeling of him by whom it is smelt, every one is aware. If you ask whether the smell, when I hold a violet to my nostrils, is in me or in the violet, it would be perfectly proper to say, in both. The same thing, however, is not in both, though the two things have the same name. What is in me is the sensation, the feeling, the point of consciousness ; and that can be in nothing but a sentient being. What is in the rose, is what I call a quality of the rose ; in fact, the antecedent of my sensation ; of which, beside its being the antecedent of my sensation, I know nothing. If I were speaking of a place in which my senses had been

variously affected, and should say, that, along with
other pleasures, I had enjoyed a succession of the most
delightful smells, I should be understood to speak of
my *sensations.* If I were speaking of a number of
unknown objects, and should say of one, that it had a
smell like that of honey ; of another, that it had a
smell like that of garlick ; I should be understood as
speaking of the *object* of each sensation, a quality of
the thing smelt.

The word smell, beside denoting the *sensation* and
the *object*, denotes also the *organ*, in such phrases as
the following ; " Sight and Hearing are two of the
inlets of my knowledge, and Smell is a third ;"
" The faculty by which I become sensible of odour is
my Smell."[3]

---

[3] It may be questioned whether, in the phrases here cited,
the word Smell stands for the olfactory organ. It would
perhaps be most correct to say, that in these cases it denotes
the abstract capacity of smelling, rather than the concrete
physical instrument. Even when smell is said to be one of
the five senses, it may fairly be doubted whether a part of the
meaning intended is, that it is one of the five *organs* of sensation. Nothing more seems to be meant, than that it is one of
five distinguishable *modes* of having sensations, whatever the
intrinsic difference between those modes may be.

In the author's footnote he recognises that the abstract
power of smelling enters into this particular application of the
word Smell ; and refers to a subsequent part of the treatise for
the meaning of Power. But he thinks that along with the
power, or as part of the conception of Power, the material
organ is also signified. It seems to me that the organ does
not enter in either of these modes, into the signification of
the word. We can imagine ourselves ignorant that we possess
physical organs ; or aware that we possess them, but not

In the phrases in which smell is called a SENSE, as when we say, that smell is one of the five senses, there is considerable complexity.   The term here imports the *organ*, it imports the *sensation*, and, in a certain way, it imports also the *object*.   It imports the organ as existing continuously, the sensation as existing only under a certain condition, and that condition the presence of the object.*

---

aware that our sensations of smell are connected with them. Yet on either of these suppositions the "power of smelling" would be perfectly intelligible, and would have the same meaning to us which it has now.—*Ed*.

* It will naturally occur to some of my readers, that, in the term sense of smelling, the idea of power is also included. They will say, that when we speak of the sense of smelling, we mean not only the organ, but the function of the organ, or its power of producing a certain effect.   This is undoubtedly true; but when the real meaning of the language is evolved, it only amounts to that which is delivered in the text.   For what does any person mean when he says that, in the sense of smelling, he has the power of smelling?   Only this, that he has an organ, and that when the object of that organ is presented to it, sensation is the consequence.   In all this, there is nothing but the organ, the object, and the sensation, conceived in a certain order.   This will more fully appear when the meaning of the relative terms, cause and effect, has been explained.—(*Author's Note.*)

SECTION II.

HEARING.

In Hearing, the same three particulars, the ORGAN, the OBJECT, and the FEELING, require to be distinguished.

The name of the organ is the Ear; and its nice and complicated structure has been described with minuteness and admiration by anatomists and physiologists.

In vulgar discourse, the object of our Sense of Hearing is a sounding body. We say that we hear the bell, the trumpet, the cannon. This language, however, is not correct. That which precedes the feeling received through the ear, is the approach of vibrating air to the ear. Certain bodies, made to vibrate in a certain way, communicate vibrations to the air, and the vibrating air, admitted into the ear, is followed by the sensation of hearing. If the air which the body makes to vibrate does not enter the ear, however the body itself may vibrate, sensation does not follow; hearing does not take place. There is, in fact, no sound. Of the circumstances in which sound is generated, part only were present. There was the organ, and there was the object, but not that juxta-position which is needed to make the antecedent of the sensation complete. Air vibrating in juxta-position to the organ, is the object of Hearing.

How air in vibration should produce the remarkable effect, called hearing, in the nerves of the ear, and no effect in those of the eye, in those of smelling, or those of taste, our knowledge does not enable us to tell.

It is not very difficult to think of the sensation of hearing, apart from the organ, and from the object, as well as from every other feeling. I hear the hum of bees. The feeling to which I give this name is a point of my own consciousness; it is an elementary part of my sensitive being; of that thread of consciousness, drawn out in succession, which I call myself. I have the hearing; it is a sensation of my own; it is my feeling, and no other man's feeling; it is a very different feeling from taste, and a very different feeling from smell, and from all my other feelings.

I hear the song of birds, I hear the lowing of oxen, I hear the sighing of the wind, I hear the roaring of the sea. I have a feeling, in each of these cases; a consciousness, which I can distinguish not only from the feelings of my other senses, but from the other feelings of the same sense. If I am asked, what takes place in me, when a trumpet is unexpectedly sounded in the next room, I answer, a sensation, a particular feeling. I become conscious in a particular way.

The number of those feelings which we are able to distinguish is very great. In this respect, the organ of hearing in man, is much more perfect than the organ of smell. The organ of hearing can distinguish, not only the voices of different classes, but of different individuals in the same class. There never, probably, was a man whose voice was not distinguishable from that of every other man, by those who were familiarly acquainted with it.

The most simple case of sound is that perhaps of a single note on a musical instrument. This note may be sounded on an endless number of instruments, and by an endless number of human voices, from no two of which will the same sound exactly be returned.

We can think of ourselves as having the feelings of this class, and having no other. In that case, our whole being would be a series of Hearings. It would be one sensation of hearing, another sensation of hearing, and nothing more. Our thread of consciousness would be the sensation, which we denominate sound. Life and sound would be two names for the same thing.

The language by which we speak of the " sense of hearing," is also imperfect. We have, indeed, the term Ear, to express the ORGAN, but we have no appropriate name for the SENSATION, nor for the OBJECT. The term sound is a name both of the sensation and the object. If I were asked, when the bell rings, whether the sound is in me, or in the bell, I might answer, in both ; not that the same thing is in both ; the things are different ; having the same name. The sensation called a sound is in me, the vibration called a sound is in the bell. Hearing is equally ambiguous ; a name both of the organ and the feeling. If asked, by which of my organs I have the knowledge of sound, I should answer, my hearing. And if asked what feeling it is I have by the ear, I still should say, hearing. Hearing is rarely made use of to denote the object of hearing, and hardly at all except by figure.

Noise is a name which denotes the object, in certain cases. There is a certain class of sounds, to which we give the name noise. In those cases, however, noise is also the name of the sensation. In fact, it is the name of the sensation first, and only by transference that of the object.

In the phrase, sense of hearing, the word has the same complexity of meaning, which we found in the word smelling, in the corresponding application of that term. When I say that I have the sense of hearing, I mean to say, that I have an organ, which organ has an appropriate object ; and that when the organ and the object are in the appropriate position, the sensation of hearing is the consequent. In the term, sense of hearing, then, is included, the organ, the object, and the sensation, with the idea of a synchronous order of the two first, and a successive order of the third. " Sense of hearing" is thus seen to be the name of a very complex idea, including five distinguishable ingredients, the idea of the organ of hearing, the idea of the sensation, the idea of the object of hearing, the idea of a synchronous order, and the idea of a successive order.[4]

---

[4] In the case of hearing, as of smell, one of the ambiguities brought to notice by the author is of questionable reality. It is doubtful if " hearing" is ever used as a name of the organ. To the question supposed in the text, " by which of my organs do I have the knowledge of sound" the correct answer would surely be, not " my hearing"—an expression which, so

applied, could only be accepted as elliptical,—but " my organ of hearing," or (still better) " my ear." Again, the phrase " I have the sense of hearing" signifies that I have a capacity of hearing, and that this capacity is classed as one of sense, or in other words, that the feelings to which it has reference belong to the class Sensations: but the organ, though a necessary condition of my having the sensations, does not seem to be implied in the name.—*Ed.*

SECTION III.

SIGHT.

In SIGHT, the organ is very conspicuous, and has an appropriate name, the Eye.

In ordinary language, the object of sight is the body which is said to be seen. This is a similar error to those which we have detected in the vulgar language relating to the senses of smell and hearing. It is Light alone which enters the eye; and Light, with its numerous modifications, is the sole object of sight.

How the particles of light affect the nerves of the eye, in the peculiar manner in which they are affected in sight, without affecting the other nerves of the body, in any similar manner, we can render no account.

That the feeling we have in sight, is very different from the feeling we have in hearing, in smelling, in tasting, or touching, every man knows. It is difficult, however, to detach the feeling we have in sight from every other feeling ; because there are other feelings which we are constantly in the habit of connecting with it ; and the passage in the mind from the one to the other is so rapid, that they run together, and cannot easily be distinguished. The different modifications of light we call colour. But we cannot think of the sensation of colour, without at the same time

thinking of something coloured, of surface or extension, a notion derived from another sense.

That the feelings of sight which we are capable of
distinguishing from one another, are exceedingly
numerous, is obvious from this, that it is by them we
distinguish the infinite variety of visible objects.
We have the sensation ; the sensation suggests the
object ; and it is only by the difference of sensation,
that the difference of object can be indicated.

Some of the things suggested by the sensations of
sight, as extension and figure, are suggested so instantaneously, that they appear to be objects of sight,
things actually seen.   But this important law of our
nature, by which so many things appear to be seen,
which are only suggested by the feelings of sight, it
requires the knowledge of other elements of the
mental phenomena to explain.

The imperfections of the language, by which we
have to speak of the phenomena of sight, deserve the
greatest attention.

We have an appropriate name for the organ ; it is
the Eye.   And we have an appropriate name for the
Object ; it is light.   But we have no appropriate
name for the Sensation.   From confusion of names,
proceeds confusion of ideas.   And from misnaming,
on this one point, not a little unprofitable discourse
on the subject of the human mind has been derived.

The word sight, in certain phrases, denotes the
sensation.   If I am asked, what is the feeling which
I have by the eye ?   I answer, sight.   But sight is also
a name of the object.   The light of day is said to be
a beautiful sight.   And sight is sometimes employed
as a name of the organ.   An old man informs us,

that his sight is failing, meaning that his eyes are failing.[5]

Colour is a name, as well of the object, as of the sensation. It is most commonly a name of the object. Colour is, properly speaking, a modification of light, though it is never conceived but as something spread over a surface ; it is, therefore, not the name of light simply, but the name of three things united, light, surface, and a certain position of the two. In many cases, however, we have no other name for the sensation. If I am asked, what feeling I have when a red light is presented to my eyes, I can only say, the colour of red ; and so of other visual feelings, the colour of green, the colour of white, and so on.

In the term sense of sight, the same complexity of meaning is involved which we have observed in the terms sense of smell, and sense of hearing. When I speak of my sense of sight, as when I speak of the attraction of the load-stone, I mean to denote an antecedent, and a consequent ; the organ with its object in appropriate position, the antecedent ; the sensation, the consequent. This is merely the philosophical statement of the fact, that, when light is received into the eye, the sensation of sight is the consequence.

Vision, a word expressive of the phenomena of

[5] The example given does not seem to me to prove that sight is ever employed as a name of the organ. When an old man says that his sight is failing, he means only that he is less capable of seeing. His eyes might be failing in some other respect, when he would not say that his sight was failing. The term " sense of sight," like sense of hearing or of smell, stands, as it seems to me, for the capability, without reference to the organ.—*Ed.*

sight, is ambiguous in the same manner. It is some-times used to denote the sense of seeing ; that is, the antecedent and consequent, as explained in the preced-ing paragraph. Thus we say, the phenomena of vision, with the same propriety as we say the pheno-mena of sight. It is sometimes employed to denote the sensation. If we ask what feeling a blind man is deprived of, it would be perfectly proper to say, vision is the feeling of which he is deprived. It is, also, employed to denote the object. What vision was that ? would be a very intelligible question, on the sudden appearance and disappearance of something which attracted the eye.[6]

---

[6] Vision, I believe, is used to denote the object of sight, only when it is supposed that this object is something unreal, *i.e.*, that it has not any extended and resisting substance behind it : or rhetorically, to signify that the object looks more like a phantom than a reality ; as when Burke calls Marie Antoinette, as once seen by him, a delightful vision.—*Ed.*

SECTION IV.

TASTE.

The ORGAN of TASTE is in the mouth and fauces.

In ordinary language, the OBJECT of taste is any thing, which, taken into the mouth, and tasted, as it is called, produces the peculiar SENSATION of this sense. Nor has philosophy as yet enabled us to state the object of taste more correctly. There are experiments which show, that galvanism is concerned in the phenomena, but not in what way.

The SENSATION, in this case, is distinguished by every body. The taste of sugar, the taste of an apple, are words which immediately recall the ideas of distinct feelings. It is to be observed, however, that the feelings of this sense are very often united with those of the sense of smell ; the two organs being often affected by the same thing, at the same time. In that case, though we have two sensations, they are so intimately blended as to seem but one ; and the flavour of the apple, the flavour of the wine, appears to be a simple sensation, though compounded of taste and smell.[7]

---

[7] Some physiologists have been of opinion that a large proportion of what are classed as tastes, including all flavours, as distinguished from the generic tastes of sweet, sour, bitter, &c., are really affections of the nerves of smell, and are mistaken for tastes only because they are experienced along with tastes, as a consequence of taking food into the mouth.—*Ed.*

It is not so easy, in the case of this, as of some of
the other senses, to conceive ourselves as having this
class of feelings and no other.   Antecedent to the sensation of taste, there is generally some motion of the
mouth, by which the object and the organ are brought
into the proper position and state.   The sensation can
hardly be thought of without thinking of this motion,
that is, of other feelings.   Besides, the organ of taste
is also the organ of another sense.   The organ of taste
has the sense of touch, and most objects of taste are
objects of touch.   Sensations of touch, therefore, are
intimately blended with those of taste.

By a little pains, however, any one may conceive
the sensations of tasting, while he conceives his other
organs to remain in a perfectly inactive state, and
himself as nothing but a passive recipient of one taste
after another.   If he conceives a mere train of those
sensations, perfectly unmixed with any other feeling,
he will have the conception of a being made up of
tastes ; a thread of consciousness, which may be called
mere taste ; a life which is merely taste.

The language employed about this sense is not less
faulty, than that employed about the other senses,
which we have already surveyed.

There is no proper name for the organ.   The word
Mouth, which we are often obliged to employ for
that purpose, is the name of this organ and a great
deal more.

There is no proper name for the object.   We are
obliged to call it, that which has taste.   The word
flavour is used to denote that quality, which is more
peculiarly the object of taste, in certain articles of
food ; and sometimes we borrow the word sapidity,

from the Latin, to answer the same purpose more extensively.

The word taste is a name for the sensation. We generally call the feeling, which is the point of consciousness in this case, by the name taste. Thus we say one taste is pleasant, another unpleasant ; and nothing is pleasant or unpleasant but a feeling.

The word taste is also a name for the object, as when we say, that any thing has taste.

It is further employed as a name of the organ. As we are said to perceive qualities by the eye, the ear, and the touch ; so we are said to perceive them by the taste.

In the phrase, sense of taste, there is the same complexity of meaning as we have observed in the corresponding phrase in the case of the other senses. In this phrase, taste expresses all the leading particulars ; the organ, the object, and the sensation, together with the order of position in the two first, and the order of constant sequence in the last.[8]

---

[8] The statement that " taste" is sometimes employed as a name of the organ, seems to me, like the similar statements respecting the names of our other senses, disputable.—*Ed.*

SECTION V.

TOUCH.

In discoursing about the ORGAN, the SENSATIONS, and the OBJECTS, of touch, more vagueness has been admitted, than in the case of any of the other senses.

In fact, every sensation which could not properly be assigned to any other of the senses, has been allotted to the touch. The sensations classed, or rather jumbled together, under this head, form a kind of miscellany, wherein are included feelings totally unlike.

The ORGAN of TOUCH is diffused over the whole surface of the body, and reaches a certain way into the alimentary canal. Of food, as merely tangible, there is seldom a distinct sensation in the stomach, or any lower part of the channel, except towards the extremity. The stomach, however, is sensible to heat, and so is the whole of the alimentary canal, as far at least as any experiment is capable of being made. It may, indeed, be inferred, that we are insensible to the feelings of touch, throughout the intestinal canal, only from the habit of not attending to them.[9]

---

[9] The surface of the sense of Touch properly so called is the skin, or common integument of the body, the interior of the mouth and the tongue, and the interior of the nose. There are common anatomical peculiarities in these organs; which distinguish them from the alimentary canal and all the other

We have next to consider the OBJECT of TOUCH.
Whatever yields resistance, and whatever is extended,
figured, hot, or cold, we set down, in ordinary language, as objects of touch.

I shall show, when the necessary explanations have
been afforded, that the idea of resistance, the idea of
extension, and the idea of figure, include more than
can be referred to the touch, as the ideas of visible
figure and magnitude include more than can be
referred to the eye. It has been long known, that
many of the things, which the feeling by the eye
seems to include, it only suggests. It is not less important to know, that the same is the case with the
tactual feeling; that this also suggests various particulars which it has been supposed to comprehend.

In the present stage of our investigation, it is not
expedient to push very far the inquiry, what it is, or
is not, proper, to class as sensations of touch, because
that can be settled with much greater advantage hereafter.

The sensations of heat and cold offer this advantage,
—that being often felt without the accompaniment of

---

interior surfaces of the body. Moreover, although, in the alimentary canal, there is solid or liquid contact with a sensitive
surface, the mode of exciting the sensitive nerves, and the
resulting sensibility, are peculiar and distinct. The mode of
action in touch is mechanical contact or pressure, mainly of
solid and resisting bodies; in digestion, the nerves are affected
through chemical and other processes—solution, absorption,
assimilation, &c. In touch, there is the peculiar feeling known
as hard contact, together with the varying discrimination of
plurality of points. In digestion, when healthy, the feeling of
contact is entirely absent.—B.

any thing visible or extended, which can be called an object, they can be more distinctly conceived as simple feelings, than most of our other sensations.[10] They are feelings very different from the ordinary sensations of touch; and possibly the only reason for classing them with those sensations was, that the organ of them, like that of touch, is diffused over the whole body. We know not that the nerves appropriated to the sensations of heat and cold are the same with those which have the sensation of touch. If they be the same, they must at any rate be affected in a very different manner.

To whatever class we may refer the sensations of heat and cold, in their moderate degrees, it seems that good reasons may be given for not ranking them with the sensations of touch, when they rise to the degree of pain. All those acute feelings which attend the disorganization, or tendency toward disorganization,

---

[10] The sensations of heat and cold are, of all sensations, the most *subjective*. The reason is that they are least connected with definite muscular energies. The rise and fall of the temperature of the surrounding air may induce sensations wholly independent of our own movements; and to whatever extent such independence exists, there is a corresponding absence of objectivity. This independence, however, is still only partial, even in the case of heat and cold; in a great number, perhaps a majority, of instances, they depend upon our movements; as in changing our position with reference to a fire, in our clothing, and so on. It is the possibility of conceiving them in the pure subject character, and apart from object relations, that constitutes them simple feelings, in the acceptation of the text. Although not in an equal degree, the same is true of sensations of hearing, on which the author made a similar remark.—*B*.

of the several parts of our frame, seem entirely distinct from the feelings of touch. Even in the case of cutting, or laceration, the mere touch of the knife or other instrument is one feeling, the pain of the cut, or laceration, another feeling, as much as, in the mouth, the touch of the sugar is one feeling, the sweetness of it another.

As we shall offer reasons hereafter to show, that the feelings of resistance, extension, and figure, are not feelings of touch, we should endeavour to conceive what feeling it is which remains when those feelings are taken away.

When we detach the feeling of resistance, we, of course, detach those of hardness and softness, roughness and smoothness, which are but different modifications of resistance. And when these, and the feelings of extension and figure, are detached, a very simple sensation seems to remain, the feeling which we have when something, without being seen, comes gently in contact with our skin, in such a way, that we cannot say whether it is hard or soft, rough or smooth, of what figure it is, or of what size. A sense of something present on the skin, and perhaps also on the interior parts of the body, taken purely by itself, seems alone the feeling of touch.

The feelings of this sense are mostly moderate, partaking very little of either pain or pleasure. This is the reason why the stronger feelings, which are connected with them, those of resistance, and extension, predominate in the groupe, and prevent attention to the sensations of touch. The sensations of touch operate as signs to introduce the ideas of resistance and extension, and are no more regarded.

The imperfection of the language which we employ, in speaking of this sense, deserves not less of our regard, than that of the language we employ, in speaking of our other senses.

We need distinct and appropriate names, for the organ, for the object, and for the sensation. We have no such name for any of them.

The word touch is made to stand for all the three. I speak of my touch, when I mean to denote my organ of touch. I speak also of my touch, when I mean to denote my sensation. And in some cases, speaking of the object, I call it touch. If I were to call a piece of fine and brilliant velvet a fine sight, another person might say, it is a fine touch as well as fine sight."

In ordinary language, the word feeling is appropriated to this sense ; though it has been found convenient, in philosophical discourse, to make the term generical, so as to include every modification of consciousness.*

When I say that I feel the table, there is a considerable complexity of meaning. Dr. Reid, and his followers, maintain, that I have not one point of

---

¹¹ It is more true of the word touch, than of the names of our other senses, that it is occasionally employed to denote the organ of touch ; because that organ, being the whole surface of the body, has not, like the organs of the special senses, a compact distinctive name. But it may be doubted if the word touch ever stands for the object of touch. If a person made use of the phrase in the text, " it is a fine touch as well as a fine sight," he would probably be regarded as purchasing an epigrammatic turn of expression at the expense of some violence to language.— *Ed.*

* " The word *feeling,* though in many cases we use it as

consciousness only, but two ; that I feel the sensation, and that I feel the table ; that the sensation is one thing, the feeling of the table another. Expositions which will be given hereafter are necessary to the complete elucidation of what takes place. But the explanations which have been already afforded will enable us to state the facts with considerable clearness. In what is called feeling the table, my organ of touch, and an object of touch, in the appropriate position, are the antecedent ; of this antecedent, sensation is the consequent. The expression, " I feel the table," includes both the antecedent and the consequent. It does not mark the sensation alone ; it marks the sensation, and, along with the sensation, its ante-cedent, namely, the organ, and its object in con-junction.

The phrase, sense of touch, or the word feeling, often synonymous, has the same complexity of mean-ing, which we have observed in the phrases, sense of hearing, sense of sight, and the rest of the senses.

When I say that I touch, or have the sense of touch, I mean to say, that I have a certain feeling, consequent upon a certain antecedent. The phrase, therefore, *notes* the sensation, and at the same time *connotes** the following things : 1st, the organ ; 2dly,

---

synonymous to *touching,* has, however, a much more extensive signification, and is frequently employed to denote our internal, as well as our external, affections. We feel hunger and thirst, we feel joy and sorrow, we feel love and hatred."—*Ad. Smith, on the External Senses.*—(*Author's Note.*)

* The use, which I shall make, of the term *connotation,* needs to be explained. There is a large class of words, which denote two things, both together ; but the one perfectly dis-the object of the organ ; 3dly, the synchronous order of the organ and object; 4thly, the successive order of the sensation ; the synchronous order being, as usual, the antecedent of the successive order.* [12]

---

tinguishable from the other. Of these two things, also, it is observable, that such words express the one, *primarily*, as it were ; the other, in a way which may be called *secondary*. Thus, *white*, in the phrase *white horse*, denotes two things, the colour, and the horse ; but it denotes the colour *primarily*, the horse *secondarily*. We shall find it very convenient, to say, therefore, that it *notes* the primary, *connotes* the secondary, signification.—(*Author's Note.*) [Reasons will be assigned further on, why the words *to connote* and *connotation* had better be employed, not as here indicated, but in a different and more special sense.—ED.]

* The terms *synchronous* order, and *successive* order, will be fully explained hereafter, when any obscurity which may now seem to rest upon them will be removed ; it may be useful at present to say, that, by synchronous order, is meant order in space, by successive order, order in time ; the first, or order in space, being nothing but the placing or position of the objects at any given time ; the second, or order in time, being nothing but the antecedence of the one, and the consequence of the other.—(*Author's Note.*)

[12] *Additional Observations on the Sense of Touch.*—The author is right in drawing a distinction between Touch proper and the sensibility to Heat and Cold, which, though principally found in the skin, extends beyond the seat of tactile sensibility, as, for example, to the alimentary canal, and to the lungs. It is a debated point, whether the nerves of Touch are also the nerves of Heat and Cold ; some persons contending for special nerves of Temperature. Such special nerves, however, have not been proved to exist.

The remark is also correct, that the feelings of temperature can be more easily attended to, as simple feelings, than the feelings of touch proper. The reason is not precisely stated. It is that radiant heat may affect the surface of the body without occasioning resistance or movement, and is thus a purely passive sensibility ; a subject-state without an object-accompaniment. When the degree of the sensation varies definitely with definite movements, it is treated as an object sensibility, or as pointing to the object world. Thus when we grow warmer as we move in one direction, and colder as we move in another, we no longer think of the feeling as a purely subject fact, but as having an object, or external embodiment.

It is also justly remarked in the text, that the severe sensations of heat, and cold, as well as those from laceration of the skin, may be properly classed with feelings of disorganization generally. At the same time, these painful feelings have a character varying with the organ affected ; the fact of injury of tissue may be the same, but the feeling will not be the same, in the skin, the nostrils, the ear, the eye, the alimentary canal.

The description above given of the feeling that remains, when the different modifications of resistance are deducted, is scarcely adequate to represent the reality. Frequently it is true of them, that they 'are mostly moderate, partaking very little of either pain or pleasure,' but there are occasions when they rise into prominence and power. We may refer to the contact of the bedclothes at night, when the body is relieved from the tight and deadening embrace of the ordinary clothing. The case of greatest moment, however, is the contact of one human being or animal with another ; such contact being the physical element in the tender as well as in the sexual affections. There is a combination of tactile sensibility and warmth in this instance, each counting for a part of the pleasure. The influence is well enough known as experienced among human beings ; but the sphere of its operation in animals has been but imperfectly explored.

If we observe carefully the first movements of a new-born animal, a mammal for example, we find that the guiding and controlling sensation of its first moments, is the contact with the mother. In that contact, it finds satisfaction and repose ; in separation, it is in discomfort and disquiet. Its earliest volitions are to retain and to recover the soft warm touch of the maternal body. When it commences sucking, and has the sensation of nourishment, a new interest springs up, perhaps still more powerful in its attractions, and able to supersede the first, or at least to put it into a second place ; yet, during the whole period of maternal dependence, the feeling of touch is a source of powerful sensibility both to the mother and to the offspring. Among animals born in litter, as pigs, kittens, &c., the embrace is equally acceptable between the fellow-progeny themselves. The sensual pleasure of this contact is the essence, the fact, of animal affection, parental and fraternal; and it is the germ, or foundation, and concomitant of tender affection in human beings. It is the experience of this agreeable contact that prepares the way for a still closer conjunction after the animal reaches puberty. Independent of, and antecedent to, that still more acute sensibility, there is a pleasure in the warm embrace of two animals, and they are ready to enter upon it, at all times when the other interests,—as nourishment, exercise and repose,—are not engrossing. The play of animals with one another clearly involves the pleasure of the embrace, even without sexuality ; and it leads to the sexual encounter at the ripe moment.—*B.*

SECTION VI.

SENSATIONS OF DISORGANIZATION, OR OF THE APPROACH TO DISORGANIZATION, IN ANY PART OF THE BODY.

That we have sensations in parts of the body suffering, or approaching to, disorganization, does not require illustration. The disorganizations of which we speak proceed sometimes from external, sometimes from internal, causes. Lacerations, cuts, bruises, burnings, poisonings, are of the former kind ; inflammation, and other diseases in the parts, are the latter.

These sensations are specifically different from those classed under the several heads of sense. The feelings themselves, if attended to, are evidence of this. In the next place, they have neither organ, nor object, in the sense in which those latter feelings have them. We do not talk of an organ of burning ; an organ of pain ; nor do we talk of an object of any of them ; we do not say the object of a cut, the object of an ache, the object of a sore.

Most of those sensations are of the painful kind ; though some are otherwise. Some slight, or locally minute inflammations, produce a sensation called itching, which is far from disagreeable, as appears from the desire to scratch, which excites it.[13]

---

[13] The author, in this passage, uses the word itching out of its ordinary sense ; making it denote the pleasant sensation

The scratching, which excites the pleasure of itching, is a species of friction, and friction, in most parts of the body, excites a sensation very different from the mere sense of touching or the simple feeling of the object. The tickling of the feather in the nose, for example, is very different from the mere feeling of the feather in touch. In some parts of the body the most intense sensations are produced by friction.

There is difficulty in classing those sensations. They are not the same with those of any of the five senses : and they are not the same with those which rise from any tendency to disorganization in the parts of the body to which they are referred. Great accuracy, however, in the classification of the sensations, is not essential to that acquaintance with them, which is requisite for the subsequent parts of this inquiry. It will suffice for our purpose, if the reader so far attend to them, as to be secure from the danger of overlooking or mistaking them, where a distinct consideration of them is necessary for developing any of the complicated phenomena in which they are concerned.[14]

---

accompanying the relief by scratching, instead of the slightly painful, and sometimes highly irritating, sensation which the scratching relieves.—*Ed.*

[14] *Organic Sens.bilities.*—The author did well to signalize these sensibilities, so powerful in their influence on human life. They are not confined to the side of pain. The same organs whose disorganization is connected with pain, are, in their healthy and vigorous working, more or less connected with pleasure. This is true not merely of the digestive functions, but of the respiration, the circulation, and others.

Nor is it difficult in their case to make up the full analogy of a sense, as having an Object, an Organ, and a characteristic Sensation. In digestion, the object is the food, the organ is the alimentary canal ; in respiration, the object is the air, and the organ the lungs. If it be said that the air is an impalpable agent and not discovered to the mind by its mode of operating, so is heat, the object of an admitted sense.

The accurate classification of these feelings may not have much speculative interest, in Psychology, but it has a great practical interest in the diagnosis of disease. For want of subjective knowledge on the part of the patient, and of a well understood nomenclature of subjective symptoms, the discrimination of disease by the feelings is usually very rough.

The best mode of arranging these sensibilities seems to be to connect them with their organs, or seats—Muscular Tissue, Bones and Ligaments, Nerves, Heart and Circulation, Lungs, Alimentary Canal. The sensations of itching and tickling are modes of skin sensibility. Tickling is an effect not well understood, although some interesting observations have been made upon it.—B.

SECTION VII.

MUSCULAR SENSATIONS, OR THOSE FEELINGS WHICH
ACCOMPANY THE ACTION OF THE MUSCLES.

There is no part of our Consciousness, which deserves greater attention than this; though, till lately,
it has been miserably overlooked. Hartley, Darwin,
and Brown, are the only philosophical inquirers into
Mind, at least in our own country, who seem to have
been aware that it fell within the province of their
speculations.

The muscles are bundles of fibres, which, by their
contraction and relaxation, produce all the motions of
the body. The nerves, with which they are supplied,
seem to be the immediate instruments of the muscular
action.

That these muscles have the power of acute sensation, we know, by what happens, when they are diseased, when they suffer any external injury, or even
when, the integuments being removed, they can be
touched, though ever so gently.

It has been said,* that if we had but one sensation,

---

* Itaque et sensioni adhæret, proprie dictæ, ut ei aliqua in-
sita sit perpetuo phantasmatum varietas, ita ut aliud ab alio
discerni posset. Si supponeremus, enim, esse hominem, oculis
quidem claris cæterisque videndi organis recte se habentibus
compositum, nullo autem alio sensu præditum, eumque ad
eandem rem eodem semper colore et specie sine ulla vel minima
varietate apparentem obversum esse, mihi certe, quicquid

and that uninterrupted, it would be as if we had no sensation at all; and, to the justice of this observation, some very striking facts appear to bear evidence. We know that the air is continually pressing upon our bodies.   But, the sensation being continual, without any call to attend to it, we lose, from habit, the power of doing so.   The sensation is as if it did not exist.   We feel the air when it is in motion, or when it is hotter or colder, to a certain degree, than our bodies; but it is because we have the habit of attending to it in those states.   As the muscles are always in contact with the same things, the sensations of the muscles must be almost constantly the same.   This is one reason why they are very little attended to, and, amid the crowd of other feelings, are, in general, wholly forgotten.   They are of that class of feelings which occur as antecedents to other more interesting feelings.   To these the attention is immediately called off, and those which preceded and introduced them are forgotten.   In such cases the thought of the less interesting sensations is merged in that of the more interesting.

If we had not direct proof, analogy would lead us to conclude, that no change could take place, in parts of so much sensibility as the muscles, without a change of feeling; in particular, that a distinguish-

---

dicant alii, non magis videre videretur, quam ego videor mihi per tactûs organa sentire lacertorum meorum ossa.   Ea tamen perpetuo et undequaque sensibilissima membrana continguntur. —Adeo sentire semper idem, et non sentire, ad idem recidunt. *Hobbes, Elem. Philos.* Pars IV. c. xxv. § 5.—(*Author's Note.*)

able feeling must attend every contraction, and relaxation. We have proof that there is such a feeling, because intimation is conveyed to the mind that the relaxation or contraction is made. I will, to move my arm ; and though I observe the motion by none of my senses, I know that the motion is made. The feeling that attends the motion has existed. Yet so complete is my habit of attending only to the motion, and not to the feeling, that no attention can make me distinctly sensible that I have it. Nay, there are some muscles of the body in constant and vehement action, as the heart, of the feelings attendant upon the action of which we seem to have no cognisance at all. That this is no argument against the existence of those feelings, will be made apparent, by the subsequent explanation of other phenomena, in which the existence of certain feelings, and an acquired incapacity of attending to them, are out of dispute.[15]

In most cases of the muscular feelings, there is not only that obscurity, of which we have immediately spoken, but great complexity ; as several muscles almost always act together ; in many of the common actions of the body, a great number.

The result of these complex feelings is often sufficiently perceptible, though the feelings, separately, can hardly be made objects of attention. The unpleasant feeling of fatigue, in part at least a muscular feeling, is one of those results. The pleasure which almost all the more perfect animals, especially the

---

[15] The paradox, of feelings which we have no cognisance of —feelings which are not felt—will be discussed at large in a future note.—*Ed.*

young, appear to feel, in even violent exercise, may be
regarded as another. The restlessness of a healthy
child ; the uneasiness in confinement, the delight in
the activity of freedom, which so strongly distinguish
the vigorous schoolboy ; seem to indicate, both a
painful state of the muscular system in rest, and a
pleasurable state of it in action. Who has not remarked the playful activity of the kitten and the
puppy ? The delight of the dog, on being permitted
to take exercise with his master, extends through the
greater part of his life.

One of the cases in which the feeling of muscular
action seems the most capable of being attended to,
is the pleasure accompanying the act of stretching,
which most animals perform in drowsiness, or after
sleep.

A very slight degree of reflection is sufficient to
evince, that we could not have had the idea of resistance, which forms so great a part of what we call our
idea of matter, without the feelings which attend
muscular action. Resistance means a force opposed
to a force ; the force of the object, opposed to the
force which we apply to it. The force which we
apply is the action of our muscles, which is only
known to us by the feelings which accompany it. Our
idea of resistance, then, is the idea of our own feelings in applying muscular force. It is true, that the
mere feeling of the muscles in action is not the only
feeling concerned in the case. The muscles move in
consequence of the Will ; and what the Will is, we
are not as yet prepared to explain. What is necessary at present is, not to shew all the simple feelings
which enter into the feeling of resistance ; but to shew

that the simple feeling of muscular action is one of them.

The feeling of resistance admits of great varieties. The feeling of a plate of iron is one thing, the feeling of a blown bladder is another, the feeling of quicksilver is a third, the feeling of water a fourth, and so on. The feeling of weight, or attraction, is also a feeling of resistance.

SECTION VIII.

SENSATIONS IN THE ALIMENTARY CANAL.

When the sensations in the alimentary canal become acutely painful, they are precise objects of attention to every body.

There is reason to believe that a perpetual train of sensations is going on in every part of it. The food stimulates the stomach. It undergoes important changes, and, mixed with some very stimulating ingredients, passes into the lower intestines; in every part of which it is still farther changed. The degree, and even the nature, of some of the changes, are different, according as the passage through the canal is slower, or quicker; they are different, according to the state of the organs, and according to the nature of the food.

Of the multitude of sensations, which must attend this process, very few become objects of attention; and, in time, an incapacity is generated, of making them objects of attention. They are not, however, as we shall afterwards perceive, feeble agents, or insignificant elements, in the trains of thought. They are of that class of feelings, to which we have already been under the necessity of alluding; a class, which serve as antecedents, to feelings more interesting than themselves; and from which the attention is so instantaneously drawn, to the more interesting feelings by which they are succeeded, that we are as little sensible of their existence, as we often are of the sound of the clock, which may strike in the room beside us, and of course affect our ear in the usual manner, and yet leave no trace of the sensations behind.

The complicated sensations in the intestinal canal, like those in the muscles, though obscure, and even unknown, as individual sensations, often constitute a general state of feeling, which is sometimes exhilarating, and sometimes depressing. The effects of opium, and of inebriating liquors, in producing exhilaration, are well known ; and though much of the pleasure in these states is owing to association, as we shall afterwards explain, yet the agreeable feelings in the stomach, are the origin and cause of the joyous associations.[16] The state of feeling in the stomach in sea-sickness, or under the operation of an emetic, is, on the contrary, one of the most distressing within our experience ; though we can neither call it a pain, nor have any more distinct conception of it, than as a state of general uneasiness.

The general effects of indigestion are well known. When the organs of digestion become disordered, and indigestion becomes habitual, a sense of wretchedness is the consequence ; a general state of feeling composed of a multitude of minor feelings, none of

---

[16] The exact mode of operation of opium and alcohol is still unknown ; but the part affected is probably the nervous substance and not the stomach. It can hardly be said with propriety that any part of the pleasure of these stimulants is due to association. No doubt the exhilarated tone of the mind is favourable to the flow of joyful ideas, which serve to heighten the pleasure ; but that pleasure could not be arrested or subdued through the absence of any supposable associations.—B.

which individually can be made an object of attention.

In the sense of wretchedness, which accompanies indigestion, and which sometimes proceeds to the dreadful state of melancholy madness, it is difficult to say, how much is sensation, and how much association. One thing is certain ; that sensations which are the origin of so much misery are of high importance to us ; whether they, or the associations they introduce, are the principal ingredient in the afflicting state which they contribute to create.

The effects of indigestion in producing painful associations, is strikingly exemplified by the horrible dreams which it produces in sleep ; not only in those whose organs are diseased ; but in the most healthy state of the stomach, when it has received what, in ordinary language, is said, whether from quantity or quality, to have disagreed with it.

The general states of feeling composed of the multitude of obscure and unnoticed feelings in the alimentary canal, though most apt to be noticed when they are of the painful kind, are not less frequently of the pleasurable kind.   That particular sorts of foods, as well as liquors, have an exhilarating effect, needs hardly to be stated.   And it is only necessary to revive the recollection of the feeling of general comfort, the elasticity, as it seems, of the whole frame, the feeling of strength, the disposition to activity and enjoyment, which every man must have experienced, when his digestion was vigorous and sound.[17]

---

[17] These effects pass beyond the influence of mere digestion. All the viscera contribute to the condition of high general

vigour and comfort here supposed. If one were to venture upon a scale of relative importance of the different organs, one would place the nervous centres first, and the digestion second.

The present section is open to several remarks. Some qualification must be given to the author's surmise 'that a perpetual train of sensations is going on in every part of the alimentary canal.' It is hardly correct to say that there are perpetual sensations in *any* part of it: during a great part of our time we are in a state of indifference as to stomachic changes; and not merely because we are not disposed to attend to them, but because they scarcely exist. The sensibility of the organ is shown, on anatomical grounds, to be mainly in the stomach, and in the rectum; these parts are supplied by the nervus vagus; and very few nerves, besides those of the sympathetic system, are found in the smaller, or in the larger intestine, so that the sensitiveness of those parts is manifested only in case of violent disorganization, as cramp, stoppage, or inflammation. Hence the feelings are principally attendant on the changes in the stomach, as when food has just been taken, and after long privation, when the state called hunger shows itself.

It is not correct to class the sensations of the alimentary canal, as a whole, with those that lose their hold of the attention, that become unheeded in themselves, and are valued only as the antecedents of other more pleasurable feelings. The remark is inapplicable to the sensations mainly characterized as pleasure or pain; nothing can be more interesting than a pleasure, except a still greater pleasure. It applies only to those slight irritations that are in themselves nothing, but may be the symptoms or precursors of ill health, or of returning good health.

The author's doctrine as to our acquiring artificially the habit of not attending to alimentary states, demands a fuller explanation. The usual cause of inattention to impressions is unbroken continuance; in accordance with the universal law of Relativity or Change, we are usually insensible to the contact of our clothing with the skin, except at the moments when we put on or take off any part of it.   In walking, and in standing, for a length of time, we are insensible to the body's weight; on rising from the recumbent position we are rendered in some degree conscious of it.   Now as the alimentary sensations—Hunger and Repletion—are intermitted and alternated with other states, they fulfil the chief condition of wakeful consciousness.

The example of the striking of the clock, adduced in the text, brings into operation a different power of the mind, which may go far to counteract the influence of change.   Under a very engrossing sensation, or occupation, we become insensible to the stimulation of the senses by other agents.   The strain of the mind in some one direction causes a sort of incapacity for going out in any other direction while the strain lasts. This is the explanation of the indifference to the striking of the clock.   By the farther influence of habit, inattention to a certain class of impressions may become habitual; as in the power of carrying on mental work in the midst of distracting noises.

The same effect may arise in connection with the alimentary feelings.   A person very much engrossed with a subject is unconscious of hunger, and does not feel the pleasures of eating. Should any one be absorbed habitually with some occupation or pursuit, such an one may contract a settled indifference to the recurring phases of alimentary sensation ; but this is an extreme and unusual case.   Any ordinary degree of interest in the avocations and pursuits of business is compatible with full attention to the feelings of hunger, and of repletion, as well as to the occasional pains and discomforts of indigestion.   We do not often choose to contract an indifference to pleasures, and we seldom succeed in acquiring an indifference to pains, although we may have moments of such indifference, under some special engrossment of mind by other things.

It is over-rating the influence of association to make it a

chief element in the pleasure of intoxicating stimulants, or in the wretched feelings of diseased digestion. These states are direct results of physical agency, and are the same throughout all stages of life, with many or with few opportunities of being associated with other feelings. They are not the cases favourable for illustrating the power of association, in the important department of the feelings.—*B.*

CHAPTER II.

IDEAS.

" Hæc in genere sors esse solet humana, ut quid in quovis
genere recte aut cogitari aut effici possit sentiant prius quam
perspiciant. Laborem autem haud ita levem illum veriti, qui in
eo impendendus erat ut, ideas operatione analytica penitus
evolventes, quid tandem velint, aut quænam res agatur, sibi ipsis
rationem sufficientem reddant, confusis, aut saltem haud satis
explicatis rationibus, ratiocinia, et scientiarum adeo systemata
superstruere solent communiter, eoque confidentius, quo ejus
quam tractant scientiæ fundamentum solidum magis ignorant."
—*Schmidt-Phiseldek, Philos. Criticæ Expositio Systematica*, t. i.
p. 561.

" Pour systematiser une science, c'est-à-dire, pour ramener une
suite de phénomènes à leur principe, à un phénomène élémentaire qui engendre successivement tous les autres, il faut saisir
leurs rapports, le rapport de génération qui les lie ; et pour cela,
il est clair qu'il faut commencer par examiner ces différens phénomènes séparément."—*Cousin, Fragm. Philos.*, p. 8.

THE sensations which we have through the medium
of the senses exist only by the presence of the object,
and cease upon its absence ; nothing being here meant
by the presence of the object, but that position of it
with respect to the organ, which is the antecedent of the
sensation ; or by its absence, but any other position.

It is a known part of our constitution, that when
our sensations cease, by the absence of their objects,
something remains. After I have seen the sun, and

by shutting my eyes see him no longer, I can still think of him. I have still a feeling, the consequence of the sensation, which, though I can distinguish it from the sensation, and treat it as not the sensation, but something different from the sensation, is yet more like the sensation, than anything else can be; so like, that I call it a copy, an image, of the sensation; sometimes, a representation, or trace, of the sensation.

Another name, by which we denote this trace, this copy, of the sensation, which remains after the sensation ceases, is IDEA. This is a very convenient name, and it is that by which the copies of the sensation thus described will be commonly denominated in the present work. The word IDEA, in this sense, will express no theory whatsoever; nothing but the bare fact, which is indisputable. We have two classes of feelings; one, that which exists when the object of sense is present; another, that which exists after the object of sense has ceased to be present. The one class of feelings I call SENSATIONS; the other class of feelings I call IDEAS.

It is an inconvenience, that the word IDEA is used with great latitude of meaning, both in ordinary, and in philosophical discourse; and it will not be always expedient that I should avoid using it in senses different from that which I have now assigned. I trust, however, I shall in no case leave it doubtful, in what sense it is to be understood.

The term Sensation has a double meaning. It signifies not only an individual sensation; as when I say, I smell this rose, or I look at my hand: but it also signifies the general faculty of sensation; that is, the complex notion of all the phenomena together, as a part of our nature.

The word Idea has only the meaning which corresponds to the first of those significations; it denotes an individual idea; and we have not a name for that complex notion which embraces, as one whole, all the different phenomena to which the term Idea relates. As we say Sensation, we might say also, Ideation; it would be a very useful word; and there is no objection to it, except the pedantic habit of decrying a new term. Sensation would in that case be the general name for one part of our constitution, Ideation for another.

It is of great importance, before the learner proceeds any farther, that he should not only have an accurate conception of this part of his constitution; but should acquire, by repetition, by complete familiarity, a ready habit of marking those immediate copies of his sensations, and of distinguishing them from every other phenomenon of his mind.

It has been represented, that the sensations of sight and hearing leave the most vivid traces; in other words, that the ideas corresponding to those sensations, are clearer than others. But what is meant hy clearer and more vivid in this case, is not very apparent.

If I have a very clear idea of the colour of the trumpet which I have seen, and a very clear idea of its sound which I have heard, I have no less clear ideas of its shape, and of its size; ideas of the sensations, neither of the eye, nor of the ear.

It is not easy, in a subject like this, to determine what degree of illustration is needful. To those who are in the habit of distinguishing their mental phenomena, the subject will appear too simple to require illustration. To those who are new to this important operation, a greater number of illustrations would be useful, than I shall deem it advisable to present.

It is necessary to take notice, that, as each of our senses has its separate class of sensations, so each has its separate class of ideas. We have ideas of Sight, ideas of Touch, ideas of Hearing, ideas of Taste, and ideas of Smell.

1. By Sight, as we have sensations of red, yellow, blue, &c., and of the innumerable modifications of them, so have we ideas of those colours. We can think of those colours in the dark ; that is, we have a feeling or consciousness, which is not the same with the sensation, but which we contemplate as a copy of the sensation, an image of it ; something more like it, than any thing else can be ; something which remains with us, after the sensation is gone, and which, in the train of thought, we can use as its representative.

2. The sensations of Touch, according to the limitation under which they should be understood, are not greatly varied. The gentle feeling, which we derive from the mere contact of an object, when we consider it apart from the feeling of resistance, and apart from the sensation of heat or cold, is not very different, as derived from different objects. The idea of this tactual feeling, therefore, is not vivid, nor susceptible of many modifications. On the other hand, our ideas of heat and cold, the feelings which we call the thought of them, existing when the sensations no longer exist, are among the most distinct of the feelings which we distinguish by the name of ideas.

3. I hear the Sound of thunder ; and I can think of it after it is gone. This feeling, the representative of the mere sound, this thinking, or having the thought of the sound, this state of consciousness, is the idea. The hearing of the sound is the primary state of consciousness ; the idea of the sound is the second-ary state of consciousness ; which exists only when the first has previously existed.

The number of sounds, of which we can have dis-tinct ideas, as well as distinct sensations, is immense. We can distinguish all animals by their voices. When I hear the horse neigh, I know it is not the voice of the ox. Why ? Because I have the idea of the voice of the ox, so distinct, that I know the sensation I have, is different from the sensation of which that is the copy or representative. We can distinguish the sounds of a great number of different musical instru-ments, by the same process. The men, women, and children, of our intimate acquaintance, we can dis-tinguish, and name, by their voices ; that is, we have an idea of the past sensation, which enables us to declare, that the present is the voice of the same person.

4. That the sensations of Taste recur in thought, when the sensation no longer exists, is a point of every man's experience. This recurring, in thought, of the feeling which we have by the sense, when the feeling by the sense is gone, is the idea of that feel-ing, the secondary state of consciousness, as we named it above.[18] That we can distinguish a very

---

[18] Discrimination and Retentiveness (the having of Ideas as the produce of Sensations) are different functions, although

great number of tastes, and distinguish them accurately, is proof that we have a vast number of distinct ideas of taste; because, for the purpose of making such distinction, we have just seen that there must be a sensation and an idea; the sensation of the present object, and the idea of the sensation of each of the other objects from which we distinguish it. You have tasted port wine, and you have tasted claret; when you taste claret again, you can distinguish it from port wine; that is, you have the idea of the taste of port wine, in conjunction with the sensation of claret. You call it bad claret. Why? Because, along with the present taste, you have the idea of another, which, when it was sensation, was more agreeable than the present sensation.

5. Since we distinguish smells, as well as tastes,

---

mutually involved, and, in all likelihood, developed in proportionate degrees in the same organ. We begin by discriminating changes of impression; this process is necessary in order to our having even a sensation; the more delicate the discriminating power, the greater the number of our primary sensations. He that can discriminate twenty shades of yellow has twenty sensations of yellow; the two statements express the same fact. These various sensations being often repeated, acquire at last an ideal persistence; they can be maintained as ideas, without the originals. The function or power of the Intellect whereby they are thus rendered self-subsisting as ideas, is not the same function as discrimination; we call it Memory, Retentiveness, Adhesiveness, Association, and so on. What may be affirmed about it, on the evidence of induction, is, that where discrimination is good, memory or retentiveness is also good. The discriminative eye for colour is accompanied with a good memory for colour; the musical ear is both discriminative and retentive.—B.

we have the same proof of the number and distinctness of the ideas of this class of sensations. There
is none of the numerous smells to which we have
been accustomed, which we do not immediately recognise. But for that recognition the idea of the
past sensation must be conjoined with the present
sensation.

6. Of that class of sensations, which I have called
sensations of disorganization, we have also ideas. We
are capable of having the thought of them when the
sensation is gone ; and that thought is the idea. A
spark from the candle flew upon my hand : I had the
sensation of burning. I at this moment think of that
sensation ; that is, I have the idea of that sensation ;
and I can think of it, as different from ten thousand
other painful sensations ; that is, I have ideas of as
many other sensations of this class.

7. The ideas of the sensations which attend the
action of the muscles are among the most important
of the elements which constitute our being. From
these we have the ideas of resistance, of compressi-
bility, of hardness, of softness, of roughness, of
smoothness, of solidity, of liquidity, of weight, of
levity, of extension, of figure, of magnitude, of whole
and of parts, of motion, of rest. It is, indeed, to be
observed, that these are all complex ideas, and that
other feelings than the mere muscular feeling are concerned in their composition. In almost all the ideas
referrible to the muscular feelings, of sufficient importance to have names, the Will is included. The
muscular action is the consequent, the Will the antecedent ; and the name of the idea, includes both.
Thus the idea of resistance is the thought, or idea, of

the feelings we have, when we will to contract certain muscles, and feel the contraction impeded.[19] [20]

There is no feeling of our nature of more importance to us, than that of resistance. Of all our sensations, it is the most unintermitted ; for, whether we sit, or lie, or stand, or walk, still the feeling of resistance is present to us. Every thing we touch, at the same time resists ; and every thing we hear, see, taste, or smell, suggests the idea of something that resists. It is through the medium of resistance, that every act by which we subject to our use the objects and laws of nature, is performed. And, of the complex states of consciousness, which the philosophy of mind is called upon to explain, there is hardly one, in which the feeling or idea of resistance is not included.

It is partly owing to this combination of something

[19] Rather, when we will to contract certain muscles, and the contraction takes place, but is not followed by the accustomed movement of the limb ; what follows, instead, being a sensation of pressure, proportioned to the degree of the contraction. It is not the muscular contraction itself which is impeded by the resisting object : that contraction takes place : but the outward effect which it was the tendency, and perhaps the purpose, of the muscular contraction to produce, fails to be produced. —*Ed.*

[20] It is unnecessary to advert to the operation of the Will, (in the first instance at least,) in considering the feelings of muscular action. The will is the principal, but not the only, source of our activity. The mere spontaneous vigour of the system may put the muscles in motion. Likewise the muscular pleasure itself operates, by the fundamental law of the will, for its own continuance ; a process not commonly called voluntary. In these circumstances, it seems advisable to consider and describe the consciousness of muscular exertion by itself, and without reference to the will.—*B.*

else with the muscular feeling, in all the states of consciousness to which we have given names, that it is
so difficult to think of the mere muscular feeling by
itself; that our notion of the muscular sensations is
so indistinct and obscure ; and that we can rather be
said to have ideas of certain general states of muscular
feeling, as of fatigue, or activity, composed of a great
number of individual feelings, than of the individual
feelings themselves.

8. As the feelings, or sensations which we have in
the intestinal canal, are almost always mixed up indis-
tinctly with other feelings, and, except in the cases of
acute pain, are seldom taken notice of but as constituting general states, we hardly have the power of
thinking of those sensations one by one ; and, in consequence, can hardly be said to have ideas of them.
They are important, as forming component parts of
many complex ideas, which have great influence on
our happiness.   But to unfold the mystery of complex
ideas, other parts of our mental process have yet to
be explained:

There is a certain distressful feeling, called the feeling of bad health, which is considerably different in
different cases, but in which sensations of the intestinal canal are almost always a material part.

Indigestion is the name of an idea, in which the
feelings of the intestinal canal are mainly concerned.

Hunger, and thirst, are also names of ideas, which
chiefly refer to sensations in the same part of our
system.[21] [22]

---

[21] Thirst is a sensation of the fauces and of the stomach ;
it is also a feeling of the body generally, due to a deficiency

It is proper to remark, that, beside the internal feelings to which I have hitherto directed the reader's attention, there are others, which might be classed, and considered apart. The blood-vessels, for example, and motion of the blood, constitute an important part of our System, not without feelings of its own ; feelings sometimes amounting to states which seriously command our attention. Of the feelings which accompany fever, a portion may reasonably be assigned to the change of action in the blood-vessels.

There are states of feeling, very distinguishable,

---

of water in the blood. It is also caused by an excess of saline ingredients in the system. In like manner, a distinction is to be drawn between Inanition, from deficiency of nutritive material in the body, and Hunger, or the state of the stomach preparatory to the act of eating. The two states must in a great measure concur : yet they may be distinct.

The account of the organic states given in this chapter would have come in appropriately under Sensation —B.

[22] I venture to think that it is not a philosophically correct mode of expression, to speak of indigestion, or of hunger and thirst, as names of ideas. Hunger and thirst are names of definite sensations ; and indigestion is a name of a large group of sensations, held together by very complicated laws of causation. If it be objected, that the word indigestion, and even the words hunger and thirst, comprehend in their meaning other elements than the immediate sensations ; that the meaning, for instance, of hunger, includes a deficiency of food, the meaning of indigestion a derangement of the functions of the digestive organs ; it still remains true that these additional portions of meaning are physical phenomena, and are not our thoughts or ideas of physical phenomena ; and must, therefore, in the general partition of human consciousness between sensations and ideas, take their place with the former, and not with the latter.—Ed.

accompanying diseased states of the heart, and of the nervous and arterial systems.

Beside the blood and its vessels, the glandular system is an important part of the active organs of the body; not without sensibility, and of course, not without habitual sensations. The same may be said of the system of the absorbents, of the lymphatics, and of the vascular system in general.

The state of the nerves and brain, the most wonderful part of our system, is susceptible of changes, and these changes are accompanied with known changes of feeling. There is a class of diseases which go by the name of nervous diseases: and though they are not a very definite class; though it is not even very well ascertained how far any morbid state of the nerves has to do with them; it is not doubtful that in some of those diseases there are peculiar feelings, which ought to be referred to the nerves. The nerves and brain may thus be, not only the organs of sensations, derived from other senses, but organs of sensations, derived from themselves. On this subject we cannot speak otherwise than obscurely, because we have not distinct names for the things which are to be expressed.

It is not, however, necessary, in tracing the simple feelings which enter into the more complex states of consciousness, to dwell upon the obscurer classes of our inward sensations; because it is only in a very general way that we can make use of them, in expounding the more mysterious phenomena. Having never acquired the habit of attending to them, and having, by the habit of inattention, lost the power of remarking them, except in their general results, we can do little more than satisfy ourselves of the cases in which they enter for more or less of the effect.

We have now considered what it is to have sensations, in the simple, uncompounded cases; and what it is to have the secondary feelings, which are the consequences of those sensations, and which we consider as their copies, images, or representatives. If the illustrations I have employed have enabled my reader to familiarize himself with this part of his constitution, he has made great progress towards the solution of all that appears intricate in the phenomena of the human mind. He has acquainted himself with the two primary states of consciousness; the varieties of which are very numerous; and the possible combinations of which are capable of composing a train of states of consciousness, the diversities of which transcend the limits of computation.[23] [24]

---

[23] *The Sensation and the Idea compared.*—Great importance, in every way, attaches to the points of agreement and of difference of the Sensation and of the Idea. By the Sensation, we mean the whole state of consciousness, under an actual or present impression of sense, as in looking at the moon, in listening to music, in tasting wine. By the Idea is meant the state of mind that remains after the sensible agent is withdrawn, or that may be afterwards recovered by the force of recollection.

1. For many purposes the sensation and the idea are identical. They are compared to original and copy, which, although not in all respects of equal value, can often answer the same ends. A perfect recollection of a process that we wish to repeat, is as good as actually seeing it. For all purposes of knowledge, and of practical guidance, a faithful remembrance is equal to the real presence. So, as regards the emotional ideas, or the recollection of states of pleasure and of pain, which

prompt our voluntary actions, in pursuit and in avoidance, the memory operates in the same way as the original fact, allowance being made for difference of degree. A pleasing melody induces us to listen to it, and to crave for its repetition ; the after recollection of it, also moves us to hear it again. If we find ourselves in the midst of distracting noises, we are impelled to escape ; the mere remembrance, at an after time, has the same influence on the will.

2. It is highly probable, if not certain, that the same nervous tracks of the brain are actuated during the sensation, and during the idea, with difference of degree corresponding to the difference of vivacity or intensity of the actual and remembered states.

Of the points wherein the Sensation and the Idea are found to differ, the most obvious is their degree of *intensity*. We are able to maintain in idea, the state of mind corresponding to the sight of the sun, the sound of a bell, or the smell of a rose, but we are conscious of a great inferiority in the degree or vividness of the state. The bright luminosity of the original sun turns into a feeble effect, without dazzle or excitement. The thrill of a fine musical air cannot be sustained by the mere memory of it, even in the freshness of the immediately succeeding moment. A certain pleasing remembrance attaches to a good dinner, but how far below the original ! Moreover, in a complicated object of sense, a great many of the parts and lineaments drop entirely out of view. Memory is unequal to retaining, without long familiarity and practice, the exact picture of a landscape, a building, or an interior. The difference in the *fulness* of the idea, as compared with the sensation, is no less remarkable than the difference of vivacity or intensity.

This inferiority in the idea as compared with the actuality is of very various amount ; being in some cases very great, and in others very slight. The difference is in proportion to the mind's power of retentiveness, a power varying according to several circumstances or conditions, which have to be distinctly enunciated by the Psychologist. For example, it is well known, that frequency of repetition enables the idea to grow in vivacity and in fulness, and to approximate in those respects to the original. It is also known, that some minds are by nature retentive, and, by a small number of repetitions, gain the point that others reach only by a greater number.

Now, that the vivacity and fulness of a remembered idea should constitute the exact measure of the mind's retentiveness in that particular instance, is a thing of course. There is no other measure of retentiveness but the power of reproducing in idea, what has been before us, in actuality, or as sensation ; and the greater the approach of the idea to the original sensation, the better is the retaining faculty.

There is an apparent exception to this general principle. The memory of the same idea, or the same feeling, in the same person, may be at one time full and vivid, and at another time meagre and faint. In particular moments, we may recall former experiences with especial force, as if there were something that co-operated with the proper force of retentiveness. What, then, are these additional or concurring forces ? Hume recognises the influence of disease in giving preternatural intensity to ideas.

The answer is that some other recollection concurs with, and adds its quota to the support of, the one in question. When, in the view of one natural prospect, we recall another with great fulness, the present sensation supplies or fills in the parts of the remembered scene ; which scene, therefore, does not exist in the mind by memory alone, but as a compound of memory and actuality. So while listening with pleasure to a band of music, we remember strongly the pleasure of some previous musical performance ; yet, the vivid consciousness of the past is not dependent upon the memory of the past, but upon the stimulus of the present ; we are more properly under sensation, than under idea. In all mental resuscitation, there is a degree of vividness and of fulness, due to the proper retentiveness of the mind for each particular thing, according to natural power, repetition, &c. Whatever is beyond this, must be ascribed to the accidental concurrence of other stimulants, either of present sensation, or of remembered impressions.

In recollection, there is an influence designated by the term " excitement," which means that portions of the brain are in a state of exalted activity. Any ideas embodied in the parts so excited, if in operation at all, are more than ordinarily vivid. Thus in fever, faded memories brighten up into vivacity and clearness. To this case the same remark applies; the result is partly memory, or the proper retentiveness of the system, and partly an excitation of the brain, through present influences. The proper power of memory is a constant quantity, varying only with repetition, and the strict conditions of memory; the intensity or fulness of a resuscitated idea is a complex result of memory proper and present stimulants, or sensations.

Difference of vividness was the only distinction adverted to by Hume in his Psychology, which resolved all our intellectual elements into Impressions and Ideas. His opening words are :—" All the perceptions of the human mind resolve themselves into two distinct kinds, which I shall call *impressions* and *ideas*. The difference between these consists in the degrees of force and liveliness, with which they strike upon the mind, and make their way into our thought or consciousness." He afterwards allows that in particular circumstances, as in sleep, in fever, or in madness, our ideas may approach in vividness to our sensations.

Another distinction between the Sensation and the Idea, is of the most vital importance. To the Sensation belongs Objective Reality; the Idea is purely Subjective. This distinction lies at the root of the question of an External World; but on every view of that question, objectivity is connected with the Sensation; in contrast to which the Idea is an element exclusively mental or subjective.

Meanings of Sensation.—The word Sensation has several meanings, not always clearly distinguished, and causing serious embroilments in philosophical controversy.

1. There being, in Sensation, the concurrence of a series of physical or physiological facts with a mental fact, the name may be inadvertently employed to express the physical, as well

as the mental element, or at all events to include the physical part as well as the mental.

The change made on the retina by light, and the nervous influences traversing the brain, may very readily be considered as entering into the phenomenon of sensation. This, however, is an impropriety. The proper use of "Sensation" is to sig-- nify the mental fact, to the exclusion of all the physical pro- cesses essential to its production.

2. In ordinary Sensation, as in looking round a room, there is a double consciousness,—objective and subjective. In the objective consciousness, we are affected with the qualities named magnitude, distance, form, colour, &c. ; these are called object properties, properties of the external and extended uni- verse. In the subject consciousness, we are alive to states of pleasure or of pain, which may go along with the other. We do not usually exist in both modes at one instant ; we pass out of one into the other. Now the word Sensation covers both, although, to the object consciousness, "Perception" is more strictly applicable ; and in contrast to Perception, Sensation would mean the subjective consciousness, the moments when we relapse from the object attitude and become subjective or self-conscious, or alive to pleasure and pain. When the mind is in the object phase, it is neutral or indifferent as respects enjoyment.

3. In Sensation, a distinction may be drawn between the present effect upon the mind, or the impression that would arise if the outward agent had operated for the first time, and the total of the past impressions of the same agent, which by its repetition are recalled to fuse with the present effect. The present view of the moon reinstates the sum total of the pre- vious views held by memory, and is not what we should ex- perience if we saw the moon for the first time. Now, if the recall of the previous impressions, or of the joint and iterated idea, be considered an addition made by the Intellect, being dependent on the retentive power of the mind, Sensation, as opposed to Intellect, would mean the force of the present im- pression and nothing more ; or the difference between the

vividness of reality, and the inferior vividness of recollection. What we can retain when we shut our eyes would represent the force of our intelligence ; the additional intensity when we resume our gaze, would represent the power of sensation or the actual experience.

This distinction suggests an important remark as to the whole nature of Sensation, namely, that there can hardly be such a thing as pure Sensation, meaning Sensation without any admixture of the Intellect. We may attribute this purity to the earliest impressions made upon the mind, but not to anything known in the experience of the adult. This mixture of Intellect with Sense is not confined to Retentiveness; the other intellectual functions, Discrimination and perception of Agreement, are inseparable from the exercise of the senses. We cannot have a sensation without a feeling of difference ; warmth is a transition from cold, and a conscious discrimination of the two facts. So, whenever we repeat a sensation, we have the consciousness of the repetition, or agreement. Were not these modes of consciousness present, we should have no sensation, indeed no consciousness. There is thus no hard line between sense and intellect. The question as to the origin of our Ideas in Sense is not a real question, until we explain what we mean by Sense, and make allowance for this unavoidable participation of Intellect in sensation.

4. Sensation is commonly used to employ the whole of our primary feelings and susceptibilities, as opposed to the Emotions which are secondary or derived. It thus confounds together two different sides of our susceptibility, the active and the passive ; the feelings arising in connection with our exertion of inward force or energy, and those arising under impressions from external things. Both are primary states of consciousness ; they are alike dependent on modifications of our sensitive tissues. But, between the two, there is a contrast, wide, deep, and fundamental, completely missed by the older Psychologists, to the detriment of their handling of such vital questions as the origin of knowledge, and the perception of a material world. The name Sensation, pointing immediately to

the operation of the five senses, gave the slip to the feelings of energy, or brought them in partially and inadequately. Yet it is the only name we have for the primary susceptibilities of the organism—including both movement and passive sensibility.—*B.*

[24] A question which, as far as I know, has been passed over by psychologists, but which ought not to be left unanswered, is this: Can we have ideas of ideas? We have sensations, and we have copies of these sensations, called ideas of them: can we also have copies of these copies, constituting a second order of ideas, two removes instead of one from sensation?

Every one will admit that we can think of a thought. We remember ourselves remembering, or imagine ourselves remembering, an object or an event, just as we remember or imagine ourselves seeing one. But in the case of a simple idea of sensation, *i.e.* the idea or remembrance of a single undivided sensation, there seems nothing to distinguish the idea of the idea, from the idea of the sensation itself. When I imagine myself thinking of the colour of snow, I am not aware of any difference, even in degree of intensity, between the image then present to my mind of the white colour, and the image present when I imagine myself to be seeing the colour.

The case, however, is somewhat different with those combinations of simple ideas which have never been presented to my mind otherwise than as ideas. I have an idea of Pericles; but it is derived only from the testimony of history: the real Pericles never was present to my senses. I have an idea of Hamlet, and of Falstaff; combinations which, though made up of ideas of sensation, never existed at all in the world of sense; they never were anything more than ideas in any mind. Yet, having had these combinations of ideas presented to me through the words of Shakespeare, I have formed what is properly an idea not of an outward object, but of an idea in Shakespeare's mind; and I may communicate my idea to others, whose idea will then be an idea of an idea in my mind. My idea of Pericles, or my idea of any person now alive whom I have never seen, differs from these in the circumstance that I am persuaded that a real object corresponding to the idea does now, or did once, exist in the world of sensation : but as I did not derive my idea from the object, but from some other person's words, my idea is not a copy of the original, but a copy (more or less imperfect) of some other person's copy : it is an idea of an idea.

Although, however, the complex idea I have of an object which never was presented to my senses, is rightly described as an idea of an idea; my remembrance of a complex idea which I have had before, does not seem to me to differ from the remembered idea as an idea differs from a sensation. There is a distinction between my visual idea of Mont Blanc and the actual sight of the mountain, which I do not find between my remembrance of Falstaff and the original impression from which it was derived. My present thought of Falstaff seems to me not a copy but a repetition of the original idea; a repetition which may be dimmed by distance, or which may, on the contrary, be heightened by intermediate processes of thought ; may have lost some of its features by lapse of time, and may have acquired others by reference to the original sources ; but which resembles the first impression not as the thought of an object resembles the sight of it, but as a second or third sight of an object resembles the first. This question will meet us again in the psychological examination of Memory, the theory of which is in no small degree dependent upon it.—*Ed.*

CHAPTER III.

THE ASSOCIATION OF IDEAS.

" To have a clear view of the phenomena of the mind, as mere affections or states of it, existing successively, and in a certain series, which we are able, therefore, to predict, in consequence of our knowledge of the past, is, I conceive, to have made the most important acquisition which the intellectual inquirer can make."
Brown, Lectures, i. 544.

THOUGHT succeeds thought; idea follows idea, incessantly. If our senses are awake, we are continually receiving sensations, of the eye, the ear, the touch, and so forth; but not sensations alone. After sensations, ideas are perpetually excited of sensations formerly received; after those ideas, other ideas: and during the whole of our lives, a series of those two states of consciousness, called sensations, and ideas, is constantly going on. I see a horse: that is a sensation. Immediately I think of his master: that is an idea. The idea of his master makes me think of his office; he is a minister of state: that is another idea. The idea of a minister of state makes me think of public affairs; and I am led into a train of political ideas; when I am summoned to dinner. This is a new sensation, followed by the idea of dinner, and of the company with whom I am to partake it. The sight of the company and of the food are other sensations; these suggest ideas without end; other sensations perpetually intervene, suggesting other ideas: and so the process goes on.

In contemplating this train of feelings, of which our lives consist, it first of all strikes the contemplator, as of importance to ascertain, whether they occur casually and irregularly, or according to a certain order.

With respect to the SENSATIONS, it is obvious enough that they occur, according to the order established among what we call the objects of nature, whatever those objects are; to ascertain more and more of which order is the business of physical philosophy in all its branches.

Of the order established among the objects of nature, by which we mean the objects of our senses, two remarkable cases are all which here we are called upon to notice; the SYNCHRONOUS ORDER, and the SUCCESSIVE ORDER. The synchronous order, or order of simultaneous existence, is the order in space; the successive order, or order of antecedent and consequent existence, is the order in time. Thus the various objects in my room, the chairs, the tables, the books, have the synchronous order, or order in space. The falling of the spark, and the explosion of the gunpowder, have the successive order, or order in time.

According to this order, in the objects of sense, there is a synchronous, and a successive, order of our sensations. I have SYNCHRONICALLY, or at the same instant, the sight of a great variety of objects; touch of all the objects with which my body is in contact; hearing of all the sounds which are reaching my ears; smelling of all the smells which are reaching my nostrils; taste of the apple which I am eating; the sensation of resistance both from the apple which is in my mouth, and the ground on which I stand; with the sensation of motion from the act of walking. I have SUCCESSIVELY the sight of the flash from the mortar fired at a distance, the hearing of the report, the sight of the bomb, and of its motion in the air, the sight of its fall, the sight and hearing of its explosion, and lastly, the sight of all the effects of that explosion.[25]

---

[25] There is here raised the interesting and important question, how far are we able to entertain synchronous sensations; in other words, whether or not we can be cognisant of a plurality of sensations at the same instant of time. There are various circumstances tending to obscure this point; the chief being the extreme rapidity of our mental transitions.

It is requisite to view the question from two sides, the side of sensation and the side of action. On the first, the appearances are more in favour of plurality; on the second, more in favour of unity.

As regards Sensation, we are incessantly solicited by a variety of agencies, outward and inward. We may be roused into consciousness, through the eye, through the ear, through the touch, through the taste, through the smell, through the organic sensibilities; and all this at the same time with the rise of emotions or ideas through purely mental causes. Nay more; even under a single sense, we may have a plurality of distinguishable impressions. Sight is the greatest example. Hearing is little inferior; witness the complexity of a band of music, and the tumult of a stormy sea. In Touch, likewise, we may have a plurality of distinguishable feelings of contact over the body.

The point to be considered, then, is, how many of these multitudinous effects, strictly synchronous in their occurrence, are capable of operating synchronously, either in directing

Among the objects which I have thus observed synchronically, or successively ; that is, from which I

---

the thoughts, or in impressing the memory. How many of them are able to work the smallest assignable change upon the consciousness ? To all appearance, more than one at a time.

Consider first the two senses most concerned in developing (out of muscular feeling as the basis) the notion of Space or Extension ; that is, Touch and Sight. It will be enough to comment upon Sight. The eye, as is known, takes in a wide prospect ; the retinas of the two eyes combined can embrace a large fraction of the surrounding visible sphere. Now, the attention at any one moment is confined to a limited portion : the precise limits are not here considered ; there being a complication of action with sensation proper, which will be adverted to afterwards. But, notwithstanding this confinement of the attention, there is a consciousness of the whole visible expanse ; as is proved in the case of any sudden change at any part ; the attention is then instantly diverted to that part. We might say that there is, at every moment, a ramified area of sensibility, at its maximum in the centre—the line of direction of the eyes, and decreasing to the extremity or circumference of the visible expanse. To one gazing at the heavens, the flash of a meteor would be felt throughout the whole area of visibility ; while it would be more certain in its effect, the nearer it was to the line of perfect vision, which is the place of special attention. A faint corruscation arising near the circumference might pass unheeded.

Next as to the sense of Hearing. Peculiar difficulties attend the explanation of this sense. There is only one main line of access to the inner ear, where the nerves are distributed, namely, the solid chain of bones of the middle ear ; and that line can hardly be supposed capable of conveying at the same instant a plurality of different series of vibrations. Yet we fancy that we hear a concurring plurality of sounds. Of what avail would be a band of a hundred performers if there were no power of taking in simultaneous pulses of sound ?

have had synchronical or successive sensations ; there
are some which I have so observed frequently ; others

There is, however, an absence of accurate investigation of this
point; no one has endeavoured to ascertain how much of the
complex effect is due to the rapid transitions of the ear from
one sound to another, how much to the concurrence of several
series of pulses in one augmented series, and how much to the
composition of successive effects in the ear into a synchronous
whole in the emotional wave, or general excitement of the
brain. It will be found, by any careful observer, that in
listening to a band, we are really occupied with very few of
the sounds at the same instant of time ; we perform a number
of rapid movements of the attention from one to another ;
while, at each moment, we are under an influence remaining
from the recently occurring beats, to which we are not now
giving our full attention.

Touch is exactly parallel to Sight, and need not be dwelt
upon. In Smell, and in Taste, we may have a plurality of
distinguishable effects at one moment : we often experience
complex odours and tastes. The above remarks will apply to
these. The undoubted tendency of the mind is to single out,
for attention, the separate constituents by turns, and to pass
with rapidity from one to another ; while it is also true that
the individual effects that are for the moment seemingly
neglected, still exercise an influence on the consciousness ;
which would be decisively shown (as in the case of sight) on
any occasion of their suddenly increasing in force, or suddenly
vanishing. Also, in their state of having fallen out of attention, they still leave an influence to modify the present sensation, the effect of their being attended to in the previous instant. Until we can measure the rapidity of those transitions
of the attention, we are not in a position to affirm absolutely
the power of double, triple, or multiple attention, although to
all practical intents such a power is possessed.

It is certain that the mind is every moment actuated and
determined by a plurality of influences, impressions, consider-

which I have so observed not frequently : in other
words, of my sensations some have been frequently

---

ations, thoughts.   Almost every act of the will is a resultant
of many motives.   Our thoughts seldom spring up at the
instance of a simple link of association ; although it may
happen that some one link is sufficing and overpowering, and
therefore governs the recall ; yet there are almost always others
aiding or checking the particular resuscitation.   Nevertheless,
such complication of antecedents is not inconsistent with the
theory of very rapid transitions of attention, there being a
certain persisting influence from each separate act.   There
would, however, be a greater theoretical simplicity, as well as
a less appearance of straining a point, if we could suppose
that the several conspiring agencies unite in a strictly synchronous whole.

Let us next view the question from the side of Activity.
Here the circumstance that would most decisively limit the
power of attention, and impose an absolute unity (qualified by
rapidity of transition) is the singleness of the muscular executive.   No one organ can perform two movements at the same
instant.   Plurality can arise only by the separate organs performing separate actions.

In such a case as playing on the pianoforte, there is a very
complicated series of muscular exertions.   The eyes are occupied with the printed music ; both hands are exerted, and
every finger performs a separate note ; the foot also may be
brought into action.   At the same time, the ear has to be on
the alert.   The plurality is here very great ; yet it seems much
greater than it is.   For, at the stage when such a performance
is possible, there is a great amount of acquirement ; many
synchronous groupings have been made by long repetition, so
as to dispense with attending to the several acts in separation.
The real attention is concentrated on one, or on a very few
acts ; so few that it is not impossible for them to be com-
manded by the mere rapidity of transition from one to another.
The performer need not attend to the notes of the music, and

synchronical, others not frequently; some frequently
successive, others not frequently. Thus, my sight of

---

to the action of the fingers at the same absolute instant of
time.

It is in the case of commencing some act entirely new to
us, that the limitation of the muscular executive is most apparent. In learning the first elements of any accomplishment
by imitating a master, the whole attention is concentrated on
single movements; at one instant on the master, and the
next instant on the act of imitating; the only synchronous
addition to this last being the remaining trace of the impression of the model. If the act is complicated, and requires
concurring movements of different organs, the attention, at
the outset, must be given to one at a time; the conjunction of
independent movements is not a primitive, but an acquired
power. Previous to acquired groupings, the restriction of the
attention to one movement is the rule.

Let us now consider the senses as compounded of passive
sensation and movement. The eye, for example, is a moving
organ under the command of the will; both eyes being moved
in one indivisible volition. Visual attention consists sometimes in moving the eyes to and fro, at other times, in fixing
them in one immoveable attitude. We have seen that so far
as the optical sensibility is concerned, there is at each instant
an effective impression of a wide area, although of very
unequal distinctness. The impressions derived from the
movements of the eye are much more limited. At the same
absolute instant of time, we can scan only a very small portion; say the outline of some isolated form, or the trace of an
isolated movement. We can run rapidly round the circumference of a round body, or along the edge of a cubical block.
In looking at a tree, we perform a series of muscular sweeps,
scarcely including, at one time, more than a single outline
course. No doubt our optical sensibility is receiving, in a
faint way, a complicated superficies; yet the ocular sweep, on
which we depend for our ideas of form, can hardly be supposed

roast beef, and my taste of roast beef, have been frequently SYNCHRONICAL; my smell of a rose, and my
sight and touch of a rose, have been frequently synchronical; my sight of a stone, and my sensations of
its hardness, and weight, have been frequently synchronical. Others of my sensations have not been
frequently synchronical: my sight of a lion, and the
hearing of his roar; my sight of a knife, and its
stabbing a man. My sight of the flash of lightning,
and my hearing of the thunder, have been often suc-
CESSIVE; the pain of cold, and the pleasure of heat,
have been often successive; the sight of a trumpet,
and the sound of a trumpet, have been often successive. On the other hand, my sight of hemlock, and
my taste of hemlock, have not been often successive:
and so on.

It so happens, that, of the objects from which we
derive the greatest part of our sensations, most of
those which are observed synchronically, are frequently
observed synchronically; most of those which are
observed successively, are frequently observed successively. In other words, most of our synchronical
sensations, have been frequently synchronical; most
of our successive sensations, have been frequently
successive. Thus, most of our synchronical sensations are derived from the objects around us, the objects which we have the most frequent occasion to
hear and see; the members of our family; the furniture of our houses; our food; the instruments of

---

to take more than one line at the same instant. The rapidity
of transition is very great; but there is a conscious transition
when we wish to combine the impression of a circle inscribed
in a square.—B.

our occupations or amusements.   In like manner, of those sensations which we have had in succession, we have had the greatest number repeatedly in succession; the sight of fire, and its warmth ; the touch of snow, and its cold ; the sight of food, and its taste.

Thus much with regard to the order of SENSATIONS; next with regard to the order of IDEAS.

As ideas are not derived from objects, we should not expect their order to be derived from the order of objects ; but as they are derived from sensations, we might by analogy expect, that they would derive their order from that of the sensations; and this to a great extent is the case.

Our ideas spring up, or exist, in the order in which the sensations existed, of which they are the copies.

This is the general law of the "Association of Ideas" ; by which term, let it be remembered, nothing is here meant to be expressed, but the order of occurrence.

In this law, the following things are to be carefully observed.

1. Of those sensations which occurred synchronically, the ideas also spring up synchronically.   I have seen a violin, and heard the tones of the violin, synchronically.   If I think of the tones of the violin, the visible appearance of the violin at the same time occurs to me.   I have seen the sun, and the sky in which it is placed, synchronically.   If I think of the one, I think of the other at the same time.

One of the cases of synchronical sensation, which deserves the most particular attention, is, that of the several sensations derived from one and the same object ; a stone, for example, a flower, a table, a chair, a horse, a man.

From a stone I have had, synchronically, the sensation of colour, the sensation of hardness, the sensations of shape, and size, the sensation of weight. When the idea of one of these sensations occurs, the ideas of all of them occur.[26]   They exist in my mind synchronically ; and their synchronical existence is called the idea of the stone ; which, it is thus plain, is not a single idea, but a number of ideas in a particular state of combination.

Thus, again, I have smelt a rose, and looked at, and handled a rose, synchronically ; accordingly the name rose suggests to me all those ideas synchronically ; and this combination of those simple ideas is called my idea of the rose.

My idea of an animal is still more complex.   The

---

[26] This must be qualified by the fact that the same individual sensation may be found in many groupings, and therefore may not bring up any one aggregate or concrete object in particular. The colour, white, is seen in conjunction with many different shapes, magnitudes, and weight ; consequently it does not suggest a specific shape or magnitude.   In such a case, the recall may be very various according to circumstances ; some individual may have a greater prominence than the rest, and be singled out on that ground ; two or three may be brought to view ; or a still greater number may be revived.

This is an important limitation of the working of the associating principle.   An individual thing is not restored, as a matter of course, unless the link of connexion points to it alone ; as is often effected by a plurality of bonds.   Thus a musical air is not suggested until as many notes are heard as to distinguish it from every other known air.—*B.*

word thrush, for example, not only suggests an idea of a particular colour and shape, and size, but of song, and flight, and nestling, and eggs, and callow young, and others.

My idea of a man is the most complex of all; including not only colour, and shape, and voice, but the whole class of events in which I have observed him either the agent or the patient.

2. As the ideas of the sensations which occurred synchronically, rise synchronically, so the ideas of the sensations which occurred successively, rise successively.

Of this important case of association, or of the successive order of our ideas, many remarkable instances might be adduced. Of these none seems better adapted to the learner than the repetition of any passage, or words; the Lord's Prayer, for example, committed to memory. In learning the passage, we repeat it; that is, we pronounce the words, in successive order, from the beginning to the end. The order of the sensations is successive. When we proceed to repeat the passage, the ideas of the words also rise in succession, the preceding always suggesting the succeeding, and no other. *Our* suggests *Father, Father* suggests *which, which* suggests *art;* and so on, to the end. How remarkably this is the case, any one may convince himself, by trying to repeat backwards, even a passage with which he is as familiar as the Lord's Prayer. The case is the same with numbers. A man can go on with the numbers in the progressive order, one, two, three, &c. scarcely thinking of his act; and though it is possible for him to repeat them backward, because he is accustomed to subtraction of numbers, he cannot do so without an effort.

Of witnesses in courts of justice it has been remarked, that eye-witnesses, and ear-witnesses, always tell their story in the chronological order; in other words, the ideas occur to them in the order in which the sensations occurred; on the other hand, that witnesses, who are inventing, rarely adhere to the chronological order.

3. A far greater number of our sensations are received in the successive, than in the synchronical order. Of our ideas, also, the number is infinitely greater that rise in the successive than the synchronical order.

4. In the successive order of ideas, that which precedes, is sometimes called the suggesting, that which succeeds, the suggested idea; not that any power is supposed to reside in the antecedent over the consequent; suggesting, and suggested, mean only antecedent and consequent, with the additional idea, that such order is not casual, but, to a certain degree, permanent.

5. Of the antecedent and consequent feelings, or the suggesting, and suggested; the antecedent may be either sensations or ideas; the consequent are always ideas. An idea may be excited either by a sensation or an idea. The sight of the dog of my friend is a sensation, and it excites the idea of my friend. The idea of Professor Dugald Stewart delivering a lecture, recals the idea of the delight with which I heard him; that, the idea of the studies in which it engaged me; that, the trains of thought which succeeded; and each epoch of my mental history, the succeeding one, till the present moment; in which I am endeavouring to present to others what appears to me valuable among

the innumerable ideas of which this lengthened train has been composed.

6. As there are degrees in sensation, and degrees in ideas; for one sensation is more vivid than another sensation, one idea more vivid than another idea; so there are degrees in association. One association, we say, is stronger than another: First, when it is more permanent than another: Secondly, when it is performed with more certainty: Thirdly, when it is performed with more facility.

It is well known, that some associations are very transient, others very permanent. The case which we formerly mentioned, that of repeating words committed to memory, affords an apt illustration. In some cases, we can perform the repetition, when a few hours, or a few days have elapsed; but not after a longer period. In others, we can perform it after the lapse of many years. There are few children in whose minds some association has not been formed between darkness and ghosts. In some this association is soon dissolved; in some it continues for life.[27]

In some cases the association takes place with less, in some with greater certainty. Thus, in repeating words, I am not sure that I shall not commit mistakes, if they are imperfectly got; and I may at one

---

[27] The difference between transient and permanent recollections turns entirely upon the strength of the association. There is not one specific mode of association suited to temporary recollection and another to permanent; the permanent contains the temporary, as the greater does the less. The reason why a feebler association will suffice for temporary purposes, is that a recent impression still retains something of the hold of a present reality. The chords struck during the

trial repeat them right, at another wrong : I am sure of always repeating those correctly, which I have got perfectly.   Thus, in my native language, the association between the name and the thing is certain ; in a language with which I am imperfectly acquainted, not certain.   In expressing myself in my own language, the idea of the 'thing suggests the idea of the name with certainty.   In speaking a language with which I am imperfectly acquainted, the idea of the thing does not with certainty suggest the idea of the name ; at one time it may, at another not.

That ideas are associated in some cases with more, in some with less facility, is strikingly illustrated by the same instance, of a language with which we are well, and a language with which we are imperfectly, acquainted.   In speaking our own language, we are not conscious of any effort ; the associations between the words and the ideas appear spontaneous.   In endeavouring to speak a language with which we are imperfectly acquainted, we are sensible of a painful effort : the associations between the words and ideas being not ready, or immediate.

7. The causes of strength in association seem all to be resolvable into two ; the vividness of the associated feelings ; and the frequency of the association.

In general, we convey not a very precise meaning,

---

actual presence have not ceased to vibrate.   It is difficult to estimate with precision the influence of recency ; we know it to be very considerable. A thing distinctly remembered for a few hours will be forgotten, or else held as a mere fragment, at the end of a month ; while anything that persists for two or three months may be considered as independent of the power of recency, and may last for years.—*B*.

when we speak of the vividness of sensations and ideas. We may be understood when we say that, generally speaking, the sensation is more vivid than the idea; or the primary, than the secondary feeling; though in dreams, and in delirium, ideas are mistaken for sensations. But when we say that one sensation is more vivid than another, there is much more uncertainty. We can distinguish those sensations which are pleasurable, and those which are painful, from such as are not so; and when we call the pleasurable and painful more vivid, than those which are not so, we speak intelligibly. We can also distinguish degrees of pleasure, and of pain; and when we call the sensation of the higher degree more vivid than the sensation of the lower degree, we may again be considered as expressing a meaning tolerably precise.

In calling one IDEA more vivid than another, if we confine the appellation to the ideas of such SENSATIONS as may with precision be called more or less vivid; the sensations of pleasure and pain, in their various degrees, compared with sensations which we do not call either pleasurable or painful; our language will still have a certain degree of precision. But what is the meaning which I annex to my words, when I say, that my idea of the taste of the pine-apple which I tasted yesterday is vivid; my idea of the taste of the foreign fruit which I never tasted but once in early life, is not vivid? If I mean that I can more certainly distinguish the more recent, than the more distant sensation, there is still some precision in my language; because it seems true of all my senses, that if I compare a distant sensation with a present, I am less sure of its being or not being a repetition of the same, than if I compare a recent sensation with a present one. Thus, if I yesterday had a smell of a very peculiar kind, and compare it with a present smell, I can judge more accurately of the agreement or disagreement of the two sensations, than if I compared the present with one much more remote. The same is the case with colours, with sounds, with feelings of touch, and of resistance. It is therefore sufficiently certain, that the idea of the more recent sensation affords the means of a more accurate comparison, generally, than the idea of the more remote sensation. And thus we have three cases of vividness, of which we can speak with some precision : the case of sensations, as compared with ideas ; the case of pleasurable and painful sensations, and their ideas, as compared with those which are not pleasurable or painful ; and the case of the more recent, compared with the more remote.[28]

---

[28] If it be admitted that in the three cases here specified the word vividness, as applied to our impressions, has a definite meaning, it seems to follow that this meaning may be extended in the way of analogy, to other cases than these. There are, for example, sensations which differ from some other sensations like fainter feelings of the same kind, in much the same manner as the idea of a sensation differs from the sensation itself : and we may, by extension, call these sensations less vivid. Again, one idea may differ from another idea in the same sort of way in which the idea of a sensation had long ago differs from that of a similar sensation received recently : that is, it is a more faded copy—its colours and its outlines are more effaced : this idea may fairly be said to be less vivid than the other.

The author himself, a few pages farther on, speaks of some complex ideas as being more " obscure" than others, merely on account of their greater complexity. Obscurity,

That the association of two ideas, but for once, does, in some cases, give them a very strong connection, is within the sphere of every man's experience. The most remarkable cases are probably those of pain and pleasure. Some persons who have experienced a very painful surgical operation, can never afterwards bear the sight of the operator, however strong the

---

indeed, in this case, means a different quality from the absence of vividness, but a quality fully as indefinite.

Mr. Bain, whose view of the subject will be found further on, draws a fundamental distinction (already indicated in a former note) between the attributes which belong to a sensation regarded in an intellectual point of view, as a portion of our knowledge, and those which belong to the element of Feeling contained in it; Feeling being here taken in the narrower acceptation of the word, that in which Feeling is opposed to Intellect or Thought. To sensations in their intellectual aspect Mr. Bain considers the term vividness to be inapplicable : they can only be distinct or indistinct. He reserves the word vividness to express the degree of intensity of the sensation, considered in what may be called its emotional aspect, whether of pleasure, of pain, or of mere excitement.

Whether we accept this restriction or not, it is in any case certain, that the property of producing a strong and durable association without the aid of repetition, belongs principally to our pleasures and pains. The more intense the pain or pleasure, the more promptly and powerfully does it associate itself with its accompanying circumstances, even with those which are only accidentally present. In the cases mentioned in the text, a single occurrence of the painful sensation is sufficient to produce an association, which neither time can wear out nor counter-associations dissolve, between the idea of the pain and the ideas of the sensations which casually accompanied it in that one instance, however intrinsically indifferent these may be.—*Ed.*

gratitude which they may actually feel towards him. The meaning is, that the sight of the operator, by a strong association, calls up so vividly the idea of the pain of the operation, that it is itself a pain.   The spot on which a tender maiden parted with her lover, when he embarked on the voyage from which he never returned, cannot afterwards be seen by her without an agony of grief.

These cases, also, furnish an apt illustration of the superiority which the sensation possesses over the idea, as an associating cause.   Though the sight of the surgeon, the sight of the place, would awaken the ideas which we have described, the mere thought of them might be attended with no peculiar effect. Those persons who have the association of frightful objects with darkness, and who are transported with terrors when placed in the dark, can still think of darkness without any emotion.

The same cases furnish an illustration of the effect of recency on the strengh of association.   The sight, of the affecting spot by the maiden, of the surgeon by the patient, would certainly produce a more intense emotion, after a short, than after a long interval. With most persons, time would weaken, and at last dissolve, the association.

So much with regard to vividness, as a cause of strong associations.   Next, we have to consider frequency or repetition ; which is the most remarkable and important cause of the strength of our associations.

Of any two sensations, frequently perceived together, the ideas are associated.   Thus, at least, in the minds of Englishmen, the idea of a soldier, and the idea of a red coat are associated ; the idea of a clergyman, and the idea of a black coat; the idea of a quaker, and of a broad-brimmed hat; the idea of a woman and the idea of petticoats. A peculiar taste suggests the idea of an apple; a peculiar smell the idea of a rose. If I have heard a particular air frequently sung by a particular person, the hearing of the air suggests the idea of the person.

The most remarkable exemplification of the effect of degrees of frequency, in producing degrees of strength in the associations, is to be found in the cases in which the association is purposely and studiously contracted; the cases in which we learn something; the use of words, for example.

Every child learns the language which is spoken by those around him. He also learns it by degrees. He learns first the names of the most familiar objects; and among familiar objects, the names of those which he most frequently has occasion to name; himself, his nurse, his food, his playthings.

A sound heard once in conjunction with another sensation; the word mamma, for example, with the sight of a woman, would produce no greater effect on the child, than the conjunction of any other sensation, which once exists and is gone for ever. But if the word mamma is frequently pronounced, in conjunction with the sight of a particular woman, the sound will by degrees become associated with the sight; and as the pronouncing of the name will call up the idea of the woman, so the sight of the woman will call up the idea of the name.

The process becomes very perceptible to us, when, at years of reflection, we proceed to learn a dead or foreign language. At the first lesson, we are told, or we see in the dictionary, the meaning of perhaps twenty words. But it is not joining the word and its meaning once, that will make the word suggest its meaning to us another time. We repeat the two in conjunction, till we think the meaning so well associated with the word, that whenever the word occurs to us, the meaning will occur along with it. We are often deceived in this anticipation; and finding that the meaning is not suggested by the word, we have to renew the process of repetition, and this, perhaps, again, and again. By force of repetition the meaning is associated, at last, with every word of the language, and so perfectly, that the one never occurs to us without the other.

Learning to play on a musical instrument is another remarkable illustration of the effect of repetition in strengthening associations, in rendering those sequences, which, at first, are slow, and difficult, afterwards, rapid, and easy. At first, the learner, after thinking of each successive note, as it stands in his book, has each time to look out with care for the key or the string which he is to touch, and the finger he is to touch it with, and is every moment committing mistakes. Repetition is well known to be the only means of overcoming these difficulties. As the repetition goes on, the sight of the note, or even the idea of the note, becomes associated with the place of the key or the string; and that of the key or the string with the proper finger. The association for a time is imperfect, but at last becomes so strong, that it is performed with the greatest rapidity, without an effort, and almost without consciousness.

In few cases is the strength of association, derived

from repetition, more worthy of attention, than in performing arithmetic. All men, whose practice is not great, find the addition of a long column of numbers, tedious, and the accuracy of the operation, by no means certain. Till a man has had considerable practice, there are few acts of the mind more toilsome. The reason is, that the names of the numbers, which correspond to the different steps, do not readily occur ; that is, are not strongly associated with the names which precede them. Thus, 7 added to 5, make 12 ; but the antecedent, 7 added to 5, is not strongly associated with the consequent 12, in the mind of the learner, and he has to wait and search till the name occurs. Thus, again, 12 and 7 make 19 ; 19 and 8 make 27, and so on to any amount ; but if the practice of the performer has been small, the association in each instance is imperfect, and the process irksome and slow. Practice, however ; that is, frequency of repetition ; makes the association between each of these antecedents and its proper consequent so perfect, that no sooner is the one conceived than the other is conceived, and an expert arithmetician can tell the amount of a long column of figures, with a rapidity, which seems almost miraculous to the man whose faculty of numeration is of the ordinary standard.

8. Where two or more ideas have been often repeated together, and the association has become very strong, they sometimes spring up in such close combination as not to be distinguishable. Some cases of sensation are analogous. For example ; when a wheel, on the seven parts of which the seven prismatic colours are respectively painted, is made to revolve rapidly, it appears not of seven colours, but of one

uniform colour, white.   By the rapidity of the succession, the several sensations cease to be distinguishable ; they run, as it were, together, and a new sensation, compounded of all the seven, but apparently a simple one, is the result.   Ideas, also, which have been so often conjoined, that whenever one exists in the mind, the others immediately exist along with it, seem to run into one another, to coalesce, as it were, and out of many to form one idea ; which idea, however in reality complex, appears to be no less simple, than any one of those of which it is compounded.

The word gold, for example, or the word iron, appears to express as simple an idea, as the word colour, or the word sound.   Yet it is immediately seen, that the idea of each of those metals is made up of the separate ideas of several sensations ; colour, hardness, extension, weight.   Those ideas, however, present themselves in such intimate union, that they are constantly spoken of as one, not many.   We say, our idea of iron, our idea of gold ; and it is only with an effort that reflecting men perform the decomposition.

The idea expressed by the term weight, appears so perfectly simple, that he is a good metaphysician, who can trace its composition.   Yet it involves, of course, the idea of resistance, which we have shewn above to be compounded, and to involve the feeling attendant upon the contraction of muscles ; and the feeling or feelings, denominated Will ; it involves the idea, not of resistance simply, but of resistance in a particular direction ; the idea of direction, therefore, is included in it, and in that are involved the ideas of extension, and of place and motion, some of the most complicated phenomena of the human mind.

The ideas of hardness and extension have been so uniformly regarded as simple, that the greatest metaphysicians have set them down as the copies of simple sensations of touch. Hartley and Darwin, were, I believe, the first who thought of assigning to them a different origin.

We call a thing hard, because it resists compression, or separation of parts; that is, because to compress it, or separate it into parts, what we call muscular force is required. The idea, then, of muscular action, and of all the feelings which go to it, are involved in the idea of hardness.

The idea of extension is derived from the muscular feelings in what we call the motion of parts of our own bodies; as for example, the hands. I move my hand along a line; I have certain sensations; on account of these sensations, I call the line long, or extended. The idea of lines in the direction of length, breadth, and thickness, constitutes the general idea of extension. In the idea of extension, there are included three of the most complex of our ideas; motion; time, which is included in motion; and space, which is included in direction. We are not yet prepared to explain the simple ideas which compose the very complex ideas, of motion, space, and time; it is enough at present to have shewn, that in the idea of extension, which appears so very simple, a great number of ideas are nevertheless included; and that this is a case of that combination of ideas in the higher degrees of association, in which the simple ideas are so intimately blended, as to have the appearance, not of a complex, but of a simple idea.

It is to this great law of association, that we trace

the formation of our ideas of what we call external objects; that is, the ideas of a certain number of sensations, received together so frequently that they coalesce as it were, and are spoken of under the idea of unity.   Hence, what we call the idea of a tree, the idea of a stone, the idea of a horse, the idea of a man.

In using the names, tree, horse, man, the names of what I call objects, I am referring, and can be referring, only to my own sensations; in fact, therefore, only naming a certain number of sensations, regarded as in a particular state of combination; that is, concomitance.   Particular sensations of sight, of touch, of the muscles, are the sensations, to the ideas of which, colour, extension, roughness, hardness, smoothness, taste, smell, so coalescing as to appear one idea, I give the name, idea of a tree.

To this case of high association, this blending together of many ideas, in so close a combination that they appear not many ideas, but one idea, we owe, as I shall afterwards more fully explain, the power of classification, and all the advantages of language.   It is obviously, therefore, of the greatest moment, that this important phenomenon should be well understood.

9. Some ideas are by frequency and strength of association so closely combined, that they cannot be separated.   If one exists, the other exists along with it, in spite of whatever effort we make to disjoin them.

For example; it is not in our power to think of colour, without thinking of extension; or of solidity, without figure.   We have seen colour constantly in combination with extension, spread, as it were, upon a surface. We have never seen it except in this connection. Colour and extension have been invariably conjoined. The idea of colour, therefore, uniformly comes into the mind, bringing that of extension along with it; and so close is the association, that it is not in our power to dissolve it. We cannot, if we will, think of colour, but in combination with extension. The one idea calls up the other, and retains it, so long as the other is retained.

This great law of our nature is illustrated in a manner equally striking, by the connection between the ideas of solidity and figure. We never have the sensations from which the idea of solidity is derived, but in conjunction with the sensations whence the idea of figure is derived. If we handle any thing solid, it is always either round, square, or of some other form. The ideas correspond with the sensations. If the idea of solidity rises, that of figure rises along with it. The idea of figure which rises, is, of course, more obscure than that of extension ; because, figures being innumerable, the general idea is exceedingly complex, and hence, of necessity, obscure. But, such as it is, the idea of figure is always present when that of solidity is present; nor can we, by any effort, think of the one without thinking of the other at the same time.

Of all the cases of this important law of association, there is none more extraordinary than what some philosophers have called, the acquired perceptions of sight.

When I lift my eyes from the paper on which I am writing, I see the chairs, and tables, and walls of my room, each of its proper shape, and at its proper distance. I see, from my window, trees, and meadows, and horses, and oxen, and distant hills. I see each of its proper size, of its proper form, and at its proper distance; and these particulars appear as immediate informations of the eye, as the colours which I see by means of it.

Yet, philosophy has ascertained, that we derive nothing from the eye whatever, but sensations of colour; that the idea of extension, in which size, and form, and distance are included, is derived from sensations, not in the eye, but in the muscular part of our frame. How, then, is it, that we receive accurate information, by the eye, of size, and shape, and distance? By association merely.[29]

The colours upon a body are different, according to its figure, its distance, and its size. But the sensations of colour, and what we may here, for brevity, call the sensations and extension, of figure, of distance, have been so often united, felt in conjunction, that the sensation of the colour is never experienced without raising the ideas of the extension, the figure, the distance, in such intimate union with it, that they not only cannot be separated, but are actually supposed to be seen. The sight, as it is called, of figure, or dis-

---

[29] We derive through the eye (1) sensations of light in its various degrees, and of colours and their shades; (2) visible form and visible magnitude, together with their changes; and also visible movements. The second group of feelings depends on the movements of the eyes; and they are feelings of activity, or of muscular expenditure. We have, besides, a certain internal muscular sensibility to the alterations of the eye-ball in adjusting for distance.—*B.*

tance, appearing, as it does, a simple sensation, is in reality a complex state of consciousness ; a sequence, in which the antecedent, a sensation of colour, and the consequent, a number of ideas, are so closely combined by association, that they appear not one idea, but one sensation.

Some persons, by the folly of those about them, in early life, have formed associations between the sound of thunder, and danger to their lives. They are accordingly in a state of agitation during a thunder storm. The sound of the thunder calls up the idea of danger, and no effort they can make, no reasoning they can use with themselves, to show how small the chance that they will be harmed, empowers them to dissolve the spell, to break the association, and deliver themselves from the tormenting idea, while the sensation or the expectation of it remains.

Another very familiar illustration may be adduced. Some persons have what is called an antipathy to a spider, a toad, or a rat. These feelings generally originate in some early fright. The idea of danger has been on some occasion so intensely excited along with the touch or sight of the animal, and hence the association so strongly formed, that it cannot be dissolved. The sensation, in spite of them, excites the idea, and produces the uneasiness which the idea imports.

The following of one idea after another idea, or after a sensation, so certainly that we cannot prevent the combination, nor avoid having the *consequent* feeling as often as we have the *antecedent*, is a law of association, the operation of which we shall afterwards find to be extensive, and bearing a principal part in some of the most important phenomena of the human mind.

As there are some ideas so intimately blended by association, that it is not in our power to separate them ; there seem to be others, which it is not in our power to combine. Dr. Brown, in exposing some errors of his predecessors, with respect to the acquired perceptions of sight, observes : " I cannot blend my notions of the two surfaces, a plane, and a convex, as one surface, both plane and convex, more than I can think of a whole which is less than a fraction of itself, or a square of which the sides are not equal." The case, here, appears to be, that a strong association excludes whatever is opposite to it.   I cannot associate the two ideas of assafœtida, and the taste of sugar. Why ?   Because the idea of assafœtida is so strongly associated with the idea of another taste, that the idea of that other taste rises in combination with the idea of assafœtida, and of course the idea of sugar does not rise.   I have one idea associated with the word pain.   Why can I not associate pleasure with the word pain ?   Because another indissoluble association springs up, and excludes it.   This is, therefore, only a case of indissoluble association ; but one of much importance, as we shall find when we come to the exposition of some of the more complicated of our mental phenomena.[30]

---

[30] Some further elucidation seems needful of what is here said, in so summary a manner, respecting ideas which it is not in our power to combine : an inability which it is essential to the analysis of some of the more complex phenomena of mind

10. It not unfrequently happens in our associated feelings, that the antecedent is of no importance

---

that we should understand the meaning of. The explanation is indicated, but hardly more than indicated, in the text.

It seems to follow from the universal law of association, that any idea could be associated with any other idea, if the corresponding sensations, or even the ideas themselves, were presented in juxtaposition with sufficient frequency. If, therefore, there are ideas which cannot be associated with each other, it must be because there is something that prevents this juxtaposition. Two conditions hence appear to be required, to render ideas incapable of combination. First, the sensations must be incapable of being had together. If we cannot associate the taste of assafœtida with the taste of sugar, it is implied, that we cannot have the taste of assafœtida along with the taste of sugar. If we could, a sufficient experience would enable us to associate the ideas. Here, therefore, is one necessary condition of the impossibility of associating certain ideas with one another. But this condition, though necessary, is not sufficient. We are but too capable of associating ideas together though the corresponding external facts are really incompatible. In the case of many errors, prejudices, and superstitions, two ideas are so closely and obstinately associated, that the man cannot, at least for the time, help believing that the association represents a real coexistence or sequence between outward facts, though such coexistence or sequence may contradict a positive law of the physical world. There is therefore a further condition required to render two ideas unassociable, and this is, that one of them shall be already associated with some idea which excludes the other. Thus far the analysis is carried in the author's text. But the question remains, what ideas exclude one another? On careful consideration I can only find one case of such exclusion : when one of the ideas either contains, or raises up by association, the idea of the absence of the other. I am aware of no case of absolute incompatibility of thought or

farther than as it introduces the consequent. In these cases, the consequent absorbs all the attention,

---

of imagination, except between the presence of something and its absence; between an affirmative and the corresponding negative. If an idea irresistibly raises up the idea of the absence of a certain sensation, it cannot become associated with the idea of that sensation; for it is impossible to combine together in the same mental representation, the presence of a sensation and its absence.

We are not yet, however, at the end of the difficulty; for it may be objected, that the idea of the absence of anything is the idea of a negation, of a nullity; and the idea of nothing must itself be nothing—no idea at all. This objection has imposed upon more than one metaphysician; but the solution of the paradox is very simple. The idea of the presence of a sensation is the idea of the sensation itself along with certain accompanying circumstances: the idea of the absence of the sensation is the idea of the same accompanying circumstances without the sensation. For example: my idea of a body is the idea of a feeling of resistance, accompanying a certain muscular action of my own, say of my hand; my idea of no body, in other words, of empty space, is the idea of the same or a similar muscular action of my own, not attended by any feeling of resistance. Neither of these is an idea of a mere negation; both are positive mental representations: but inasmuch as one of them includes the negation of something positive which is an actual part of the other, they are mutually incompatible: and any idea which is so associated with one of them as to recall it instantly and irresistibly, is incapable of being associated with the other.

The instance cited by the author from Dr. Brown, is a good illustration of the law. We can associate the ideas of a plane and of a convex surface as two surfaces side by side; but we cannot fuse the two mental images into one, and represent to ourselves the very same series of points giving us the sensations we receive from a plane surface and those we receive

and the antecedent is instantly forgotten. Of this a very intelligible illustration is afforded by what happens in ordinary discourse. A friend arrives from a distant country, and brings me the first intelligence of the last illness, the last words, the last acts, and death of my son. The sound of the voice, the articulation of every word, makes its sensation in my ear ; but it is to the ideas that my attention flies. It is my son that is before me, suffering, acting, speaking, dying. The words which have introduced the ideas, and kindled the affections, have been as little heeded, as the respiration which has been accelerated, while the ideas were received.

It is important in respect to this case of association

---

from a convex surface both at once. That this cannot but be so, is a corollary from the elementary law of association. Not only has no instance ever occurred in our experience of a surface which gave us at the same moment both these sets of sensations ; but whenever in our experience a surface originally plane, came to give us the sensations we receive from a convex surface (as for instance when we bend a flat sheet of paper), it, at the very same moment, ceased to be, or to appear, a plane. The commencement of the one set of sensations has always been simultaneous with the cessation of the other set, and this experience, not being affected by any change of circumstances, has the constancy and invariability of a law of nature. It forms a correspondingly strong association ; and we become unable to have an idea of either set of sensations, those of planeness or those of convexity, without having the idea of the disappearance of the other set, if they existed previously. I believe it will be found that all the mental incompatibilities, the impossibilities of thought, of which so much is made by a certain class of metaphysicians, can be accounted for in a similar manner.—*Ed.*

to remark, that there are large classes of our sensations, such as many of those in the alimentary duct, and many in the nervous and vascular systems, which serve, as antecedents, to introduce ideas, as consequents; but as the consequents are far more interesting than themselves, and immediately absorb the attention, the antecedents are habitually overlooked; and though they exercise, by the trains which they introduce, a great influence on our happiness or misery, they themselves are generally wholly unknown.

That there are connections between our ideas and certain states of the internal organs, is proved by many familiar instances. Thus, anxiety, in most people, disorders the digestion. It is no wonder, then, that the internal feelings which accompany indigestion, should excite the ideas which prevail in a state of anxiety. Fear, in most people, accelerates, in a remarkable manner, the vermicular motion of the intestines. There is an association, therefore, between certain states of the intestines, and terrible ideas; and this is sufficiently confirmed by the horrible dreams to which men are subject from indigestion; and the hypochondria, more or less afflicting, which almost always accompanies certain morbid states of the digestive organs. The grateful food which excites pleasurable sensations in the mouth, continues them in the stomach; and, as pleasures excite ideas of their causes, and these of similar causes, and causes excite ideas of their effects, and so on, trains of pleasurable ideas take their origin from pleasurable sensations in the stomach. Uneasy sensations in the stomach, produce analogous effects. Disagreeable sensations are asso-

ciated with disagreeable circumstances ; a train is introduced, in which, one painful idea following another,
combinations, to the last degree afflictive, are sometimes introduced, and the sufferer is altogether over-
whelmed by dismal associations.[31] [32]

---

[31] There is more than association in the case here supposed.
Fear, anxiety, and painful emotions generally, cause disorder
in the digestive and other vital functions, as a part of their
nature.   Every mental state can be proved to have its coun-
terpart physical state ; joy, sorrow, fear, are each embodied in
a distinct group of physical effects in the nervous system, the
muscular movements, and the organic processes.   The physical side of agreeable emotions, as a rule, is a heightened tone
of the purely animal functions.   The physical side of fear is a
complicated series of effects, one of them being the depression
of the organic processes, digestion among the rest.   In this
respect, however, it more or less resembles severe pain, sorrow,
shame, remorse, and other states, characterised by the general
phrase " depressing passions ;" the depression being both mental and physical.

The reciprocal agency described in the text, whereby the
painful sensations of indigestion induce fear, is not dependent
on the association of ideas, but on the deep connections of the
emotional states with one another, through their physical accompaniments.   A painful feeling of indigestion has much in
common with states of depression due to mental causes, as,
for example, the shock of a misfortune, fear, sorrow, and the
like.   From this alliance it favours the ideas of depressing
states.   It does more ; it directly reduces that vigorous tone
of the system, which is the support of the courageous and
sanguine disposition ; and hence, surrenders the mind an easy
prey to any chance incentive of alarm or anxiety.—B.

[32] The law of association laid down in this section ranks
among the principal of what may be termed the laws of Obli-
viscence.   It is one of the widest in its action, and most im-

In illustration of the fact, that sensations and ideas, which are essential to some of the most important

---

portant in its consequences of all the laws of the mind; and the merit of the author, in the large use he makes of it is very great, as, though it is the key that unlocks many of the more mysterious phenomena of the mind, it is among the least familiar of the mental laws, and is not only overlooked by the great majority of psychologists, but some, otherwise of merit, seem unable to see and understand the law after any quantity of explanation.

The first, however, of the examples by which the author illustrates this law, is not marked by his usual felicity. Its shortcomings are pointed out by Mr. Bain in the preceding note. The internal feelings (says the author) which accompany indigestion, introduce trains of ideas (as in the case of horrible dreams, and of hypochondria) which are acutely painful, and may embitter the whole existence, while the sensations themselves, being comparatively of little interest, are unheeded and forgotten. It is true that the sensations in the alimentary canal, directly produced by indigestion, though (as every one knows) in some cases intense, are in others so slight as not to fix the attention, and yet may be followed by melancholy trains of thought, the connection of which with the state of the digestion may be entirely unobserved : but by far the most probable supposition appears to be, that these painful trains are not excited by the sensations, but that they and the sensations are joint or successive effects of a common organic cause. It is difficult to comprehend how these obscure sensations can excite the distressing trains of ideas by the laws of association ; for what opportunity have these sensations usually had of becoming associated, either synchronously or successively, with those ideas ? The explanation, in the text, of this difficulty, seems surprisingly insufficient. Anxiety, in most people, disorders the digestion ; and consequently, according to the author, the sensations of indigestion excite the ideas which prevail in a state of anxiety. If that were the

operations of our minds, serve only as antecedents to
more important consequents, and are themselves so

true explanation, the only persons with whom indigestion
would depress the spirits, would be those who had suffered
previous depression of spirits, sufficient in duration and intensity
to disorder the digestion, and to keep it disordered long enough
to effect a close and inseparable cohesion between even very
slight sensations of indigestion and painful ideas excited by
other causes. Surely this is not the fact. The theory has a
true application in the case of the confirmed hypochondriac.
When the sensations have been repeatedly experienced along
with the melancholy trains of thought, a direct association is
likely to grow up between the two ; and when this has been
effected, the first touch of the sensations may bring back in
full measure the miserable mental state which had coexisted
with them, thus increasing not only the frequency of its recurrence, but, by the conjunction of two exciting causes, the
intensity of the misery. But the origin of the state must
be looked for elsewhere, and is probably to be sought in
physiology.

The other example in the text seems still less relevant.
Fear tends to accelerate the peristaltic motion, therefore there
is a connection between certain states of the intestines and
terrible ideas. To make this available for the author's purpose,
the consequence of the connection ought to be, that accelera-
tion of the peristaltic motion excites ideas of terror. But does
it ? The state of indigestion characteristic of hypochondria
is not looseness of the bowels, but is commonly attended with
the exact opposite. The author's usual acuteness of discern-
ment seems to have been, in these cases, blunted by an
unwillingness to admit the possibility that ideas as well as
sensations may be directly affected by material conditions.
But if, as he admits, ideas have a direct action on our bodily
organs, a *prima facie* case is made out for the localization of
our ideas, equally with our sensations, in some part of our
bodily system; and there is at least no antecedent presumption

habitually overlooked, that their existence is unknown, we may recur to the remarkable case which we have just explained, of the ideas introduced by the sensations of sight. The minute gradations of colour, which accompany varieties of extension, figure, and distance, are insignificant. The figure, the size, the distance, themselves, on the other hand, are matters of the greatest importance. The first having introduced the last, their work is done. The consequents remain the sole objects of attention, the antecedents are forgotten ; in the present instance, not completely ; in other instances, so completely, that they cannot be recognised. [33] [34]

---

against the supposition that the action may be reciprocal—that as ideas sometimes derange the organic functions, so derangements of organic functions may sometimes modify the trains of our ideas by their own physical action on the brain and nerves, and not through the associations connected with the sensations they excite.—*Ed.*

[33] Perhaps the most remarkable case of sensations overlooked on their own account, and considered only as a means of suggesting something else, is the visual, or retinal, magnitude of objects seen by the eye. This is probably the most delicate sensibility within the compass of the mind ; and yet we habitually disregard it for all things near us, and use it solely for perceiving real magnitude as estimated by our locomotive and other members. The visual magnitude of a table, or other article in a room, is never thought of for itself; although incessantly fluctuating we never think of the fluctuations ; we pass from these to the one constant perception, named the true or real magnitude. It is only for remote objects,—as the sun and moon, the clouds, the distant hills,—that the retinal magnitude abides with us in its own proper character. In looking down a vista, we may also be aroused to the feeling of

11. Mr. Hume, and after him other philosophers, have said that our ideas are associated according to

---

retinal magnitude. For perspective drawing, it is necessary that we should arrest the strong tendency to pass from the visible, to the real, forms and dimensions of things.—*B*.

[34] The reader, it may be hoped, is now familiar with the important psychological fact, so powerfully grasped and so discerningly employed by Hartley and the author of the Analysis,—that when, through the frequent repetition of a series of sensations, the corresponding train of ideas rushes through the mind with extreme rapidity, some of the links are apt to disappear from consciousness as completely as if they had never formed part of the series. It has been a subject of dispute among philosophers which of three things takes place in this case. Do the lost ideas pass through the mind without consciousness? Do they pass consciously through the mind and are they then instantly forgotten? Or do they never come into the mind at all, being, as it were, overleaped and pressed out by the rush of the subsequent ideas?

It would seem, at first sight, that the first and third suppositions involve impossibilities, and that the second, therefore, is the only one which we are at liberty to adopt. As regards the first, it may be said—How can we have a feeling without feeling it, in other words, without being conscious of it? With regard to the third, how, it may be asked, can any link of the chain have been altogether absent, through the pressure of the subsequent links? The subsequent ideas are only there because called up by it, and would not have arisen at all unless it had arisen first, however short a time it may have lasted. These arguments seem strong, but are not so strong as they seem.

In favour of the first supposition, that feelings may be unconsciously present, various facts and arguments are adduced by Sir William Hamilton in his Lectures; but I think I have shewn in another work, that the arguments are inconclusive, and the facts equally reconcilable with the second of the three

three principles ; Contiguity in time and place, Causation, and Resemblance.   The Contiguity in time and

---

hypotheses.   That a feeling should not be felt appears to me
a contradiction both in words and in nature.   But, though a
feeling cannot exist without being felt, the organic state which
is the antecedent of it may exist, and the feeling itself not follow.
This happens, either if the organic state is not of sufficient
duration, or if an organic state stronger than itself, and conflicting with it, is affecting us at the same moment.   I hope
to be excused for quoting what I have said elsewhere on this
subject (Examination of Sir William Hamilton's Philosophy,
ch. 15).

" In the case, for instance, of a soldier who receives a wound
" in battle, but in the excitement of the moment is not aware
" of the fact, it is difficult not to believe that if the wound
" had been accompanied by the usual sensation, so vivid a
" feeling would have forced itself to be attended to and re-
" membered.   The supposition which seems most probable is,
" that the nerves of the particular part were affected as they
" would have been by the same cause in any other circum-
" stances, but that, the nervous centres being intensely
" occupied with other impressions, the affection of the local
" nerves did not reach them, and no sensation was excited.   In
" like manner, if we admit (what physiology is rendering more
" and more probable) that our mental feelings, as well as our
" sensations, have for their physical antecedents particular
" states of the nerves ; it may well be believed that the ap-
" parently suppressed links in a chain of association, those
" which Sir William Hamilton considers as latent, really are
" so ; that they are not, even momentarily, felt ; the chain of
" causation being continued only physically, by one organic
" state of the nerves succeeding another so rapidly that the
" state of mental consciousness appropriate to each is not pro-
" duced.   We have only to suppose, either that a nervous
" modification of too short duration does not produce any sen-
" sation or mental feeling at all, or that the rapid succession of

place, must mean, that of the sensations ; and so far
it is affirmed, that the order of the ideas follows that

" different nervous modifications makes the feelings produced
" by them interfere with each other, and become confounded
" in one mass. The former of these suppositions is extremely
" probable, while of the truth of the latter we have positive
" proof. An example of it is the experiment which Sir W.
" Hamilton quoted from Mr. Mill, and which had been noticed
" before either of them by Hartley. It is known that the seven
" prismatic colours, combined in certain proportions, produce
" the white light of the solar ray. Now, if the seven colours
" are painted on spaces bearing the same proportion to one
" another as in the solar spectrum, and the coloured surface so
" produced is passed rapidly before the eyes, as by the turning
" of a wheel, the whole is seen as white. The physiological
" explanation of this phenomenon may be deduced from
" another common experiment. If a lighted torch, or a bar
" heated to luminousness, is waved rapidly before the eye, the
" appearance produced is that of a ribbon of light ; which is
" universally understood to prove that the visual sensation
" persists for a certain short time after its cause has ceased.
" Now, if this happens with a single colour, it will happen with
" a series of colours : and if the wheel on which the prismatic
" colours have been painted, is turned with the same rapidity
" with which the torch was waved, each of the seven sensations
" of colour will last long enough to be contemporaneous with
" all the others, and they will naturally produce by their com-
" bination the same colour as if they had, from the beginning,
" been excited simultaneously. If anything similar to this
" obtains in our consciousness generally (and that it obtains in
" many cases of consciousness there can be no doubt) it will
" follow that whenever the organic modifications of our nervous
" fibres succeed one another at an interval shorter than the
" duration of the sensations or other feelings corresponding to
" them, those sensations or feelings will, so to speak, overlap
" one another, and becoming simultaneous instead of succes-

of the sensations. Contiguity of two sensations in time, means the successive order. Contiguity of two

---

" sive, will blend into a state of feeling, probably as unlike the
" elements out of which it is engendered, as the colour white is
" unlike the prismatic colours. And this may be the source of
" many of those states of internal or mental feeling which we
" cannot distinctly refer to a prototype in experience, our ex-
" perience only supplying the elements from which, by this
" kind of mental chemistry, they are composed. The elemen-
" tary feelings may then be said to be latently present, or to be
" present but not in consciousness. The truth, however, is
" that the feelings themselves are not present, consciously or
" latently, but that the nervous modifications which are their
" usual antecedents have been present, while the consequents
" have been frustrated, and another consequent has been pro-
" duced instead."

In this modified form, therefore, the first of the three hypotheses may possibly be true. Let us now consider the third,
that of the entire elision of some of the ideas which form the
associated train. This supposition seemed to be inadmissible,
because the loss of any link would, it was supposed, cause the
chain itself to break off at that point. To make the hypothesis
possible, it is only, however, necessary to suppose, that, while
the association is acquiring the promptitude and rapidity which
it ultimately attains, each of the successive ideas abides for a
brief interval in our consciousness after it has already called
up the idea which is to succeed it. Each idea in the series,
though introduced, not by synchronous, but by successive
association, is thus, during a part of its continuance, synchronous with the idea which introduced it : and as the rapidity
of the suggestions increases by still further repetition, an idea
may become synchronous with another which was originally
not even contiguous to it, but separated from it by an intervening link ; or may come into immediate instead of mediate
sequence with such an idea. When either of these states of
things has continued for some time, a direct association of the

sensations in place, means the synchronous order. We have explained the mode in which ideas are associated, in the synchronous, as well as the successive order, and have traced the principle of contiguity to its proper source.

Causation, the second of Mr. Hume's principles, is the same with contiguity in time, or the order of succession. Causation is only a name for the order established between an antecedent and a consequent; that is, the established or constant antecedence of the one,

---

synchronous or of the successive kind will be generated between two ideas which are not proximate links in the chain; A will acquire a direct power of exciting C, independently of the intervening idea B. If, then, B is much less interesting than C, and especially if B is of no importance at all in itself, but only by exciting C, and has therefore nothing to make the mind dwell on it after C has been reached, the association of A with C is likely to become stronger than that of A with B: C will be habitually excited directly by A; as the mind runs off to the further ideas suggested by C, B will cease to be excited at all; and the train of association, like a stream which breaking though its bank cuts off a bend in its course, will thenceforth flow in the direct line AC, omitting B. This supposition accounts more plausibly than either of the others for the truly wonderful rapidity of thought, since it does not make so large a demand as the other theories on our ability to believe that a prodigious number of different ideas can successively rush through the mind in an instant too short for measurement.

The result is, that all the three theories of this mental process seem to be quite possible; and it is not unlikely that each of them may be the real process in some cases, either in different persons, or in the same persons under different circumstances. I can only remit the question to future psychologists, who may be able to contrive crucial experiments for deciding among these various possibilities.—*Ed.*

and consequence of the other. Resemblance only remains, as an alleged principle of association, and it is necessary to inquire whether it is included in the laws which have been above expounded. I believe it will be found that we are accustomed to see like things together. When we see a tree, we generally see more trees than one ; when we see an ox, we gene- rally see more oxen than one ; a sheep, more sheep than one ; a man, more men than one. From this observation, I think, we may refer resemblance to the law of frequency, of which it seems to form only a particular case.[35]

---

[35] The reason assigned by the author for considering asso- ciation by resemblance as a case of association by contiguity, is perhaps the least successful attempt at a generalisation and simplification of the laws of mental phenomena, to be found in the work. It ought to be remembered that the author, as the text shows, attached little importance to it. And perhaps, not thinking it important, he passed it over with a less amount of patient thought than he usually bestowed on his analyses.

Objects, he thinks, remind us of other objects resembling them, because we are accustomed to see like-things together. But we are also accustomed to see like things separate. When two combinations incompatible with one another are both realised in familiar experience, it requires a very great prepon- derance of experience on one side to determine the association specially to either. We are also much accustomed to see un- like things together ; I do not mean things contrasted, but simply unlike. Unlikeness, therefore, not amounting to con- trast, ought to be as much a cause of association as likeness. Besides, the fact that when we see (for instance) a sheep, we usually see more sheep than one, may cause us, when we think of a sheep, to think of an entire flock ; but it does not explain why, when we see a sheep with a black mark on its

Mr. Hume makes contrast a principle of association, but not a separate one, as he thinks it is compounded

---

forehead, we are reminded of a sheep with a similar mark, formerly seen, though we never saw two such sheep together. It does not explain why a portrait makes us think of the original, or why a stranger whom we see for the first time reminds us of a person of similar appearance whom we saw many years ago. The law by which an object reminds us of similar objects which we have been used to see along with it, must be a different law from that by which it reminds us of similar objects which we have not been used to see along with it. But it is the same law by which it reminds us of dissimilar objects which we have been used to see along with it. The sight of a sheep, if it reminds us of a flock of sheep, probably by the same law of contiguity, reminds us of a meadow ; but it must be by some other law that it reminds us of a single sheep previously seen, and of the occasion on which we saw that single sheep.

The attempt to resolve association by resemblance into association by contiguity must perforce be unsuccessful, inasmuch as there never could have been association by contiguity without a previous association by resemblance. Why does a sensation received this instant remind me of sensations which I formerly had (as we commonly say), along with it ? I never had them along with this very sensation. I never had this sensation until now, and can never have it again. I had the former sensations in conjunction not with it, but with a sensation exactly like it. And my present sensation could not remind me of those former sensations unlike itself, unless by first reminding me of the sensation like itself, which really did coexist with them. There is thus a law of association anterior to, and presupposed by, the law of contiguity : namely, that a sensation tends to recall what is called the idea of itself, that is, the remembrance of a sensation like itself, if such has previously been experienced. This is implied in what we call *recognising* a sensation, as one which has been felt before ;

of Resemblance and Causation.   It is not necessary
for us to show that this is an unsatisfactory account

---

more correctly, as undistinguishably resembling one which has
been felt before.   The law in question was scientifically enunciated, and included, I believe for the first time, in the list of
Laws of Association, by Sir William Hamilton, in one of the
Dissertations appended to his edition of Reid : but the fact itself
is recognised by the author of the Analysis, in various passages
of his work ; more especially in the second section of the
fourteenth chapter.   There is, therefore, a suggestion by resemblance—a calling up of the idea of a past sensation by a
present sensation like it—which not only does not depend on
association by contiguity, but is itself the foundation which
association by contiguity requires for its support.

When it is admitted that simple sensations remind us of one
another by direct resemblance, many of the complex cases of
suggestion by resemblance may be analysed into this elementary case of association by resemblance, combined with an
association by contiguity.   A flower, for instance, may remind
us of a former flower resembling it, because the present flower
exhibits to us certain qualities, that is, excites in us certain
sensations, resembling and recalling to our remembrance
those we had from the former flower, and these recall the entire
image of the flower by the law of association by contiguity.
But this explanation, though it serves for many cases of complex phenomena suggesting one another by resemblance, does
not suffice for all.   For, the resemblance of complex facts
often consists, not solely, or principally, in likeness between the
simple sensations, but far more in likeness of the manner of
their combination, and it is often by this, rather than by the
single features, that they recall one another.   After we had
seen, and well observed, a single triangle, when we afterwards
saw a second there can be little doubt that it would at once
remind us of the first by mere resemblance.   But the suggestion would not depend on the sides or on the angles, any or
all of them ; for we might have seen such sides and such

of contrast. It is only necessary to observe, that, as a case of association, it is not distinct from those which we have above explained.

A dwarf suggests the idea of a giant. How? We call a dwarf a dwarf, because he departs from a certain standard. We call a giant a giant, because he departs from the same standard. This is a case, therefore, of resemblance, that is, of frequency.

Pain is said to make us think of pleasure; and this is considered a case of association by contrast. There is no doubt that pain makes us think of relief from it; because they have been conjoined, and the great vividness of the sensations makes the association strong. Relief from pain is a species of pleasure; and one pleasure leads to think of another, from the resemblance. This is a compound case, therefore, of vividness and frequency. All other cases of contrast, I believe, may be expounded in a similar manner.

I have not thought it necessary to be tedious in expounding the observations which I have thus stated; for whether the reader supposes that resemblance is, or is not, an original principle of association, will not affect our future investigations.

12. Not only do simple ideas, by strong association, run together, and form complex ideas: but a

---

angles uncombined, or combined into some other figure. The resemblance by which one triangle recalls the idea of another is not resemblance in the parts, but principally and emphatically in the manner in which the parts are put together. I am unable to see any mode in which this case of suggestion can be accounted for by contiguity; any mode, at least, which would fit all cases of the kind.—*Ed.*

complex idea, when the simple ideas which compose it have become so consolidated that it always appears as one, is capable of entering into combinations with other ideas, both simple and complex. Thus two complex ideas may be united together, by a strong association, and coalesce into one, in the same manner as two or more simple ideas coalesce into one. This union of two complex ideas into one, Dr. Hartley has called a duplex idea.[37] Two also of these duplex, or doubly compounded ideas, may unite into one; and these again into other compounds, without end. It is hardly necessary to mention, that as two complex ideas unite to form a duplex one, not only two, but more than two may so unite; and what he calls a duplex idea may be compounded of two, three, four, or any number of complex ideas.

Some of the most familiar objects with which we are acquainted furnish instances of these unions of complex and duplex ideas.

Brick is one complex idea, mortar is another complex idea; these ideas, with ideas of position and quantity, compose my idea of a wall. My idea of a plank is a complex idea, my idea of a rafter is a complex idea, my idea of a nail is a complex idea. These, united with the same ideas of position and quantity, compose my duplex idea of a floor. In the same manner my complex idea of glass, and wood, and others, compose my duplex idea of a window; and

---

[37] I have been unable to trace in Hartley the expression here ascribed to him. In every passage that I can discover, the name he gives to a combination of two or more complex ideas is that of a *decomplex* idea.—*Ed.*

these duplex ideas, united together, compose my idea of a house, which is made up of various duplex ideas. How many complex, or duplex ideas, are all united in the idea of furniture? How many more in the idea of merchandize? How many more in the idea called Every Thing?[38] [39]

---

[38] This chapter raises questions of the most fundamental kind relating to our intellectual constitution. The Association of Ideas, comprehensively viewed, involves everything connected with the mental persistence and reproduction of ideas; being offered as adequate to explain the operations named Memory, Reason, and Imagination.

Conditions of the Growth of Association, or of the Retentiveness of the Mind.—A practical, as well as a theoretical, interest attaches to the precise statement of the conditions or circumstances that regulate the growth of our associations, in other words our mental culture generally. All agree in the efficacy of the two conditions mentioned in the text; the vividness of the feelings associated, and the frequency of the association, that is repetition or practice. It is well remarked, however, that the phrase " vividness of the sensations or ideas" does not convey a very precise meaning. The proper attribute of a sensation, or an idea, considered as an *intellectual* element, is greater or less distinctness; when an object seen or remembered is seen or remembered distinctly and fully, and without any unusual labour or effort, there is nothing more to be desired, so far as concerns our intelligence. If, however, the object is accompanied with *feeling*—with pleasure or pain—a new element is introduced, to which other epithets are applicable. A feeling is more or less strong or intense; and the addition of an intense feeling to an intellectual conception is a sum, combining both sets of attributes—distinctness and adequacy in the conception, and intensity in the feeling. An object whose perception or conception is thus accompanied with the animation of strong feeling, is called lively, or vivid;

in the absence of feeling, these epithets are unsuitable. Hence, the associating stimulus expressed by " vividness" is better expressed by the "strength of the feelings." Any strong feeling impresses on the mind whatever is the object of it, or is in any way mixed up with it. We remember by preference the things that have given us either pleasure or pain ; and the effect may be produced by mere excitement although neither pleasurable nor painful ; the influence of a surprise being a case in point. Our *interest* in a thing is but another name for the pleasure that it gives us ; and to inspire interest is to aid the memory. Hamilton's Law of *Preference* refers to this source ; and appears to exclude, or not to recognise, the efficacy of feelings not pleasurable, namely, such as are either painful or neutral. The comprehensive law should include all the feelings, although there are specific characters attaching to the influence of each of the three modes. Pleasure is the most effectual in stamping the memory, as it is the most powerful in detaining the attention and the thoughts. Pain has a conflicting operation ; as affecting the will, it repels the object ; but as mere excitement it retains it ; we cannot forget what is disagreeable, merely because we wish to forget it. The stimulant of pain, as applied in education, is an indirect pleasure. ·It is not intended to make the subject of the lesson disagreeable, but to render painful all diversions from that towards other subjects ; so that comparatively the most pleasing course to a pupil may be to abide by the task prescribed.

The influence of the Feelings upon Retentiveness is not throughout in proportion to their degree, whether they are pleasurable, painful, or neutral. We have to introduce a modifying circumstance into the case, namely, that great strength of feeling absorbs the forces of the system, and diminishes the power available for cementing an intellectual association   A strong feeling once aroused, while inflaming the attention upon whatever is bound up with it, necessarily engages us with itself. The plastic process of fixing a train or aggregate of ideas has but a share of the energies awakened under feeling.

It is possible also to stimulate attention, and thereby to

quicken memory, without the excitement of the feelings, as in pure voluntary attention. For although the will, in the last resort, is stimulated by an end (which must involve the feelings), yet we may be strongly moved without being under the excitement of the feelings that enter into the final end. Our volitions may be energetic, without the presence of strong emotions, notwithstanding that, apart from our possessing such emotions, we should not be strongly moved to action. Thus, a difference is made between the influence of the feelings and the influence of the will ; both being powers to impress the memory.

The two considerations now advanced,—namely, the want of strict concomitance between strength of feeling and the stimulus to memory, and the operation of the will in the abeyance of present feeling,—make it desirable to find some other mode of stating the element or condition that qualifies the influence of Frequency or Repetition, in the growth of memory and association. Perhaps the best mode of singling out the operative circumstance is to describe it as " Concentration of Mind ;" the devotion of the mental forces to the thing to be done or remembered —the withdrawal of power from other exercises, to expend it on the exercise in hand. Every circumstance that at once rouses the mental and nervous energies, and keeps them fixed upon any subject of study or the practice of any art, is a circumstance in aid of acquisition. No fact more comprehensive, more exactly in point, can be assigned than the one now stated. What remains is to apply it in the detail, or to point out the occasions and conditions that favour, and those that obstruct, the concentration of the mental energy. It is under this view that we can best appreciate the efficacy of pleasure (interest in the subject), of pain, of mere excitement, and of voluntary attention. We can also see, as an obvious corollary, the advantage of having the mind unoccupied, or disengaged for the work, and the disadvantage of being diverted, or distracted by other objects. Fear, care, anxiety, are hostile to culture by lowering the tone or energy of the mind ; while what power is left concentrates itself upon the subject matter of the anxious feeling. On the other hand, general vigour of the system, good health, easy circumstances, are all in favour of mental improvement, provided the force thus made available can be reserved and devoted to that end.

Thus the two leading conditions of the plastic process are Frequency of Repetition, and Mental Concentration. For practical purposes, these are all that we need to consider, at least as regards the same individual. We have no art or device for training either body or mind but what is comprised under one or other of these heads. There are methods of superseding the labour of new acquirement, by adapting existing acquirements to new cases ; but no means can be assigned for the original construction of adhesive links, apart from these two circumstances.

Still, in a large and exhaustive view of the Retentive power of the mind, we should not omit to allow for the differences between one mind and another in respect of Natural Aptitude for acquiring. When two persons engaged in the same lesson, for equal periods of time, and with about equal concentration of mind, make very unequal progress, we must admit a difference in natural or constitutional plasticity on that particular subject. Sometimes we find extraordinary progress made in acquisition generally ; the same person excelling in languages, in sciences, in practical arts, and in fine arts. More commonly, however, we find an aptitude for some subject in particular, combined with deficiency in other things. One person has great mechanical acquirements, another lingual, and so on.

The first case is sufficiently common to justify the assumption of degrees of acquisitive or plastic aptitude on the whole, or a variety in the cerebral endowment corresponding to the adhesion of trains of actions and ideas that have been more or less frequently brought together. If the differences among human beings are not so broad as to make this apparent, we may refer to the differences between the lower animals and man. The animals have the power of acquiring, but so limited is that power in comparison with human beings, that people have often doubted its existence.

The second case, the inequality of the same person's progress in different subjects, may be looked at in another way. We may view it as incident to the better or worse quality, for all purposes, of the special organs concerned. Thus to take musical acquisition. This is commonly attributed to a good ear, meaning a delicate sense of musical notes. as shown in their nice discrimination. Discriminating is a different function from remembering ; yet, we can only doubt that the fact of being able to discriminate acutely is accompanied by the power of remembering or retaining the impressions of the sense. The superiority of endowment that shows itself in the one function, embraces also the other. Hence we are entitled to say that the special retentiveness for any one subject, or department of training, varies with the local endowment involved : which is not to maintain an identical proposition, for the local endowment may be held as tested by delicacy of discrimination, a distinct fact from memory. Thus, a delicate sense of shades of colour would entail a good visual memory for spectacle ; a delicate ear for articulation would indicate a memory for shades and varieties of pronunciation, thereby counting as a part of the verbal memory. So, delicate discrimination in the tactile muscles would be followed by rapid acquirements in manipulative or manual art.

The Ultimate Analysis of the Laws of Association.—It is easy to reduce all the laws ever assigned, as governing the reproduction of our ideas, to three, Contiguity, Similarity, and Contrast. It is open to question whether these can be resolved any farther. The author has endeavoured to reduce Similarity to Contiguity, but his reasons show that he had not deeply considered the workings of similarity. Hamilton's criticisms on the attempt (Reid, p. 914) are just and irrefragable. By far the most important examples of the working of similarity are such as, by their very nature, preclude a former contiguity : as, for example, Franklin's identification of Electricity and lightning.

There is, nevertheless, a considerable degree of subtlety in the relationship of the two principles. There may be good reasons for treating them as distinct, but in their working they are inextricably combined. There can be no contiguity without similarity, and no similarity without contiguity. When, looking at a river, we pronounce its name, we are properly said to exemplify contiguity; the river and the name by frequent association are so united that each recalls the other. But mark the steps of the recall. What is strictly present to our view is the impression made by the river while we gaze on it. It is necessary that this impression should, by virtue of similarity or identity, re-instate the previous impression of the river, to which the previous impression of the name was contiguous. If one could suppose failure in the re-instatement of the former idea of the river, under the new presentation, there would be no opportunity given to the contiguous bond to come into operation. In that accumulation of the impressions of contiguous ideas, ending at last in a firm association, there must be a process of similarity to the extent of reviving the sum of the past at the instance of the present. This is a case of similarity that we give little heed to, because it is sure and unfailing; we concern ourselves more with what is liable to uncertainty, the acquired strength of the contiguous adhesion. Yet it strictly comes under the case of reproduction through similarity.

Consider again, what may be called a case of Similarity proper, as when a portrait recalls the original. The sensuous effects possessed in common by the portrait and by its subject bring about a restoration of the idea of the subject, in spite of certain differences or discrepancies. The interest of this case is owing to the fact that a partial likeness, a likeness in unlikeness, will often reproduce a past idea; thus enabling us to assemble in the mind a number of things differing in some respects because they agree in other respects. This is not identifying a thing with itself, viewed at a former time, but assimilating one thing with other things placed far asunder in nature, and having many features of difference.

Let us try and express the consecutive steps of this case of reproduction. The thing now present to the mind has certain peculiarities in common with one or more things formerly present ; as when, in a portrait, the outline and colouring resembles a subject original. These sensible effects make alive the previous recurrence of them, or put us in the cerebral and mental attitude formerly experienced by the corresponding effects of the resembling object. We are aware, by the liveliness of our impression, that we have gone in upon an old track ; we have the peculiar consciousness called the consciousness of Identity or Agreement. This is one step, but not the whole. In order that the complete restoration may be effected, the features of community must be in such firm contiguous alliance with the features of difference—the *special* part of the previous subject—that the one shall reinstate the idea of the other. The points common to a present portrait and a past original must be so strongly coherent with the remaining features of the original, that the one cannot be awakened without the other following. Here, then, in the very heart of Similarity, is an indispensable bond of Contiguity ; showing that it is not possible for either process to be accomplished in separation from the other. The mutual coherence of parts, now described as essential to reproduction, may be too weak for the purpose, and the recovering stroke of similarity will in that case fail.

It might, therefore, be supposed that Similarity is, after all, but a mode of Contiguity, namely, the contiguity or association of the different features or parts of a complex whole. The inference is too hasty. Because contiguity is a part of the fact of the restoration of similars, it is not the entire fact. There is a distinct and characteristic step preceding the play of this mutual coherence of the parts of the thing to be recovered. The striking into the former track of the agreeing part of the new and the old, is a mental movement by itself, which the other follows, but does not do away with. The effect above described, as the consciousness of agreement or identity, the flash of a felt similarity, is real and distinct. We are conscious of it by itself ; there are occasions when we have it without the other, that is to say, without the full re-instatement of the former object in its entireness. We often aware of an identity without being able to say what is the thing identified ; as when a portrait gives us the impression that we have seen the original, without enabling us to say who the original is. We have been affected by the stroke of identity or similarity ; but the restoration fails from the feebleness of the contiguous adherence of the parts of the object identified. There is thus a genuine effect of the nature of pure similarity, or resemblance, and a mode of consciousness accompanying that effect ; but there is not the full energy of reproduction without a concurring bond of pure contiguity. A portrait may fail to give us the consciousness of having ever seen the original. On the supposition that we have seen the original, this would be a failure of pure similarity.

Thus in every act of reproducing a past mental experience, there is a complication, involving both contiguity proper and similarity proper. When the similarity amounts to identity, as when a new impression of a thing puts us in the track of the old impressions of the same thing, the effect is so sure, so obvious, so easily arrived t, that we do not need to think of it, to make a question of it. It does not prevent us from regarding the operation of recalling a name when we see the thing, or recalling a thing when we hear the name, as pure contiguity. The strength of the coherence may be deficient, and the restoration may fail on this account ; it can never fail on account of insufficient similarity. No inconvenience will arise from speaking of this case as if it were Contiguity and nothing else.

The situation of Similarity in Diversity is quite distinct. The diversity obstructs the operation of similarity ; we cannot be sure that the new shall put us on the track of the old. It is always a question whether such similarities shall be felt at all ; whether we shall experience the flash, the peculiar consciousness, of agreement in difference. It is a farther question, whether the internal coherence of the thing identified is enough to restore it in completeness. This last step may be allowed to be a case of proper contiguity ; while the flash of identity struck between a present and a past, never coupled in the mind before, is an effect *sui generis*, and not resolvable into any mode or incident of contiguity.

The circumstances of this identifying stroke are so numerous and far-reaching as to demand a special exemplification. Some of the broadest distinctions of intellectual character can be grounded on the distinctive aptitudes of the mind for Contiguity and for Similarity.

Learning, Acquisition, Memory, Habit, all designate the plastic adherence of contiguous impressions. The processes of Classification, Reasoning, Imagination, and the Inventive faculty generally, depend upon the identifying stroke of likeness in unlikeness. Some forms of intellectual strength, as a whole, are best represented by a highly energetic Adhesiveness; distinction as a learner, a follower of routine, turns upon this power. Other, and higher, forms of intelligence depend upon far-reaching strokes of similarity; the identification of likeness shrouded in diversity, expresses much of the genius of the poet, the philosopher, the man of practice.

There remains the consideration of Contrast, as a link of association. It is easy to show that both Contiguity and Similarity may enter into the association of contrasts. All contrasts that we are interested in are habitually coupled in language, as light and dark, heat and cold, up and down, life and death. Again contrasts suppose a common genus, that is a generic similarity; at least until we ascend to the highest contrast of all, the subject mind, and the object or extended world. Cold and Hot are grades of the common attribute called Temperature. As these links of contiguity and similarity are present, and of considerable strength, they practically lead to the mutual suggestion of contrasting things.

Still, we cannot overlook the deeper circumstance that in contrast there is *relation*, and therefore mutual implication, so that the two members must always be virtually present, although they are not equally attended to. Heat has no meaning, no existence, but as a change from cold; the north implicates the south. We have two modes of regarding these relationships, which are distinguished by language, as if we could abstract the one side from the other; that is, we think of heat apart from cold, and of the north apart from the south. But if one side is present, both must be present, and nothing is wanted but a motive, to make us reverse the conception, and bring into prominence the side that was in abeyance, cold instead of heat, south instead of north.

This view of Contrast is variously expressed by Hamilton. (Reid, Note D * * *).

Contrast, therefore, as an associating link, would draw from three sources, Relativity, Contiguity, and Similarity. It would also be heightened, in many instances, by the presence of strong feelings or emotions, as in the contemplation of startling changes, and the vicissitudes of things. Being one of the effects habitually introduced in Art and in Oratory, we are more than ordinarily impressed by the things so made use of—infancy beside old age, squalor following on splendour, abasement succeeding to elevation.

The associating principle of Contrast cannot be put forward as a basis of distinction in intellectual character. There is no such a thing as a special aptitude for Contrasts. There may be, in certain minds given to emotion, a fondness for the impressive or emotional contrasts; but there is no intellectual gift, subsisting apart from other powers and rising and falling independently, for the mutual recall of contrasting qualities. Whenever we feel a difference we make a contrast; the two differing things, are contrasting things, and are both known in one indivisible act of thought. To be unable to bring up the contrast of a subject present to the view, is not to know the subject; we cannot possess intelligently the conception of "up," and be oblivious to, or incapable of remembering, "down." Forgetfulness in this department is not the snapping of a link, as in Contiguity, or the dulness that cannot reach a similitude; it is the entire blank of conception or knowledge. The north pole of a magnet cannot be in the view, and the south pole in oblivion.—*B*.

[39] The author and Mr. Bain agree in rejecting Contrast as an independent principle of association. I think they might

have gone further, and denied it even as a derivative one. All the cases considered as examples of it seem to me to depend on something else. I greatly doubt if the sight or thought of a dwarf has intrinsically any tendency to recall the idea of a giant. Things certainly do remind us of their own absence, because (as pointed out by Mr. Bain) we are only conscious of their presence by comparison with their absence; and for a further reason, arising out of the former, viz. that, in our practical judgments, we are led to think of the case of their presence and the case of their absence by one and the same act of thought, having commonly to choose between the two. But it does not seem to me that things have any special tendency to remind us of their positive opposites. Black does not remind us of white more than of red or green. If light reminds us of darkness, it is because darkness is the mere negation, or absence, of light. The case of heat and cold is more complex. The sensation of heat recalls to us the absence of that sensation: if the sensation amounts to pain, it calls up the idea of relief from it; that is, of its absence, associated by contiguity with the pleasant feeling which accompanies the change. But cold is not the mere absence of heat; it is itself a positive sensation. If heat suggests to us the idea of the sensation of cold, it is not because of the contrast, but because the close connection which exists between the outward conditions of both, and the consequent identity of the means we employ for regulating them, cause the thought of cold and that of heat to be frequently presented to us in contiguity.—*Ed.*

CHAPTER IV.

NAMING.

"I endeavour, as much as I can, to deliver myself from those fallacies which we are apt to put upon ourselves, by taking words for things. It helps not our ignorance to feign a knowledge where we have none, by making a noise with sounds without clear and distinct significations. Names made at pleasure, neither alter the nature of things, nor make us understand them, but as they are signs of, and stand for, determined ideas."— *Locke, Hum. Und.* b. ii. ch. 13, § 18.

WE have now surveyed the more simple and obvious phenomena of the human mind. We have seen, first, that we have SENSATIONS; secondly, that we have IDEAS, the copies of those sensations; thirdly, that those ideas are sometimes SIMPLE, the copies of one sensation; sometimes COMPLEX, the copies of several sensations so combined as to appear not several ideas, but one idea; and, fourthly, that we have TRAINS of those ideas, or one succeeding another without end.

These are simple facts of our nature, attested by experience; and my chief object in fixing upon them the attention of the reader has been, to convey to him that accurate and steady conception of them, which is requisite for the successful prosecution of the subsequent inquiries.

After delineating the simple and elementary states of consciousness, it follows, in order, that we should endeavour to show what is contained in those that are complex.   But in all the more complicated cases of human consciousness something of the process of Naming is involved.   These cases, of course, cannot be unfolded, till the artifice of Naming is made known. This, therefore, is necessarily an intermediate inquiry; and one to which it is necessary that we should devote a particular degree of attention.

There are two purposes, both of great importance, for which marks of our ideas, and sensations ; or signs by which they may be denoted ; are necessary.   One of these purposes is, That we may be able to make known to others what passes within us.   The other is, That we may secure to ourselves the knowledge of what at any preceding time has passed in our minds.

The sensations and ideas of one man are hidden from all other men ; unless they have recourse to some expedient for disclosing them.   We cannot convey to another man our sensations and ideas directly. Our means of intercourse with other men are through their senses exclusively.   We must therefore choose some SENSIBLE OBJECTS, as SIGNS of our inward feelings. If two men agree, that each shall use a certain sensible sign, when one of them means to make known to the other that he has a certain sensation, or idea, they, in this, and in no other way, can communicate a knowledge of those feelings to one another.

Almost all the advantages, which man possesses above the inferior animals, arise from his power of acting in combination with his fellows ; and of accomplishing, by the united efforts of numbers, what could not be accomplished by the detached efforts of individuals. Without the power of communicating to one another their sensations and ideas, this co-operation would be impossible. The importance, therefore, of the invention of signs, or marks, by which alone that communication can be effected, is obvious.

Among sensible objects, those alone which are addressed to the senses of seeing and hearing have sufficient precision and variety to be adapted to this end. The language of Action, as it has been called, that is, certain gesticulations and motions, has very generally, especially among rude people, whose spoken language is scanty, been found in use to indicate certain states, generally complicated states, of mind. But, for precision, variety, and rapidity, the flexibility of the voice presented such obvious advantages, not to mention that visible signs must be altogether useless in the dark, that sounds, among all the varieties of our species, have been assumed as the principal medium by which their sensations and ideas were made known to one another.

There can be little doubt that, of the two uses of marks, Communicating our thoughts, and Recording them, the advantage of the first would be the earliest felt; and that signs for Communicating would be long invented, before any person would see the advantage of Recording his thoughts. After the use of signs for Communication had become familiar, it would not fail, in time, to appear that signs might be employed for Recordation also; and that, from this use of them, the highest advantages might be derived.

In respect to those advantages, the following particulars are to be observed.

1. We cannot recall any idea, or train of ideas, at will. Thoughts come into the mind unbidden. If they did not come unbidden, they must have been in the mind before they came into it ; which is a contradiction. You cannot bid a thought come into the mind, without knowing that which you bid ; but to know a thought is to have the thought : the knowledge of the thought, and the thought's being in the mind, are not two things but one and the same thing, under different names.

If we cannot recall at pleasure a single idea, we are not less unable to recall a train. Every person knows how evanescent his thoughts are, and how impossible it is for him to begin at the beginning of a past train, if it is not a train of the individual objects familiar to his senses, and go on to the end, neither leaving out any of the items which composed it, nor allowing any which did not belong to it, to enter in.

2. It is most obvious that, by ideas alone, the events which are passed, are to us any thing. If the objects which we have seen, heard, smelt, tasted, and touched, left no traces of themselves; if the immediate sensation were every thing, and a blank ensued when the sensation ended, the past would be to us as if it had never been. Yesterday would be as unknown as the months we passed in the womb, or the myriads of years before we were born.

3. It is only by our ideas of the past, that we have any power of anticipating the future. And if we had no power of anticipating the future, we should have no principle of action, but the physical impulses, which we have in common with the brutes. This great law of our nature, the anticipation of the future from the

past, will be fully illustrated in a subsequent part of this inquiry : at present, all that is required is, the admission, which will probably not be refused, of this general truth : That the order, in which events *have been observed* to take place, is the order in which they are *expected* to take place ; that the order in which they have taken place is testified to us only by our ideas ; and that upon the correctness, with which they are so testified, depends the faculty we possess of converting the powers of nature into the instruments of our will ; and of bringing to pass the events which we desire.

4. But all this power depends upon the order of our ideas.   The importance, therefore, is unspeakable, of being able to insure the order of our ideas ; to make, in other words, the order of a train of ideas correspond unerringly with a train of past sensations. We have not, however, a direct command over the train of our ideas.   A train of ideas may have passed in our minds corresponding to events of great importance; but that train will not pass again, unvaried, except in very simple cases, without the use of *expedients*.

5. The difference between the *occasions* of our IDEAS, and the *occasions* of our SENSATIONS, affords a resource for this purpose.   Over the occasions of our sensations we have an extensive power.   We can command the smell of a rose, the hearing of a bell, the sight of a tree, the sensation of heat or of cold, and so on.   Over the occasions of our ideas we have little or no direct power. Our ideas come and go.   There is a perpetual train of them, one succeeding another ; but we cannot will any link in that chain of ideas ; each link is determined by the foregoing ; and every man knows, how impossible

it is, by mere willing, to make such a train as he desires. Thoughts obtrude themselves without his bidding; and thoughts which he is in quest of will not arise.

By the power, however, which we have over the occasions of our sensations, we can make sure of having a train of sensations exactly the same as we have had before. This affords us the means of having a train of ideas exactly the same as we have had before. If we choose a number of sensible objects, and make use of them as marks of our ideas, we can ensure any succession which we please of the sensible objects; and, by the association between them and the ideas, a corresponding succession of the ideas.

6. To one of the two sets of occasions, upon which Signs are thus useful, *evanescent* Signs are the best adapted; *permanent* signs are absolutely necessary for the other. For the purposes of speech, or immediate communication, sounds are the most convenient marks. Sounds, however, perish in the making. But for the purpose of retracing a train of ideas, which we have formerly had, it is necessary we should have marks which do not perish. Marks, addressed to the sight, or the touch, have the requisite permanence; and, of the two, those addressed to the eye have the advantage. Of marks addressed to the eye, two kinds have been adopted; either marks immediately of the ideas intended to be recalled; such as the picture-writing, or hieroglyphics, of some nations: or, visible marks, by letters, of the audible marks employed in oral communication. This latter kind has been found the most convenient, and in use among the largest, and most intelligent portion of our species.

According to this scheme, spoken language is the use of immediate marks of the ideas; written language, is the use of secondary marks of the ideas. The written marks are only signs of the audible marks ; the audible marks, are signs of the ideas.[40]

---

[40] This exposition of Naming in its most general aspect, needs neither explanation nor comment. It is one of those specimens of clear and vigorous statement, going straight to the heart of the matter, and dwelling on it just long enough and no longer than necessary, in which the Analysis abounds.—*Ed.*

SECTION I.

NOUNS SUBSTANTIVE.

The power of Language essentially consists, in two things; first, in our having marks of our SENSATIONS, and IDEAS: and, secondly, in so arranging them, that they may correctly denote a TRAIN of those mental states or feelings. It is evident, that if we convey to others the ideas which pass in our own minds, and also convey them in the order in which they pass, the business of COMMUNICATION is completed. And, if we establish the means of reviving the ideas which we have formerly had, and also of reviving them in the order in which we formerly had them, the business of RECORDATION is completed. We now proceed to show, by what contrivances, the expedient of Marking is rendered efficient to those several ends.

The primary importance to men, of being able to make known to one another their SENSATIONS, made them in all probability begin with inventing marks for that purpose; in other words, making Names for their SENSATIONS. Two modes presented themselves. One was to give a name to each single sensation. Another was to bestow a name on a cluster of sensations, whenever they were such as occur in a cluster. Of this latter class, are all names of what are called External Objects; rose, water, stone, and so on. Each of these names is the mark of as many sensations (sight, touch, smell, taste, sound) as we are said to derive from those objects. The name rose, is the mark of a sensation of colour, a sensation of shape, a sensation of touch, a sensation of smell, all in conjunction. The name water, is the mark of a sensation of colour, a sensation of touch, a sensation of taste, and other sensations, regarded not separately, but as a compound.[41]

There is a convenience in giving a single mark to any number of sensations, which we thus have in clusters; because there is hence a great saving of marks. The sensations of sight, of touch, of smell, and so on, derived from a rose, might have received marks, and have been enumerated, one by one; but the term rose, performs all this much more expeditiously, and also more certainly.

The occasions, however, are perpetual, on which we need marks for sensations, not in clusters, but taken separately. And language is supplied with

---

[41] It is not intended to be understood that all this complex meaning entered into the names as originally given. The process of naming seems to have been this: Each object was designated by a term expressive of some one prominent quality, and of that only. Thus *rose* is referred with every probability to the same root as the adjective *red* (compare Greek ῥόδον, a rose, ἐρυθρὸς red, German *roth*, Latin *rutilus*), and thus meant " the ruddy" (flower). Other objects would doubtless also be called " ruddy," and would dispute the epithet with the rose; but by a process of natural selection, each would settle down in possession of the term found best suited to distinguish it; which would thus cease to be an attributive, and become a name substantive with a complex connotation derived from association. All names of objects whose origin can be traced are found to be thus simple in their primary signification. The stars (Sans. *staras*) were so called because they were " strewers" (of light).—*F*.

names of this description. We have the terms, red,
green, hot, cold, sweet, bitter, hard, soft, noise, stench,
composing in the whole a numerous class. For many
sensations, however, we have not names in one word ;
but make a name out of two or more words : thus, for
the sensation of hearing, derived from a trumpet, we
have only the name, "sound of a trumpet ;" in the
same manner, we have "smell of a rose," "taste of an
apple," "sight of a tree," "feeling of velvet."

Of those names which denote clusters of sensations,
it is obvious (but still very necessary) to remark, that
some include a greater, some a lesser number of sensations. Thus, stone includes only sensations of touch,
and sight. Apple, beside sensations of touch and
sight, includes sensations of smell and taste.

We not only give names to clusters of sensations,
but to clusters of clusters ; that is, to a number of
minor clusters, united into a greater cluster. Thus
we give the name wood to a particular cluster of
sensations, the name canvas to another, the name
rope to another. To these clusters, and many others,
joined together in one great cluster, we give the name
ship. To a number of these great clusters united
into one, we give the name fleet, and so on. How
great a number of clusters are united in the term
House ? And how many more in the term City ?

Sensations being infinitely numerous, all cannot
receive, marks or signs. A selection must be made.
Only those which are the most important are named.

Names, to be useful, cannot exceed a certain number.
They could not otherwise be remembered. It is,
therefore, of the greatest importance that each name
should accomplish as much as possible. To this end,

the greater number of names stand, not for individuals only, but classes. Thus the terms red, sweet, hot, loud, are names, not of one sensation only, but of classes of sensations; that is, every sensation of a particular kind. Thus also the term, rose, is not the name of one single cluster, but of every cluster coming under a certain description. As rose denotes one class, stone denotes another, iron another, ox another, and so on.[42]

As we need marks for SENSATIONS, we need marks also for IDEAS.

The Ideas which we have occasion to name, are, first, Simple Ideas, the copies of simple sensations; secondly, Complex Ideas, the copies of several sensations, combined. Of those complex ideas, also, there is one species, those copied directly from sensations, in the formation of which the mind has exercised but little control; as the ideas of rose, horse, stone, and of what are called the objects of sense in general. There is another species of complex ideas which, though derived also from the senses, are put together in a great degree at our discretion, as the ideas of a

---

[42] Economy in the use of names is a very small part of the motive leading to the creation of names of classes. If we had a name for every individual object which exists in the universe, and could remember all those names, we should still require names for what those objects or some of them have in common; in other words, we should require classification, and class names. This will be obvious if it is considered that had we no names but names of individuals, we should not have the means of making any affirmation respecting any object; we could not predicate of it any qualities. But of this more largely in a future note.—*Ed.*

centaur, a mountain of gold, of comfort, of meanness; all that class of ideas in short which Mr. Locke has called mixed modes.

We may thus distinguish three classes of ideas, which we have occasion to name : 1, simple ideas, the copies of single sensations : 2, complex ideas, copied directly from sensations : 3, complex ideas, derived indeed from the senses, but put together in arbitrary combinations. The two former classes may be called Sensible, the last Mental Ideas.

With respect to ideas, of the first two classes, those which are the direct copies of our sensations, either singly, or in groups; it is of great importance to observe, and also to remember, that, for the most part, the words, which are employed as marks of the Sensations, are made to serve the further purpose of being marks also of the Ideas. The same word is at once the name of the sensations, and the ideas.

If any person were asked, whether the word BEING is the name of a Sensation, or of an Idea ; he would immediately reply, that it is the name of an Idea. In like manner, if he were asked, whether the word ANIMAL is the mark of a cluster of Sensations, or of a cluster of Ideas ; he would with equal readiness say, of a cluster of Ideas. But if we were to ask, whether the name Sheep is the name of a cluster of Sensations, or of a cluster of Ideas ; he would probably say, that Sheep is the name of Sensations ; in the same manner as rose, or apple. Yet, what is the difference ? Only this, that ANIMAL is the more general name, and includes sheep along with other species; and that BEING is still more general, and includes animal along with vegetable, mineral, and other

genera. If sheep, therefore, or stone, be a name of
sensations, so is animal or being; and if animal, or
being, be a name of ideas, so is sheep or stone a name
of ideas. The fact is, they are all names of both.
They are names of the Sensations, primarily; but are
afterwards employed as names also of the Ideas or
copies of those sensations.

It thus appears, that the names generally of what
are called the objects of sense are equivocal; and
whereas it would have been a security against confusion to have been provided with appropriate names,
one, in each instance, for the Sensation, and one for
the Idea, the same name has been made to serve as
the mark for both. The term horse is not only made
to stand for the sensations of sight, of hearing, of
touch, and even of smell, which give me occasion for
the use of the term horse; but it stands also for the
ideas of those sensations, as often as I have occasion
to speak of that cluster of ideas which compose my
notion of a horse. The term tree denotes undoubtedly
the Idea in my mind, when I mean to convey the
idea tree into the mind of another man; but it also
stands for the sensations whence I have derived my
idea of a tree.

Thus, too, if I mean to name my simple ideas;
those, for example, of sight; I have no other names
than red, blue, violet, &c.; but all these are names of the
sensations. When forced to distinguish them, I must
use the awkward expressions, my sensation of red, my
idea of red. Again; sound of a trumpet, is the name,
as well of the sensation, as the idea; flight of a bird,
the name, as well of the sensation, as the idea; light
the name as well of the sensation as the idea; pain

the name as well of the sensation as the idea; heat
the name as well of the sensation as the idea.[43]

As we have remarked, in regard to SENSATIONS,
singly, or in clusters, that they are too numerous to
receive names but in classes, that is names common
to every individual of a class, the same is obviously
true of the IDEAS. The greater number of names of
Sensible Ideas are names of classes : man is the name
of a class ; lion, horse, eagle, serpent, and so on, are
names of classes.

Ideas, of the third class, those which the mind
forms arbitrarily, are innumerable ; because the combinations capable of being formed of the numerous
elements which compose them, exceed computation.
All these combinations cannot receive names. The
memory can manage but a moderate number. Of
possible combinations, therefore, a small proportion
must be selected for naming. These, of course, are
the combinations which are suggested by the occasions of life, and conduce to the ends which we
pursue.

We arrange those ideas, also, in classes ; to the
end that every name may serve the purpose of marking, as extensively as possible. Thus the term fear is

---

[43] In strict propriety of language all these are names only
of sensations, or clusters of sensations ; not of ideas. A
person studious of precision would not, I think, say heat,
meaning the idea of heat, or a tree, when he meant the idea
of a tree. He would use heat as the name only of the sensation of heat, and tree as the name of the outward object, or
cluster of sensations ; and if he had occasion to speak of the
idea, he would say, my idea (or the idea) of heat ; my idea
(or the idea) of a tree.—*Ed.*

applicable to a state of mind, of which the instances form a class. In like manner, courage is the name of a class ; temperance, ignorance, piety, and so on, names of classes. Republic, aristocracy, monarchy, are names, each of them, not of an individual government, a government at one time and place, but of a class, a sort of government, at any time and place.

The names of the ideas which are thus mentally clustered, are exempt from that ambiguity which we saw belonged to the names of both classes of sensible ideas. The names of sensible ideas generally stand for the sensations as well as the ideas. The names of the mental ideas are not transferable to sensations. But they are subject to another uncertainty, still more fertile in confusion, and embarrassment.

As the combinations are formed arbitrarily, or in other words, as the ideas of which they are composed, are more or less numerous, according to pleasure, and each man of necessity forms his own combination, it very often happens, that one man includes something more or something less than another man in the combination to which they both give the same name. Using the same words, they have not exactly the same ideas. In the term piety, for example, a good catholic includes many things which are not included in it by a good protestant. In the term good manners, an Englishman of the present day does not include the same ideas which were included in it by an Englishman two centuries ago ; still less those which are included in it by foreigners of habits and usages dissimilar to our own. Prudence, in the mind of a man of rank and fortune, has a very different meaning from what it bears in the minds of the

frugal and industrious poor.   Under this uncertainty
in language, it not only happens that men are often
using the same expressions when they have different
ideas ; but different, when they have the same ideas.[44]

---

[44] There is some need for additional elucidation of the class
of complex ideas distinguished (under the name of Mixed
Modes) by Locke, and recognised by the author of the
Analysis, as " put together in a great degree at our discretion ;"
as " those which the mind forms arbitrarily," so that "the
ideas of which they are composed are more or less numerous
according to pleasure, and each man of necessity forms his
own combination." From these and similar phrases, interpreted literally, it might be supposed that in the instances
given, a centaur, a mountain of gold, comfort, meanness, fear,
courage, temperance, ignorance, republic, aristocracy, monarchy,
piety, good manners, prudence—the elements which constitute
these several complex ideas are put together premeditatedly,
by an act of will, which each individual performs for himself,
and of which he is conscious.   This, however, happens only
in cases of invention, or of what is called creative imagination.   A centaur and a mountain of gold are inventions :
combinations intentionally made, at least on the part of the
first inventor ; and are not copies or likenesses of any combination of impressions received by the senses, nor are supposed to have any such outward phenomena corresponding to
them.   But the other ideas mentioned in the text, those of
courage, temperance, aristocracy, monarchy, &c., are supposed
to have real originals outside our thoughts.   These ideas, just
as much as those of a horse and a tree, are products of generalization and abstraction : they are believed to be ideas of
certain points or features in which a number of the clusters of
sensations which we call real objects agree : and instead of
being formed by intentionally putting together simple ideas,
they are formed by stripping off, or rather, by not attending to,
such of the simple sensations or ideas entering into the

clusters as are peculiar to any of them, and establishing an extremely close association among those which are common to them all. These complex ideas, therefore, are not, in reality, like the creations of mere imagination, put together at discretion, any more than the complex ideas, compounded of the obvious sensible qualities of objects, which we call our ideas of the objects. They are formed in the same manner as these, only not so rapidly or so easily, since the particulars of which they are composed do not obtrude themselves upon the senses, but suppose a perception of qualities and sequences not immediately obvious. From this circumstance results the consequence noticed by the author, that this class of complex ideas are often of different composition in different persons. For, in the first place, different persons abstract their ideas of this sort from different individual instances; and secondly, some persons abstract much better than others; that is, take more accurate notice of the obscurer features of instances, and discern more correctly what are those in which all the instances agree. This important subject will be more fully entered into when we reach that part of the present work which treats of the ideas connected with General Terms. —*Ed.*

SECTION II.

NOUNS ADJECTIVE.

As the purpose of language is to denote sensations and ideas; to mark them for our own use, or to give indication of them to our fellow men; it is obvious that the names of sensations and ideas are the fundamental parts of language. But as ideas are very numerous, and the limits of the human memory admit the use of only a limited number of marks or names, various contrivances are employed to make one name serve as many purposes as possible.

Of the contrivances for making the use of each word as extensive as possible, we have already adverted to one of great importance; that of arranging ideas in classes, and making one name stand for each individual of the class. When the classes are large, one word or mark serves to name or indicate many individuals.

But when, for the sake of economizing names, those classes have been made as large as possible, we often find occasion for breaking them down into smaller parcels, or sub-classes, and speaking of these sub-classes by themselves.

An example will render what is here expressed sufficiently plain. The term sound, is the name of a large class of ideas or sensations; for it is equally the name of both; the sound of thunder, the sound of a cannon, the whistling of the wind, the voice of a man, the howling of a dog, and so on.

Among these sounds I perceive differences ; some affect me in one way, and I wish to mark them as doing so ; some affect me in another way, and I wish to mark them as affecting me in that particular way.

It is obvious that names might be invented for these subordinate classes, to mark such of them as we have occasion to mark ; and the cases are numerous, in which this is the expedient adopted. Thus the term animal is the name of a large class. But we have occasion to speak apart of various portions of this class, to all the more important of which portions, we have given particular names. Horse is the name of one portion, man of another, sheep of another, and so of the rest.

There is, however, another mode of naming subordinate classes ; a mode by which the use of names is greatly economized, and of which the utility is therefore conspicuous.

The subordinate class is distinguished from the rest of the greater class by some peculiarity, something in which the individuals of it agree with one another, and do not agree with the rest. Thus to recur to the example of sound. One set of sounds affect me in a certain way, a way peculiar to that set. Wishing to distinguish these sounds from others by a mark, I call them *loud*. Another set of sounds affect me in another way, and I call them *low;* a third set in another way, and I call them *harsh;* a fourth in another way, and I call them *sweet*. By means of those adjectives applied as marks upon the mark of the great class, I have the names of four species, or sub-classes ; 1, loud sounds ; 2, low sounds ; 3, harsh sounds ; 4, sweet sounds; and the number might be greatly enlarged.

It thus appears that, as nouns substantive are marks of ideas, or sensations, nouns adjective are marks put upon nouns substantive, or marks upon marks; in order to limit the signification of the noun substantive; and instead of its marking a large class, to make it mark a subdivision of that class. Thus the word, rose, is the mark of a large class : apply to it the adjective *yellow*, that is, put the mark yellow upon the mark rose, and you have the name, yellow rose, which is a sub-division, or species, of the class Rose.

This peculiarity of naming, this putting of marks upon marks, in order to modify the meaning of a certain mark, is a contrivance which deserves the greatest attention. It is one of the principal expedients for the great purpose of economizing names, and performing the business of marking with the smallest number of marks; but, like the rest of the contrivances for this purpose, it contributes to obscure the simple process of naming; and when not distinctly known and attended to, operates as a source of confusion and error.

The use of adjectives, in economizing names, is most conspicuous, in the case of those subdivisions which apply to the greatest number of classes. There is one distinction which applies to most classes; the distinction between what pleases, and what does not please us, no matter on what account. The first we call good, the second evil. These two terms serve to mark a very great number of subordinate classes, and, of course, save, to a great extent, the multiplication of names.

Thus, in the case of the senses, we have the word taste, the mark of one great class of sensations. Tastes we divide into sub-classes by the words good and evil; good tastes being one class, bad tastes another. If we had invented separate marks for each of these two classes, we should have had three names, to mark the class taste with these its two primary subdivisions; and we should have had occasion for the same number of names in the case of each of the five senses; or, fifteen different names. But the adjectives, good, and evil, they being applicable to all the senses, save us the invention of names for the subclasses of the other four senses; as we say good smells, bad smells, in the same manner as good tastes, and bad tastes. They save, therefore, eight names out of fifteen, or more than one-half.

The economizing power of adjectives is still more remarkable, when we depart from simple sensations and ideas, and apply them as marks upon the names of the complex, which are far more numerous. Thus, the term horse is the mark of a complex idea, and the name of a class of objects. We say good horse and bad horse, good dog and bad dog, good house and bad house, and so in cases without number; in each of which, the repetition of the two adjectives, good, and bad, saves us the use and embarrassment of separate names.

It deserves to be remarked, that the terms good and evil apply much more generally to that class of complex ideas, in the formation of which the mind has but little control; namely, those of external objects; than they do to the other class of complex ideas which the mind makes up in an arbitrary manner to suit its own convenience. Ideas of the latter description are very often made up according to the distinction of good and evil. Thus, the idea glory, is composed of ingredients all of which belong to the classes, good; and the idea good, is multifariously included in the name. After the same manner, the idea of evil is multifariously included in the complex idea disgrace. Good is implied in the term virtue, evil in the term vice; good is implied in the term wealth, evil in the term poverty; good is implied in the term power, evil in the term weakness. In some cases, the ideas of this class are so general, that good and evil are both included; and, in such cases, adjectives are necessary to mark the subdivisions or species. Thus, we say good manners, bad manners; good sense, bad sense; good conduct, bad conduct; and so on.

Next to the adjectives which form the numerous sub-classes of good and evil, those which mark degrees are of the most extensive application, and in the operation of sub-marking save the greatest number of names. Thus the terms, great, and little, are applicable to a great proportion of the marks of complex ideas of both formations. We say a great tree, a little tree; a great man, a little man; a great crime, a small crime; great blame, little blame; great honour, little honour; great value, little value; great weight, little weight; great strength, little strength, and so on.

Different adjectives differ in the number of classes to the subdivision of which they are subservient. Thus hot and cold are only applicable where diversities of temperature are included; round, square, and so on, where figure is included; white or black, where colour; and so on.

Beside the use of adjectives, in dividing great classes into smaller ones, without multiplication of names; they sometimes answer another purpose. It often happens that, in the cluster of sensations or ideas which have one name; we have occasion to call attention particularly to some one ingredient of the cluster. Adjectives render this service, as well as that of marking a class. This rose, I say, is red; that rose is yellow: this stone is hot, that stone is cold. The term, red rose, or yellow rose, is the name of a class. But when I say, this rose is red, where an individual is named, I mark emphatically the specific difference; namely, red, or yellow; which constitutes that subdivision of the genus rose, to which the individual belongs.[45]

---

[45] In the concluding paragraph we find the first recognition by the author that class names serve any purpose, or are introduced for any reason, except to save multiplication of names. Adjectives, it is here said, answer also the purpose of calling attention to some one ingredient of the cluster of sensations combined under one name. That is to say, they enable us to *affirm* that the cluster contains that ingredient: for they do not merely call attention to the ingredient, or remind the hearer of it: the hearer, very often, did not know that the cluster contained the ingredient, until he was apprised by the proposition.

But surely it is not only adjectives which fulfil either office, whether of giving information of an ingredient, or merely fixing the attention upon it. All general names do so, when used as predicates. When I say that a distant object which I am pointing at is a tree, or a building, I just as much call attention to certain ingredients in the cluster of sensations constituting the object, as I do when I say, This rose is red. So far is it from being true that adjectives are distinguished from substantives by having this function in addition to that of economizing names, that it is, on the contrary, much more nearly true of adjectives than of the class-names which are nouns substantive, that the economizing of names is the principal motive for their institution. For though general names of some sort are indispensable to predication, adjectives are not. As is well shewn in the text, the peculiarity, which really distinguishes adjectives from other general names, is that they mark cross divisions. All nature having first been marked out into classes by means of nouns substantive, we might go on by the same means subdividing each class. We might call the large individuals of a class by one noun substantive and the small ones by another, and these substantives would serve all purposes of predication; but to do this we should need just twice as many additional nouns substantive as there are classes of objects. Since, however, the distinction of large and small applies to all classes alike, one pair of names will suffice to designate it. Instead therefore of dividing every class into sub-classes, each with its own name, we draw a line across all the classes, dividing all nature into large things and small, and by using these two words as adjectives, that is, by adding one or other of them as the occasion requires to every noun substantive which is the name of a class, we are able to mark universally the distinction of large and small by two names only, instead of many millions.—*Ed.*

SECTION III.

VERBS.

1. There is one class of complex ideas, of so particular a nature, and of which we have so frequent occasion to speak, that the means of sub-dividing them require additional contrivances. Marks put upon marks are still the instrument. But the instrument, to render it more effectual to this particular purpose, is fashioned in a particular way. I allude to the class of words denominated Verbs; which are, in their essence, adjectives, and applied as marks upon marks; but receive a particular form, in order to render them, at the same time, subservient to other purposes.

The mode of their marking, and the peculiarity of their marking power may easily, I hope, be thus conceived.

A billiard-ball affects my senses, in a particular manner. On account of this, I call it round; and the term round is ever after a mark to me of a portion of the sensations which I derive from it. It affects me in another manner. I call it on that account white, and the term white is to me a mark of this other mode in which it affects me: and in the same manner as I call it white, round, on account of such and such sensations, I call it Moving, on account of certain other sensations, of which the term Moving is to me a perpetual mark.

The manner of affecting me on account of which I call it moving, I learn from experience to be peculiarly entitled to my regard. I find that it is a mode of affecting me, which belongs to almost all bodies ; and I find that upon this attribute of theirs the greatest part of my interesting sensations depend. I am therefore deeply concerned in the knowledge of motions ; and have the strongest inducement to divide them into such classes as may in the highest degree facilitate that knowledge.

Motions are divided in a great variety of ways for a variety of purposes. Sometimes we divide them according to their subjects. Thus, the motion of a bird is one class of motions ; the motion of a horse another ; so the motion of a serpent, the motion of an arrow, the motion of a wheel. At other times we form classes of motions according to the manner. Thus we have running, flying, rolling, leaping, staggering, throwing, striking, and so on.

Of all the classifications of motions, however, that which deserves the greatest attention is the distinction of them into the motions which originate within the moving body, and those which originate without it. Of the motions which originate within the moving body, the principal are the living motions of animals. We find, also, that of all the motions of animals, those of men are the most important to men. The motions of men are divided into a great number of classes. On account of one set of motions we call a man walking ; on account of another sort we call him running ; another, writing ; another, dancing ; another, fencing ; another, boxing ; another, building ; and so on. We have also frequent occasion for a name which shall embrace all these motions of men. For this purpose the word Acting is employed : and the term Action denotes any of the motions, which originate within a man as the moving body. It is no objection to this account of the use of the word action, that it is sometimes employed in cases in which the motion is not the principal object of attention ; as in the act of singing, or that of speaking. Here, though it is not the motion, but the effect of the motion, which is the object of attention to the hearer, the act of the singer or speaker is not the less truly a motion.

The word action, when thus invented, and used, is afterwards applied metaphorically to motions which do not originate in the moving body, as when we say the action of a sword ; and also to certain processes of the mind, which, as they are accompanied with the feeling we call effort, resembling that which accompanies the voluntary motions, are sometimes classed along with them, and, by an extension of the meaning of the word, receive the name of actions. In this manner, remembering, computing, comparing, even hearing, and seeing, are denominated actions.

2. In applying the term Acting, or the terms expressive of the several kinds of acting, the Time of the action is a material circumstance. The grand divisions of time are the Past, the Present, and the Future. There is great utility in a short method of marking these divisions of time in conjunction with the mark of the action. This is effected by the Tenses of Verbs.

3. When the name of an act is applied to an agent, the agent is either the person speaking, the person spoken to, or some other person. The word denoting

the action is, by what are called the Persons of the
verb, made to connote these diversities. Thus *amo*
notes the act, and connotes the person speaking as the
actor; *amas* notes the act, and connotes the person
spoken to, as the actor; *amat* notes the act, and connotes some person, as the actor, who is neither the
person speaking, nor the person spoken to.[46]

4. When the names of actions are applied to agents,
they are applied to one or a greater number. A short
method of connoting this grand distinction of numbers is effected by the marks of the Singular and Plural
number. Thus *amo* notes the act, and connotes one
actor; *amamus* notes the act, and connotes more than
one actor.

5. In applying the names of actions to the proper
subjects of them, there are three Modes of the action,
one or other of which is always implied. The first is,
when the action has no reference to any thing previously spoken of. The second is, when it has a reference to something previously spoken of. The third is,
when it has a reference to some state of the will of

---

[46] There is here a fresh instance of the oversight already
pointed out, that of not including in the function for which
general names are required, their employment in Predication.
Amo, amas, and amamus, cannot, I conceive, with any propriety be called names of actions, or names at all. They are
entire predications. It is one of the properties of the kind of
general names called verbs, that they cannot be used except in
a Proposition or Predication, and indeed only as the predicate
of it: (for the infinitive is not a verb, but the abstract of a
verb). What else there is to distinguish verbs from other
general names will be more particularly considered further
on.—*Ed.*

the speaker or person spoken of. These diversities of mode are connoted by the Moods of the verb. The Indicative is used when no reference is made to any thing which precedes : the Subjunctive, when a reference is made to something which precedes : and the Optative, and Imperative, when the reference is to the state of the will of the speaker or the person spoken of.

Such are the contrivances to make the marks or names of action, by their connotative powers, a more and more effectual instrument of notation. Accurately speaking, they are adjectives, so fashioned as to connote, a threefold distinction of agents, with a twofold distinction of their number, a threefold distinction of the manner of the action, and a threefold distinction of its time ; and, along with all this, another important particular, about to be explained, namely, the COPULA in PREDICATION.[47]

---

[47] The imperfection of this theory of Verbs is sufficiently apparent. They are, says the author, a particular kind of Adjectives. Adjectives, according to the preceding Section, are words employed to enable us, without inconvenient multiplication of names, to subdivide great classes into smaller ones. Can it be said, or would it have been said by the author, that the only, or the principal reason for having Verbs, is to enable us to subdivide classes of objects with the greatest economy of names ?

Neither is it strictly accurate to say that Verbs are always marks of motion, or of action, even including, as the author does, by an extension of the meaning of those terms, every process which is attended with a feeling of effort. Many verbs, of the kind which grammarians call neuter or intransitive verbs, express rest, or inaction : as sit, lie, and in some cases, stand. It is true however that the verbs first invented, as

6. We have, last of all, under this head, to consider the marking power of a very peculiar, and most comprehensive word, the SUBSTANTIVE VERB, as it has been called by grammarians, or the word expressive of BEING. The steps, which we have already traced, in the process of naming, will aid us in obtaining a true conception of this, which is one of the most important steps, in that process.

We have seen that, beside the names of particular species of motions, as walking, running, flying, there was occasion for a general name which might include

far as we know anything of them, expressed forms of motion, and the principal function of verbs still is to affirm or deny action. Or, to speak yet more generally, it is by means of verbs that we predicate events. Events, or changes, are the most important facts, to us, in the surrounding world. Verbs are the resource which language affords for predicating events. They are not the names of events; all names of events are substantives, as sunrise, disaster, or infinities, as *to rise*, and infinitives are logically substantives. But it is by means of verbs that we assert, or give information of, events; as, The sun rises, or, Disaster has occurred. There is, however, a class of neuter verbs already referred to, which do not predicate events, but states of an unchanging object, as lie, sit, remain, exist. It would be incorrect, therefore, to give a definition of Verbs which should limit them to the expression of events. I am inclined to think that the distinction between nouns and verbs is not logical, but merely grammatical, and that every word, whatever be its meaning, must be reputed a verb, which is so constructed grammatically that it can only be used as the predicate of a proposition. Any meaning whatever is, in strictness, capable of being thrown into this form: but it is only certain meanings, chiefly actions or events, which there is, in general, any motive for putting into this particular shape.—*Ed.*

the whole of those motions.   For this purpose, the
names Action and Acting were employed.   It is now
to be remembered, that those sensations which we
mark by the names of action, as walking, running,
&c., are but part of the sensations which we derive
from objects; that we have other sensations, and
clusters of sensations, from them, on account of which
we apply to them other names; as when we call a
man tall, on account of certain sensations; dark, on
account of certain other sensations, and so on.   Now,
as we had occasion for a name to include the separate
clusters, called walking, running, flying, rolling, falling, and so on, and for that purpose adopted the
name Acting; so, having from objects other sensations than those marked by the word acting, we have
occasion for a name which shall include both those
sensations, and those comprehended in the word acting
along with them : in short, a word that shall embrace
all sensations, of whatever kind, which any object is
capable of exciting in us.   This purpose is effected by
the word affirmative of Existence.   When we affirm
of any thing that it EXISTS, that it IS : what we mean,
is, that we may have sensations from it; nothing,
without ourselves, being known to us, or capable of
being known, but through the medium of our senses.

    There is the same occasion for making the Substan-
tive Verb connote the three distinctions of TIME PAST,
TIME PRESENT, and TIME FUTURE, as in the case of
other verbs; also to connote the distinctions of
PERSONS and NUMBERS; and, lastly, to connote the
THREE MODES, that in which there is no reference to
any thing preceding, that in which there is a reference
to something preceding, and that in which reference

is made to the will of one of the PERSONS. Accordingly the Substantive Verb has TENSES, MOODS, NUMBERS, and PERSONS, like any other verb.

Such is the nature and object of the Substantive Verb. It is the most GENERICAL of all the words, which we have characterized, as marks upon marks. These are the words usually called ATTRIBUTIVES. According to the view which we have given of them, they may be more appropriately denominated, SECONDARY MARKS. The names of the larger classes, as tree, horse, strength, we may call PRIMARY MARKS. The subsidiary names by which smaller classes are marked out of the larger; as when we say, tall tree, great strength, running horse, walking man; that is, all attributives, or marks applied upon marks; we may call SECONDARY MARKS.

SECTION IV.

PREDICATION.

The purposes of language are two. We have occasion to mark sensations or ideas singly; and we have occasion to mark them in trains; in other words, we have need of contrivances to mark not only sensations and ideas; but also the order of them. The contrivances which are necessary to mark this order are the main cause of the complexity of language.

If all names were names of one sort, there would be no difficulty in marking a train of the feelings which they serve to denote. Thus, if all names were names of individuals, as John, James, Peter, we should have no difficulty in marking a train of the ideas of these individuals; all that would be necessary would be to set down the marks, one after another, in the same order in which, one after another, the ideas occurred.

If all names were names of Species, as man, horse, eagle, the facility of marking the order of the ideas which they represent would be the same. If the idea man occurred first, the idea horse second, the idea eagle third; all that would be necessary would be to put down the name or mark man the first, the name or mark horse the second, and the order of marks would represent the order of ideas.

But we have already seen, that the facility of communication requires names of different degrees of

comprehensiveness ; names of individuals, names of
classes, and names both of the larger and the smaller
classes.   For the younger and less instructed part of
my readers, it may be necessary to mention, that the
names of the smaller classes, are called names of
Species, or specific names ; the names of the larger
classes, names of Genera, or generic names.   Thus,
the term animal, denotes a large class ; a class which
contains the smaller classes, man, horse, dog, &c. The
name animal, therefore, is called a Genus, or a generic
name ; the name man, a Species, or a specific name.

In using names of these different kinds ; names of
individuals when the idea is restricted to one individual ; and, for brevity, the names of classes ; the
names of the less when necessary, of the large when
practicable; there is perpetual need of the substitution
of one name for another. When I have used the names,
James and John, Thomas and William, and many
more, having to speak of such peculiarities of each, as
distinguish him from every other, I may proceed to
speak of them in general, as included in a class.
When this happens, I have occasion for the name of
the class, and to substitute the name of the class, for
the names of the individuals.   By what contrivance
is this performed ?   I have the name of the individual,
John ; and the name of the class *man ;* and I can set
down my two names ; *John, man ;* in juxta-position.
But this is not sufficient to effect the communication
I desire ; namely, that the word man is a mark of the
same idea of which John is a mark, and a mark of
other ideas along with it, those to wit, of which James,
Thomas, &c. are marks.   To complete my contrivance,
I invent a mark, which, placed between my marks,

John and *man*, fixes the idea I mean to convey, that *man*, is another mark to that idea of which *John* is a mark, while it is a mark of the other ideas, of which *James*, *Thomas*, &c., are marks. For this purpose, we use in English, the mark " is." By help of this, my object is immediately attained. I say, *John* "is" a *man*. I, then, use the word *man*, instead of the word *John*, with many advantages ; because every thing which I can affirm of the word *man*, is true not only of *John*, but of *James*, and *Peter*, and every other individual of the class.

The joining of two names by this peculiar mark is the act which has been denominated, PREDICATION ; and it is the grand contrivance by which the marks of sensations and ideas are so ordered in discourse, as to mark the order of the trains, which it is our purpose to communicate, or to record.

The form of expression, " John is a man," is called a Proposition. It consists of three marks. Of these, " John," is denominated the SUBJECT ; " man," the PREDICATE ; and " is," the COPULA. To speak generally, and in the language of the grammarians, the nominative of the verb is the *subject* of the proposition; the substantive, or adjective, which agrees with the nominative, is the *predicate*, and the verb is the *copula*.

By a few simple examples, the reader may render familiar to himself the use of PREDICATION, as the grand expedient, by which language is enabled to mark not only sensations and ideas, but also the order of them.[48]

---

[48] The theory of Predication here set forth, stands in need of further elucidation, and perhaps of some correction and addition.

The account which the author gives of a Predication, or Pro-

For the more complete elucidation of this important
part of the business of Naming, it is necessary to

---

position, is, first, that it is a mode of so putting together the
marks of sensations and ideas, as to mark the order of them.
Secondly, that it consists in substituting one name for another,
so as to signify that a certain name (called the predicate), is a
mark of the same idea which another name (called the subject)
is a mark of.

It must be allowed that a predication, or proposition, is intended to mark some portion of the order either of our sensations or of our ideas, *i.e.*, some part of the coexistences or
sequences which take place either in our minds, or in what we
term the external world. But what sort of order is it that a
predication marks ? An order supposed to be believed in.
When *John*, or *man*, are said to be marks of an individual object, all there is in the matter is that these words, being associated with the idea of the object, are intended to raise that
idea in the mind of the person who hears or reads them. But
when we say, John is a man, or, John is an old man, we intend to do more than call up in the hearer's mind the images
of John, of a man, and of an old man. We intend to do more
than inform him that we have thought of, or even seen, John
and a man, or John and an old man, together. We inform him
of a fact respecting John, namely, that he *is* an old man, or at
all events, of our belief that this is a fact. The characteristic
difference between a predication and any other form of speech,
is, that it does not merely bring to mind a certain object
(which is the only function of a mark, merely as such); it
asserts something respecting it. Now it may be true, and I
think it is true, that every assertion, every object of Belief,—
everything that can be true or false—that can be an object of
assent or dissent—is some order of sensations or of ideas: some
coexistence or succession of sensations or ideas actually experienced, or supposed capable of being experienced. And
thus it may appear in the end that in expressing a belief, we
are after all only declaring the order of a group or series of

remark, that Logicians have classed Predications,
under five heads ; 1st, when the *Genus* is predicated,

---

sensations or ideas. But the order which we declare is not
an imaginary order; it is an order believed to be real. Whatever
view we adopt of the psychological nature of Belief, it is necessary to distinguish between the mere suggestion to the mind
of a certain order among sensations or ideas—such as takes
place when we think of the alphabet, or the numeration table
—and the indication that this order is an actual fact, which is
occurring, or which has occurred once or often·r, or which, in
certain definite circumstances, always occurs ; which are the
things indicated as true by an affirmative predication, and as
false by a negative one.

That a predication differs from a name in doing more than
merely calling up an idea, is admitted in what I have noted as
the second half of the author's theory of Predication. That
second half points out that every predication is a communication, intended to act, not on the mere ideas of the listener, but
on his persuasion or belief: and what he is intended to believe, according to the author, is, that of the two names which
are conjoined in the predication, one is a mark of the same
idea (or let me add, of the same sensation or cluster of sensations) of which the other is a mark. This is a doctrine of
Hobbes, the one which caused him to be termed by Leibnitz,
in words which have been often quoted, " plus quam nomi-
nalis." It is quite true that when we predicate B of A—when
we assert of A that it is a B—B must, if the assertion is true,
be a name of A, *i.e.*, a name applicable to A ; one of the innumerable names which, in virtue of their signification, can be
used as descriptive of A : but is this the information which we
want to convey to the hearer ? It is so when we are speaking
only of names and their meaning, as when we enunciate a definition. In every other case, what we want to convey is a
matter of fact, of which this relation between the names is but
an incidental consequence. When we say, John walked out
this morning, it is not a correct expression of the communica-

of any subject ; 2dly, when the *Species* is predicated ;
3dly, when the *Specific Difference* is predicated ; 4thly,

---

tion we desire to make, that "having walked out this morning" or "a person who has walked out this morning" are two
of the innumerable names of John. They are only accidentally and momentarily names of John by reason of a certain
event, and the information we mean to give is, that this event
has happened. The event is not resolvable into an identity
of meaning between names, but into an actual series of sensations that occurred to John, and a belief that any one who had
been present and using his eyes would have had another series
of sensations, which we call seeing John in the act of walking
out. Again, when we say, Negroes are woolly-haired, we mean
to make known to the hearer, not that woolly-haired is a name
of every negro, but that wherever the cluster of sensations signified by the word negro, are experienced, the sensations signified by the word woolly-haired will be found either among
them or conjoined with them. This is an order of sensations :
and it is only in consequence of it that the name woolly-haired
comes to be applicable to every individual of whom the term
negro is a name.

There is nothing positively opposed to all this in the author's
text : indeed he must be considered to have meant this, when
he said, that by means of substituting one name for another,
a predication marks the order of our sensations and ideas. The
omission consists in not remarking that what is distinctively
signified by a predication, as such, is Belief in a certain order
of sensations or ideas. And when this has been said, the
Hobbian addition, that it does so by declaring the predicate to
be a name of everything of which the subject is a name, may
be omitted as surplusage, and as diverting the mind from the
essential features of the case. Predication may thus be defined, a form of speech which expresses a belief that a certain
coexistence or sequence of sensations or ideas, did, does, or,
under certain conditions, would take place : and the reverse of
this when the predication is negative. *Ed.*

when a *Property* is predicated ; 5thly, when an *Accident* is predicated. These five classes of names, the things capable of being predicated, are named PREDICABLES. The five Predicables, in Latin, the language in which they are commonly expressed, are named *Genus, Species, Differentia, Proprium, Accidens.*

We have already seen, perhaps at sufficient length, the manner in which, and the end for which, the Genus, and the Species are predicated of any subject. It is, that the more comprehensive name, may be substituted for the less comprehensive ; so that each of our marks may answer the purpose of marking, to as great an extent as possible. In this manner we substitute the word *man,* for example, for the word *Thomas,* when we predicate the Species of the individual, in the proposition, " Thomas is a man ;" the word *animal,* for the word *man,* when we predicate the Genus of the Species, in the proposition, " man, is an animal." [49]

---

[49] If what has been said in the preceding note is correct, it is a very inadequate view of the purpose for which a generic or specific name is predicated of any subject, to say that it is in order that " the more comprehensive name may be substituted for the less comprehensive, so that each of our marks may answer the purpose of marking to as great an extent as possible." The more comprehensive and the less comprehensive name have each their uses, and the function of each not only could not be discharged with equal convenience by the other, but could not be discharged by it at all. The purpose, in predicating of anything the name of a class to which it belongs, is not to obtain a better or more commodious name for it, but to make known the fact of its possessing the attributes which constitute the class, and which are therefore signified by the class-name. It is evident that the name of one class cannot possibly perform this office vicariously for the name of another.—*Ed.*

We have already, also, taken notice of the artifice, by which smaller classes are formed out of larger, by the help of secondary marks. Of these secondary marks, the principal classes are designated by the terms *Differentia, Proprium, Accidens.* No very distinct boundaries, are, indeed, marked by these terms ; nor do they effect a scientific division ; but, for the present purpose, the elucidation of the end to which Predication is subservient, they are sufficient.

Differentia is always an Attributive, applicable to a Genus, and which, when combined with it, marks out a Species ; as the word *rational,* which is applicable to the Genus *animal,* and when applied to it, in the phrase "rational animal," marks out a Species, and is synonymous with the word *man.* In a similar manner the word *sensitive* is applicable to *body,* and marks out the subordinate Genus, *animal.*

Proprium is also an Attributive, and the Attributives classed under this title differ from those classed under the title *differentia,* chiefly in this ; That those classed under *differentia,* are regarded as more expressly involved in the definition of the Species which they seem to cut out from the Genus. Thus, both *rational,* and *risible,* when applied to *animal,* cut out of it the class Man ; but *rational* is called DIFFERENTIA, *risible* PROPRIUM, because *rational,* is strictly involved in the definition of *man ; risible* is not. Some Attributives are classed under the title *proprium,* which, when applied to the genus, do not constitute the same Species, constituted by the *differentia,* but a different Species ; as *bipes,* two-footed animal, is the name of a class including at least the two classes of men, and birds ; *hot-blooded animal,* is the name of a class so large as to include man, horse, lion, dog, and the greater part of the more perfectly organized Species. There are some Attributives, classed under the title *proprium*, which cut out of the Genus a class even less than that which is cut by the *differentia*; as, for example, the word *grammatical*. This word grammatical, applied to the word animal, in the term "grammatical animal," separates a class so small, as to include only part of the Species man, those who are called Grammarians. Such Attributives, for an obvious reason, are applicable, as well to the name of the Species, as to that of the Genus. Thus, we say, "a grammatical man," as well as "a grammatical animal," and that with greater propriety, as cutting out the sub-species from the Species more immediately.

The Attributives, classed under the title *accidens*, are regarded, like those classed under *differentia*, and *proprium*, as applicable to the class cut out by the *differentia*, but applicable to it rather fortuitously than by any fixed connection. The term *lame* is an example of such Attributives. The term *lame*, however, applied to the name of the Species, does not the less take out of it a sub-species, as "lame man," "lame horse."

With respect to these classes of Attributives (*Differentia, Proprium, Accidens*) this is necessary to be observed, and remembered; that they differ from one another only by the accident of their application. Thus, when *rational*, applied to the Genus *animal*, constitutes the Species man, all other Attributives applied to that Species are either *accidens*, or *proprium*; but these Attributives themselves may be the *differentia* in the case of other classes. Thus, *warm-blooded*, applied to *man*, stands under the class *proprium*; but

when applied to the animals which stand distinguished
from the cold-blooded, as constituting a class, it becomes the *differentia*, and *rational*, with respect to this
comprehensive class, is only an *accidens*.[50]

---

[50] The author says, that no very distinct boundaries are
marked by the three terms, Differentia, Proprium, and
Accidens, nor do they effect a scientific division. As used,
however, by the more accurate of the school logicians, they
do mark out distinct boundaries, and do effect a scientific
division.

Of the attributes common to a class, some have been taken
into consideration in forming the class, and are included in
the signification of its name. Such, in the case of man, are
rationality, and the outward form which we call the human
These attributes are its Differentiæ ; the fundamental differences which distinguish that class from the others most nearly
allied to it. The school logicians were contented with one
Differentia, whenever one was sufficient completely to circum-
scribe the class. But this was an error, because one attribute
may be sufficient for distinction, and yet may not exhaust the
signification of the class-name. All attributes, then, which
are part of that signification, are set apart as Differentiæ.
Other attributes, though not included among those which constitute the class, and which are directly signified by its name,
are consequences of some of those which constitute the class,
and always found along with them. These attributes of the
class are its Propria. Thus, to be bounded by three straight
lines is the Differentia of a triangle : to have the sum of its
three angles equal to two right angles, being a consequence of
its Differentia, is a Proprium of it. Rationality is a Differentia
of the class Man : to be able to build cities is a Proprium, being
a consequence of rationality, but not, as that is, included in
the meaning of the word Man. All other attributes of the class,
which are neither included in the meaning of the name, nor
are consequences of any which are included, are Accidents,

We now arrive at a very important conclusion ; for it thus appears, that all Predication, is Predication of Genus or Species, since the Attributives classed under the titles of *Differentia, Proprium, Accidens*, cannot be used but as part of the name of a Species. But we have seen, above, that Predication by Genus and Species is merely the substitution of one name for another, the more general for the less general ; the fact of the substitution being marked by the *Copula.* It follows, if all Predication is by Genus and Species, that all Predication is the substitution of one name for another, the more for the less general.

It will be easy for the learner to make this material fact familiar to himself, by attending to a few instances. Thus, when it is said that man is rational, the term rational is evidently elliptical, and the word animal is understood. The word rational, according to grammatical language, is an adjective, and is significant only in conjunction with a substantive. According to logical language, it is a connotative term, and is without a meaning when disjoined from the object, the property or properties of which it connotes.[51]

---

however universally and constantly they may be true of the class ; as blackness, of crows.

The author's remark, that these three classes of Attributives differ from one another only in the accident of their application, is most just. There are not some attributes which are always Differentiæ, and others which are always Propria, or always Accidents. The same attribute which is a Differentia of one genus or species, may be, and often is, a Proprium or an Accidens of others, and so on.—*Ed.*

[51] I am unable to feel the force of this remark. Every predication ascribes an attribute to a subject. Differentiæ, Pro-

With respect, however, to such examples as this
last, namely, all those in which the predicate consists

---

pria, and Accidents, agree with generic and specific names in
expressing attributes, and the attributes they express are the
whole of their meaning.   I therefore cannot see why there
should not be Predication of any of these, as well as of Genus
and Species.   These three Predicables, the author says, cannot
be used but as part of the name of a genus or species : they
are adjectives, and cannot be employed without a substantive
understood.   Allowing this to be logically, as it is grammatically, true, still the comprehensive and almost insignificant
substantive, "thing" or "being," fully answers the purpose ;
and the entire meaning of the predication is contained in the
adjective.   These adjectives, as the author remarks, are connotative terms ; but so, on his own shewing elsewhere, are all
concrete substantives, except proper names.   Why, when it is
said that man is rational, must "the word animal" be "understood ?"   Nothing is understood but that the being, Man, has
the attribute of reason.   If we say, God is rational, is animal
understood ?   It was only the Greeks who classed their gods
as ζῶα ἀθάνατα.

The exclusion of the three latter Predicables from predication probably recommended itself to the author as a support to
his doctrine that all Predication is the substitution of one name
for another, which he considered himself to have already demonstrated so far as regards Genus and Species.   But proofs
have just been given that in the predication of Genus and
Species no more than in that of Differentia, Proprium, or
Accidens, is anything which turns upon names the main consideration.   Except in the case of definitions, and other merely
verbal propositions, every proposition is intended to communicate a matter of fact : This subject has that attribute—This
cluster of sensations is always accompanied by that sensation.

Let me remark by the way, that the word *connote* is here
used by the author in what I consider its legitimate sense—
that in which a name is said to connote a property or proper-

of the genus and differentia, the proposition is a mere definition ; and the predicate, and the subject, are precisely equivalent. Thus, " rational animal" is precisely the same class as " man ;" and they are only two names for the same thing ; the one a simple, or single worded name ; the other a complex, or double-worded, name. Such propositions therefore are, properly speaking, not Predications at all. When they are used for any other purpose than to make known, or to fix, the meaning of a term, they are useless, and are denominated identical propositions.[52]

The preceding expositions have shown the peculiar use of the *Copula.* The Predication consists, essentially, of two marks, whereof the first is called the Subject, the latter the Predicate ; the Predicate being set down as a name to be used for every thing of which the Subject is a name ; and the *Copula* is merely a mark necessary to shew that the Predicate is to be taken and used as a substitute for the Subject.

There is a great convenience in giving to the *Copula* the same powers of connotation, in respect of Time,

---

ties belonging to the object it is predicated of. He afterwards casts off this use of the term, and introduces one the exact reverse : but of this hereafter.—*Ed.*

[52] In this passage the author virtually gives up the part of his theory of Predication which is borrowed from Hobbes. According to his doctrine in this place, whenever the predicate and the subject are exactly equivalent, and "are only two names for the same thing," the predication serves only " to make known, or to fix, the meaning of a term," and "such propositions are, properly speaking, not Predications at all." —*Ed.*

Manner, Person, and Number, as we have seen to be usefully annexed to the Verb.

It is necessary to explain a little this convenience ; and the explanation will have another advantage, that it will still farther illustrate the manner in which Predication serves the great purpose of marking the Order of ideas in a Train.

If the sensations or ideas in a train were to be marked as merely so many independent items, the mode of marking the order of them would be simple ; the order of the marks itself might suffice.   If this, for example, were the train ; smell of a rose, sight of a rat, sound of a trumpet, touch of velvet, prick of a pin, these names placed in order might denote the order of the sensations.

In the greater number of instances, however, it is necessary to mark the train as the train of somebody ; and for this purpose additional machinery is required. Suppose that the train I have to mark is the train of John, a train of the sensations of John ; what are the marks for which I shall have occasion ?   It is first of all evident that I must have a mark for John, and a mark for each of the sensations.   Suppose it is my purpose to represent John as having a sensation by each of his senses, sight, smell, &c., how must I proceed ?   I have first the word John, for the mark of the person ; and I have the word seeing, for the mark of the sensation.   But beside the marks, " John," " seeing," I have occasion for a mark to show that I mean the mark " seeing" to be applied to the mark " John," and not to any other.   For that purpose I use the word " is."   I say " John is seeing," and the first sensation of John's train is now sufficiently denoted. In the same manner I proceed with the rest; John is smelling, John is tasting, John is hearing, John is touching.

But I have often occasion to speak not only of John's present sensations, but of his past or his future sensations; not of John as merely now seeing, hearing, &c., but as having been, or as going to be, the subject of these sensations. The *Copula* may be so contrived as most commodiously to connote the main distinctions of Time: not merely to mark the connection between the two marks which form the subject and the predicate of the proposition, but to mark, along with this, either past, or present, or future, Time. Thus, if I say John is seeing, the copula marks present time along with the peculiar connection between the predicate and the subject; if I say John was seeing, it connotes past time; if I say John will be seeing, it connotes future time.

As, in explaining the functions of verbs, there appeared a convenience in the contrivance by which they were made to connote three Manners; first, when no reference is made to any thing which is previously spoken of; secondly, when a reference is made to something which is previously spoken of; thirdly, when a reference is made to the will of one of the PERSONS; it will now be seen that there is the same convenience in making the *Copula* connote these references by a similar contrivance. Thus, when we speak of a man having sensations, we may speak of him as having them or as not having them, in consequence of something previously spoken of; or we may speak of him as having them in consequence of our will. It is, therefore, useful, that the *Copula* should

have moods as well as tenses.   The same thing may
be said of persons and numbers; of which no illustration seems to be required.

We come next to an observation respecting the
Copula, to which the greatest attention is due.   In
all Languages, the Verb which denotes EXISTENCE has
been employed to answer the additional purpose of
the *Copula* in Predication.   The consequences of this
have been most lamentable.   There is thus a double
meaning in the *Copula*, which has produced a most
unfortunate mixture and confusion of ideas.   It has
involved in mystery the whole business of Predication;
the grand contrivance by which language is rendered
competent to its end.   By darkening Predication, it
has spread such a veil over the phenomena of mind,
as concealed them from ordinary eyes, and allowed
them to be but imperfectly seen by those which were
the most discerning.

In our own language, the verb, TO BE, is the important word which is employed to connote, along with
its Subject, whatever it be, the grand idea of EXIS-
TENCE.   Thus, if I use the first person singular of its
indicative mood, and say, " I am," I affirm EXISTENCE
of myself.   " I am," is the equivalent of " I am EXIST-
ING."   In the first of these expressions, " I am," the
mark " am" involves in it the force of two marks; it
involves the meaning of the word " existing," and the
marking power or meaning of the *Copula*.   In the
second expression " I am existing," the word " am"
ought to serve the purpose of the *Copula* only.   But
in reality its connotation of EXISTENCE still adheres to
it; and whereas the expression ought to consist of the
three established parts of a Predication ; 1, the *subject*

" I ;" 2, the *predicate* EXISTING ; and 3, the *copula ;* it in reality consists of, 1, the subject " I ;" 2, the predicate EXISTING ;   3, the *Copula ;*   which signifies, 4, EXISTING, over again.

Let us take, as another case, that in which the subject and predicate of my intended proposition are, the word " I" and " reading."   I want for the purpose of predication only a *Copula* to signify nakedly that the mark " reading" is applied to the mark " I ;" but instead of this I am obliged to use a word which connotes EXISTENCE, along with the force of the *Copula ;* and when I say " I am reading," not only *reading* is predicated of me, but EXISTING also.   Suppose, again, my subject is " John," my predicate " dead," I am obliged to use for my *Copula* the word " is," which connotes EXISTENCE, and I thus predicate of John both *existence* and *death.*

It may be easily collected, from this one example, what heterogeneous and inconsistent ideas may be forced into connection by the use of the Substantive Verb as the *Copula* in Predication ; and what confusion in the mental processes it tends to produce.   It is in the case, however, of the higher abstractions, and the various combinations of ideas which the mind, in the processes of enquiring and marking, forms for its own convenience, to obtain a greater command over its stores and greater facility in communicating them, that the use of the verb which conjoins the Predication of EXISTENCE with every other Predication, has produced the wildest confusion, and been the most deeply injurious.   Is it any wonder, for example, that *Chance,* and *Fate,* and *Nature,* have been personified, and have had an EXISTENCE ascribed

to them, as objects, when we have no means of predicating anything whatsoever of them, without predicating such EXISTENCE at the same time. If we say
that " chance is nothing ;" we predicate of it, by the
word " is," both *existence* and *nothingness.*

When this is the case, it is by no means to be
wondered at, that philosophers should so long have
inquired what those EXISTENCES are which abstract
terms were employed to express ; and should have
lost themselves in fruitless speculations about the
nature of entity, and quiddity, substance, and quality,
space, time, necessity, eternity, and so on.

It is necessary here to take notice of a part of the
marking power of Verbs, which could not be explained
till the nature of the *copula* was understood.

Every Verb involves in it the force of the *copula.*
It combines the marking powers of an *adjective,* and
of the *copula ;* and all Verbs may be resolved into
those elements. Thus, " John walks," is the same
with " John is walking." Verbs, therefore, are attributives, of the same nature as adjectives, only with
additional connotative powers ; and they cut smaller
classes out of larger, in the manner of adjectives.
Thus " John walks," is an expression, the same in
import as the Predication " John is a walking man ;"
and, walking men, standing men, running men, lying
men, are all sub-species of the Species Man.

The same unhappy duplicity of meaning, which is
incurred by using the *Substantive* Verb as the *copula*
in Predication, is inflicted on *other* Verbs, in that part
of their marking power by which they exhibit the
connection between the two terms of a Predication.

The *copula,* included in Verbs, is not the PURE *copula,*

but the ACTUAL *copula*; the *copula* familiar and in constant use; namely, the Substantive Verb. From this it results, that whatever the peculiar attribute, which is predicated by means of any verb, EXISTENCE is always predicated along with it. Thus, when I say "John walks," which is equivalent to "John is walking," I predicate both existence, and walking, of John. When I say, "Caliban existed not," which is the same as "Caliban was not existing," I predicate both existence, and non-existence, of the imaginary being Caliban. By the two first words of the Predication, "Caliban was," existence is predicated of him; by the addition of the compound term "not existing," the opposite is predicated of him.

The instances, in which the more complicated formations of the mind are the subjects of this double Predication, are those which, from the importance of their consequences, deserve the greatest degree of attention. Thus, when we say "virtue exalts," both *existing*, and *exalting*, are predicated of virtue. When we say that "passion impels," both *existence*, and *impulsion*, are predicated of passion. When we say that "Time generates," and "Space contains all things," we affirm *existence* of space and time, by the same expression by which we affirm of the one, that it generates; of the other, that it contains. This constancy of Predication, forcing the same constancy in the junction of the ideas, furnishes a remarkable instance of that important case of association, of which we took notice above, where, by frequency of association, two ideas become so joined, that the one constantly rises, and cannot be prevented from rising, in combination with the other. Thus it is,

that Time forces itself upon us as an *object.* So it is
with Space. We cannot think of Space, we cannot
think of Time, without thinking of them as existent.
With the ideas of space and time, the idea of EXIS-
TENCE, as it is predicated of objects, is so associated,
by the use of the Substantive Verb as the *copula* in
predication, that we cannot disjoin them. The same
would have been the case with Chance, and Fate, and
Nature; if our religious education did not counteract
the association. It was precisely the same, among
the Greeks and Romans, whose religious education
had not that effect.[53] [54]

---

[53] The account of predication above given is in conformity
with the phenomena of the family of languages known as the
Indo-European. Logicians, in fact, in treating of this subject
have had almost exclusive regard to Greek and Latin and the
literary languages of modern Europe, which are all of one type.
It might therefore be presumed that the theory thus formed
would be found not to fit in all its parts when applied to languages of an altogether different structure. The mental process
must doubtless be the same in all; but the words that express
the several parts may be used in new and unprecedented ways.
Were naturalists to construct a scheme of the animal organism
without ever having seen any other animals than those of the
vertebrate type, the theory would certainly fail in generality;
certain organs or functions would be set down as essential to
animal existence which acquaintance with other classes of creatures shows can be quite well dispensed with. Similarly, the
current theory of predication, when viewed in the light of a
wider and deeper knowledge of the organism of speech, seems
to attach an exaggerated importance to the peculiar predicative
power presumed to be inherent in verbs, and especially in the
verb of existence. It is now a well known fact that in the mono-
syllabic class of languages, in which a third part of the human
race express their thoughts, there is no distinction among the

We have now observed, wherein Predication consists, and the instruments by which it is performed.

---

parts of speech. In Chinese, for example, the word *ta* expresses
indifferently great, greatness, to be great, to make great or mag-
nify, greatly. It is only position that determines in each case
how the word is to be understood ; thus traditional convention
assigns to *ta fu* the meaning of "a great man," and to *fu ta*
that of "the man is great." Being habituated to the constant
use of the verb *is* in such a case as the latter, we are apt to
suppose that the expression derives its predicative force from
its suggesting the verb of existence, which the mind instinc-
tively and necessarily supplies for itself. How little ground
there is for this presumed necessity, has been conclusively
shown by the late Mr. Garnett, in his profound and exhaustive
essay on the Nature and Analysis of the Verb. Speaking of
the theory that makes the essential difference between the verb
and other parts of speech to reside in the verb substantive,
which is to be supplied by the mind in all cases where the
functions of the verb proper are to be called into requisition,
he observes : "This theory presupposes the existence of a verb
substantive in the languages in question, and consciousness of
that existence and of the force and capabilities of the element
in those who speak them. Unfortunately the Spanish grammarians, to whom we are indebted for what knowledge we
possess of the Philippine dialects, unanimously concur in stating
that there is no verb substantive either in Tagalá, Pampanga,
or Bisaya, nor any means of supplying the place of one, except
the employment of pronouns and particles. Mariner makes a
similar remark respecting the Tonga language ; and we may
venture to affirm that there is not such a thing as a true verb
substantive in any one member of the great Polynesian family.

"It is true that the Malayan, Javanese and Malagassy
grammarians talk of words signifying *to be ;* but an attentive
comparison of the elements which they profess to give as such,
shows clearly that they are no verbs at all, but simply pronouns
or indeclinable particles, commonly indicating the time, place

We have also, in part, contemplated the End which
it is destined to fulfil; that is, to mark the order in
which sensations and ideas follow one another in a

---

or manner of the specified action or relation. It is not therefore easy to conceive how the mind of a Philippine islander, or
of any other person, can supply a word totally unknown to it,
and which there is not a particle of evidence to show that it
ever thought of."

Of the substitutes put in place of the substantive verb, by
far the most common are pronouns, and particles indicating
position. Thus in Coptic, the descendant of the ancient
Egyptian, the demonstrative *pe*, "this," after a noun singular
masculine, or *te* when the noun is feminine, is'equivalent to *is ;*
and *ne*, "these," after a plural, to *are.* In the ancient hiero-
glyphic monuments the function of the substantive verb is
performed by the same means. Even in the Semitic languages,
which have substantive verbs, pronouns are habitually used
instead of them ; so that *I I,* or *I he*, stands for *I am*, and *we
we* or *we they*, for *we are.* " Thou art my King" (Ps. 44, 5)
is in the Hebrew " Thou *he* my King ;" " We are the servants
of the God of heaven" (Ezra 5, 11) is in Chaldee " We *they*
servants of the God of heaven ;" " I am the light of the world,"
is in Arabic " I *he* the light of the world."

Although such modes of expression are foreign to the Indo-
European languages, even they furnish abundant evidence of
the predicative power of pronouns and particles. If any word
required to have inherent in it the peculiar affirmative power
attributed to verbs, it is the word *yes*. Accordingly Tooke
derives it from the French imperative *a-yez :* forgetting, or not
knowing, that the Anglo-Saxon *gese* or *yea* (cognate with the
Sanscrit pronoun *ya*) was in existence long before the French
ayez. The fact is that Eng. *yes*, Ger. *ja*, and the corresponding
words in the other European languages are oblique cases of
demonstrative pronouns, and mean simply " in this (manner),"
or " thus." The Italian *si* (yes) is from Lat. *sic*, (thus) ; the
Provençal *oc* is from Lat. *hoc ;* and the modern Fr. *oui* was

train. On this last part of the subject, however, the following observations are still required.

The trains, the order of which we have occasion to

---

originally a combination of *hoc illo,* and passed through the stages of *ocil* and *oïl* into its present form.

The consideration of these and a multitude of similar phenomena suggests, that the Sanscrit *as-mi,* Gr. *ei-mi,* Lat. *s-um* (for *es-um*), Eng. *a-m,* may have had for its root the demonstrative pronoun *sa,* and meant primarily " that (or there) as to me." Be that as it may, all philologists are agreed that the verbs now used to express *being* in the abstract, expressed originally something physical and palpable. Thus Ital. *stato,* Fr. *été,* *been,* are from the Lat. *statum,* the participle of *sto,* "to stand ;" and *exist* itself meant " to stand out or be prominent." Eng. *be,* Lat. *fu-* is identical with Gr. *phy-* " to grow ;" and, according to Max Müller, *as* the root of *as-mi* meant " breath" or " breathing." It may then be safely affirmed that no word had for its primary function to express mere existence ; it seems enough for the purpose of predication that existence be implied.

With regard to ordinary verbs, the analytic processes of comparative grammar show no traces of a substantive verb entering into their structure. It is now an accepted doctrine of philology that, as a rule, the root of a verb is of the nature of an abstract noun ; and that it became a verb simply by the addition of a pronominal affix—as in the Greek δί-δω-μι, δί-δω-ς, δί-δω-σι, in which the terminations were originally -μι,-σι τι. The habits of thought arising out of the present analytic state of the Indo-European languages naturally lead us to conceive these pronominal affixes as nominatives. But *gift I* does not seem a very natural way of getting at the meaning " I give ;" and therefore Mr. Garnett maintains that the affixes were originally in an oblique case—the genitive or the instrumental—so that the literal meaning was " gift of me," or " giving by me." That this is the nature of the verb in the agglutinate languages—by far the most numerous class—it seems hardly possible to dispute; for in these the

mark, may for the elucidation of the present subject,
be divided into two classes.   We have occasion to

---

affixes remain rigidly distinct and little disguised.   Thus,
according to Garnett, the Wotiak, in order to express "my
son," "thy son," &c., joins oblique cases of the personal
pronouns to the noun *pi* in the following way :—

> pi-ĭ . . . . son of me
> pi-ed . . . son of thee
> pi-ez . . . son of him
> pi-mi . . . son of us
> pi-dy . . . son of you
> pi-zy . . . son of them

In an exactly similar way the preterite of the verb to speak
stands thus —

> bera-i . . . speech of me=I spoke
> bera-d . . . speech of thee
> bera-z . . . speech of him
> bera-my . . speech of us
> bera-dy . . speech of you
> bera-zy . . speech of them

In the Fiji language *loma* means " heart" or " will;" and
loma-qu (heart of me) may, according to the connection, signify either " my heart or will," or " I will."

In the inflected languages the affixes are so amalgamated
with the root and otherwise obliterated that there is no such
direct evidence of their nature ; but a great many facts tend
to show that the structure of the verb was originally the same
as in the agglutinate family.

If this analysis of the verb is correct, the affirmation of existence found no expression in the early stages of language ;
*the real copula connecting the subject with the predicate was
the proposition contained in the oblique case of the pronominal affix.—F.*

[54] The interesting and important philological facts adduced
by Mr. Findlater, confirm and illustrate in a very striking
manner the doctrine in the text, of the radical distinction

mark, either, first, The series of the objects we have
seen, heard, or otherwise perceived by our senses ; or,

---

between the functions of the copula in predication, and those
of the substantive verb ; by shewing that many languages
have no substantive verb, no verb expressive of mere exist-
tence, and yet signify their predications by other means ; and
that probably all languages began without a substantive verb,
though they must always have had predications.

The confusion between these two different functions in the
European languages, and the ambiguity of the verb To Be,
which fulfils them both, are among the most important of the
minor philosophical truths to which attention has been called
by the author of the Analysis.   As in the case of many other
luminous thoughts, an approach is found to have been made
to it by previous thinkers.   Hobbes, though he did not reach
it, came very close to it, and it was still more distinctly anticipated by Laromiguière, though without any sufficient perception of its value.   It occurs in a criticism on a passage of
Pascal, and in the following words.   " Quand on dit, l'être
est, *etc.* le mot *est*, ou le verbe, n'exprime pas la même chose
que le mot être, sujet de la définition.   Si j'énonce la proposition suivante : Dieu est existant, je ne voudrais pas dire
assurément, Dieu existe existant : cela ne ferait pas un sens ;
de même, si je dis que Virgile est poëte, je ne veux pas donner
à entendre que Virgile existe.   Le verbe *est*, dans la proposition, n'exprime donc pas l'existence réelle ; il n'exprime
qu'un rapport spécial entre le sujet et l'attribut, le rapport du
contenant au contenu," &c.   (Leçons de Philosophie, 7me ed.
vol. i. p. 307.)   Having thus hit upon an unobvious truth in
the course of an argument directed to another purpose, he
passes on and takes no further notice of it.

It may seem strange that the verb which signifies existence
should have been employed in so many different languages as
the sign of predication, if there is no real connection between
the two meanings.   But languages have been built up by the
extension of an originally small number of words, with or

secondly, A train of thoughts which may have passed in our minds.

1. When we come to record a train of the objects we have perceived, that is, a train of sensations, the sensations have become ideas ; for the objects are not now acting on our senses, and the sensations are at an end.

The order of the objects of our senses, is either the order of time, or the order of place. The first is the order of SUCCESSION ; when one object comes first, another next, and so on. The second is the order of POSITION ; when the objects are considered as simultaneous, but different in distance and direction from a particular point.

Let us observe in what manner the artifice of Pre-

---

without alterations of form, to express new meanings, the choice of the word being often determined by very distant analogies. In the present case, the analogy is not distant. All our predications are intended to declare the manner in which something affects, or would affect, ourselves or others. Our idea of existence is simply the idea of something which affects or would affect us somehow, without distinction of mode. Everything, therefore, which we can have occasion to assert of an existing thing, may be looked upon as a particular mode of its existence. Since snow is white, and since snow exists, it may be said to exist white ; and if a sign was wanted by which to predicate white of snow, the word exists would be very likely to present itself. But most of our predications do relate to existing things : and this being so, it is in the ordinary course of the human mind that the same sign should be adhered to when we are predicating something of a merely imaginary thing (an abstraction, for instance) and that, being so used, it should create an association between the abstraction and the notion of real existence.—*Ed.*

dication is adapted to the marking of a train in either of those orders : and first, with respect to a train in the order of Time.

Of this the following may be taken as a simple example. "The sun rises ; clouds form ; clouds cover the sky ; lightning flashes ; thunder roars." It is easy in these expressions to observe, what were the sensations, and in what order they succeeded one another. It is also observable, that the order is denoted by so many Predications ; and that Predication is our only expedient for denoting their order. First sensation, "sight of the sun ;" second sensation, "rising of the sun ;" these two denoted shortly and in their order by the Predication, "the sun rises." Third sensation, "sight of clouds ;" fourth sensation, "forming of clouds ;" these two again shortly denoted in their order by the Predication, "clouds form." The next, "clouds cover the sky," needs no further explanation ; but there is a peculiar artifice of language in the two following Predications ; "lightning flashes," "thunder roars," which deserves to be well understood. "Lightning flashes ;" here there is but one sensation, the sensation of sight, which we call a flash. But there are various kinds of flashes ; this is a peculiar one, and I want to mark peculiarly what it is. It is not a flash on the earth, but a flash in the sky ; it will not, however, sufficiently distinguish the flash in question, to say, the sky flashes, because other flashes come from the sky. What then is my contrivance ? I form the fancy of a cause of this particular flash, though I know nothing concerning it, and for this unknown cause I invent a name, and call it lightning. I have then an expression which always accurately marks the sensation I mean to denote : I say, "the lightning flashes," " a flash of lightning," and so on. " Thunder roars," is another case of the same artifice. The noise here is the only sensation ; but in order to distinguish it from all other noises, I invent a name for its unknown cause, and by its means can mark the sensation with perfect precision.

The Fictions, after this manner resorted to, for the purpose of marking ; though important among the artifices of naming ; have contributed largely to the misdirection of thought.

By the unfortunate ambiguity of the *Copula*, EXISTENCE is affirmed of them in every Predication into which they enter. The idea of EXISTENCE becomes, by this means, inseparable from them ; and their true nature, as Creatures of the mind, and nothing more, is rarely, and not without difficulty, perceived.

The mode in which a train, in the order of place, is marked by the artifice of Predication, may be thus exemplified : "The house is on a hill ; a lawn is in front ; a stable is on the left hand ; a garden is on the right ; a wood is behind." It is not necessary, after the exposition of the preceding example, to exhibit the detail of the marking performed by these Predications. The reader can trace the sensations, the order of them, and the mode of the marking, according to the specimen which has just been exhibited.

2. The trains of thought which pass in our minds, are sequences, the items of which are connected in three principal ways : 1st, as cause and effect ; 2dly, as resembling ; 3dly, as included under the same name. A short illustration of each of these cases will

complete the account of predication, as a contrivance for marking the order of ideas.

To illustrate a sequence, connected as Cause and Effect, let me suppose that I have a flint and steel in my hand, which I am about to strike, one against the other, but at that instant perceive a barrel of gunpowder open, close before me. I withhold the stroke in consequence of the train of thought which suggests to me the ultimate effect. If I have occasion to mark the train, I can only do it by a series of Predications, each of which marks a sequence in the train of causes and effects. " I strike the flint on the steel," first sequence. " The stroke produces a spark," second sequence. " The spark falls on gunpowder," third sequence. " The spark ignites the gunpowder," fourth sequence. " The gunpowder ignited makes an explosion," fifth sequence. The ideas contained in these propositions must all have passed through my mind, and this is the only mode in which language enables me to mark them in their order.[55]

---

[55] It is necessary again to notice the consistent omission, throughout the author's theory of Predication, of the element Belief. In the case supposed, the ideas contained in all the propositions might have passed through the mind, without our being led to assert the propositions. I might have thought of every step in the series of phenomena mentioned, might have pictured all of them in my imagination, and have come to the conclusion that they would not happen. I therefore should not have made, either in words or in thought, the predication, This gunpowder will explode if I strike the flint against the steel. Yet the same ideas would have passed through my mind in the same order, in which they stand in the text. The only deficient link would have been the final one, the Belief. —Ed.

The sequences of which the items are connected by Resemblance will not require much illustration. I see A, who suggests B to me by his stature. B suggests C by the length of his nose. C suggests D by the similarity of their profession, and so on. The series of my thoughts is sufficiently obvious. How do I proceed when I have occasion to mark it? I use a series of predications. "I see A;" this predication marks the first item, my sight of A. "A is tall," the second. "A man of like tallness is B," the third; and so on.

The mode in which thoughts are united in a Syllogism, is the leading example of the third case. Let us consider the following very familiar instance. "Every tree is a vegetable: every oak is a tree: therefore, every oak is a vegetable." This is evidently a process of naming. The primary idea is that of the object called an oak; from the name oak, I proceed to the name tree, finding that the name oak, is included in the name tree; and from the name tree, I proceed to the name vegetable, finding that the name tree is included in the name vegetable, and by consequence the name oak. This is the series of thoughts, which is marked in order, by the three propositions or predications of the syllogism.[56]

---

[56] For the present I shall only remark on this theory of the syllogism, that it must stand or fall with the theory of Predication of which it is the sequel. If, as I have maintained, the propositions which are the premises of the syllogism are not correctly described as mere processes of naming, neither is the formula by which a third proposition is elicited from these two a process of mere naming. What it is, will be considered hereafter.—*Ed.*

The Predications of Arithmetic are another instance of the same thing. "One and one are two." This again is a mere process of naming. What I call one and one, in numbering things, are objects, sensations, or clusters of sensations; suppose, the striking of the clock. The same sounds which I call one and one, I call also two; I have for these sensations, therefore, two names which are exactly equivalent: so when I say, one and one and one are three: or when I say, two and two are four: ten and ten are twenty: and the same when I put together any two numbers whatsoever. The series of thoughts in these instances is merely a series of names applicable to the same thing, and meaning the same thing.

Beside the two purposes of language, of which I took notice at the beginning of this inquiry; the recording of a man's thoughts for his own use, and the communication of them to others; there is a use, to which language is subservient, of which some account is yet to be given. There are complex sensations, and complex ideas, made up of so many items, that one is not distinguishable from another. Thus, a figure of one hundred sides, is not distinguishable from one of ninety-nine sides. A thousand men in a crowd are not distinguishable from nine hundred and ninety-nine. But in all cases, in which the complexity of the idea arises from the repetition of the same idea, names can be invented upon a plan, which shall render them distinct, up to the very highest degree of complication. Numbers are a set of names contrived upon this plan, and for this very purpose. Ten and the numbers below ten, are the repetition of so many ones: twenty, thirty, forty, &c., up to a hundred, are

the repetition of so many tens : two hundred, three
hundred, &c., the repetition of so many hundreds ;
and so on.   These are names, which afford an immediate reference to the ones or units, of which they are
composed ; and the highest numbers are as easily distinguished by the difference of a unit as the lowest.
All the processes of Arithmetic are only so many
contrivances to substitute a distinct name for an indistinct one.   What, for example, is the purpose of
addition ?   Suppose I have six numbers, of which I
desire to take the sum, 18, 14, 9, 25, 19, 15 ; these
names, eighteen, and fourteen, and nine, &c., form a
compound name ; but a name which is not distinct.
By summing them up, I get another name, exactly
equivalent, one hundred, which is in the highest degree distinct, and gives me an immediate reference to
the units or items of which it is composed ; and this
is of the highest utility.

That the Predications of Geometry are of the same
nature with those of Arithmetic, is a truth of the
greatest importance, and capable of being established
by very obvious reasoning.   It is well known, that all
reasoning about quantity can be expressed in the form
of algebraic equations.   But the two sides of an algebraic equation are of necessity two marks or two names
for the same thing ; of which the one on the right-
hand side is more distinct, at least to the present purpose of the inquirer, than the one on the left-hand
side; and the whole purpose of an algebraic investigation, which is a mere series of changes of names, is to
obtain, at last, a distinct name, a name the marking
power of which is perfectly known to us, on the right-
hand side of the equation.   The language of geometry

itself, in the more simple cases, makes manifest the
same observation. The amount of the three angles of
a triangle, is twice a right angle. I arrive at this
conclusion, as it is called, by a process of reasoning :
that is to say, I find out a name " twice a right angle,"
which much more distinctly points out to me a certain
quantity, than my first name, " amount of the three
angles of a triangle ;" and the process by which I
arrive at this name is a successive change of names,
and nothing more ; as any one may prove to himself
by merely observing the steps of the demonstration.[57]

There is one important class of words, the NAMES
of NAMES ; of which we shall have occasion to take
account more particularly hereafter, and of which it
is necessary here to speak only as they form a variety
of Predication. A few examples will make the case

---

[57] I cannot see any propriety in the expression that when
we infer the sum of the three angles of a triangle to be twice
a right angle, the operation consists in finding a second name
which more distinctly points out the quantity than the first
name. When we assent to the proof of this theorem, we do
much more than obtain a new and more expressive name for a
known fact ; we learn a fact previously unknown. It is true
that one result of our knowledge of this theorem is to give
us a name for the sum of the three angles, " the marking
power of which is perfectly known to us :" but it was not for
want of knowing the marking power of the phrase " sum of
the three angles of a triangle" that we did not know what that
sum amounted to. We knew perfectly what the expression
" sum of the three angles" was appointed to mark. What we
have obtained, that we did not previously possess, is not a
better mark for the same thing, but an additional fact to mark
—the fact which is marked by predicating of that sum, the
phrase " twice a right angle."—*Ed.*

intelligible. WORD is a *generical* name for all Names. It is not the name of a Thing, as chair is the name of a thing, or watch, or picture. But word is a *name* for these several *names;* chair is a word, watch is a word, picture is a word, and so of all other names. Thus grammatical and logical terms are names of names. The word *noun,* is the name of one class of words. *verb* of another, *preposition* of another, and so on. The word *sentence,* is the name of a series of words put together for a certain purpose; the word *paragraph* the same ; and so *oration, discourse, essay, treatise,* &c. The words *genus* and *species,* are not names of things, but of names. Genus is not the name of any thing called animal or any thing called body ; it is a name of the *names* animal, body, and so on ; the *name* animal is a *genus,* the *name* body is a *genus;* and in like manner is the *name* man a *species,* the *name* horse, the name crow, and so on. The name *proposition,* the name *syllogism,* are names of a series of words put together for a particular purpose; and so is the term *definition;* and the term *argument.* It will be easily seen that these words enter into Predication precisely on the same principles as other words. Either the more distinct is predicated of the less distinct, its equivalent; or the more comprehensive of the less comprehensive. Thus we say, that nouns and verbs are declinables ; preposition and adverb indeclinables ; where the more comprehensive terms are predicated of the less. Thus we say, that adjectives and verbs are attributes ; where the more distinct is predicated of the less.[58]

---

[58] This exposition of the class of words which are properly names of names, belongs originally to Hobbes, and is highly

important. They are a kind of names, the signification of which is very often misunderstood, and has given occasion to much hazy speculation. It should however be remarked that the words genus and species are not solely names of names ; they are ambiguous. A genus never indeed means (as many of the schoolmen supposed) an abstract entity, distinct from all the individuals composing the class ; but it often means the sum of those individuals taken collectively ; the class as a whole, distinguished on the one hand from the single objects comprising it, and on the other hand from the class name.—*Ed.*

SECTION V.

PRONOUNS.

The principal part of the artifice of Naming is now explained. We have considered the nature of the more necessary marks, and the manner in which they are combined so as to represent the order of a train. Beside those marks, which are the fundamental part of language, there are several classes of auxiliary words or marks, the use of which is, to abbreviate expression, and to render it, what is of great importance, a more rapid vehicle of thought. These are usually comprehended under the titles of pronoun, adverb, preposition, and conjunction ; a classification which, for our present purpose, has the best recommendation, that of being familiarly known.

It is to be distinctly understood, that in the account which is here to be given of the subsidiary parts of speech, it is but one part of the explanation of them which will be attempted. The ideas, which many of them stand for, are of the most complicated kind, and have not yet been expounded. We are, therefore, not yet prepared to point out the items which they mark. Our present business is only to indicate the mode in which they are used in Predication, as part of the great contrivance for marking the order of a train of ideas, and for economizing the number of words.

It is also necessary to observe, that I have limited myself, in this part, to brief indications, without going into minute development, the length of which, it appeared to me, would not be compensated by the advantage.

In all speech their is a *speaker;* there is some *person spoken to ;* and there is some *person* or *thing spoken of.* These objects constitute three Classes, marks of which are perpetually required. Any artifice, therefore, to abridge the use of marks, of such frequent recurrence, was highly to be desired. One expedient offered itself obviously, as likely to prove of the highest utility. *Speakers* constituted one class, with numerous names ; *persons spoken to,* a second class ; *persons* and *things spoken of,* a third. A *generical* name might be invented for each class ; a name, which would include all of a class, and which singly might be used as the substitute of many. For this end were the Personal Pronouns invented and such is their character and office. " I," is the generical mark which includes all marks of the class, *speakers.* " Thou," is a generical mark, which includes all marks of the class, *persons spoken to.* " He," " she," " it," are marks, which include all marks of the class, *persons* or *things spoken of.*

By forming Adjectives from certain kinds of Nouns we obtain a useful class of specific names. From wool we make woollen ; and woollen, attached to various generic names, furnishes us with specific names ; thus we say woollen cloth, which is a species of cloth ; woollen yarn, which is a species of yarn ; woollen garment, which is a species of garment. So, from the word gold we make golden, which furnishes us with a greater number of specific names ; from wood wooden, which furnishes us with a still greater number. Adjectives are formed in like manner from the personal pronouns : from I, my or mine; from Thou, thy or thine; from He, She, It, his, hers, its ; also from the plurals of them, ours, yours, theirs. These adjectives answer a purpose of very frequent recurrence ; that of singling out, from any class of objects, a sub-class, or an individual, bearing a peculiar relation, to the *person speaking*, the *person spoken to*, or the *person* or *thing spoken of.* Thus, when I say, my sheep or my oxen, I denote a sub-class of those animals, those which stand in the relation of property to the speaker; when I say thy sheep or oxen, I denote a sub-class in the same relation to the person spoken to ; and when I say his sheep or oxen, a sub-class, standing in that relation to the person spoken of. When I say my son, thy wife, his father, I single out individuals having that relation.

The Demonstrative Pronouns, This and That, are of great utility. They serve to individualize any thing in a class. One of these marks put upon a specific mark, makes it an individual mark. Thus, the mark " man," is the name of a class : put upon it the mark this, or that; this man, and that man, are marks, signs, or names, of individuals. In this manner innumerable individual names can be made, without adding a single word to the cumbrous materials of language.

The nature of the Relative Pronoun is not difficult to understand. It supplies the place of a personal pronoun and a conjunction, in connecting a Predication with the subject, or predicate of another proposition. Thus, " John received a wound, *which* occasioned his death," is of the same import as " John received a wound, *and it* occasioned his death." This

is a case in which the Relative connects a subsequent
predication with the *predicate* of an antecedent predication. The following are cases in which it connects
a subordinate predication with the *subject* of the principal one : " Erasmus, *who* was a lover of truth, but of
a timid character, hesitated between the new and the
old religion." Erasmus, *and he* was a lover of truth,
&c. " The man *who* spoke to you is my father."
" The man spoke to you, *and he* is my father."[59]

---

[59] There is really no well marked distinction between relative pronouns and demonstrative pronouns, either in their
origin or in their use. Of the demonstrative roots *ka, sa, ta,
ja,* derivatives from the gutteral *ka* prevail as relatives in Latin
and its modern descendants (Lat. *qui,* It. *che,* Fr. *qui*), and in
the Teutonic languages (Goth. *hva,* Eng. *who,* Ger. *wer,
welch*), but by no means exclusively. In Greek the relative
differs little from the article, which is also used as a demonstrative and a personal pronoun. Modern Italian uses as a
demonstrative a compound of the Latin *qui* with *iste* and *illa*
—*questo, quella.* In German the relative proper, viz. *welch,*
is comparatively little used, its place being supplied by the
article *der,* which is merely an unemphatic demonstrative ; and
in English *that* is perhaps as often used as who or which.
The relative serves for two purposes, which it is useful to
distinguish. (1) It may add on either a clause containing an
independent proposition, as in the example in the text, " John
received a wound, which occasioned his death ;" or a clause
dependent in some way upon the preceding—*e.g.* assigning the
reason of it, as, " It was unjust to punish the servant, *who*
only did what he was ordered." (2) The clause introduced by
the relative may serve simply to limit or define a noun, in the
way that an adjective or another noun in apposition does, as
" The man *who* spoke to you is my father." It is in this
latter use of the relative, and in no other, that it is permissible

The Interrogative is easily explained. It is merely the Relative, in a very elliptical form of expression. The interrogative sentence, " *Who* gave you that book ?" when the subaudition is supplied, is thus expressed : The person gave you the book, *and him* I will you to name to me. " *What* is the hour of the day ?" is an elliptical form of,—It is an hour of the day, *and it* I will you to tell me.

---

in English to use *that ;* to substitute *that* for *which* in the first of the other two sentences, or for *who* in the second, would give a different meaning. Now it is only in the cases in which *that* could *not* be substituted for who or which that the relative involves the force of a conjunction ; and it is not always *and* that is the conjunction involved. The conjunction has no verbal expression, and never had ; it is only suggested, and the mind supplies that which best suits the logical connection. When the predication of the relative clause is co-ordinate with the preceding, as in the first example, *and* is the proper conjunction to supply. In the sentence about the punishment of the servant, *who* is equivalent to *for he ;* and in that about Erasmus, in the text, to *inasmuch as he.* When the relative clause merely defines, no conjunction of any kind is even implied. In such a sentence as " He rewarded the man that rescued him," the relative clause is the answer to a question naturally suggested by " He rewarded the man"—what man ? " The or that (man) rescued him ;" which is equivalent to, " his rescuer." To resolve it into " And that man rescued him," gives quite a different meaning ; namely, that he rewarded some man (otherwise known to the hearers) for something (likewise known to them), and that this man now rescued him.—*F.*

SECTION VI.

ADVERBS.

The power of this class of words, in the great busi-ness of marking, and the extent of the service ren-dered by them, will be so easily seen, that a few words will suffice to explain them. Adverbs may be reduced under five heads; 1, Adverbs of Time; 2, Adverbs of Place; 3, Adverbs of Quantity; 4, Adverbs of Quality; 5, Adverbs of Relation. They are mostly abridgments, capable of being substituted for longer marks. And they are always employed for the pur-pose of putting a modification upon the Subject, or the Predicate, of a Proposition. A few examples will suffice for the further elucidation of this subject. "Anciently," is an adverb of time. It is of the same import as the expression, "In distant past time." It is applied to modify the subject, or predicate, of a pro-position, as in the following example : "A number of men anciently in England had wives in common." "Had wives in common," is the predicate of the above proposition, and it is modified, or limited, in respect to time, by the word "anciently." Adverbs of place it is easy to exemplify in the same manner. Under adverbs of quantity all those which mark degrees may be included ; as greatly, minutely : Thus, "He enlarged greatly upon patriotism :" "Greatly" here means "in many words;" and it modifies the predicate, "enlarged," &c. Adverbs of quality and relation are exceedingly numerous, because they are easily made from the words which connote the quality or relation : thus, from hard, hardly ; from loud, loudly ; from sweet, sweetly ; from warm, warmly : again, from father, paternally ; from son, filially ; from magistrate, magisterially ; from high, highly ; from expensive, expensively ; and so on. In all this no difficulty is presented which requires removing.[60]

---

[60] In many cases, and even in some of the examples given, the adverb does not modify either the subject or the predicate, but the application of the one to the other. "Anciently," in the proposition cited, is intended to limit and qualify not men, nor community of wives, but the practice by men of community of wives : it is a circumstance affecting not the subject or the predicate, but the predication. The qualification of past and distant time attaches to the fact asserted, and to the copula, which is the mark of assertion. The reason of its seeming to attach to the predicate is because, as the author remarked in a previous section, the predicate, when a verb, includes the copula.—*Ed.*

SECTION VII.

PREPOSITIONS.

It is easy to see in what manner Prepositions are employed to abridge the process of discourse. They render us the same service which, we have seen, is rendered by adjectives, in affording the means of naming minor classes, taken out of larger, with a great economy of names. Thus, when we say, "a man with a black skin," this compound name, "a man with a black skin;" is the name of a sub-class, taken out of the class man; and when we say, "a black man with a flat nose and woolly hair;" this still more compound name is the name of a minor class, taken out of the sub-class, "men with a black skin."

Prepositions always stand before some word of the class called by grammarians nouns substantive. And these nouns substantive they connect with other nouns substantive, with adjectives, or with verbs. We shall consider the use of them, in each of those cases.

1. Substantives are united to Substantives by prepositions, on purpose to mark something added, something taken away, something possessed or owned. Thus, a man with a dog, a horse without a saddle, a man of wealth, a man of pleasure, and so on.

It was first shewn by Mr. Horne Tooke, that prepositions, in their origin, are verbs, or nouns. Thus the prepositions in English, which note the modifications effected by adding to, or taking from, were originally concrete words, which, beside something connoted by them, marked particularly *junction*, or *disjunction*. In the use of them as prepositions, that part of their signification, which we have called the connotation, has been dropped; and the notation alone remains. Prepositions, therefore, are a sort of abstract terms, to answer a particular purpose. To express my idea of a man with a dog (a very complex idea, consisting of two clusters; one, that which is marked by the term man; the other, that which is marked by the term dog); it is not enough that I set down the term Man, and the term Dog; it is necessary, besides, that I have a mark for that particular *junction* of them, which my mind is making. For that mark I use the preposition " with." " Without" denotes disjunction in a similar manner, and requires no further explanation. The preposition " of," by which possession or ownership is denoted, (formerly, as remarked by Mr. Gilchrist, written *og, oc, ac,* &c.), is *eke,* or add. If we suppose that our verb *have* is of the same origin, *of* is merely the verb, which signifies possessing; and the learner may thus conceive the nature of its different applications.* " A man of wealth," a man hav(ing) wealth; " a field of ten acres," a field hav(ing) ten acres; so, " a house of splendour;" " a woman of gallantry;" in all of which cases, beside the two clusters of ideas, marked by the two names which the preposition connects, there is an idea of possession coming between.

Here, however, a peculiarity is to be noted. When there is a possessor, there is something possessed.

---

* See note at p. 209.

The preposition, therefore, which marks the relation between the possessor and the possessed, stands ambiguously between the active and the passive power. It, therefore, partakes more of the active or the passive signification, according to the position of the words which it is employed to connect. In the instances previously given, we have seen that it had clearly an active signification. In the following it has clearly a passive. "The book of John;" the book *of*, hav(ed) John. "The Creator of the world;" Creator hav(ed). "The wealth of Crœsus;" wealth hav(ed).

Of is employed in a partitive sense, when one of the words denotes a part of the other; as "half of the army;" "many of the people;" "much of the loss." In this case the idea of possession is sufficiently obvious to support the analogy. The parts are possessed, had, by the whole. "Part of the debt," part hav(ed) the debt.

It is easy to see how the preposition with a substantive, serves the purpose of a new adjective. Thus, in the expression, "a man with one eye," the words, "with one eye," might have been supplied by an adjective, having the same meaning or marking power; and the French language actually has such an adjective, in the mark *borgne*. We say, a man with red hair, and we have the adjective, red-haired; a man of wealth, and we have the adjective, wealthy; a man of strength, and we have the adjective, strong; cases which distinctly exemplify our observation.

2. We come now to shew in what manner, and with what advantage, prepositions are employed to connect Substantives with Adjectives. The following

classes of adjectives will furnish sufficient illustration of this part of the subject: 1, Adjectives of place or position ; Adjectives of time or succession ; 3, Adjectives signifying profit or disprofit ; 4, Adjectives of plenty or want ; 5, Adjectives signifying an affection or state of the mind.

Adjectives of position, such as near, distant, high, low, have the ordinary power of adjectives, as marks upon marks ; and an additional power, which will best be explained by examples. When we say " a distant house," " a neighbouring town ;" the words " distant," and " neighbouring," are not only marks upon " house," and " town," but refer to something else : " a *distant* house," is a house distant from *something ;* " a *neighbouring* town," is a town neighbouring *something :* it may mean " a house distant from my house," " a town neighbouring my house :" in these cases, we should say that the adjective has both a notation, and a connotation. The adjective *distant*, for example, notes *house*, and connotes *my house ;* neighbouring, notes *town*, connotes *my house.* It is next, however, to be observed, that the connotation, in such cases, would be vague without a mark to determine it. The expression would be very imperfect, if, after the word high, we were merely to put the word " hill ;" and say, " the house is high the hill ;" or, " the house is distant the post-town." Prepositions supply this defect. We say, " the house is high *on* the hill ;" " the house is distant *from* the post-town." In the case of some adjectives, their juxta-position makes the reference sufficiently precise ; and in that case, the preposition may be dispensed with ; as, near the town, near the road,·&c.

It is observable, that the adjectives of position are not numerous. Some very general ones are used; and the sub-species are formed out of them by the aid of prepositions. Thus we have the word placed, which includes all positions; and this, joined with a substantive and a preposition, marks positions of all kinds: thus we can say, placed on the right hand, placed on the left hand, placed behind the house, placed before the house, placed above it, placed below it, placed in it, and so on.

It is not my intention to inquire into the precise meaning of each of the prepositions. It is sufficient to have given a sample of the inquiry, as in the case of the prepositions which connect substantives with substantives; and to have shewn the mode of their signification, as a kind of abstract terms, either active or passive.

The varieties of time or succession are not many, and the words to denote them, proportionally few. Previous, simultaneous, posterior, are the principal adjectives; and the terms to which these words of reference point, are marked by prepositions: thus we say, previous to, simultaneous to, and also with; " with," as we have seen, denoting junction, sameness of time.

Adjectives of profit or disprofit, need prepositions to mark their connexion with the things benefited or hurt; as, hurtful to the crop; good for the health. These adjectives afford a good example of the manner in which generical adjectives are divided into numerous sub-species, without the inconvenience of new names, by the aid of the prepositions: thus, hurtful, which notes all kinds of hurtfulness, is made to note

its various species, in the following manner : hurtful
to the health, hurtful to the eyes, hurtful to the
stomach, hurtful to the crops, hurtful to the reputa-
tion: all different species of hurtfulness, which might
be noted by adjectives severally appropriated to them.

There is nothing particular to be remarked of the
manner in which adjectives of plenty, or want, or
those signifying an affection of the mind, are connected with the objects they connote, by prepositions;
we shall, therefore, proceed to shew the manner in
which verbs are connected with substantives, by their
means.

3. All verbs are adjectives, either active or passive,
put into a particular form, for the sake of a particular
connotation. All actions, saving those which begin
and end in the actor, have a reference to a patient, or
something acted on; and the being acted on; the passion as it is called ; has a reference to the actor. Action, therefore, and passion, are relative terms, standing in the order of cause and effect; agent and patient,
are the names of the subjects of the action and the
passion, the cause and the effect.

Most actions are motions, or named by analogy to
motions. In applying terms denoting motion, there
is particular occasion for marking the two points of
termination ; the point at which it began, and the
point at which it ended. This is effected by the
name of the two places, and a preposition. The contrivance will be sufficiently illustrated by an obvious
example : " John travelled from London to Dover :"
" Travelled," the name of the motion ; London, the
point of commencement ; Dover, the point of termination: from, a word denoting commencement, connect-

ing London with travelled; to, a word signifying completion, connecting the word Dover, with the word travelled.

Some verbs, which imply motion, have their main, or only reference, to the point of its termination. Thus, he stopped at Dover : he struck him on the head : he stabbed him in the side. These prepositions, whatever their precise import, which we shall not now stop to inquire, mark, when thus applied to the name of the place at which the respective motions terminated, the connexion of the two names, that of the motion, and that of its point of termination.

With respect to motions, we have occasion to mark, not only the points of their commencement and termination, but also their direction. The direction of a motion, by which we mean the position of the moving body, at the several points of its course, can only be marked by a reference to other bodies, whose position is known. Thus, "He walked through the field." The direction of the walk, or the position of the walking man, at the several moments of it, is marked by a reference to the field whose position is known to me, and a word which means from side to side. The expression, "It flew in a straight line," is less full and particular in its marking, but clear and distinct, as far as it goes, by reference to a modification of position ; namely, a line, with which I am perfectly familiar.

In using verbs of action and passion, that is, words which mark a certain cluster of ideas, we have occasion to modify such clusters, by adding to, or taking from them, not only ideas of Position, as above, but various other ideas ; of which the idea of

the Cause, or End, of the action, the idea of the Instrument with which it was performed, and the idea
of the Manner of the performance, are among the
principal. "John worked;" to this, a mark of a
certain cluster of ideas, I want to make an addition,
that of the Cause or End of his working. That End
is, Bread. To mark this as the cause of his working,
it is not enough to set down the name bread ; I need
a mark to fix its connexion with the working, and the
kind of its connexion. I say, "John worked for
(cause) bread." "John was robbed for (cause of the
robbery) his money." The ideas of manner and
instrument are commonly annexed by one preposition; "John worked with (joining) diligence," the
manner; "John worked with a spade," the same idea,
as "John with (joined) a spade worked;" spade, the
instrument. "John worked by the job, worked by
the day;" manner: "John worked by machinery,"
the instrument. "He was killed with barbarity,
with a cudgel."

We say, done with hurry, or in a hurry, done in
haste. "In," which seems to mark a modification of
position, is here applied to that which does not admit
of position. Hurry and haste seem in such expressions to be personified ; to be things which surround
an action, and in the midst of which it is done.

We have compound names for many actions. Thus
we may say, "he hurt John," or "he did hurt to
John," "he gave a lecture to John," or, "he lectured
John." The reason why a preposition is required
before the patient, in the case of the compound name
of the action, and not of the single name, is, that the
word which stands with respect to the verb in the

immediate relation of the recipient or patient of the
action, is not the man, but the thing done.   Thus, in
the phrase, " he did hurt to John," it is not John
which is done, but hurt : in the phrase, " he gave a
lecture to John," it is not John who is given, but a
lecture.   There are here as it were, two patients,
lecture, the primary, John, the secondary ; juxta-
position marks the connexion of the primary ; but a
preposition is necessary, to mark that of the secondary.

The following phrases seem to admit of a similar
explanation.   " He reminded him of his promise ;"
" he accused him of perjury ;" " he deprived him of
his wife :" the secondary patients being " promise,"
" perjury," " wife."   He reminded him of his
promise (hav(ed) his promise) ; the promise being the
thing had or conceived in the reminding : accused him
of perjury ; perjury being the thing had in the accusation, the matter of the accusation : deprived him of his
wife ; his wife being the matter of the deprivation ;
the thing hav(ed) in it.[61]

---

[61] The ingenious speculations of Mr. Tooke did great
service to the cause of philology in England, by awakening
a very general interest in the subject.   But his knowledge of
the cognate languages was far too circumscribed to warrant
his sweeping inductions.   In his day, in fact, the accesses had
not yet been opened up to this new mine, nor the right veins
struck that have since yielded such rich results.   Accordingly nearly all Tooke's derivations are now discredited, and
among others his account of prepositions.   One or two English
prepositions, of comparatively recent formation, seem to be
formed from nouns ; as *among* Ang. Sax. *gemang* or *ongemang*,
gemang meaning " mixture ;" and *against*, Ang. Sax. *on-gegen*
in which *gegen*, from its use in cognate dialects, appears to be

a noun, though its primary meaning is not very clear. These however still involve a preposition which has to be accounted for. *Between,* again, is *by twain,* "near two;" and *except, save, during* were originally participles in the case absolute ; "except this" was originally "this excepted," Lat. hoc excepto. But the simple prepositions *in, of, by* belong to the radical elements of language, and are more independent of nouns and verbs than nouns and verbs are of them. Comparative philology, which did not exist in Tooke's days, has shewn, that, besides predicative roots, as they are called—that is syllables expressive of some action or property, such as "to go," "to eat," "to be bright," "to speak," &c., which form the bases of nouns, adjectives, and verbs—there was a class of roots denoting simply relations in space, that is, place or direction (here or this, there or that, up, down, away, &c.). It is easy to see how the audible marks of such notions, at first, doubtless, vague enough, would be rendered precise and intelligible by gesticulations ; or perhaps the gesticulations were the original signs, and the words mere involuntary exclamations accompanying them, and in time taking their place. These syllables have been called local, demonstrative, or pronominal roots, and play a most important part in language. They are joined to other roots to form derivatives of various kinds ; and it is of them that the inflexional endings of nouns and verbs are built up. Singly or in combination, they constitute the pronouns, personal as well as demonstrative. Abstract as are now the meanings of *I, he,* they were once patent to the senses ; *ma* was an emphatic "here," calling attention to the speaker ; *sa* or *ta,* "there, that," something different from both speaker and hearer. Most of the prepositions originated in roots of this class. The roots of some of them, at least, **are** identical with those of pronouns ; others express direction, and thus imply motion. Thus *up* means, "(motion) from below to above ;" in the root FR (as in *for, from*), which is represented in Sans. Gr. and Lat. by PR (pro), the ground idea is, motion or removal from the speaker, in the front direction. *Of* is the Gothic *af,* Old Ger. *aba* or *apa,* Sans. *apa,* Gr. ἀπὸ

Lat. *a* or *ab*. It is not easy to determine the precise physical relation primarily expressed by this particle ; probably "proceeding from," or "descending or depending from." If there is any connection between *of* and *have*, it is more likely that *have* is derived from *of* than the reverse. That not a few verbs have this kind of origin, is now recognised ; the English *utter* from *out* is a signal example.

The primary relations expressed by prepositions were always physical or sensible ; but the transition to the abstruse mental relations which they now serve to mark (cause instrumentality, superiority, &c.) is, as a rule, sufficiently obvious. For example, "issuing or proceeding from" passes insensibly into "being part of," "belonging to," "in the possession of."—*F.*

SECTION VIII.

CONJUNCTIONS.

The Conjunctions are distinguished from the Prepositions, by connecting Predications ; while the Prepositions connect only Words.

There are seeming exceptions, however, to this description, the nature of which ought to be understood. They are all of one kind ; they all belong to those cases of Predication, in which either the subject or the predicate consists of enumerated particulars ; and in which the Conjunction is employed to mark the enumeration. Thus we say, "Four, and four, and two, are ten." Here the *subject* of the predication consists of three enumerated particulars, and the conjunction seems to connect words, and not predications. In like manner, we say, " His bag was full of hares, and pheasants, and partridges." In this last case, the *predicate* is composed of enumerated particulars. In these instances, the words called conjunctions, appear to perform the business of prepositions, in joining *words :* and in fact, they may be supplied by prepositions. Thus, instead of " four, and four, and two, are ten," we may say " four, with four, with two, are ten :" and, in the same way, " His bag was full of hares, and pheasants, and partridges," may be put " full of hares, with pheasants, with partridges." And nothing can be more simple than such a variety in the use of such words.

With means *join; and* means *add.*[62]   These are words of the same kind, and the same import ; and nothing but use has appropriated the one to the joining of words rather than predications, the other to the joining of predications rather than words.

Our object, however, on the present occasion, is distinct, both from that of the grammarian, and that of the etymologist.   We have shewn, that a set of marks are exceedingly useful to connect single words, and by what contrivances this end is accomplished ; it remains for us to shew, what use there is of marks

---

[62] This is according to Tooke's etymology, who traces *and* to an Ang. Sax. verb *anan*, to add.   Unfortunately, Anglo-Saxon scholars deny that there is such a verb.   The nearest to it is *unnan*, which means, however, merely "to wish well to," "to favour."   No satisfactory account has been given of *and*, but the analogy of other conjunctions would connect it with a demonstrative root.   J. Grimm is inclined to consider it as a nasalised form of the Lat. *et ;* which in its turn may be an inversion of Greek τὲ, just as *ac* is of καὶ.

All conjunctions are essentially adverbs, and derive their connective power from their adverbial meaning.   This is well seen in *also,* the radical meaning of which is " all (quite) in that (the same) way."   Most of the adverbs used as conjunctions are obviously oblique cases of pronouns ; so, as, than, when, where, tum, ubi, quam, quum.   In Gothic, *jah*, (Old Ger. *ja*, Finnish *ja;* of the same origin as Eng. *yes*) takes the place of *and*, and means "in that or the same (manner)."   The Gr. καὶ and the Lat. que," and," are similarly oblique cases from the root *ka*, and equivalent to " in which or that (manner)."   The identity of manner or circumstance constitutes the mental bond.   It is easy to see how a preposition used adverbially and expressing proximity, distance, or other relative position, would connect predications or ideas ; *e.g.* " *After* he had rested a little, he began again."—*F.*

to connect Predications; and by what contrivances
that object is attained.

The occasions for the use of marks to connect Predications, seem to be of two kinds.

First, When two Predications are to be marked, as
following one another.

Secondly, When they are to be marked, as modified,
the one by the other.

1. Those of the first kind need but few words for
their explanation.

I may say, "Newton was a mathematician,"
"Locke was a metaphysician," "Milton was a poet."
So stated, these Predications do not mark any particular order in my thoughts. I desire, however, to
show, that the ideas thereby expressed, were *proximate*
parts of the train in my mind. The word *and*, which
means *add*, placed between every pair, affords the
requisite indication.

Like *and*, the conjunction *nor* marks predications in
sequence. It differs from *and* only in uniting *negative*
predications. "The act is not honourable, *nor* is the
man honest." In this case, it is obvious that *nor*,
whatever its origin, has the meaning of *and not*. The
predications then are two negative predications, the
sequence of which, is marked by the word *and*.

But, though it has been otherwise classed, and
called adversative, is of the same kind, and simply
marks the sequence. Thus we say, "Catiline was a
brave man, but Catiline was a wicked man." The
meaning of *but* is scarcely different from that of *and*,
addition being the fundamental idea signified by both
of them. The *opposition* between the two predications
is signified by the predications themselves, not by the

connective.[63]   In fact, the sense would not be changed, if we substituted *and* for *but*.   It is only because, in use, *but* has been commonly confined to the sequence of two *opposing* predications, that the word *but* is no sooner expressed, than an *opposing* predication is anticipated.   This is a simple case of association.

2. It is not necessary for us to do more than exemplify the principal cases in which one Predication is modified by another.

" The space is triangular, *if* it is bounded by three straight lines."

" The space is triangular, *because* it is bounded by three straight lines."

" The space is bounded by three straight lines,. *therefore* it is triangular."

In each of these three propositions, there are two predications ; the one of which is dependent on the other.   The dependence is that of necessary consequence.   The triangularity is the consequence of being bounded by three straight lines.

In order to have names for two Predications thus related, we may call the one the *conditioning*, the other the *conditioned*.   In the above instances, " The space is bounded by three straight lines," is the *conditioning*

---

[63] This is not strictly correct.   *But* is compounded of the two prepositions or local particles *by* and *out* (Ang. Sax. *bi utan*) ; and the force of it, in the example given in the text, may be thus paraphrased : " Catiline was a brave man ; *but* (*by*, near or beside that fact, put another fact, which is *out*, away, or different from it, namely) Catiline was a wicked man."   This is something more than a simple case of association ; the opposition is expressed as well as the addition.—*F*.

predication; "The space is triangular," is the *conditioned*.

There are two states of the conditioning predication; one, in which it is contingent; another, in which it is positive. Observe, now, the simple contrivance for marking the dependence of the *conditioned* upon the *conditioning* predication, in all the above cases.

In the first of the examples, "The space is triangular, *if* it is bounded by three straight lines," the *conditioning* predication is contingent. The word *if*, which is equivalent to *give*,[64] prefixed to the conditioning predication, marks it both as the conditioning predication, and as contingent.

In the second of the examples, "The space is triangular, because it is bounded by three straight lines," the *conditioning* predication is positive; the word *because* (having the meaning of, *cause be*, or *cause is*)[65] prefixed to it, marks it as at once the conditioning predication, and also positive. If *for* had been the

---

[64] That *if* has no connection with *give*, is manifest from the cognate forms; Goth. *jabai*, Frisic *jef*, Ang. Sax. *gif*, Old Ger. *ibu*, Lettish *ja*, all meaning primarily "in which or in that case, or supposition." "*Jabai*—from which the other Germanic forms are descended—appears to have originally been a dative or instrumental case of *ja*, analogous to *tubya* = Latin *tibi*: compare *ibi*, *ubi*, Gr. βίηφι, Slavonic *tebje* = tibi."—*Garnett.—F.*

[65] The syllable *be*, in "because," "before," &c., is the simple preposition *by*, Sans. *abhi*, Gr. επì, "near," "close to." *Therefore* is *for that;* in which *for* is a preposition, meaning primarily "position in front," and thence, by metaphor, the relation of motive or cause.—*F.*

mark instead of because, the artifice would have been still the same, as *for* has the meaning of *cause.*

In the third of the examples, " The space is bounded by three straight lines, *therefore* it is triangular ;" the order of the predications is inverted, the *conditioning* being put first. In this case, therefore, we need a mark to show that the last predication is conditioned, and conditioned by the preceding. This is done by prefixing to it the compound word, *therefore,* of which the first part *there* is equivalent to *that,* and *fore* or *for* means *cause.* The expression in its elementary form being, " The space is bounded by three straight lines ; for that, or cause that, the space is triangular."

In these cases we have examples of what are called, the Suppositive, the Causal, and the Illative conjunctions.

The following are examples of what are called the Disjunctive.

" The ship was well manned ; *else* it would have been lost."

" *Unless* the ship had been well manned, it would have been lost."

In these two examples, the conditioning predications are, " The ship was well manned ;" " The ship had been well manned :" the *conditioned* is, " it would have been lost," in both instances.

The dependence here, between the *conditioning* and *conditioned,* is that of physical consequence. The ship's not being lost, was the consequence of its being well manned. The contrivance for marking this dependence is akin to that which we have traced in the former instance.

In the first of the two examples, the *conditioning*

predication stands first. How do I mark that the next is *conditioned*, and conditioned as a physical consequent? I interpose the word *else*. This is part of an obsolete verb, signifying, *to dismiss, to turn out, to take away.*[66] And the sentence is thus resolved: "The ship was well manned," *take away that* (take away the cause, the effect is taken away also) "she would have been lost."

Other conjunctions of the disjunctive kind, as they are called, would here have answered the same purpose with *else*. "The ship was well manned, *otherwise*, she would have been lost." *Otherwise* here is precisely of the same import as *else*. "The ship was well manned;" that being dismissed, that being *other* than it was; "it would have been lost."

"The ship was well manned, *or* it would have been lost." *Or*, in German *oder*, is *other*. The resolution of this sentence, therefore, is the same as the former.

In the second of the two examples, "*Unless* the ship had been well manned, it would have been lost," the contrivance is the same, with a mere change of position. *Unless*, is a word of the same import, rather the same word, as *else*. *Unless* is PREFIXED to the *conditioning* predication, whereas *else* is SUFFIXED; and that is the difference.[67] The word *except*, which signifies *take*

---

[66] *Else* is the genitive of an obsolete adjective, in Gothic *alis*, corresponding to Lat. *alius;* and is analogous with Lat. *alias.—F.*

[67] *Unless* is simply *on less*, corresponding to Fr. *à moins*, and is equivalent to *if not.—F.*

away, may be substituted for *unless*. A peculiar application of *if* (*give*) may here also be exemplified. *If* with the negative, (*if not*,) has a similar signification with unless, except; " *If* the ship had not been well manned, &c."

Let us now pass to another case.

"*Although* the ship was well manned, it was lost." The two predications may change places, without change of meaning. " The ship was lost, *although* it was well manned."

What (as above) was to be marked by *else*, *unless*, *if not*, *except*, and so on, was the connexion between a cause and its usual effect; that is, the manning of a ship, and the safety of the ship. What is to be marked in this case is the want of connexion between a cause and its usual effect. It is done by similar means.

Although is part of an obsolete verb, *to allow*, *to grant*.[68] The two predications are: "The ship was well manned," "The ship was lost." I want to mark between my two predications not only a connexion, that of the antecedence and consequence of the predicated events, but the existence of a consequent differing from that by which the antecedent is usually followed. *Although*, prefixed to the predication of the antecedent event, gives notice of another predication, that of the consequent, and of a consequent differing from that by which the antecedent might have been

---

[68] *Although* is a compound pronominal adverb resembling Lat. *tamen*, and means "(the case being) quite thus (yet)."—*F*.

followed : *Grant* such an antecedent, such and not such was the consequent.

The same connection is marked by other conjunctions. "The ship was well manned, *nevertheless* it was lost." *Nevertheless,* means *not less for that.*[69] "*Notwithstanding* the ship was well manned, it was lost." *Notwithstanding,* is, *not being able to prevent, maugre, in spite of.* The resolution of the above sentences is obvious. "The ship was well manned, *yet* it was lost." *Yet* is the verb *get,* and has here the force of *although, grant.* "The ship was well manned, *yet* (or got, that being got, had, granted) it was lost."[70] "The ship was well manned, *still,* it was lost." *Still* is part of an obsolete verb, *to put, to fix, to establish.* "The ship was well manned, *still* (that put, that supposed) it was lost."[71]

A few more cases will exemplify all that is material in the marking power of the conjunctions.

"We study, *that,* we may be learned." The connexion here, again, is that of cause and effect. "We study :" "We may be learned," are the two predications, between which the connexion in question is to

---

[69] *Nevertheless* means literally, "not less by (or for) that." In this compound *the* is not the article, but an adverb, in Ang. Sax. *thy,* "by that much," and corresponds to Lat. *eo* in the expression *eo minus.—F.*

[70] *Yet* is of pronominal origin like Gr. ἔτι, Ger. *jetzt,* and has no connection with the verb *get.—F.*

[71] *Still* seems to be the adjective *still,* quiet, used adverbially, and having the force of "undisturbed, uninterrupted by that."—*F.*

be marked. The demonstrative pronoun performs the service. " We may be learned, *that* we study :" we study ; what ? to be learned.

" John is more learned than James is eloquent." The conjunction here is a relative term, and consists of the *two* words, *more than.* The two predications are, " John is learned," " James is eloquent." The connexion between them is, that they are the two parts of a comparison turning upon the point of greatness in degree. The two words *more than*, suffice to mark that connexion. *Than* is but a mode of spelling and pronouncing *that,* which use has appropriated to this particular case. " John is learned, more that (that being the more, the other of course is the less), James is eloquent."[72]

As, obsolete as a pronoun, only exists as a conjunction. It is a word of the same import with *that.* The following will suffice in exemplification of the marking property which it retains. " Virgil was *as* great a poet as Cicero an orator." The two predications are, " Virgil was a. great poet," " Cicero was a great orator." They also are connected as the two parts of a comparison, turning upon the point of equality in degree. *As,* or *that,* suffices to mark that connexion. " Virgil was a great poet," *that* (namely great) Cicero was an orator. We shall see afterwards, in the composition of RELATIVE TERMS, that every such term consists of two words, or the same word taken twice. The conjunction here is a relative term, and consists

---

[72] *Than* is only another form of *then,* and marks that the one comes after the other, and is therefore inferior.—*F*.

of two words, namely, *as*, or *that*, taken twice. " Virgil was a poet great, that that, an orator was Cicero ;" the first *that* marking *great as poet;* the second *that*, marking *great as orator*.[73]

---

[73] *As* is an oblique case of the demonstrative root *sa*, and is equivalent to " in this (degree) ;" and the nature of the connection is this : Virgil was a poet great in this degree ; Cicero was an orator great in this degree ; that is, the degree of greatness was the same in both.—*F*.

CHAPTER V.

CONSCIOUSNESS.

" It is not easy for the mind to put off those confused notions and prejudices it has imbibed from custom, inadvertency, and common conversation. It requires pains and assiduity to examine its ideas, till it resolves them into those clear and distinct simple ones out of which they are compounded; and to see which, amongst its simple ones, have or have not a necessary connexion and dependence one upon another. Till a man doth this in the primary and original notions of things, he builds upon floating and uncertain principles, and will often find himself at a loss."—*Locke, Hum. Und.* b. ii. c. 13. s. 28.

IT will now be instructive to retrace our steps, to look back upon the space we have passed, and contemplate the progress we have made toward our journey's end.

We have become acquainted with the elementary feelings of our nature ; *first,* those derived immediately from our bodies, whether by impressions made on the surface of them, or unseen causes operating on them within ; *secondly,* the feelings which, after the above mentioned feelings have ceased, are capable of existing as copies or representatives of them.

We have also observed the manner in which those *secondary* Feelings, to which we have given the name of IDEAS, flow, either into *groups,* or into *trains.* And we have explored the system of contrivances, to which mankind have had recourse, for MARKING those feelings, and the trains of them ; so as either to fix the knowledge of them for one's own use, or to make communication of them to others.

In what has been thus already presented, it will be seen that several expositions of considerable importance are included.

Sensations, and Ideas, are both feelings. When we have a sensation we feel, or have a feeling ; when we have an idea we feel, or have a feeling.

Having a SENSATION, and having a feeling, are not two things. The thing is one, the names only are two. I am pricked by a pin. The sensation is one ; but I may call it sensation, or a feeling, or a pain, as I please. Now, when, having the sensation, I say I feel the sensation, I only use a tautological expression : the sensation is not one thing, the feeling another ; the sensation is the feeling. When, instead of the word feeling, I use the word conscious, I do exactly the same thing, I merely use a tautological expression. To say I feel a sensation, is merely to say I feel a feeling ; which is an impropriety of speech. And to say I am conscious of a feeling, is merely to say that I feel it. To have a feeling is to be conscious ; and to be conscious is to have a feeling. To be conscious of the prick of the pin, is merely to have the sensation. And though I have these various modes of naming my sensation, by saying, I feel the prick of a pin, I feel the pain of a prick, I have the sensation of a prick, I have the feeling of a prick, I am conscious of the feeling ; the thing named in all these various ways is one and the same.

The same explanation will easily be seen to apply to IDEAS. Though, at present, I have not the sensation, called the prick of a pin, I have a distinct idea of it. The having an idea, and the not having it, are distinguished by the existence or non-existence of a certain feeling. To have an idea, and the feeling of that idea, are not two things ; they are one and the same thing. To feel an idea, and to be conscious of that feeling, are not two things ; the feeling and the consciousness are but two names for the same thing. In the very word feeling all that is implied in the word Consciousness is involved.

Those philosophers, therefore, who have spoken of Consciousness as a feeling, distinct from all other feelings, committed a mistake, and one, the evil consequences of which have been most important ; for, by combining a chimerical ingredient with the elements of thought, they involved their inquiries in confusion and mystery, from the very commencement.

It is easy to see what is the nature of the terms CONSCIOUS, and CONSCIOUSNESS, and what is the marking function which they are destined to perform. It was of great importance, for the purpose of naming, that we should not only have names to distinguish the different classes of our feelings, but also a name applicable equally to all those classes. This purpose is answered by the concrete term Conscious ; and the abstract of it, Consciousness. Thus, if we are in any way sentient ; that is, have any of the feelings whatsoever of a living creature ; the word Conscious is applicable to the feeler, and Consciousness to the feeling: that is to say, the words are GENERICAL *marks*, under which all the names of the subordinate classes of the feelings of a sentient creature are included. When I smell a rose, I am conscious ; when I have the idea of a fire, I am conscious ; when I remember, I am conscious ; when I reason, and when I believe, I am conscious ; but believing, and being conscious of belief, are not two things, they are the same thing ; though this same thing I can name, at one time without the aid of the generical mark, while at another time it suits me to employ the generical mark.[74] [75]

---

[74] The mistake of Reid in raising Consciousness to a separate faculty has been commented on by Brown, Hamilton, and others. It must be allowed that to feel and to be conscious are not two things but the same thing : that is to say, the use of the term consciousness, whether in common life or in philosophical discussion, does not point to knowing, and exclude feeling.

Consciousness is the widest word in our vocabulary. By common consent it embraces everything that "mind" embraces ; while one mode of extricating the great problem of Perception from self contradictions, makes it mean more than mind strictly means. We speak of the *object-consciousness* as our attitude in being cognisant of the extended universe; while our attitude under feeling, and thought, we call *subject-consciousness*, or mind.

The object-consciousness follows one set of laws, the laws of matter and space, as propounded in Mathematics, Natural Philosophy, and so on. The subject-consciousness follows a different set of laws, such as the laws of pleasure and pain, and the association of ideas, treated of in Psychology. We are conscious objectively, in counting the stars, we are conscious subjectively, in feeling oppressed by their number.

The subject-consciousness comprises all our feelings and thoughts ; it enters into volition ; and it makes a part of sensation, in which both attitudes are conjoined. This consciousness may be faint and limited, or it may be intense and variegated. We may be in a state of pleasure with little or nothing of thought accompanying; we are still properly said to be conscious or under consciousness. But we may add to the mere fact of pleasure, the *cognition of the state*, as a state of pleasure, and as a state belonging to us at the time. This is not the same thing as before : it is something new superposed upon the previous consciousness. When we take note of the fact that we are pleased, we proceed beyond the bare experience of the present pleasure, to an intellectual act of comparison, assimilation, or classification with past pleasures; we probably introduce the machinery of language to express ourselves as pleased; all this is so much *extra* consciousness. These knowing operations are not involved in mere feeling ; we may feel without them. Indeed, if the cognitive powers are brought into very active exercise upon our feelings, as in the self-dissection of the Psychologist, the feelings themselves are apt to subside.

It is thus correct to draw a line between feeling, and knowing that we feel; although there is great delicacy in the operation. It may be said, in one sense, that we cannot feel without knowing that we feel, but the assertion is verging on error ; for feeling may be accompanied with a minimum of cognitive energy, or as good as none at all; or it may be accompanied with an express application of our knowing powers, which is purely optional on our part, and even hostile to the full development of the feeling as feeling, as pleasure or pain.

Reid wanted a name to express the act of scrutinizing or examining the mind, and to correspond with such names as Perception, Observation, for the study of the extended or object universe. He used Consciousness for this purpose; a word that had been probably more applied to our cognitive energies than to our experience of mere feeling in its simplest manifestation. It is not often that "consciousness" is employed as the popular designation of states of feeling as such, states of marked enjoyment or suffering. On the other hand, the word is frequently made use of to designate the act of cognizing or thinking of our states of feeling; for which, however, self-consciousness is undoubtedly the more proper appellative.

Hamilton terms "consciousness" a "condition" of our feelings and mental operations; more correctly it is the operations themselves; the consciousness is not the condition of the feeling, but the feeling itself. More material is the opinion, held by Hamilton in common with most of the German philosophers, that the foundation of all consciousness is knowing; that we feel, only as we know that we feel. He says, "It is evident that every mental phenomenon is either an act of knowledge, or only possible through an act of knowledge: for *consciousness is a knowledge—a phenomenon of cognition.*" ("Metaphysics," Lect. xi.) Now although we may not be able to rebut this singular assertion by pointing to a state of feeling such as to entirely exclude knowledge, we may ask, do the two properties, said to be thus implicated, rise and fall in steady concomitance; the more the knowledge, the greater the feeling? The answer must be negative. A favourite doctrine of Hamilton, containing a certain amount of truth, affirms an inverse ratio between knowing and feeling; which it is difficult to reconcile with the present doctrine. A new distinction must be laid down between the kind of knowing that constitutes "feeling," and the kind of knowing that constitutes "knowing" in the strict sense of knowledge. We may concede to Hamilton that feeling must always be *within reach* of a cognitive exertion, but it cannot be conceded that an actual cognitive exertion is essential to the manifestation of the feeling. Such exertion unless kept within narrow limits of intensity cools down instead of promoting the emotional state.

The facts of the case appear to be best represented, by allowing the state of Feeling to stand on its own independent foundation as a mode of the subject-consciousness, or of mind. There may, and almost always does, go along with it a certain degree of cognitive effort. We can scarcely be under feeling, without performing some function of an intellectual kind; the divisions of the mental energies do not imply that they can exist in absolute separation. The act of discriminating the degree of feeling,—of pronouncing a pleasure to be greater than, or equal to, some other pleasure,—is properly an intellectual, or cognitive exercise; but this discrimination does not make the feeling. So a feeling cannot exist without impressing the memory in some degree, which is an intellectual function; one may truly affirm that we do not feel unless, immediately afterwards, we remember that we felt. It is an incident or concomitant of feeling to leave an impression behind, but this does not characterize or define the state of feeling. Being an accompaniment or concomitant of an emotional excitement, we may point to memory as a proof of its existence and a criterion of its degree, but we should confuse all the boundaries of mental phenomena, if we treated memory or retentiveness otherwise than as an intellectual property, a property whose sphere is intellect and not feeling.—*B*.

[75] Those psychologists who think that being conscious of a feeling is something different from merely having the feeling, generally give the name Consciousness to the mental act by which we refer the feeling to ourself; or, in other words, regard it in its relation to the series of many feelings, which constitutes our sentient life. Many philosophers have thought that this reference is necessarily involved in the fact of sensation: we cannot, they think, have a feeling, without having the knowledge awakened in us at the same moment, of a Self who feels it. But of this as a primordial fact of our nature, it is impossible to have direct evidence; and a supposition may be made which renders its truth at least questionable. Suppose a being, gifted with sensation but devoid of memory; whose sensations follow one after another, but leave no trace of their existence when they cease. Could this being have any knowledge or notion of a Self? Would he ever say to himself, *I* feel; this sensation is *mine* ? I think not. The notion of a Self is, I apprehend, a consequence of Memory. There is no meaning in the word Ego or I, unless the I of to-day is also the I of yesterday; a permanent element which abides through a succession of feelings, and connects the feeling of each moment with the remembrance of previous feelings. We have, no

doubt, a considerable difficulty in believing that a sentient being can exist without the consciousness of Itself. But this difficulty arises from the irresistible association which we, who possess Memory, form in our early infancy between every one of our feelings and our remembrance of the entire series of feelings of which it forms a part, and consequently between every one of our feelings and our Self. A slight correction, therefore, seems requisite to the doctrine of the author laid down in the present chapter. There is a mental process, over and above the mere having a feeling, to which the word Consciousness is sometimes, and it can hardly be said improperly, applied, viz. the reference of the feeling to our Self. But this process, though separable in thought from the actual feeling, and in all probability not accompanying it in the beginning, is, from a very early period of our existence, inseparably attendant on it, though, like many other mental processes, it often takes place too rapidly to be remembered at the next instant.

Other thinkers, or perhaps the same thinkers on other occasions, employ the word Consciousness as almost a synonyme of Attention. We all know that we have a power, partly voluntary, though often acting independently of our will, of *attending* (as it is called) to a particular sensation or thought. The essence of Attention is that the sensation or thought is, as it were, magnified, or strengthened : it becomes more intense as a whole, and at the same time more distinct and definite in its various parts, like a visible object when a stronger light is thrown upon it : while all other sensations or thoughts which do or which might present themselves at the same moment are blunted and dimmed, or altogether excluded. This heightening of the feeling we may call, if we please, heightening the consciousness of the feeling ; and it may be said that we are made more conscious of the feeling than we were before : but the expression is scarcely correct, for we are not more conscious of the feeling, but are conscious of more feeling.

In some cases we are even said to be, by an act of attention, made conscious of a feeling of which we should otherwise have been unconscious : and there is much difference of opinion as to what it is which really occurs in this case. The point has received some consideration in a former Note, but there may be advantage in again recalling it to remembrance. It frequently happens (examples of it are abundant in the Analysis) that certain of our sensations, or certain parts of the series of our thoughts, not being sufficiently pleasurable or painful to compel attention, and there being no motive for attending to them voluntarily, pass off without having been attended to ; and, not having received that artificial intensification, they are too slight and too fugitive to be remembered. We often have evidence that these sensations or ideas have been in the mind ; because, during their short passage, they have called up other ideas by association. A good example is the case of reading from a book, when we must have perceived and recognized the visible letters and syllables, yet we retain a remembrance only of the sense which they conveyed. In such cases many psychologists think that the impressions have passed through the mind without our being conscious of them. But to have feelings unconsciously, to have had them without being aware, is something like a contradiction. All we really know is that we do not remember having had them ; whence we reasonably conclude that if we had them, we did not attend to them ; and this inattention to our feelings is what seems to be here meant by being unconscious of them. Either we had the sensations or other feelings without attending to them, and therefore immediately forgot them, or we never, in reality, had them. This last has been the opinion of some of the profoundest psychologists. Even in cases in which it is certain that we once had these feelings, and had them with a lively consciousness (as of the letters and syllables when we were only learn ing to read) yet when through numberless repetitions the process has become so rapid that we no longer remember having those visual sensations, these philosophers think that they are elided,—that we cease to have them at all. The usual impressions are made on our organs by the written characters, and are transmitted to the brain, but these organic states, they think, pass away without having had time to excite the sensations corresponding to them, the chain of association being kept up by the organic states without need of the sensations. This was apparently the opinion of Hartley; and is distinctly that of Mr. Herbert Spencer. The conflicting suppositions are both consistent with the known facts of our mental nature. Which of them is the true, our present knowledge does not, I think, enable us to decide.

The author of the Analysis often insists on the important doctrine that we have many feelings, both of the physical and of the mental class, which, either because they are permanent and unchangeable, or for the contrary reason, that they are extremely fugitive and evanescent, and are at the same time uninteresting to us except for the mental processes they originate, we form the habit of not attending to; and this habit, after a time, grows into an incapacity; we become unable to attend to them, even if we wish. In such cases we are usually not aware that we have had the feelings; yet the author seems to be of opinion that we really have them. He says, for example, in the section on Muscular Sensations (ch. i. sect. vii.) " We know that the air is continually pressing upon our " bodies. But the sensation being continual, without any call " to attend to it, we lose from habit, the power of doing so. " The sensation is as if it did not exist." Is it not the most reasonable supposition that the sensation does not exist; that the necessary condition of sensation is change; that an unchanging sensation, instead of becoming latent, dwindles in intensity, until it dies away, and ceases to be a sensation? Mr. Bain expresses this mental law by saying, that a necessary condition of Consciousness is change; that we are conscious only of changes of state. I apprehend that change is necessary to consciousness of feeling, only because it is necessary to feeling: when there is no change, there is, not a permanent feeling of which we are unconscious, but no feeling at all.

In the concluding chapter of Mr. Bain's great work, there is an enumeration of the various senses in which the word Consciousness is used. He finds them no fewer than thirteen.—*Ed.*

CHAPTER VI.

CONCEPTION.

"The generalizations of language are already made for us, before we have ourselves begun to generalize; and our mind receives the abstract phrases without any definite analysis, almost as readily as it receives and adopts the simple names of persons and things. The separate co-existing phenomena, and the separate sequences of a long succession of words, which it has been found convenient to comprehend in a single word, are hence, from the constant use of that single word, regarded by the mind almost in the same manner, as if they were only one phenomenon, or one event."—*Inquiry into the Relation of Cause and Effect. By Thomas Brown, M.D.* Note M, p. 567.

THE philosophers, who erected CONSCIOUSNESS into what they called a Power of the mind, have bestowed the same rank upon CONCEPTION.

When we have a Sensation, we are not said, in the ordinary use of the word, to Conceive. If burned with the candle, I do not say, "I conceive the pain;" I do not say, if I smelt putrescence, that "I conceive the stench." It even seems to be not without a sort of impropriety, if the term is ever applied to mark a simple Idea. We should not, in ordinary language, say, "I conceive red," "I conceive green." We say, however, "I conceive a horse," "I conceive a tree," "I conceive a ship;" we say also, "I conceive an argument," " I conceive a plan." In these examples, which may be taken as a sufficient specimen of the manner in which the term Conception is used, we see that it is applied exclusively to cases of the secondary feelings ; to the Idea, not the Sensation ; and to the case of compound, not of single ideas. With this use, the etymology of the word very accurately corresponds: I conceive, that is, *I take together*, a horse ; that is, the several ideas, combined under the name horse, and constituting a compound idea. The term conception, we have seen, applies not only to those combinations of ideas, which we call the ideas of external objects, but to those combinations which the mind makes for its own purposes.

It thus appears, that the word CONCEPTION is a *generical* name, like CONSCIOUSNESS ; but less comprehensive. We call ourselves conscious, when we have any sensation, or any idea. We say that we conceive, only when we have some complex idea. It remains to be inquired, whether by saying we conceive, or have a conception, we mean any thing whatsoever beside having an idea.

If I say, I have the idea of a horse, I can explain distinctly what I mean. I have the ideas of the sensations of sight, of touch, of hearing, of smelling, with which the body and actions of a horse have impressed me ; these ideas, all combined, and so closely, that their existence appears simultaneous, and one. This is my IDEA of a horse. If I say, I have a CONCEPTION of a horse, and am asked to explain what I mean, I give the same account exactly, and I can give no other. My CONCEPTION of the horse, is merely my taking together, in one, the simple ideas of the sensations which constitute my knowledge of the horse ; and my IDEA of the horse is the same thing.

We may notice here, however, one of those curious illusions, which the intimate associations of ideas with words, so often, and sometimes so inconveniently, occasion. The term " I conceive," has the form of an active verb ; and with *the form of an active verb* THE IDEA OF ACTION is so frequently conjoined, that we are rarely able to separate them. By this means, the idea of activeness is often mixed up with other ideas, when it is wholly misplaced and illusive. I use the same form of expression when I say, I dream ; as when I say, I study, I argue, I imagine. In these cases the idea of what I call activity is properly included : in the expression I dream, it is not properly included ; though the active form of the verb so invariably calls up a certain idea of activity, and so strongly tends to mix it with the other ideas, that in using the term, " I dream," we seem to consider ourselves as, somehow, agents. Even in using the term, "I die," we cannot escape the illusion ; though the ideas are so highly incongruous. It would be obviously absurd to affirm that we are less active when we say we have an idea, than when we say we have a conception, yet there is constantly a feeling, when we use the phrase " I conceive," as if we were in some manner active ; and no such feeling, when we use the phrase " I have an idea." The terms, therefore, the concrete "conceive," and its abstract "conception," are somewhat inconvenient, and misguiding, as they infuse into the complex ideas to which they are applied, an ingredient which does not belong to them.

The relation which the words, CONSCIOUSNESS, and

CONCEPTION, bear to one another, is now, therefore, apparent. Consciousness is the more *generical* of the two names. Conception is the name of a class *included under* the name Consciousness. Consciousness applies to sensations, and to ideas, whether simple or complex ; to all the feelings, whatsoever they may be, of our sentient nature. Conception applies only to ideas ; and to ideas, only in a state of combination. It is a generical name including the several classes of complex ideas.[76]

---

[76] The doctrine of this chapter is as just as it is admirably stated. A conception is nothing whatever but a complex idea, and to conceive is to have a complex idea. But as there must always have been some cause why a second name is used when there is already a first, there is generally some difference in the occasions of their employment : and a recognition of this difference is necessary to the completeness of the exposition. It seems to me that conception and to conceive are phrases appropriated to the case in which the thing conceived is supposed to be something external to my own mind. I am not said to conceive my own thoughts ; unless it be in the case of an invention, or mental creation ; and even then, to conceive it, means to imagine it realized, so that it may be presented to myself or others as an external object. To conceive something is to understand what it is ; to adapt my complex idea to something presented to me objectively. I am asked to conceive an iceberg : it is not enough that I form to myself some complex idea ; it must be a complex idea which shall really resemble an iceberg, *i.e.*, what is called an iceberg by other people. My complex idea must be made up of the elements in my mind which correspond to the elements making up the idea of an iceberg in theirs.

This is connected with one of the most powerful and misleading of the illusions of general language. The purposes of general names would not be answered, unless the complex idea connected with a general name in one person's mind were composed of essentially the same elements as the idea connected with it in the mind of another.   There hence arises a natural illusion, making us feel as if, instead of ideas as numerous as minds, and merely resembling one another, there were one idea, independent of individual minds, and to which it is the business of each to learn to make his private idea correspond.   This is the Platonic doctrine of Ideas in all its purity : and as half the speculative world are Platonists without knowing it, hence it also is that in the writings of so many psychologists we read of *the* conception or *the* concept of so and so ; as if there was a concept of a thing or of a class of things, other than the ideas in individual minds—a concept belonging to everybody, the common inheritance of the human race, but independent of any of the particular minds which conceive it.   In reality, however, this common concept is but the sum of the elements which it is requisite for the purposes of discourse that people should agree with one another in including in the complex idea which they associate with a class name.   As we shall presently see, these are only a part, and often but a small part, of each person's complex idea, but they are the part which it is necessary should be the same in all.—*Ed.*

CHAPTER VII.

IMAGINATION.

THE IMAGINATION is another term, the explanation of which will be found to be included in the expositions which have previously been given.

The phenomena classed under this title are explained, by modern Philosophers, on the principles of Association. Their accounts of the mental process, to which the name Imagination is applied, include their explanation of the laws of Association, or the manner in which ideas succeed one another in a train, with little else, except remarks on the causes to which diversity in the several kinds of Imagination may be traced.

It is not to be overlooked that the term IMAGINATION is here used in the sense which is given to it by philosophers when they rank it as a particular power of the mind; for it is no doubt true, that it is often used, in vulgar speech, as synonymous with Conception, and with Supposition, and with Conjecture; as the verb, to imagine, is, with the verbs, to discover, to suppose, conjecture, believe, and perhaps others.

We have seen that Consciousness, and Conception, are names of feelings, *taken one by one :* Consciousness of *any* of our feelings so taken ; Conception of *a parti-cular class* of them, namely, complex ideas. IMAGINA-TION is not a name of any one idea. I am not said to imagine, unless I combine ideas successively in a less or greater number. An imagination, therefore, is the name of a *train*. I am said to have an imagi-nation when I have a train of ideas ; and when I am said to imagine, I have the same thing ; nor is there any train of ideas, to which the term imagination may not be applied.

In this comprehensive meaning of the word Imagi-nation, there is no man who has not Imagination, and no man who has it not in an equal degree with any other. Every man imagines, nay, is constantly, and unavoidably, imagining. He cannot help ima-gining. He can no more stop the current of his ideas, than he can stop the current of his blood.

In the phrase we have just employed, "there is no man who has not imagination," it is meant, that there is no man who now has not, who has not always had, and who will not always have a train of ideas. Imagination, therefore, is a word connoting *indefinite time ;* it is, to use the language of the Greek gramma-rians, aoristical. When it connotes, which by the strain of the passage it may be made to do, a *par-ticular time*, it marks a *particular train*. When it connotes *time indefinitely*, it marks *trains indefinitely*, any train at any time.

The having or doing a thing at any time, means the potentiality of having or doing it. Imagination, then, has two meanings. It means either some one train, or the potentiality of a train. These are two meanings which it is very necessary not to confound.

There is great diversity of trains. Not only has the same individual an endless variety of trains; but a different character belongs to the whole series of trains which pass through the minds of different individuals or classes of individuals. The different pursuits in which the several classes of men are engaged, render particular trains of ideas more common to them than other trains. One man is a merchant; and trains respecting the goods in which he deals, the markets in which he buys, and those in which he sells, are habitual in his mind. Another man is a lawyer, and ideas of clients, and fees, and judges, and witnesses, and legal instruments, and points of contestation, and the practice of his court, are habitually passing in his mind. Ideas of another kind occupy the mind of the physician; of another kind still, the mind of the warrior. The statesman is occupied with a train different from that of any of the classes that have been mentioned; and one statesman with a very different train from another, according as his mind is running upon expedients which may serve the purpose of the day, or arrangements which may secure the happiness of the population from generation to generation. A peculiar character belongs to the train which habitually occupies the mind of the mathematician. The mind of the metaphysician is also occupied by a train distinguished from that of other classes. And there is one man, yet to be mentioned, the poet, the peculiarity of whose trains has been a subject of particular observation. To such a degree, indeed, have the trains of the poet been singled out for distinction, that the word Imagination, in a more restricted sense, is appropriated to them. We do not

call the trains of the lawyer, or the trains of the merchant, imagination.   We do not speak of them as
imagining, when they are revolving, each, the ideas
which belong to his peculiar occupation ; it is only to
the poet, that the epithet of imagining is applied.
His trains, or trains analogous to his, are those which
receive the name of Imagination.

It is then a question, to which we should find an
answer, whether, in that by which the trains of the
poet differ from the trains of other men, there be any
thing which, being wholly absent from that by which
the trains of other classes are distinguished, lays a
foundation for this peculiarity of naming.

The trains of one class differ from those of another,
the trains of the merchant, for example, from those of
the lawyer, not in this, that the ideas follow one another by any other law, in the mind of the one, and
the mind of the other ; they follow by the same laws
exactly ; and are equally composed of ideas, mixed
indeed with sensations, in the minds of both.   The
difference consists in this, that the ideas which flow
in their minds, and compose their trains, are ideas of
different things. The ideas of the lawyer are ideas of
the legal provisions, forms, and distinctions, and of
the actions, bodily, and mental, about which he is con-
versant. The ideas of the merchant are equally ideas
of the objects and operations, about which he is concerned, and the ends toward which his actions are
directed ; but the objects and operations themselves,
are remarkably different. The trains of poets, also, do
not differ from the trains of other men, but perfectly
agree with them, in this, that they are composed of
ideas, and that those ideas succeed one another, accord-

ing to the same laws, in their, and in other minds. They are ideas, however, of very different things. The ideas of the poet are ideas of all that is most lovely and striking in the visible appearances of nature, and of all that is most interesting in the actions and affections of human beings. It thus, however, appears most manifestly, that the trains of poets differ from those of other men in no other way, than those of other men differ from one another ; that they differ from them by this only, that the ideas of which they are composed, are ideas of different things. There is also nothing surprising in this, that, being trains of pleasurable ideas, they should have attracted a peculiar degree of attention ; and in an early age, when poetry was the only literature, should have been thought worthy of a more particular naming, than the trains of any other class. These reasons seem to account for a sort of appropriation of the name Imagination, to the trains of the poet. An additional reason may be seen in another circumstance, which also affords an interesting illustration of a law of association already propounded ; namely, the obscuration of the antecedent part of a train, which leads to a subsequent, more interesting than itself. In the case of the lawyer, the train leads to a decision favourable to the side which he advocates. The train has nothing pleasurable in itself. The pleasure is all derived from the end. The same is the case with the merchant. His trains are directed to a particular end. And it is the end alone, which gives a value to the train. The end of the metaphysical, and the end of the mathematical inquirer, is the discovery of truth :

their trains are directed to that object ; and are, or
are not, a source of pleasure, as that end is or is not
attained. But the case is perfectly different with the
poet. His train is its own end. It is all delightful,
or the purpose is frustrate. From the established laws
of association, this consequence unavoidably followed ;
that, in the case of the trains of those other classes,
the interest of which was concentrated in the end,
attention was withdrawn from the train by being fixed
upon the end ; that in the case of the poet, on the
other hand, the train itself being the only object, and
that pleasurable, the attention was wholly fixed upon
the train ; that hence the train of the poet was provided with a name ; that in the cases of the trains of
other men, where the end only was interesting, it was
thought enough that the end itself should be named,
the train was neglected.

In conformity with this observation, we find, that
wherever there is a train which leads to nothing beyond itself, and has any pretension to the character
of pleasurable (the various kinds of reverie, for example), it is allowed the name of Imagination. Thus
we say that Rousseau indulged his imagination, when,
as he himself describes it, lying on his back, in his
boat, on the little lake of Bienne, he delivered himself
up for hours to trains, of which, he says, the pleasure
surpassed every other enjoyment.

Professor Dugald Stewart has given to the word
Imagination, a technical meaning ; without, as it appears to me, any corresponding advantage. He con-
fines it to the cases in which the mind forms new
combinations ; or, as he calls them, creations ; that is,

to cases in which the ideas which compose the train
do not come together in the same combinations in
which sensations had ever been received. But this is
no specific difference. This happens, in every train
of any considerable length, whether directed to any
end, or not so directed. It is implied in every wish
of the child to fly, or to jump over the house; in a
large proportion of all his playful expressions, as puss
in boots, a hog in armour, a monkey preaching, and
so on. It is manifested in perfection in every dream.
It is well known that, for the discovery of truths in
philosophy, there is a demand for new trains of
thought, multitudes of which pass in review before
the mind, are contemplated, and rejected, before the
happy combination is attained, in which the discovery
is involved. If imagination consists in bringing trains
before the mind involving a number of new combinations, imagination is probably more the occupation of
the philosopher than of the poet.

Mr. Stewart appears not to have understood the
real distinction between the use of the words Conception, and Imagination; that the one is the name of a
single idea, the other that of a train. He also involves, without seeming to be wholly aware of it, the
idea of a train destined to a particular end in the
meaning which he bestows on the word Imagination.
Imagination is with him, not the name of a train
having merely new combinations, but of a train having new combinations, and those destined to some
end. But this is not more the character of the trains
which belong to the painter and the poet, as his language appears to imply, than it is of the lawyer, or
the metaphysician; or, indeed, the professors of many

of the vulgar arts ; the tailor, for example, and the
mantua-maker.[77]

---

[77] The foregoing analysis of the Imagination brings to
view some of the important points of distinction between it
and the other faculties ; for example, the circumstance that the
trains and constructions of the Imagination are their own ends,
and not a means to farther ends, as in the constructions of
science and of the industrial arts. All creative originality is
not imagination ; the steam-engine was not a product of this
faculty.

The main features that distingnish the Imagination seem to
be these three :—

1. It is a faculty of the CONCRETE, like Perception and
Memory, and not of the Abstract, as the scientific faculties.
When we imagine a thing, we picture it to the mind, as far as
we are able, in its full concrete reality. Our imagination of a
scene in the tropics is of the character of an actual perception ;
it embraces, or should embrace, whatever would strike the view
of any one surveying the reality.

2. Imagination rises above Perception and Memory, in being
a CONSTRUCTIVE faculty. It alters, re-arranges, puts together
the materials of perception and memory to satisfy certain demands of the mind. In this respect, it is more than Conception, which as viewed by the author, is also a faculty of the
concrete, but introduces no novelty of combination. Conception may involve a great constructive effort, as when we try to
picture to ourselves a poet's creation by the help of his language ; nevertheless, the term imagination loses its charac
teristic force, and leaves an important meaning without a name,
if applied to this conceiving or realizing effort. The imaginative stretch belongs to the poet or artist ; the power of conceiving is what the reader of a poem brings into exercise.

3. Imagination is swayed by some PRESENT EMOTION. This
is another way of expressing the author's view that it is an end
in itself. If we were to use the general word "feeling,"
we should encounter the difficulty of separating imagination

from common industry, which is all intended to gain pleasures or ward off pains.

The brief designation "present emotion" approximates to, but does not fully bring out, the precise operation of the feelings in the constructions of Imagination. When, actuated by the love of the marvellous, any one invents a fabulous story, or highly exaggerates a real occurrence, the process is a typical instance of the imaginative workings.

The Fine Arts are the domain of Imagination ; the one goes far to specify the other. If the coincidence were exact, Imagination would be defined by a definition of the Æsthetic emotions. Now, although any original construction, selected and put together to gratify an Æsthetic emotion, is a work of Imagination, yet imagination is not exhausted by fine art. The picture that an angry man draws of his enemy would be called an effort of imagination, but not a work of fine art. All our emotions,—Wonder, Fear, Love, Anger, Vanity—determine the constructions of the intellect, when called into active exercise ; and for these constructions we have no other name but imagination, whether they may, or may not give pleasure as works of art.

Perhaps this exceptional region may be marked out by a statement of the perverting influence, or bias, of the feelings in matters of truth and falsehood, or in works of utility. When the true and the useful, instead of being determined by their own ends, or their proper criteria, are swayed by extraneous emotions—giving birth to mythical or fictitious creations—we have the corrupting substitution of Imagination for Reason in men's judgments and opinions.

Thus, Fear is a potent spur to Imagination ; its creations may not be æsthetically agreeable, and therefore may not come under the definition of Fine Art ; yet they are fairly to be described as perverting the judgment of true and false.—*B.*

CHAPTER VIII.

CLASSIFICATION.

" Dans l'ordre historique, la philosophie transcendante a de-
vancé la philosophie élémentaire. Il ne faut point s'en étonner ;
les grands problèmes de la métaphysique et de la morale se pré-
sentent à l'homme, dans l'enfance même de son intelligence, avec
une grandeur et une obscurité qui le séduisent et qui l'attirent.
L'homme, qui se sent fait pour connoître, court d'abord à la vérité
avec plus d'ardeur que de sagesse ; il cherche à deviner ce qu'il
ne peut comprendre, et se perd dans des conjectures absurdes
ou téméraires. Les théogonies et les cosmogonies sont antérieures
à la saine physique, et l'esprit humain a passé à travers toutes
les agitations et les délires de la métaphysique transcendante
avant d'arriver à la psychologie."—*Cousin, Frag. Philos.* p. 75.

THE process by which we connect what we call the
objects of our senses, and also our ideas, into certain
aggregates called classes, is of too much importance
not to have attracted the attention of those who have
engaged in the study of mind.   Yet it is doubtful,
whether metaphysicians have regarded CLASSIFICATION
as an original power of the mind, or have allowed that
what is included under that name might be resolved
into simpler elements. The term Abstraction, I think,
they have generally taken as the name of a distinct,
and original, power, not susceptible of further analysis.
But, in doing so, it seems (for the language of writers

is too loose on this subject, to allow us the use of more affirmative terms), they have restricted the name to the power of forming such ideas as are represented by the terms, hardness, softness, length, breadth, space, and so on. And this operation they rather consider as subservient to classification, than as that operation itself. The process, however, of grouping individuals into classes, has been regarded as sufficiently mysterious. The nature of it has been the object of deep curiosity; and the erroneous opinions which were entertained of it bewildered, for many ages, the most eminent philosophers; and enfeebled the human mind.

What (it was inquired) is that which is really done by the mind, when it forms individuals into classes; separates such and such things from others, and regards them, under a certain idea of unity, as something by themselves? Why is the segregation thought of? And for what end is it made? These questions all received answers; but it was many ages before they received an answer approaching the truth; and it is only necessary to read with care the writings of Plato and of Aristotle, and of all philosophers, with very few exceptions, from theirs to the present time, to see, that a misunderstanding of the nature of General Terms is that which chiefly perplexed them in their inquiries, and involved them in a confusion, which was inextricable, so long as those terms were unexplained.

The process in forming those classes was said to be this. The Mind leaves out of its view this, and that, and the other thing, in which individuals differ from one another; and retaining only those in which they all agree, it forms them into a class. But what is

this forming of a class ? What does it mean ? When
I form a material aggregate ; when ɪ collect a library ;
when I build a house ; when I even raise a heap of
stones ; I move the things, whatever they may be,
and place them, either regularly or irregularly, in a
mass together. But when I form a class, I perform
no operation of this sort. I touch not, nor do I in
any way whatsoever act upon the individuals which I
class. The proceeding is all mental. Forming a
class of individuals, is a mode of regarding them. But
what is meant by a mode of regarding things ? This
is mysterious ; and is as mysteriously explained, when
it is said to be the taking into view the particulars
in which individuals agree. For what is there, which
it is possible for the mind to take into view, in that
in which individuals agree ? Every colour is an individual colour, every size is an individual size, every
shape is an individual shape. But things have no
individual colour in common, no individual shape in
common, no individual size in common ; that is to
say, they have neither shape, colour, nor size in common. What, then, is it which they have in common,
which the mind can take into view ? Those who
affirmed that it was something, could by no means
tell. They substituted words for things ; using vague
and mystical phrases, which, when examined, meant
nothing. Plato called it ἰδέα, Aristotle, εἶδος, both,
words taken from the verb to see ; intimating, something as it were seen, or viewed, as we call it. At
bottom, Aristotle's εἶδος, is the same with Plato's ἰδέα,
though Aristotle makes a great affair of some very
trifling differences, which he creates and sets up between them. The Latins, translated both ἰδέα, and

εἶδος, by the same words, and were very much at a loss for one to answer the purpose ; they used *species*, derived in like manner from a verb to see, but which, having other meanings, was ill adapted for a scientific word ; they brought, therefore, another word in aid, *forma*, the same with ὅραμα, derived equally from a verb signifying to see, which suited the purpose just as imperfectly as *species ;* and as writers used both terms, according as the one or the other appeared best to correspond with their meaning, they thickened by this means the confusion.

After a time, unfortunately a long time, it began to be perceived, that what was thus represented as the object of the mind in the formation of classes, was chimerical and absurd ; when a set of inquirers appeared, who denied the existence of all such objects, affirmed that ideas were all individual, and that nothing was general but names. The question rose to the dignity of a controversy ; and to the hateful violence of a religious controversy. They who affirmed the existence of general ideas were called Realists, they who denied their existence Nominalists. There can be no doubt, that of the two the Nominalists approached, by far, the nearest to the truth ; and their speculations tended strongly to remove from mental science the confusion in which the total misapprehension of abstract terms had involved it. But the clergy brought religion into the quarrel, and as usual on the wrong side. Realism was preached as the doctrine which alone was consistent with orthodoxy ; the Nominalists were hunted down ; and persecution, well knowing her object, clung to the books as well as the men ; so that the books of the Nominalists, though the art of printing tended strongly to preserve them, were suppressed and destroyed, to such a degree, that it is now exceedingly difficult to collect them; and not easy to obtain copies even of the most remarkable.

The opinion, that the particulars in which the individuals of a class agree were distinct Objects of the Mind, soon made them distinct EXISTENCES; they were the Essence of things; the Eternal Exemplars, according to which individual things were made; they were called UNIVERSALS, and regarded as alone the Objects of the Intellect. They were invariable, always the same; individuals, not the objects of intellect but only the low objects of sense, were in perpetual flux, and never, for any considerable period, the same. Universals alone have Unity; they alone were the subject of science; Individuals were innumerable, every one different from another; and cognoscible only by the lower, the sensitive part of our nature.

Endless were the subtleties into which ingenious men were misled, in the contemplation of those Fictions; and wonderful were the attributes which they bestowed upon them. " It is, then, on these *permanent* Phantasms," says Mr. Harris, copying the ancient Philosophers, " that the human mind first works, and by an energy as spontaneous and familiar to its nature, as the seeing of colour is familiar to the eye, it discerns at once what in MANY IS ONE; what in things DISSIMILAR and DIFFERENT is SIMILAR and the SAME. By this it comes to behold a kind of *superior* Objects; a new Race of Perceptions, more comprehensive than those of sense; a Race of Perceptions, *each one of which, may be found entire and whole in the separate in-*

dividuals of an infinite and fleeting multitude, without departing from the unity and permanence of its own nature." Here we have something sufficiently mystical; a thing which is, at once, ONE, and MANY; which is ONE, it seems, by its very nature, and yet may exist, *entire and whole,* in the separate *individuals* of an infinite MULTITUDE. This is a *specimen* of their Doctrine; a specimen of what they call THE SUBLIME in Intellection.

But this is not all. For as, when we form a minor class, as *man,* there is a certain ONE, the object of intellect, complete in every individual; MANY, therefore, and at the same time, ONE; so when we form a larger class, *animal,* there is a certain ONE, the object of intellect, complete in every one of those individuals. And when we go still higher, as to the grand class, BODY, there is always a ONE, the object of intellect, complete in every one of those more numerous individuals. When we mount up to the very summit, and embrace all things in one class, BEING, there is in like manner a ONE, the object of intellect, complete in every individual that exists. This is the grand ONE; the ONE pre-eminently. This is *the* ONE; το ἕν; ONE-NESS; ONE in the abstract. This was a conception deemed truly SUBLIME. The loftiest epithets were bestowed upon τό ἕν, *the* ONE. It was DIVINE; it was more than that; for being not concrete, but abstract, it was DIVINITY. All things were contained in *the* ONE; and *the* ONE was in all things. *The* ONE was the source and principle of Being. It was immutable, eternal.

* Hermes, b. iii. ch. 4.

These ONES they also called by the names of *Internal Forms*, and *Intelligible Forms.* Thus Harris : " Let us suppose any man to look for the first time upon *some Work of Art;* as, for example, upon a Clock ; and, having sufficiently viewed it, at length to depart. Would he not retain, when absent, an Idea of what he had seen ? And what is it, *to retain such Idea ? It is to have* A FORM INTERNAL *correspondent to* THE EXTERNAL ; only with this difference, that the *Internal Form is devoid of the Matter; the External is united with it*, being seen in the metal, the wood, and the like. Now, if we suppose this Spectator to view *many such Machines,* and not simply to view, but to consider every part of them, so as to comprehend how those parts all operate to one End, he might be then said to possess a kind of INTELLIGIBLE FORM, by which he would not only understand and know the clocks, which he had seen *already,* but every Work, also, of like Sort, which he might see *hereafter.*"

We might here remark upon the mystical jargon, which is thus employed to obscure the simple fact, that after a man has seen an individual of a particular kind he has the idea of that individual ; and after he has seen various individuals of the same kind, he has ideas of the various individuals, and has them combined by association. But we must hear Mr. Harris a little further.

After telling us that there are two orders of these *immutable* INTELLIGIBLE FORMS ; *one* belonging to the Contemplator of objects, and subsequent to their existence ; *another* belonging to the Maker of them, being the archetype, according to which they were formed ; he thus proceeds : " The WHOLE VISIBLE

WORLD, exhibits nothing more than so many passing
pictures of these IMMUTABLE ARCHETYPES. Nay,
through these it attains even a Semblance of Immortality, and continues throughout ages to be SPECIFI-
CALLY ONE, amid those infinite particular changes,
that befall it every moment. May we be allowed
then to credit those speculative men, who tell us, *it is
in these permanent and comprehensive* FORMS *that the*
DEITY *views at once, without looking abroad, all possible
productions both present, past, and future; that this great
and stupendous view is but a view of himself, where all
things lie enveloped in their Principles and Exemplars,
as being essential to the fulness of this universal Intellection ?*"

I shall exhibit but one other specimen of the mode
of speculating about these imaginary Beings, from
another great master of the ancient philosophy, Cudworth. Both Aristotle and Plato, he says, "acknowledged two sorts of Entities, the one mutable, or subject
to flux and motion, such as are especially individual
corporeal things; the other immutable, that always
rest or stand still, which are the proper objects of
certain, constant, and immutable knowledge, that
therefore cannot be mere nothings, non-entities.

" Which latter kind of being, that is, the immutable essence, as a distinct thing from individual sensibles, Aristotle plainly asserts against Heraclitus, and
those other flowing philosophers in these words : ' We
would have these philosophers to know, that besides
sensible things that are always mutable, there is
another kind of being or entity of such things as are
neither subject to motion, corruption, nor generation.'
And elsewhere he tells us, that this immovable essence

is the object of theoretical knowledge, of the first philosophy, and of the pure mathematics.

" Now these immutable entities are the universal *rationes*, or intelligible natures and essences of all things, which some compare to unities, but Aristotle to numbers ; which formally considered, are indivisible : saith he, ' The essences of things are like to numbers ;' because if but the least thing be added to any number, or subtracted from it, the number is destroyed.

" And these are the objects of all certain knowledge. As for example, the objects of geometry are not any individual material triangles, squares, circles, pyramids, cubes, spheres, and the like; which because they are always mutable, nothing can be immutably affirmed of them ; but they are those indivisible and unchangeable *rationes* of a triangle, square, circle ; which are ever the same to all geometricians, in all ages and places, of which such immutable theorems as these are demonstrated, as that a triangle has necessarily three angles equal to two right angles.

" But if any one demand here, where this 'ἀκίνητος οὐσία, these immutable entities do exist ? I answer, first, that as they are considered formally, they do not properly exist in the individuals without us, as if they were from them imprinted upon the understanding, which some have taken to be Aristotle's opinion ; because no individual material thing is either universal or immutable. And if these things were only lodged in the individual sensibles, then they would be unavoidably obnoxious to the fluctuating waves of the same reciprocating Euripus, in which all individual material things are perpetually whirled. But because they perish not together with them, it is a certain argument that they exist independently upon them. Neither in the next place, do they exist somewhere else apart from the individual sensibles, and without the mind, which is that opinion that Aristotle justly condemns, but either unjustly or unskilfully attributes to Plato. For if the mind looked abroad for its objects wholly without itself, then all its knowledge would be nothing but sense and passion. For to know a thing is nothing else but to comprehend it by some inward ideas that are domestic to the mind, and actively exerted from it. Wherefore these intelligible ideas or essences of things, those forms by which we understand all things, exist no where but in the mind itself; for it was very well determined long ago by Socrates, in Plato's Parmenides, that these things are nothing but *noëmata* : 'these species or ideas are all of them nothing but *noëmata*, or notions that exist no where but in the soul itself.' Wherefore, to say that there are immutable natures and essences, and rationes of things, distinct from the individuals that exist without us, is all one as if one should say, that there is in the universe above the orb of matter and body, another superior orb of intellectual being, that comprehends its own immediate objects, that is, the immutable *rationes* and ideas of things within itself, by which it understands and knows all things without itself.

"And yet notwithstanding though these things exist only in the mind, they are not therefore mere figments of the understanding : for if the subjects of all scientifical theorems were nothing but figments, then all truth and knowledge that is built upon them would be a mere fictitious thing ; and if truth itself, and the intellectual nature be fictitious things, then what can be real or solid in the world ?　But it is evident, that though the mind thinks of these things at pleasure, yet they are not arbitrarily framed by the mind, but have certain, determinate, and immutable natures of their own, which are independent upon the mind, and which are not blown away into nothing at the pleasure of the same being that arbitrarily made them.

" But we all naturally conceive that those things have not only an eternal, but also a necessary existence, so that they could not ever but be, such and so many as they are, and can never possibly perish or cease to be, but are absolutely undestroyable.

" Which is a thing frequently acknowledged in the writings of both those famous philosophers, Plato and Aristotle.　The former of them calling those things, ' things that were never made, but always are,' and ' things that were never made, nor can be destroyed.' ' Things ingenerable and unperishable ;' *Quæ* Plato *negat gigni sed semper esse* (as Tully expresseth it) *et ratione et intelligentia contineri.*　And Philo the Platonical Jew, calls the τὰ Νοητὰ, which are the same things we speak of, ἀναγκαιόταται οὐσίαι, the most necessary essences, that is, such things as could not but be, and cannot possibly not be.　And Aristotle himself calls the *rationes* of things in his metaphysics, not only χωριστὰ and ἀκίνητα, things separate from matter and immutable, but also ἀΐδια, or eternal ; and in his ethics likewise, he calls geometrical truths ἀΐδια, eternal things, l. 3, c. 5 ; ' where he makes the geometrical truth concerning the incommensurability betwixt the

diameter and the side of a square, to be an eternal
thing.' Elsewhere he tells us, that 'Science, properly so called, is not of things corruptible and contingent,' but of things necessary, incorruptible and
eternal. Which immutable and eternal objects of
science, in the place before quoted, he described thus:
'Such a kind of entity of things has neither motion
nor generation, nor corruption,' that is, such things
as were never made, and can never be destroyed. To
which, he saith, the mind is necessarily determined.
For science or knowledge has nothing either of fiction
or of arbitrariness in it, but is 'the comprehension
of that which immutably is.'

"Moreover, these things have a constant being,
when our particular created minds do not actually
think of them, and therefore they are immutable in
another sense likewise, not only because they are
indivisibly the same when we think of them, but also
because they have a constant and never-failing entity;
and always are, whether our particular minds think
of them or not. For the intelligible natures and
essences of a triangle, square, circle, pyramid, cube,
sphere, &c., and all the necessary geometrical verities
belonging to these several figures, were not the creatures of Archimedes, Euclid, or Pythagoras, or any
other inventors of Geometry; nor did then first
begin to be; but all these *rationes* and verities had a
real and actual entity before, and would continue still,
though all the geometricians in the world were quite
extinct, and no man knew them or thought of them.
Nay, though all the material world were quite swept
away, and also all particular created minds annihilated together with it; yet there is no doubt but the

intelligible natures or essences of all geometrical
figures, and the necessary verities belonging to them,
would notwithstanding remain safe and sound. Wherefore these things had a being also before the material
world and all particular intellects were created. For
it is not at all conceivable, that ever there was a time
when there was no intelligible nature of a triangle,
nor any such thing cogitable at all, and when it was
not yet actually true that a triangle has three angles
equal to two right angles, but that these things were
afterward arbitrarily·made and brought into being out
of an antecedent nothing or non-entity; so that the
being of them bore some certain date, and had a
youngness in them, and so by the same reason might
wax old, and decay again; which notion he often
harps upon, when he speaks of the "Εἴδη, or forms of
things, as when he says, 'there is no generation of
the essence of a sphere,' that is, it is a thing that is
not made; but always is: and elsewhere he pronounces universally of the "Εἴδη, 'The forms of material things are without generation and corruption,'
and 'that none makes the form of any thing, for it is
never generated.' Divers have censured Aristotle in
some of such passages too much to confound physics
and metaphysics together; for indeed these things
are not true in a physical, but only in a metaphysical
sense. That is, the immediate objects of intellection
and science, are eternal, necessarily existent, and
incorruptible."*

Under the influence of such notions as these, men

---

* " A Treatise concerning Eternal and Immutable Morality.
By Ralph Cudworth, D.D."—pp. 241—250.

were led away from the real object of Classification ; which remained, till a late period in metaphysical inquiry, not at all understood. Yet the truth appears by no means difficult to find, if we only observe the steps, by which the mind acquires its knowledge, and the exigencies which give occasion to the contrivances to which it resorts.

Man first becomes acquainted with individuals. He first names individuals. But individuals are innumerable, and he cannot have innumerable names. He must make one name serve for many individuals. It is thus obvious, and certain, that men were led to class solely for the purpose of economizing in the use of names. Could the processes of naming and discourse have been as conveniently managed by a name for every individual, the names of classes, and the idea of classification, would never have existed. But as the limits of the human memory did not enable men to retain beyond a very limited number of names ; and even if it had, as it would have required a most inconvenient portion of time, to run over in discourse, as many names of individuals, and of individual qualities, as there is occasion to refer to in discourse, it was necessary to have contrivances of abridgment ; that is, to employ names which marked equally a number of individuals, with all their separate properties; and enabled us to speak of multitudes at once.[78]

---

[78] The doctrine that "men were led to class solely for the purpose of economizing in the use of names," is here reasserted in the most unqualified terms. The author plainly says that if our memory had been sufficiently vast to contain a name

It was impossible that this process should not be involved in obscurity, and liable to great misapprehen-

---

for every individual, the names of classes and the idea of classification would never have existed. Yet how (I am obliged to ask) could we have done without them? We could not have dispensed with names to mark the points in which different individuals resemble one another : and these are class-names. The fact that we require names for the purpose of making affirmations—of predicating qualities—is in some measure recognised by the author, when he says "it would have required a most inconvenient portion of time to run over in discourse as many names of individuals *and of individual qualities* as there is occasion to refer to in discourse." But what is meant by an individual quality? It is not *individual* qualities that we ever have occasion to predicate. It is true that the qualities of an object are only the various ways in which we or other minds are affected by it, and these affections are not the same in different objects, except in the sense in which the word same stands for exact similarity. But we never have occasion to predicate of an object the individual and instantaneous impressions which it produces in us. The only meaning of predicating a quality at all, is to affirm a resemblance. When we ascribe a quality to an object, we intend to assert that the object affects us in a manner similar to that in which we are affected by a known class of objects. A quality, indeed, in the custom of language, does not admit of individuality : it is supposed to be one thing common to many ; which, being explained, means that it is the name of a resemblance among our sensations, and not a name of the individual sensations which resemble. Qualities, therefore, cannot be predicated without general names ; nor, consequently, without classification. Wherever there is a general name there is a class : classification, and general names, are things exactly coextensive. It thus appears that, without classification, language would not fulfil its most important function. Had we no names but those of individuals, the

sion, so long as the manner, in which words become significant, was unexplained. After this knowledge was imparted, and pretty generally diffused, the value of it seemed for a long time to be little understood.

Words become significant purely by association. A word is pronounced in conjunction with an idea ; it is pronounced again and again ; and, by degrees, the idea and the word become so associated, that the one can never occur without the other. To take first the example of an individual object. The word, St. Paul's, has been so often named in conjunction with the idea of a particular building, that the word, St. Paul's, never occurs without calling up the idea of the building, nor the idea of the building without calling up the name, St. Paul's. The effect of association is similarly exemplified in connecting the visible mark with the audible. Children learn first to speak. They learn next to read. In learning to speak, they associate the audible mark with their sensations and ideas; the sound tree is associated with the sight of the tree, or the idea of the tree. In learning to read, a new association has to be formed. The *written word* is a *visible* sign of the *audible* sign. What reading accomplishes, by degrees, is, to associate the visible sign so closely with the audible, that at the same instant with the sight of the word the sound of it, and with the sound of it the sense, occurs.

After the explanations which have been already

names might serve as marks to bring those individuals to mind, but would not enable us to make a single assertion respecting them, except that one individual is not another. Not a particle of the knowledge we have of them could be expressed in words.—*Ed.*

given, no difficulty can remain about the manner in which names come to signify the *individuals* of which they are appointed to be the marks.

Let us now, proceeding to the simplest cases first, and by them expounding such as are more complicated, suppose that our name of one individual is applied to another individual. Let us suppose that the word, foot, has been first associated in the mind of the child with one foot only; it will in that case call up the idea of that one, and not of the other. Here is one name, and one thing named. Suppose next, that the same name, foot, begins to be applied to the child's other foot. The sound is now associated not constantly with one thing, but sometimes with one thing, and sometimes with another. The consequence is, that it calls up sometimes the one, and sometimes the other. Here two things, the two feet, are both of them associated with one thing, the name. The one thing, the name, has the power of calling up both, and in rapid succession. The word foot suggests the idea of one of the feet; this foot with its name, is a complex idea; and this complex idea suggests its like, the other foot with its name.

This is a peculiar and a highly important case of association; but not the less simple and indisputable. We have already sufficiently exemplified the two grand cases of the formation of complex ideas by association; —that in which the ideas of synchronous sensations are so concreted by constant conjunction as to appear, though numerous, only one; of which the ideas of sensible objects, a rose, a plough, a house, a ship, are examples;—and that in which the ideas of successive sensations are so concreted; of which, the idea of a tune in music, the idea of the revolution of a wheel, of a walk, a hunt, a horse-race, are instances.

It is easy to see wherein the present case agrees with, and wherein it differs from, those familiar cases. The word, man, we shall say, is first applied to an individual ; it is first associated with the idea of that individual, and acquires the power of calling up the idea of him ; it is next applied to another individual, and acquires the power of calling up the idea of him ; so of another, and another, till it has become associated with an indefinite number, and has acquired the power of calling up an indefinite number of those ideas indifferently. What happens ? It does call up an indefinite number of the ideas of individuals, as often as it occurs ; and calling them up in close connexion, it forms them into a species of complex idea.

There can be no difficulty in admitting that association does form the ideas of an indefinite number of individuals into one complex idea ; because it is an acknowledged fact. Have we not the idea of an army ? And is not that precisely the ideas of an indefinite number of men formed into one idea ? Have we not the idea of a wood, or a forest ; and is not that the idea of an indefinite number of trees formed into one idea ? These are instances of the concretion of synchronous ideas. Of the concretion of successive ideas indefinite in number, the idea of a concert is one instance, the idea of a discourse is another, the idea of the life of a man is another, the idea of a year, or of a century, is another, and so on. The idea, which is marked by the term " race of man," is complex in both ways, for it is not only the idea of the present generation, but of all successive generations.

It is also a fact, that when an idea becomes to a certain degree complex, from the multiplicity of the ideas it comprehends, it is of necessity indistinct. Thus the idea of a figure of one thousand sides is incurably indistinct ; the idea of an army is also indistinct ; the idea of a forest, or the idea of a mob. And one of the uses of language, is, to enable us, by distinct marks, to speak with distinctness of those combinations of ideas, which, in themselves, are too numerous for distinctness. Thus, by our marks of numbers, we can speak, with the most perfect precision, of a figure not only of a thousand, but of ten thousand sides, and deduce its peculiar properties ; though it is as impossible, by the idea, as by the sensations, to distinguish one of a thousand, from one of a thousand and one, sides.

Thus, when the word man calls up the ideas of an indefinite number of individuals, not only of all those to whom I have individually given the name, but of all those to whom I have in imagination given it or imagine it will ever be given, and forms all those ideas into one,—it is evidently a very complex idea, and, therefore, indistinct ; and this indistinctness has, doubtless, been the main cause of the mystery, which has appeared to belong to it. That this, however, is the process, is an inevitable result of the laws of association.

It thus appears, that the word, *man*, is not a word having a very simple idea, as was the opinion of the Realists ; nor a word having no idea at all, as was that of the Nominalists ; but a word calling up an indefinite number of ideas, by the irresistible laws of association, and forming them into one very complex, and indistinct, but not therefore unintelligible, idea.

It is thus to be seen, that appellatives, or general names, are significant, in two modes. We have frequently had occasion to recur to the mode in which the simple ideas of sensation are associated or concreted, so as to form what we call the complex ideas of objects. Thus, I have the complex ideas of this pen, this desk, this room, this man, this handwriting. The simple ideas, so concreted into a complex idea in the case of each individual, are one thing signified by each appellative ; and this complex idea of the individual, concreted with another, and another of the same kind, and so on without end, is the other of the things which are signified by it. Thus, the word rose, signifies, first of all, a certain odour, a certain colour, a certain shape, a certain consistence, so associated as to form one idea, that of the individual ; next, it signifies this individual associated with another, and another, and another, and so on ; in other words, it signifies the class.

The complexity of the idea, in the latter of the two cases, is distinguished by a peculiarity from that of the former. In applying the name to the odour, and colour, and so on, of the rose, concreted into one idea, the name is not the name of each of the sensations taken singly, only of all taken together. In applying the name to rose, and rose, and rose, without end, the name is at once a name of each of the individuals, and also the name of the complex association which is formed of them. This too, is itself a peculiar association. It is not the association of a name with a number of particulars clustered together as one ; but the association of a name with each of an indefinite number of particulars, and all those particulars associated back again with the name.

This peculiarity may require a little further explanation. It is well known, that between an idea, and the name which stands for it, there is a double association. The name calls up the idea in close association, and the idea calls up the name in equally close association ; and this they have a tendency to do in a series of repetitions ; the name bringing up the idea, the idea the name, and then the name the idea again, and so on, for any number of times. This is, in great part, the way in which language is learned, as we observe by the repetitions to which children are prone. And this, indeed, is what, in many cases, we • mean when we speak of dwelling upon an idea. It is a familiar observation, that no idea dwells in the mind, or can ; for it has innumerable associations, and whatever association occurs, of course, displaces that by which it is introduced. But if the idea which thus displaces it, again calls it up, and these two go on calling up one another, that which is the more interesting of the two appears to be that which alone is occupying the attention. This alternation is frequent between the name and the idea.

Now, then, let the word, man, be supposed, first of all, the name of an individual ; it becomes associated with the idea of the individual, and acquires the power of calling up that idea. Let us next suppose it applied to one other individual, and no more : it becomes associated with this other idea ; and it now has the power of calling up either. The following is, then, a very natural train :—1, The name occurs ; 2, the name suggests the idea of one of the individuals; 3, that idea suggests the name back again ; 4, the name suggests the idea of the second individual. All this may pass, and, after sufficient repetition, does pass, with the rapidity of lightning. Suppose, now, that the name is associated, with the ideas not of two individuals, but of many; the same train may go on; the name exciting the idea of one individual, that idea the name, the name another individual, and so on, to an indefinite extent; all in that small portion of time of which the mind takes no account. The combination thus formed stands in need of a name. And the name, man, while it is the name of every individual included in the process, is also the name of the whole combination; that is, of a very complex idea.

One other question, respecting classification, may still seem to require solution; namely, what it is by which we are determined in placing such and such things together in a class in preference to others; what, in other words, is the principle of Classification ? I answer, that, as it is for the purpose of naming, of naming with greater facility, that we form classes at all; so it is in furtherance of that same facility that such and such things only are included in one class, such and such in another. Experience teaches what sort of grouping answers the purposes of naming best; under the suggestions of that experience, the application of a general word is tacitly and without much of reflection regulated; and by this process, and no other, it is, that Classification is performed. It is the aggregation of an indefinite number of individuals, by their association with a particular name.

It may seem that this answer is still very general,

and that to make the explanation sufficient, the suggestions by which experience recommends this or that classification should be particularized. For the purpose of the present chapter, however, namely, to shew that the business of Classification is merely a process of naming, and is all resolvable into association, the observation, though general, is full and satisfactory. The detail of the purposes to be answered by general terms belongs more properly to the next head of Discourse, and as far as the development of the mental phenomena seems to require it, will there be presented.

It may still be useful to advert to the three principal cases into which Classification may be resolved ; 1, that of objects considered as synchronical ; 2, that of objects considered as successive ; 3, that of feelings. The first is exemplified in the common classes of sensible objects, as men, horses, trees, and so on ; and requires no further explanation. The second is exemplified in the classes of events, denoted by such words, as Birth, Death, Snowing, Thundering, Freezing, Flying, Creeping. By these words there is always denoted one antecedent and one consequent, generally more, sometimes a long train of them. And it is obvious that each of them is, at once, the name of each instance individually, and of all taken generally together. Thus, Freezing, is not the name of an individual instance of freezing only, but of that and of all other instances of Freezing. The same is the case with other words of a still more general, and thence more obscure signification, as Gravitation, Attraction, Motion, Force, &c. ; which words have this additional source of confusion, that they are ambiguous, being both abstract and concrete. When we say that there is a third case of classification, relating to Feelings, it does not mean that the two former do not relate to feelings : for when we say, that we classify objects, as men, horses, &c. ;—or events, as the sequences named births, deaths, and so on ;—it is obvious that our operation is about our own feelings, and nothing else ; as the objects, and their successions, are, to us, the feelings merely which we thus designate. But as there are feelings which we do thus designate ; and feelings which we do not ; it is convenient, for the purpose of teaching, to treat of them apart. The Feelings, of this latter kind, which we classify, are either single feelings, or trains. Thus, Pain is the name of a single feeling, and the name both of an individual instance, and of indefinite instances, forming a most extensive class. Memory is the name not of a single feeling or idea, but of a train ; and it is the name not only of a single instance, but of all instances of such a train, that is, of a class. The same is the case with Belief. It is the name of a train consisting of a certain number of links ; and it is the name not only of an individual instance of such trains, but of all instances, forming an extensive class. Imagination is another instance of the same sort of classification. So also is Judgment, and Reasoning, and Doubting, and we might name many more.

It is easy to see, among the principles of Association, what particular principle it is, which is mainly concerned in Classification, and by which we are rendered capable of that mighty operation ; on which, as its basis, the whole of our intellectual structure is reared. That principle is Resemblance. It seems to be similarity or resemblance which, when we have applied a name to one individual, leads us to apply it to another, and another, till the whole forms an aggregate, connected together by the common relation of every part of the aggregate to one and the same name. Similarity, or Resemblance, we must regard as an Idea familiar and sufficiently understood for the illustration at present required. It will itself be strictly analysed, at a subsequent part of this Inquiry.

So deeply was the sagacious mind of Plato, far more philosophical than that of any who succeeded him, during many ages, struck with the importance of Classification, that he seems to have regarded it as the sum of all philosophy ; which he described, as being the faculty of seeing " the ONE in the MANY, and the MANY in the ONE ;" a phrase which, when stripped from the subtleties of the sophists whom he exposed, and from the mystical visions of his successors, of which he never dreamed, is really a striking expression of what in classification is the matter of fact. His error lay, in misconceiving the ONE ; which he took, not for the aggregate, but something pervading the aggregate.[79] [80]

---

[79] The two chapters (VII. and VIII.) of Mr. James Mill's Analysis are highly instructive, and exhibit all his customary force and perspicuity. But in respect to Classification and Abstraction, I think that the ancient philosophers of the Sokratic school generally, are entitled to more credit than he allows them ; and moreover that in respect to the difference of opinion between Plato and Aristotle, he has assigned an undue superiority to the former at the expense of the latter.

The reader would take very inadequate measure of these

ancient philosophers, if he judged them from the two citations
out of Harris and Cudworth, produced by Mr. James Mill as
setting forth the most successful speculations of the ancient
world.   Both these passages are brought to illustrate " the
mystical jargon" (p. 253) with which the ancients are said to
have obscured a clear and simple subject.   The mysticism in
both citations is to a certain extent real; but it depends also
in part on the use of a terminology now obsolete, rather than
on confusion of ideas.   In regard to the citation from Harris,
it is a passage in which that author passes into theology, and
includes God and Immortality : topics upon which mystical
language can seldom be avoided : moreover, if we compare the
remarks on Harris (p. 251) with p. 271, we shall find Mr. James
Mill ridiculing as mystical, when used by Harris, the same
language (about "the One in the Many") which, when employed
by Plato, he eulogises as follows—" a phrase which, when
" stripped from the subtleties of the sophists whom he (Plato)
" exposed, and from the mystical visions of his successors, of
" which he never dreamed, is really a striking expression of
" what in classification is the matter of fact."

I wish I could concur with Mr. James Mill in exonerating
Plato from these mystical visions, and imputing them exclusively to his successors.   But I find them too manifestly proclaimed in the Timæus, Phædon, Phædrus, Symposion,
Republic, and other dialogues, to admit of such an acquittal :
I also find subtleties quite as perplexing as those of any sophist
whom he exposed.   Along with these elements, the dialogues
undoubtedly present others entirely disparate, much sounder
and nobler.   I have in another work endeavoured to render a
faithful account of the multifarious Platonic aggregate, stamped
in all its parts,—whether of negative dialectic, poetical fancy,
or ethical dogmatism,—with the unrivalled genius of expression belonging to the author.   The misfortune is that his Neo-
Platonic successors selected by preference his dreams and
visions for their amplifying comment and eulogy, leaving
comparatively unnoticed the instructive lessons of philosophy

accompanying them. To this extent the Neo-Platonists fully deserve the criticism here bestowed on them.

The long passage, extracted in the Analysis from Cudworth, contains two grave mis-statements, respecting both Plato and Aristotle ; which deserve the more attention because they seem to have misled Mr. James Mill himself. Respecting Universals, Cudworth, after saying that they do not exist in the individual sensibles, proceeds as follows (p. 255-256)—

1. "Neither, in the next place, do they exist somewhere "else apart from the individual sensibles, and without the "mind : which is that opinion that Aristotle justly condemns, "but either unjustly or unskilfully attributes to Plato.

2. "Wherefore these intelligible ideas or essences of things, "those forms by which we understand all things, exist no- "where but in the mind itself: for it was very well determined "long ago by Socrates, in Plato's Parmenides, that these "things are nothing but *noëmata :* these species or ideas are "all of them nothing but *noëmata,* or notions that exist no- "where but in the soul itself."

Now, neither of these assertions of Cudworth will be found accurate : neither the "determination" which he ascribes to the Platonic Sokrates—nor the censure of "unjust or unskilful" which he attaches to Aristotle. It is indeed true that the opinion here mentioned is enunciated by Sokrates in Plato's Parmenides. But far from being given as a "determination," it is enunciated only to be refuted and dropt.[a] In that dialogue, Sokrates is introduced as a youthful and ardent aspirant in philosophy, maintaining the genuine Platonic theory of self-existent and separate Ideas. He finds himself unable to repel several acute objections tendered against the theory by the veteran Parmenides: he is driven from position to position : and one among them, not more tenable than the rest, is the suggestion cited by Cudworth. Yet Parmenides, though his objections remain unanswered and though he alludes to others

---

[a] Plato Parmenid. p. 132, C, D.

not specified,—concludes by declaring[a] that nevertheless the Platonic theory of Ideas cannot be abandoned : it must be upheld as a postulate essential to the possibility of general reasoning and philosophy.

Even in the Parmenides itself, therefore, where Plato accumulates objections against the theory of separate and self-existent Ideas, we still find him reiterating his adherence to it. And when we turn to his other dialogues, Phædrus, Phædon, Symposion, Republic, Kratylus, &c., we see that theory so emphatically proclaimed and so largely illustrated, that I wonder how Cudworth can blame Aristotle for imputing it to him.

It is by Cudworth, probably, that Mr. James Mill has been misled, when he says—p. 249—"At bottom, Aristotle's εἶδος "is the same as with Plato's ἰδέα, though Aristotle makes a "great affair of some very trifling differences, which he creates "and sets up between them."—I have pointed out Cudworth's mistake, and I maintain that the difference between Plato and Aristotle on this subject was grave and material. The latter denied, what the former affirmed, self-existence and substantiality of the Universal Ideas, apart from and independent of particulars.

Having cited with some comments the extracts from Cudworth and Harris, Mr. James Mill observes, " Under the "influence of such notions as these, men were led away from "the real object of Classification, which remained, till a late "period of metaphysical enquiry, not at all understood. Yet "the truth appears by no means difficult to find, if we only "observe the steps by which the mind acquires its knowledge, "and the exigencies which give occasion to the contrivances "to which it resorts" (p. 259).—He then proceeds, clearly and forcibly, to announce his own theory of classification, intended to dispel the mystery with which others have surrounded

---

[a] Plato Parmenid. p. 135, B, C.

I have given an account of this acute but perplexing dialogue, in the twenty-fifth chapter of my work on Plato and the other Companions of Sokrates.

it (p. 264). "The word *man* is first applied to an indi-
" vidual : it is first associated with the idea of that individual,
" and acquires the power of calling up the idea of him : it is
" next applied to another individual, and acquires the power
" of calling up the idea of him : so of another and another,
" till it has acquired the power of calling up an indefinite
" number of those ideas indifferently. What happens ? It
" does call up an indefinite number of the ideas of individuals,
" as often as it occurs : and calling them up in close combi-
" nation, it forms them into a species of complex idea."
" It thus appears that the word *man* is not a word having
" a very simple idea, as was the opinion of the Realists :
" nor a word having no idea at all, as was that of the Nomi-
" nalists : but a word calling up an indefinite number of ideas,
" by the irresistible laws of association, and forming them into
" one very complex and indistinct, but not therefore unintelli-
" gible, idea" (p. 265).—" As it is for the purpose of naming,
" and of naming with greater facility, that we form classes at
" all ; so it is in furtherance of that same facility that such
" and such things only are included in one class, such and
" such things in another. Experience teaches us what sort of
" grouping answers this purpose best : under the suggestions
" of that experience, the application of a general word is
" tacitly and without much of reflection regulated : and by
" this process and no other, it is, that Classification is per-
" formed. It is the aggregation of an indefinite number of
" individuals, by their association with a particular name"
(p. 268).—" It is Similarity or Resemblance, which, when we
" have applied a name to one individual, leads us to apply it
" to another and another—till the whole forms an aggregate,
" connected together by the common relation of the aggregate
" to one and the same name" (p. 271).

Such is the theory of Mr. James Mill. Its great peculiarity
is that it neither includes nor alludes to Abstraction. It
admits in Classification nothing more than the one common
name associated with an aggregate indefinite and indistinct, of
similar concrete individuals. I shall now consider the manner

in which the Greek philosophers of the fourth century B.C. dealt with the same subject, and how far they merit the censure of having imported unnecessary mystery into it.

It is impossible to understand Plato unless we take our departure from his master Sokrates. Now it is precisely in regard to Classification, and the meaning and comprehension of general terms, that the originality and dialectical acuteness of Sokrates were most conspicuously manifested. He was the first philosopher (as Aristotle[a] tells us) who set before himself the Universal as an express object of investigation,— and who applied himself to find out and test the definition of universal terms. He wrote nothing; but he passed most part of his long life in public, and in talking indiscriminately with every one. Oral colloquy, and cross-examining interrogation, were carried by him to a pitch of excellence never equalled. Not only did he disclaim all power of teaching, but he explicitly avowed his own ignorance; professing to be a mere seeker of truth from others who knew better, and to be anxious only for answers such as would stand an accurate scrutiny. To this peculiar scheme the topics on which he talked were adapted: for he avoided all recondite themes, and discussed only matters relating to man and society: such as What is the Holy? What is the Unholy? What are the Beautiful and the Mean—the Just and Unjust? Temperance? Madness? Courage? Cowardice? A City? A man fit for citizenship? Command of Men? A man fit for commanding men? Such is the specimen-list given by Xenophon[b] of the themes chosen by Sokrates. We see that they are all general, and embodied in universal terms. But the terms as well as the themes were familiar to all: every man believed himself thoroughly to understand the meaning of the former—every one had convictions ready-made and decided on the latter. When Sokrates first opened the colloquy, respondents were surprised to be questioned about such subjects, upon which they presumed

---

[a] Aristot. Metaphys. A. p. 987, b. 1, M. p. 1078, b. 30,
[b] Xenophon, Memorab. I., 1—16.

that every one must know as well as themselves. But this confidence speedily vanished when they came to be tested by inductive[a] interrogatories : citation of appropriate particulars, included or not included in the generalities which they laid down. The result proved that they could not answer the questions without speedily contradicting themselves : that they did not understand the comprehension of their own universal terms : and that upon all these matters, on which they talked so confidently, they had never applied themselves deliberately to learn, nor could they say how their judgments had been acquired or certified.[b]

The conviction formed in the mind of Sokrates, after long persistence in such colloquial cross-examination, is consigned in his defence before the Athenian judicature, pronounced a month before his death. He declared that what he found every where was real ignorance, combined with false persuasion of knowledge : that this was the chronic malady of the human mind, which it had been his mission to expose : that no man was willing to learn, because no man believed that he stood in need of learning : that, accordingly, the first step indispensable to all effective teaching, was to make the pupil a willing learner, by disabusing his mind of the false persuasion of knowledge, and by imparting to him the stimulus arising from a painful consciousness of ignorance.

Such was the remarkable psychological scrutiny instituted by Sokrates on his countrymen, and the verdict which it suggested to him. I have already observed that his great intellectual bent was to ascertain the definition of general terms, and to follow these out to a comprehensive and consistent classification.[c] It must be added that no man was ever less inclined to mysticism than Sokrates : and that he was thus

---

[a] So Aristotle calls them—λόγους ἐπακτικούς.—Metaph. M. p. 1078, b. 28.

[b] Xenophon, Memorab. IV. 2—13—30—36.

[c] Xenophon, Memor. IV. 5, 12; IV. b. 1—7—10—15. ὧν ἕνεκα σκοπῶν σὺν τοῖς συνοῦσιν, τί ἕκαςον εἴη τῶν ὄντων, οὐδέποτε ἔληγε.

exempt from those misleading influences which (according to
Mr. James Mill, p. 260) "have led men away from the real
"object of Classification, and prevented them from understand-
"ing it till a late period in metaphysical enquiry." Sokrates
did not come before his countrymen with classifications of his
own, originated or improved—nor did he teach them how the
process ought to be conducted. His purpose was, to test and
appreciate that Classification which he found ready-made and
current among them. He pronounced it to be worthless and
illusory.

Now I wish to point out that what Sokrates thus depreciated,
is exactly that which this Chapter of the Analysis lays before
us as Classification generally. I agree with the Analysis that
Classification, up to a certain point, grows out of the principle
of Association and the exigencies of the human mind, by steps
instructively set forth in that work. But such natural growth
reaches no higher standard than that which Sokrates tested and
found so lamentably deficient, even among a public of unusual
intelligence. It does not deserve the name of a "mighty
operation" (bestowed upon it by Mr. James Mill, p. 270). It
is a rudimentary procedure, indispensable as a basis on which
to build, and sufficing in the main for social communication,
when no science or reasoned truth is required : but failing
altogether to realise what has been understood by philosophers,
from Sokrates downward, as the true and full purpose of Classification. So long as the Class is conceived to be only what the
Analysis describes, an indistinct aggregate of resembling individuals denoted by the same name, without clearly understanding wherein the resemblance consists, or what facts and
attributes are *connoted* by the name[a]—(I use the word *connote*,

---

[a] The necessity of determining the *connotation* of the Class-
term is distinctly put forward by Sokrates—Xenophon, Memorab.
III. 14, 2. λόγῳ ὄντος περὶ ὀνομάτων, ἐφ' οἵῳ ἔργῳ ἕκαςον
εἴη—Ἔχοιμεν ἂν (ἔφη) εἰπεῖν, ἐπὶ ποίῳ ποτὲ ἔργῳ ἄνθρωπος
ὀψόφαγος καλεῖται; &c., also the remarkable passage IV.,
6. 13—15, Plato, Sophistes, p. 218 B. τοὔνομα μόνον ἔχομεν
κοινῇ· τὸ δὲ ἔργον, ἐφ' ᾧ καλοῦμεν, &c.

not in the sense of the Analysis, but in the sense of Mr. John
Stuart Mill)—so long will Classification continue to be, as
Sokrates entitled it, a large persuasion of knowledge with little
reality to sustain it.

I pass now from Sokrates to Plato. It is true, as we read
in the Analysis, (p. 271) that Plato "was so deeply struck
"with the importance of Classification, that he seems to have
"regarded it as the sum of all philosophy." But what Plato
thus admired was not the Classification that he found prevalent around him, such as this chapter of the Analysis depicts.
Here Plato perfectly agreed with Sokrates. Among his im-
mortal dialogues, several of the very best are devoted to the
illustration of the Sokratic point of view : to the cross-examination and exposure of the minds around him, instructed as
well as vulgar, in respect to the general terms familiarly used
in speech. The Platonic questions and answers are framed
to shew how little the respondents understand beneath those
current generalities on which every one talks with confidence
and fluency—and how little they can avoid contradiction or in-
consistency, when their class-terms are confronted with particulars. In fact, Plato goes so far as to intimate that these
uncertified classifications,—generated in each man's mind by
merely learning the application of words, and imbibed unconsciously, without special teaching, through the contagion of
ordinary society—are rather worse than ignorance : inasmuch
as they are accompanied by a false persuasion of knowledge.
It would be (in the opinion of Plato) a comparative improvement, if this state of mental confusion, creating a false persuasion of knowledge, were broken up ; and if there were substituted in place thereof positive ignorance, together with the
naked and painful consciousness of being really ignorant.
Only in this way could the mind of the learner be stimulated
to active effort in the acquisition of genuine knowledge.[a]

Accordingly, when it is said that Plato was "deeply struck

---

[a] Plato, Sophistes, p. 230—231. Symposion, p. 204 A, Menon
p. 84, A. D.

"with the importance of Classification," we must understand
the phrase as applying to Classification, not as he found it
prevalent, but as he idealized it. And the scheme that he
imagined was not merely different from that which he found,
but in direct repugnance to it. He denounced altogether the
aggregate of individuals; he declared the class-constituent to
reside in a reality apart from them, separate and self-existent
—the Idea or Form. He enjoined the student of philosophy
to fix his contemplation on these Class-Ideas, the real Realities, in their own luminous region : and for that purpose, to
turn his back upon the phenomenal, particulars, which were
mere transitory, shadowy, incoherent projections of these
Ideas[a]—and from the study of which no true knowledge could
be obtained. Of the two statements in the Analysis—(p. 271)
that " Plato never dreamed of the mystical visions of his succes-
" sors,"—and that " his error (respecting Classification) lay in
" misconceiving the One ; which he took, not for the aggregate,
" but something pervading the aggregate"—neither one nor
the other appears to me accurate. In regard to the second of
the two, indeed, you may find various passages of Plato which,
if construed separately, would countenance it : for Plato does
not always talk Realism—nor always consistently with himself. But still his capital and peculiar theory was, Realism.
The Platonic One was not something pervading the aggregate
of particulars, but an independent and immutable reality,
apart from the aggregate : and Plato, when he thus conceived

---

[a] This is what we read in the memorable simile of the Cave,
in Plato, Republic, VII., p. 514—519. The language used
throughout this simile is περιάγειν, περιακτέον, περιαγωγή, &c.
He supposes that the natural state of man is to have his face
and vision towards the particular phenomena, and his back towards the universal realities : the great problem is, how to make
the man face about, turn his back towards phenomena, and his
eyes towards Universals—τὰ ὄντα—τὰ νοητά. Nothing can be
learnt from observation however accute, of the phenomena. The
same point is enforced with all the charm of Platonic expression
in Republ. V. 478, 479, VI., 493, 494. Symposion, p. 210—211,
Phædon, p. 74—75.

the One, illustrating it by the vast hypotheses embodied in the
Republic, Phædon, Phædrus, Symposion, Menon, &c., is the
true originator of those " mystical visions " against which the
Analysis justly protests.   Such visions were doubtless suggested to Plato by " his deep sense of the importance of
Classification :" but they are his own, though continued and
amplified, without his decorative genius, by Neo-Platonic
successors.   His theory of classification was the first ever
propounded ; and that theory was Realism.   The doctrine here
ascribed to him by Mr. James Mill is much more Aristotelian
than Platonic.   The main issue raised by Aristotle against Plato
was, upon the essential separation, and separate objective existence, of the Abstract and Universal : Plato affirmed it, Aristotle
denied it.[a]   Aristotle recognised no reality apart from the
Particular, to which the Universal was attached as a predicate,
either essential or accidental to its subject.   The Aristotelian
Universal may thus be called, in relation to a body of similar
particulars, not the aggregate but something pervading the
aggregate.   But this is not Plato's view : it is the negation of
the Platonic Realism.

When we read in the Analysis (p. 265) that " the word *man*
" is not a word having a very simple idea, as was the opinion
" of the Realists ; nor a word having no idea at all, as was that of
" the Nominalists"—this language seems to me not well-chosen.

---

[a] According to Plato, it is τὸ ἓν παρὰ τὰ πολλά.   According to
Aristotle, it is ἓν κατὰ πολλῶν—ἓν καὶ τὸ αὐτὸ ἐπὶ πλειόνων
μὴ ὁμώνυμον ἓν ἐπὶ πολλῶν.   Analyt. Poster. I. 11, p. 77, a.
6. Metaphys. I. 9, p. 990, b. 7—13.
Whoever reads the portions of Plato's dialogues indicated in
my last preceding foot note, will see how material this difference
is between the two philosophers.
In the remarkable passage of the Analyt. Post. I. 24, p. 85,
a. 30, b. 20, Aristotle notices the Platonic hypothesis that the
Universal has real objective, separate, existence apart from its
particulars (τὸ καθόλου ἐστί τι παρὰ τὰ καθ' ἕκαστα) as an illusion,
mischievous and misleading—frequent, but not unavoidable.
See the antithesis between Plato and Aristotle, on the subject
of Universals, more copiously explained in the recent work of
Professor Bain, Mental and Moral Science, Appendix, pp. 6—20.

As to the Realists—the Platonic Ideas are conceived as eternal, immutable, grand, dignified, &c., but Aristotle[a] contends that they cannot all be simple : for the Idea of Man (e.g.) can hardly be simple, when there exists distinct Ideas of Animal and of Biped.   As to the Nominalists—we cannot surely say that they conceived the universal term as "having no idea at all." A doctrine something like this is ascribed (on no certain testimony) to Stilpon, in the generation succeeding Aristotle : the word Man (Stilpon is said to have affirmed[b]) did not mean John more than William or Thomas or Richard, &c., therefore it did not mean either one of them : therefore it had no meaning at all.   So also William of Ockham is said to have declared that Universal Terms were mere "flatus vocis :" but this (as Prantl has shewn[c]) was a phrase fastened upon him by his opponents, not employed by himself.   Still less can it be admitted that Hobbes and Berkeley conceived the Universal Term as "having no idea at all."   They denied indeed Universal Ideas in the Realistic sense : they also denied what Berkeley calls "determinate abstract Ideas :" but both of them explained (Berkeley especially) that the Universal term meant, any particular idea, considered as representing or standing for all other particular ideas of the same sort.[d] Whether this be the best and most complete explanation or not, it can hardly have been present to Mr. James Mill's mind, when he said that the Universal term had no idea at all in the opinion of the Nominalists.

There is one other remark to be made, respecting the view of Classification presented in the eighth Chapter of the Analysis. We read in the beginning of that Chapter—p. 249—"Forming "a class of things is a mode of regarding them.   But what is "meant by a mode of regarding things ?   This is mysterious :

---

[a] Aristot. Metaphys. Z. 1039, a. 27, 1040, a. 23.

[b] See Grote, Plato and the other Companions of Sokrates, Vol. III., ch. 38, p. 523.

[c] Prantl, Geschichte der Logik, Vol. III., Sect. 19, p. 327.

[d] Berkeley, Principles of Human Knowledge, Introduction, Sect. 12, 15, 16.

" and is as mysteriously explained, when it is said to be the taking
" into view the particulars in which individuals agree. For what
" is there which it is possible for the mind to take into view, in
" that in which individuals agree ? Every colour is an indi-
" vidual colour, every size is an individual size, every shape
" is an individual shape. But things have no individual
" colour in common, no individual shape in common, no indi-
" vidual size in common: *that is to say, they have neither shape,*
" *colour, nor size in common.* What then is it which they
" have in common which the mind can take into view ? Those
" who affirmed that it was something, could by no means tell.
" They substituted words for things : using vague and mystical
" phrases, which when examined meant nothing."

Here we find certain phrases, often used both in common
speech and in philosophy, condemned as mystical and obscure.
In the next or ninth Chapter (on Abstraction, p. 295 seq.), we
shall see the language substituted for them, and the theory by
which the mystery is supposed to be removed. I cannot but
think that the theory of Mr. James Mill himself is open to quite
as many objections as that which he impugns. He finds fault
with those who affirm that the word *cube* or *sphere* is applied
to a great many different objects by reason of the shape which
they have in common ; and that they may be regarded so far
forth as *cube* or *sphere*. But surely this would not have been
considered as either incorrect or mysterious by any philosopher, from Aristotle downward. When I am told that it is
incorrect, because the shape of each object is an *individual*
shape, I dissent from the reason given. In my judgment, the
term *individual* is a term applicable, properly and specially,
to a concrete object—to that which Aristotle would have
called a Hoc Aliquid. The term is not applicable to a quality
or attribute. The same quality that belongs to one object,
may also belong to an indefinite number of others. It is this
common quality that is *connoted* (in the sense of that word
employed by Mr. John Stuart Mill) by the class-term : and if
there were no common quality, the class-term would have no
connotation. In other words, there would be no class : nor

would it be correct to apply to any two objects the same concrete appellative name.

But when we come to the following Chapterof the Analysis (ch. ix. on Abstraction, p. 296), we read as follows—"Let "us suppose that we apply the adjective *black* first to the word "Man. We say 'black man.' But we speedily see that *for* "*the same reason* for which we say black man, we may say "black horse, black cow, black coat, and so on. The word "*black* is thus associated with innumerable modifications of "the sensation *black*. By frequent repetition, and the gradual "strengthening of the association, these modifications are at "last called up in such rapid succession that they appear com- "mingled, and no longer many ideas, but one. *Black* is there- "fore no longer an individual, but a general name. It marks "not the particular black of a particular individual, but the "black of every individual and of all individuals."

To say that we apply the word *black* to the horse *for the same reason* as we applied it to the man, is surely equivalent to saying that the colour of the horse is the same as that of the man : that blackness is the colour which they have in common. It is quite true that we begin by applying the name to one individual object, then apply it to another, and another, &c. ; but always for the same reason—to designate (or *connote*, in the phraseology of Mr. John Stuart Mill) the same colour in them all, and to denote the objects considered under one and the same point of view. It may be that in fact there are differences in shade of colour : but the class-name leaves these out of sight. When we desire to call attention to them, we employ other words in addition to it. Every attribute is considered and named as One, which is or may be common to many individual objects : the objects only are individual.

It is to be regretted, I think, that Mr. James Mill disconnected Classification so pointedly from Abstraction, and insisted on explaining the former without taking account of the latter. Such disconnection is a novelty, as he himself states (p. 294) : previous expositors thought that " abstraction was included in classification"—and, in my judgment, they were

right in thinking so, if (with Mr. James Mill) we are to consider Classification as a " great operation." An aggregate of
concretes is not sufficient to constitute a Class, in any scientific
sense, or as available in the march of reasoned truth. You
must have, besides, the peculiar mode of regarding the aggregate : (a phrase which Mr. James Mill deprecates as mysterious,
but which it is difficult to exchange for any other words more
intelligible) you must have "that separating one or more of
" the ingredients of a complex idea from the rest, which has
"received the name of Abstraction"—to repeat the very just explanation given by him, p. 295—though that too, if we look
at p. 249, he seems to consider as tainted with mystery.

We proceed afterwards to some clear and good additional
remarks—p. 298. A class-term, as *black*, "is associated
" with two distinguishable things, but with the one much more
" than with the other :—the clusters, with which it is asso-
" ciated, are variable : the *peculiar* sensation with which it is
" associated, is invariable. It is constantly, and therefore
" much more strongly, associated with the sensation, than
" with any of the clusters. It is at once a name of the clusters
" and a name of the sensation : but it is more *peculiarly* a
" name of the sensation." Again shortly afterwards,—the abstract term is justly described as "marking *exclusively* one part
" (of the cluster), upon which such and such effects depend,
" no alteration being supposed in any other part of it."[a]

This process of marking exclusively, and attending to, one
constant portion of a complex state of consciousness, amidst a

---

[a] The abstract term is coined for the express purpose of
marking one part of a cluster simultaneously present to the
mind, and fixing attention upon it without the other parts—but
the concrete term is often made to serve the same purpose, by
means of the adverb quatenus, καθόσον, ᾗ, &c. These phrases
are frequent both in Plato and Aristotle : the stock of abstract
terms was in their day comparatively small. It is needless to
multiply illustrations of that which pervades the compositions of
both : a very good one appears in Plato, Republ. I., p. 340 D,
341 C, 342.

great variety of variable adjuncts—is doubtless one fundamental characteristic in Abstraction and Classification. A
mystery was spread around it by Plato—first through his
ascribing to the Constant a separate self-existence, apart from
the Variables—still more by his hyperbolical predicates respecting these self-existent transcendental Entia. Plato[a] however
in other passages gives many just opinions, respecting Classification, which are no way founded on Realism, and are equally
admissible by Nominalists: and portions of Aristotle may be
indicated, which describe the process of abstraction as clearly
as any thing in Hobbes or Berkeley.[b]

One farther remark may be made upon these two Chapters
of the Analysis. Mr. James Mill seems to take little or no
thought of Classification and Abstraction, except as performed
by Adjectives. But the adjective presupposes a substantive,
which is alike an appellative; and which has already performed
its duty in the way of abstracting and classifying. This fact
seems to be overlooked in the language of some sentences
in the present Chapter: for example—" Some successions
" are found to depend upon the clusters called *objects*, all
" taken together. Thus a tree, a man, a stone, are the ante-

---

[a] The two Platonic dialogues, Sophïstes and Politikus, (in
which processes of Classification are worked out,) give precepts,
for correct and pertinent classification, not necessarily involving
the theory of Realism, but rather putting it out of sight; though
in one special part of the Sophïstes, the debate is made to turn
upon it. The main purpose of Plato is to fix upon some fact or
phenomenon, clear and appropriate, as the groundwork for distinguishing each class or sub-class—and to define thereby each
class-term (*i.e.*, to determine its *connotation*, in the sense of Mr.
John Stuart Mill). Plato deprecates the mere following out of
resemblances as a most slippery proceeding (ὀλισθηρότατον γένος
—Sophist. 231 A). The commonly received classes carry with
them in his opinion, no real knowledge, but only the false persuasion of knowledge: he wants to break them up and remodel
them.

[b] See especially Aristot. De Memoriâ et Reminiscentiâ, c. 1,
p. 449, b. 13. De Sensu et Sensili, c. 6, p. 445, b. 17. De
Animâ III. 8, p. 432, a. 9.

" cedents of certain consequents, as such : and not on account
" of any particular part of the cluster. Other consequents
" depend not upon the whole cluster, but upon some particular
" part : thus a tall tree produces certain effects which a tree
" not tall cannot produce," &c.

I think that the phraseology of this passage is not quite
clear. " The whole cluster all taken together " is not a tree as
such—a man as such—a stone as such—but this particular
man, tree, or stone, as it stands : John, Thomas, Caius or
Titius, clothed with all his predicates, acting or suffering in
some given manner. When we speak of a man *as such* or
quatenus man—we do not include the whole cluster, but only
those attributes *connoted* (in Mr. John Stuart Mill's sense of
the word) by the name *man :* we speak of him as a member
of the class *Man.* What I wish to point out is—That Man is a
class-term, just as much as *tall* or *short :* only it is the name
of a larger class, while tall man is a smaller class under it.
The school-logicians did not consider substantives as connotative, but only adjectives : Mr. James Mill has followed them
as to this extent of the word, though he has inverted their
meaning of it (see p. 299). Mr. John Stuart Mill, while declining to adopt the same inversion, has enlarged the meaning
of the word *connotative,* so as to include appellative substantives as well as adjectives.—*G.*

[80] Rejecting the notion that classes and classification would
not have existed but for the necessity of economizing names,
we may say that objects are formed into classes on account of
their resemblance. It is natural to think of like objects
together ; which is, indeed, one of the two fundamental laws
of association. But the resembling objects which are spontaneously thought of together, are those which resemble each
other obviously, in their superficial aspect. These are the only
classes which we should form unpremeditatedly, and without
the use of expedients. But there are other resemblances
which are not superficially obvious ; and many are not brought
to light except by long experience, or observation carefully
directed to the purpose ; being mostly resemblances in the

manner in which the objects act on, or are acted on by, other things. These more recondite resemblances are often those which are of greatest importance to our interests. It is important to us that we should think of those things together, which agree in any particular that materially concerns us. For this purpose, besides the classes which form themselves in our minds spontaneously by the general law of association, we form other classes artificially, that is, we take pains to associate mentally together things which we wish to think of together, but which are not sufficiently associated by the spontaneous action of association by resemblance. The grand instrument we employ in forming these artificial associations, is general names. We give a common name to all the objects, we associate each of the objects with the name, and by their common association with the name they are knit together in close association with one another.

But in what manner does the name effect this purpose, of uniting into one complex class-idea all the objects which agree with one another in certain definite particulars? We effect this by associating the name in a peculiarly strong and close manner with those particulars. It is, of course, associated with the objects also ; and the name seldom or never calls up the ideas of the class-characteristics unaccompanied by any other qualities of the objects. All our ideas are of individuals, or of numbers of individuals, and are clothed with more or fewer of the attributes which are peculiar to the individuals thought of. Still, a class-name stands in a very different relation to the definite resemblances which it is intended to mark, from that in which it stands to the various accessory circumstances which may form part of the image it calls up. There are certain attributes common to the entire class, which the class-name was either deliberately selected as a mark of, or, at all events, which guide us in the application of it. These attributes are the real meaning of the class-name—are what we intend to ascribe to an object when we call it by that name. With these the association of the name is close and strong : and the employment of the same name by different persons, provided they employ it with a precise adherence to the meaning, ensures that they shall all include these attributes in the complex idea which they associate with the name. This is not the case with any of the other qualities of the individual objects, even if they happen to be common to all the objects, still less if they belong only to some of them. The class-name calls up, in every mind that hears or uses it, the idea of one or more individual objects, clothed more or less copiously with other qualities than those marked by the name; but these other qualities may, consistently with the purposes for which the class is formed and the name given, be different with different persons, and with the same person at different times. What images of individual horses the word horse shall call up, depends on such accidents as the person's taste in horses, the particular horses he may happen to possess, the descriptions he last read, or the casual peculiarities of the horses he recently saw. In general, therefore, no very strong or permanent association, and especially no association common to all who use the language, will be formed between the word horse and any of the qualities of horses but those expressly or tacitly recognised as the foundations of the class. The complex ideas thus formed consisting of an inner nucleus of definite elements always the same, imbedded in a generally much greater number of elements indefinitely variable, are our ideas of classes; the ideas connected with general names; what are called General Notions: which are neither real objective entities, as the Realists held, nor mere names, as supposed to be maintained by the Nominalists, nor abstract ideas excluding all properties not common to the class, such as Locke's famous Idea of a triangle that is neither equilateral nor isosceles nor scalene. We cannot represent to ourselves a triangle with no properties but those common to all triangles: but we may represent it to ourselves sometimes in one of those three forms, sometimes in another, being aware all the while that all of them are equally consistent with its being a triangle.

One important consequence of these considerations is, that

the meaning of a class-name is not the same thing with the complex idea associated with it. The complex idea associated with the name man, includes, in the mind of every one, innumerable simple ideas besides those which the name is intended to mark, and in the absence of which it would not be predicated. But this multitude of simple ideas which help to swell the complex idea are infinitely variable, and never exactly the same in any two persons, depending in each upon the amount of his knowledge, and the nature, variety, and recent date of his experience. They are therefore no part of the meaning of the name. They are not the association common to all, which it was intended to form, and which enables the name to be used by all in the same manner, to be understood in a common sense by all, and to serve, therefore, as a vehicle for the communication, between one and another, of the same thoughts. What does this, is the nucleus of more closely associated ideas, which is the constant element in the complex idea of the class, both in the same mind at different times, and in different minds.

It is proper to add, that the class-name is not solely a mark of the distinguishing class-attributes, it is a mark also of the objects. The name man does not merely signify the qualities of animal life, rationality, and the human form, it signifies all individual men. It even signifies these in a more direct way than it signifies the attributes, for it is predicated of the men, but not predicated of the attributes; just as the proper name of an individual man is predicated of him. We say, This is a man, just as we say, This is John Thompson: and if John Thompson is the name of one man, Man is, in the same manner, a name of all men. A class name, being thus a name of the various objects composing the class, signifies two distinct things, in two different modes of signification. It signifies the individual objects which *are* the class, and it signifies the common attributes which constitute the class. It is predicated only of the objects; but when predicated, it conveys the information that these objects possess those attributes. Every concrete class-name is thus a connotative name. It marks both the objects and their common attributes, or rather, that portion of their common attributes in virtue of which they have been made into a class. It *denotes* the objects, and, in a mode of speech lately revived from the old logicians, it *connotes* the attributes. The author of the Analysis employs the word connote in a different manner; we shall presently examine which of the two is best.

We are now ready to consider whether the author's account of the ideas connected with General Names is a true and sufficient one. It is best expressed in his own words. "The "word Man, we shall say, is first applied to an individual; "it is first associated with the idea of that individual, and "acquires the power of calling up the idea of him; it is next "applied to another individual, and acquires the power of "calling up the idea of him; so of another, and another, till "it has become associated with an indefinite number, and has "acquired the power of calling up an indefinite number of "those ideas indifferently. What happens? It does call up "an indefinite number of the ideas of individuals, as often as it "occurs, and calling them up in close connexion, it forms them "into a species of complex idea. . . . When the word man "calls up the ideas of an indefinite number of individuals, "not only of all those to whom I have individually given the "name, but of all those to whom I have in imagination given "it, or imagine it will ever be given, and forms all those ideas "into one,—it is evidently a very complex idea, and therefore "indistinct; and this indistinctness has doubtless been the "main cause of the mystery which has appeared to belong "to it. That this however is the process, is an inevitable "result of the laws of association."

In brief, my idea of a Man is a complex idea compounded of the ideas of all the men I have ever known and of all those I have ever imagined, knit together into a kind of unit by a close association.

The author's description of the manner in which the class-association begins to be formed, is true and instructive; but does any one's idea of a man actually include all that the author finds in it ?   By an inevitable result of the laws of association, it is impossible to form an idea of a man in the abstract ; the class-attributes are always represented in the mind as part of an image of an individual, either remembered or imagined ; this individual may vary from time to time, and several images of individuals may present themselves either alternatively or in succession : but is it necessary that the name should recal images of all the men I ever knew or imagined, or even all of whom I retain a remembrance ?   In no person who has seen or known many men, can this be the case.   Apart from the ideas of the common attributes, the other ideas whether of attributes or of individual men, which enter into the complex idea, are indefinitely variable not only in kind but in quantity.   Some people's complex idea of the class is extremely meagre, that of others very ample.   Sometimes we know a class only from its definition, i.e. from an enumeration of its class-attributes, as in the case of an object which we have only read of in scientific books : in such a case the idea raised by the class-name will not be limited to the class-attributes, for we are unable to conceive any object otherwise than clothed with miscellaneous attributes : but these, not being derived from experience of the objects, may be such as the objects never had, nor could have ; while nevertheless the class, and the class-name, answer their proper purpose ; they cause us to group together all the things possessing the class-attributes, and they inform us that we may expect those attributes in anything of which that name is predicated.

The defect, as it seems to me, of the view taken of General Names in the text, is that it ignores this distinction between the meaning of a general name, and the remainder of the idea which the general name calls up.   That remainder is uncertain, variable, scanty in some cases, copious in others, and connected with the name by a very slight tie of association, continually overcome by counter-associations.   The only part of the complex idea that is permanent in the same mind, or common to several minds, consists of the distinctive attributes marked by the class-name.   Nothing else is universally present, though something else is always present : but whatever else be present, it is through these only that the class-name does its work, and effects the end of its existence. We need not therefore be surprised that these attributes, being all that is of importance in the complex idea, should for a long time have been supposed to be all that is contained in it. The truest doctrine which can be laid down on the subject seems to be this—that the idea corresponding to a class-name is the idea of a certain constant combination of class-attributes, accompanied by a miscellaneous and indefinitely variable collection of ideas of individual objects belonging to the class.—*Ed.*

CHAPTER IX.

ABSTRACTION.

"I think, too, that he (Mr. Locke) would have seen the advantage of 'thoroughly weighing,' not only (as he says) 'the *imperfections* of Language;' but its *perfections* also : For the perfections of Language, not properly understood, have been one of the chief causes of the imperfections of our knowledge."—*Diversions of Purley, by John Horne Tooke, A.M., i. 37.*

THE two cases of Consciousness, CLASSIFICATION, and ABSTRACTION, have not, generally, been well distinguished.

According to the common accounts of Classification, ABSTRACTION was included in it. When it is said, that, in order to classify, we leave out of view all the circumstances in which individuals differ, and retain only those in which they agree ; this separating one portion of what is contained in a complex idea, and making it an object of consideration by itself, is the process which is named Abstraction, at least a main part of that process.

It is necessary now to inquire what are the purposes to which this separating of the parts of a complex idea, and considering and naming the separated parts by themselves, is subservient.

We have already observed the following remarkable things in the process of naming : 1, Assigning names of those clusters of ideas called objects ; as man, fish ; 2, Generalizing those names, so as to make them represent a class ; 3, Framing adjectives by which minor classes are cut out of larger.

Those adjectives are all names of some separate portion of a cluster, and are, therefore, all instruments of abstraction, or of that separating one or more of the ingredients of a complex idea from the rest, which has received the name of Abstraction. One purpose of Abstraction, therefore, is the formation of those *subspecies*, the formation of which is required for certain purposes of speech.

These observations will be rendered familiar by examples. We say, tall man, red flower, race horse. In my complex idea of a man, or the cluster of ideas of sense to which I affix that mark, are included, certain ideas of colour, of figure, size, and so on. By the word tall, I single out a portion of those ideas, namely, the part relating to size, or rather size in one direction, and mark the separation by the sign or name. In my complex idea of a flower, colour is always one of the ingredients. By applying the adjective red, I single out this one from the rest, and point it out for peculiar consideration. The explanation is obvious, and need not be pursued in a greater number of instances.

Words of this description all denote differences ; either such as mark out species from genera, or such as mark out individuals from species. Of this latter sort the number is very small ; of which the reason is obvious ; individual differences are too numerous to receive names, and are marked by contrivances of abridgment which will be spoken of hereafter.

To explain this notation of differences; the same examples will suffice. In the phrase " tall man," the adjective " tall" marks the difference between such a man, and " short man," or " middle-sized man." Of the genus man, tall men are one species; and the difference between them and the rest of the genus is marked by the word tall. Of the genus flower, red flowers form a species, and the difference between them and the rest of the genus is marked by the adjective red. Of the genus horse, race horse forms a species, and the difference between this species and the rest of the genus is marked by the word race.

It is of importance further to observe, that adjectives singling out ideas which are not differences, that is, ideas common to the whole class, are useless : as, tangible wood; coloured man; sentient animal. Such epithets express no more than what is expressed by the name without them.

Another thing requiring the attention of the student is the mode in which these differential adjectives are generalized. As the word man, applied first to one individual, then to another, becomes associated with every individual, and every variety of the species, and calls them all up in one very complex idea; so are these adjectives applied to one class after another, and by that means at last call up a very complicated idea. Let us take the word " black" for an example; and let us suppose that we apply this adjective first to the word man. We say " black man." But we speedily see that for the same reason for which we say black man we may say black horse, black cow,

black coat, and so on. The word black is thus associated with innumerable modifications of the sensation black. By frequent repetition, and the gradual
strengthening of the association, these modifications
are at last called up in such rapid succession that they
appear commingled, and no longer many ideas, but
one. Black is therefore no longer an individual but a
general name. It marks not the particular black of
a particular individual; but the black of every individual, and of all individuals.[81] The same is the case

---

[81] The example which the author has here selected of a
general name, sets in a strong light the imperfection of the
theory of general names, laid down by him in the preceding
chapter. A name like "black," which marks a simple sensation, is an extreme case of the inapplicability of the theory.
Can it be maintained that the idea called up in our minds by
the word black, is an idea compounded of ideas of black men,
black horses, black cows, black coats, and the like? If I can
trust my own consciousness, the word need not, and generally
does not, call up any idea but that of a single black surface.
It is still not an abstract idea, but the idea of an individual
object. It is not a mere idea of colour; it is that, combined
with ideas of extension and figure, always present but extremely
vague, because varying, even from one moment to the next.
These vague ideas of an uncertain extension and figure, combined with the perfectly definite idea of a single sensation of
colour, are, to my consciousness, the sole components of the complex idea associated with the word black. I am unable to find
in that complex idea the ideas of black men, horses, or other
definite things, though such ideas may of course be recalled by it.
    In such a case as this, the idea of a black colour fills by itself
the place of the inner nucleus of ideas knit together by a closer
association, which I have described as forming the permanent
part of our ideas of classes of objects, and the meaning of
the class-names.—*Ed.*

with all other words of the same class. Thus I
apply the word sweet, first to the lump of sugar in
my mouth, next to honey, next to grapes, and so on.
It thus becomes associated with numerous modifications of the sensation sweet ; and when the association
is sufficiently strengthened by repetition, calls them
up in such close succession, that they are converted
into one complex idea. We are also to remember, that
the idea and the name have a mutual power over one
another. As the word black calls up the complex
idea, so every modification of black calls up the name;
and in this, as in other cases, the name actually forms
a part of the complex idea.

The next thing, which I shall observe, deserves in
a high degree, the attention of the learner. In the
various applications of that species of marks which
we are now considering, they are associated with two
distinguishable things ; but with the one much more
than the other. Thus, when we say black man, black
horse, black coat, and so of all other black things, the
word black is associated with the cluster, man, as often
as black man is the expression; with the cluster horse,
as often as black horse is the expression, and so on
with infinite variety : but at the same time that it is
associated with each of those various clusters, it is
also associated with the peculiar sensation of colour
which it is intended to mark. The CLUSTERS, therefore, with which it is associated, are variable ; the
PECULIAR SENSATION with which it is associated is
invariable. It is much more constantly, and therefore much more strongly associated with the
SENSATION than with any of the CLUSTERS. It is
at once a name of the clusters, and a name of the

sensation; but it is more peculiarly a name of the SENSATION.

We have, in a preceding note, observed, that such words have been called *connotative;* and I shall find much convenience in using the term NOTATION to point out the sensation or sensations which are peculiarly marked by such words, the term CONNOTATION to point out the clusters which they mark along with this their principal meaning.

Thus the word, black, NOTES that of which black is more peculiarly the name, a particular colour; it CONNOTES the clusters with the names of which it is joined: in the expression, black man, it connotes man; black horse, it connotes horse; and so of all other cases. The ancient Logicians used these terms, in the inverse order; very absurdly, in my opinion.[82]

---

[82] The word Connote, with its substantive Connotation, was used by the old logicians in two senses; a wider, and a narrower sense. The wider is that in which, up to this place, the author of the Analysis has almost invariably used it; and is the sense in which he defined it, in a note to section 6 of his first chapter. "There is a large class of words which denote "two things both together; but the one perfectly distinguish-"able from the other. Of these two things, also, it is observable, "that such words express the one primarily as it were; the "other in a way which may be called secondary. Thus white, "in the phrase white horse, denotes two things, the colour and "the horse; but it denotes the colour primarily, the horse "secondarily. We shall find it very convenient to say, there-"fore, that it *notes* the primary, *connotes* the secondary "signification."

This use of terms is attended with the difficulty, that it may often be disputed which of the significations is primary and

In using these connotative names, it is often highly convenient to drop the connotation; that is, to leave out the connoted cluster.

---

which secondary. In the example given, most people would agree with the author that the colour is the primary signification; the word being associated with the objects, only through its previous association with the colour. But take the other of the two words, horse. That too is connotative, and in the same manner. It signifies any and every individual horse, and it also signifies those attributes common to horses, which led to their being classed together and receiving that common name. Which, in this case, is the primary, and which the secondary signification? The author would probably say, that in this case, unlike the other, horse is the primary signification, the attributes the secondary. Yet in this equally with the former case, the attributes are the foundation of the meaning: a thing is called a horse to express its resemblance to other horses; and the resemblance consists of the common attributes. The question might be discussed, pro and con, by many arguments, without any conclusive result. The difference between primary and secondary acceptations is too uncertain, and at best too superficial, to be adopted as the logical foundation of the distinction between the two modes of signification.

The author, however, has, throughout the preceding chapters, regarded words as *connoting* any number of things which though included in their signification, are not, in his judgment, what they primarily signify. He said, for example, that a verb notes an action, and connotes the agent (as either me, thee, or some third person), the number of agents (as one or more), the time (as past, present, or future), and three modes, "that in which there is no reference to anything preceding, that in which there is a reference to something preceding, and that in which reference is made to the will of one of the Persons." I cite this complicated case, to shew by a striking example the great latitude with which the author uses the word Connote.

A mark is needed, to show when it is meant that the connotation is dropped. A slight mark put upon the connotative term answers the purpose; and shews

---

But in the present chapter he follows the example of some of the old logicians in adopting a second and more restricted meaning, expressive of the peculiar connotation which belongs to all concrete general names; viz. that twofold manner of signification, by which every name of a class signifies, on the one hand, all and each of the individual things composing the class, and on the other hand the common attributes, in consideration of which the class is formed and the name given, and which we intend to affirm of every object to which we apply the name. It is difficult to overrate the importance of keeping in view this distinction, or the danger of overlooking it when not made prominent by an appropriate phrase. The word Connote, which had been employed for this purpose, had fallen into disuse. But, though agreeing with the old logicians in using the word Connote to express this distinction, the author exactly reverses their employment of it. In their phraseology, the class-name connotes the attributes : in his, it notes the attributes, and connotes the objects. And he declares that in his opinion, their mode of employing the term is very absurd.

We have now to consider which of these two modes of employing it is really the most appropriate.

A concrete general name may be correctly said to be a mark, in a certain way, both for the objects and for their common attributes. But which of the two is it conformable to usage to say that it is the name of? Assuredly, the objects. It is they that are called by the name. I am asked, what is this object called? and I answer, a horse. I should not make this answer if I were asked what are these attributes called. Again, I am asked, what is it that is called a horse? and I answer, the object which you see; not the qualities which you see. Let us now suppose that I am asked, what is it that is called black; I answer, all *things* that have this particular colour.

when it is not meant that anything should be connoted. In regard to the word black, for example, we merely annex to it the syllable *ness;* and it is immediately

---

Black is a name of all black things. The name of the colour is not black, but blackness. The name of a thing must be the name which is predicated of the thing, as a proper name is predicated of the person or place it belongs to. It is scarcely possible to speak with precision, and adhere consistently to the same mode of speech, if we call a word the name of anything but that which it is predicated of. Accordingly the old logicians, who had not yet departed widely from the custom of common speech, considered all concrete names as the names of objects, and called nothing the name of an attribute but abstract names.

Now there is considerable incongruity in saying that a word connotes, that is, signifies secondarily, the very thing which it is a name of. To connote, is to mark something along with, or in addition to, something else. A name can hardly be said to mark the thing which it is a name of in addition to some other thing. If it marks any other thing it marks it in addition to the thing of which it is itself the name. In the present case, what is marked in addition, is that which is the cause of giving the name; the attributes, the possession of which by a thing entitles it to that name. It therefore seems more conformable to the original acceptation of the word Connote, that we should say of names like man or black that they connote humanity or blackness, and *de*note, or are names of, men and black objects; rather than, with the author of the Analysis, that they note the attributes, and connote the things which possess the attributes.

If this mode of using the terms is more consonant to propriety of language, so also is it more scientifically convenient. It is of extreme importance to have a technical expression exclusively consecrated to signify the peculiar mode in which the name of a class marks the attributes in virtue of which it is a class, and is called by the name. The verb " to note,"

indicated that all connotation is dropped: so, in sweetness ; hardness ; dryness ; lightness. The new words, so formed, are the words which have been denominated

---

employed by the author of the Analysis as the correlative of "to connote," is far too general to be confined to so specific a use, nor does the author intend so to confine it. " To connote," on the contrary, is a phrase which has been handed down to us in this restricted acceptation, and is perfectly fitted to be used as a technical term. There is no more important use of a term than that of fixing attention upon something which is in danger of not being sufficiently taken notice of. This is emphatically the case with the attribute-signification of the names of objects. That signification has not been seen clearly, and what has been seen of it confusedly has bewildered or misled some of the most distinguished philosophers. From Hobbes to Hamilton, those who have attempted to penetrate the secret of the higher logical operations of the intellect have continually missed the mark for want of the light which a clear conception of the connotation of general names spreads over the subject. There is no fact in psychology which more requires a technical name ; and it seems eminently desirable that the words Connote and Connotative should be exclusively employed for this purpose ; and it is for this purpose that I have myself invariably employed them.

In studying the Analysis, it is of course necessary to bear in mind that the author does not use the words in this sense, but sometimes in a sense much more vague and indefinite, and, when definite, in a sense the reverse of this. It may seem an almost desperate undertaking, in the case of an unfamiliar term, to attempt to rectify the usage introduced by the actual reviver of the word : and nothing could have induced me to attempt it, but a deliberate conviction that such a technical expression is indispensable to philosophy, and that the author's mode of employing these words unfits them for the purpose for which they are needed, and for which they are well adapted. I fear, however, that I have rarely succeeded in associating

ABSTRACT ; as the connotative terms from which they are formed have been denominated CONCRETE ; and, as these terms are in frequent use, it is necessary that the meaning of them should be well remembered.

It is now also manifest what is the real nature of ABSTRACT terms ; a subject which has in general presented such an appearance of mystery. They are simply the CONCRETE terms, with the connotation dropped. And this has in it, surely, no mystery at all.[83]

---

the words with their precise meaning, anywhere but in my own writings. The word Connote, not unfrequently meets us of late in philosophical speculations, but almost always in a sense more lax than the laxest in which it is employed in the Analysis, meaning no more than to *imply*. To such an extent is this the case, that able thinkers and writers do not always even confine the expression to names, but actually speak of Things as connoting whatever, in their opinion, the existence of the Things implies or presupposes.—*Ed*.

[83] After having said that a concrete general name notes an attribute, that this, one of the sensations in a cluster, and connotes the objects which have the attribute, i.e. the clusters of which that sensation forms a part; the author proceeds to say that an abstract name is the concrete name with the connotation dropped.

This seems a very indirect and circuitous mode of making us understand what an abstract name signifies. Instead of aiming directly at the mark, it goes round it. It tells us that one name signifies a part of what another name signifies, leaving us to infer what part. A connotative name with the connotation dropped, is a phrase requiring to be completed by specifying what is the portion of signification left. The concrete name with its connotation signifies an attribute, and also the objects which have the attribute. We are now instructed

It hence, also, appears that there can be no
ABSTRACT term without an implied CONCRETE, though
cases are not wanting, in which there is much occasion for the ABSTRACT term but not much for the CON-
CRETE ; in which, therefore, the concrete is not in use,
or is supplied by another form of expression.

---

to drop the latter half of the signification, the objects. What
then remains ? The attribute. Why not then say at once
that the abstract name is the name of the attribute ? Why
tell us that x is a plus b with b dropped, when it was as easy
to tell us that x is a ?

The noticeable thing however is that if a stands merely for
the sensation, x really is a little more than a : the connotation (in the author's sense of the term) of the concrete name
is not *wholly* dropped in the abstract name. The term blackness, and every other abstract term, includes in its signification
the existence of a black object, though without declaring what
it is. That is indeed the distinction between the name of an
attribute, and the name of a kind or type of sensation. Names
of sensations by themselves are not abstract but concrete
names. They mark the type of the sensation, but they do not
mark it as emanating from any object. " The sensation of
black" is a concrete name, which expresses the sensation apart
from all reference to an object. " Blackness" expresses the
same sensation with reference to an object, by which the sensation is supposed to be excited. Abstract names thus still
retain a limited amount of connotation in both the author's
senses of the term—the vaguer and the more specific sense. It
is only in the sense to which I am anxious to restrict the term,
that any abstract name is without connotation.

An abstract name, then, may be defined as the name of an
attribute ; and, in the ultimate analysis, as the name of one
or more of the sensations of a cluster ; not by themselves, but
considered as part of any or all of the various clusters, into
which that type of sensations enters as a component part.—*Ed.*

In irregular and capricious languages, as our own, the dropping of the connotation of the concrete terms is not marked in a uniform manner; and this requires some illustration. Thus, heavy is a concrete term, and we shew the dropping of the connotation, by the same mark as in the instances above, saying heaviness; but we have another term which is exactly the equivalent of heaviness, and frequently used as the abstract of heavy; that is, weight. Friend is a concrete, connotative term, in the substantive form. Its connotation is dropped by another mark, the syllable ship; thus, friendship; in like manner, generalship; brothership; cousinship. The syllable age is another of the marks we use for the same purpose; pilotage, parsonage, stowage.

Among concrete connotative words, we have already had full opportunity of observing that verbs constitute a principal class. Those words all NOTE some *motion* or *action;* and CONNOTE an *actor.* There is the same frequency of occasion to leave out the connotation in the case of this class of connotative words, as in other classes. Accordingly ABSTRACT terms are formed from them, as from the connotative adjectives and substantives. The infinitive mood is such an abstract term; with this peculiarity, that, though it leaves out the connotation of the *actor*, it retains the connotation of *time*.[84]

---

[84] The infinitive mood does not always express time. At least, it often expresses it aoristically, without distinction of tense. "To love" is as abstract a name as "love," "to fear," as "fear": they are applied equally to past, present, and future. The infinitives of the past and future, as *amavisse, amaturus esse,* do, however, include in their signification a particular time.—*Ed.*

It is convenient, however, to have abstract terms from the verbs, which leave out also the connotation of time ; such are the substantive *amor* from *amo*, *timor* from *timeo*, and so on.

Verbs have not only an active but a passive form. In the passive form, it is not the *action*, but the *bearing* of the action, which is NOTED; and not the *actor*, but the *bearer* of the action, that is CONNOTED. In this case, also, there is not less frequent occasion to drop the connotation. By the simple contrivance of a slight alteration in the connotative term, the important circumstance of dropping the connotation is marked. In the case of the passive as the active form of verbs, the infinitive mood drops the connotation of the person, but retains that of the time. Other abstract terms, formed from the passive voice, leave out the connotation both of person and time. Thus from *legor*, there is *lectio;* from *optor, optatio ;* from *dicor, dictio;* and so on.

It is to be remarked that the Latin mode of forming abstract terms from verbs, by the termination " tio,' has been adopted to a great extent in English. A large proportion of our abstract terms are thus distinguished ; as action, association, imagination, navigation, mensuration, friction, motion, station, faction, legislation, corruption, and many others.

It is also of extreme importance to mark a great defect and imperfection, in this respect, of the Latin language. Such words as *lectio, dictio, actio,* are derived with equal readiness either from the supine, *lectum, dictum, actum ;* or from the participle, *lectus, dictus, actus.* The supine is *active*, the participle, *passive.* From this circumstance probably it is, that

these abstract terms in the Latin language possess
both the active and passive signification ; and by this
most unfortunate ambiguity have proved a fertile
source of obscurity and confusion. This defect of the
Latin language is the more to be lamented by us, that
it has infected our own language; for as we have
borrowed from the Latin language a great proportion
of our abstract terms, we have transplanted the mischievous equivocation along with them. This
ambiguity the Greek language happily avoided : thus
it had πρᾶξις and πρᾶγμα the first for the active signification of *actio*, the latter the passive.[85]

Of the abstract terms, of genuine English growth,
derived from the concrete names of action, or verbs,
the participle of the past tense supplied a great number, merely dropping the adjective, and assuming the
substantive form. Thus, weight, a word which we
had occasion to notice before, is the participle weighed,
with the connotation dropped : stroke is merely
struck ; the *thing* struck, the connotation, being left
out : thought is the past participle passive of the
verb to think, and differs from the participle in nothing, but that the participle, the adjective, has the
connotation ; the abstract, the substantive, has it not.
Whether the concrete, or the abstract, is the term
employed, is in such cases always indicated by the
context ; and, therefore, no particular mark to distinguish them is required.

---

[85] I apprehend that πρᾶγμα is not an abstract but a concrete term, and does not express the attribute of being done,
but the thing done—the effect which results from the completed action.—*Ed.*

In our non inflected language, a facility is afforded in forming a non-connotative from the connotative, in the active voice of verbs ; because the connotative word is always distinguished by the presence of the persons of the verb, or that of some part of the auxiliary verb. The same word, therefore, answers for the abstract, as for the concrete ; it being of course the abstract, when none of the marks of the concrete are present. Thus the word love, is both the verb or the connotative, and the substantive or the non-connotative ; thus also fear, walk, ride, stand, fight, smell, taste, sleep, dream, drink, work, breath, and many others.

We have in English, formed from verbs, a great many abstracts or non-connotatives, which terminate in " th," as truth, health, dearth, stealth, death, strength. It may be disputed whether these words are derived from one part of the verb or another ; but, in all other respects, the nature of them is not doubtful. The third person singular of the present, indicative active, ends in " th ;" and, therefore, they may be said to be that part of the verb with the connotation dropped. The termination, however, of the past participle is " d," and we know that " th" and " d," are the same letter under a slight difference of articulation ; and, therefore, they may just as well be derived from the past participle, and as often at least as they have a passive signification, no doubt are. Thus the verb trow, to think, has either troweth, or trowed ; from one of which, but more likely from the last, we have truth : the verb to heal, has either healeth, or healed ; from one of which, but more likely the last, we have health : the verb to string has stringeth, or stringed ;

from one of which we have strength; thus from dieth,
or died, death; from stealeth, or stealed, stealth;
mirth in the same manner, from a verb now out of
use; so heighth, length, breadth.[86]

---

[86] The abstracts in *th* belong to a very early stage of the
language. We cannot now form words like *health, truth*, as
we can abstracts in *-ness*. As in the case of adjectives in *-en*
(wooden), and of preterites and participles like *fell, fallen*,
that particular part of the vital energy of the language that
produced them, is dead—ossified, as it were; and we cannot
exemplify their formation by any process now going on. To
account for many of them, we must suppose them formed
from roots different from any now existing as separate words
—roots from which the corresponding verbs and adjectives that
we are acquainted with have been themselves derived by
augmentation or other change. This being the case, it is impossible to say with certainty whether the immediate root of
any particular abstract in *-th* was a verb, a noun, or an adjective; and, indeed, the question need hardly be raised, since
a primitive root was of the nature of all three.

The structure of these derivatives is better seen in some
of the other Teutonic dialects than in the English or the Anglo-
Saxon, in which the affix is reduced to a mere consonant.
Thus, for Eng. *depth* the Gothic has *diupi-tha*; for *heigh-th*,
hauhi-tha. In Old High German the affix *-tha* becomes *-da*,
and we have *heili-da* corresponding to Eng. *heal-th*; *strenki-
da*, to *streng-th*; besides a great number of analogous forms,
such as *evi-da*, "eternity" (from the same root as *ever*; compare Lat. *aetas* for *aevitas*). In modern German comparatively few of these derivatives survive; and in those that do,
the *-da* of the Old German has passed into *-de*, as in *ge-baer-de*,
the way of 'bearing' oneself, behaviour; equivalent to Latin
habi-tus. The modern German equivalents of *bread-th*,
leng-th, are *breit-e, läng-e*; but in some of the popular dialects the older forms *breite de, läng-de* are still retained; and

It would be interesting to give a systematic account of the non-connotatives, derived from English

---

in Dutch *warm-te* corresponds to *warm-th*, and *grôt-te* is *great-ness*. When we recollect that *th* or *d* in the Germanic languages represents in such cases the *t* of the Greek and Latin (compare Gr. μέλιτ (ος), honey with Goth. *milith;* Lat. *alter* with Eng. *other*), we cannot help seeing how analogous is the formation of the class of words we are now considering to that of Latin past participles (ama-tus, dic-tus, auditus). In the case of those abstracts that seem to come more naturally from an adjective root than from a verb, we can conceive the adjective formed on the analogy of the past participle ; just as there are in English adjectives having no possible verbal root, yet simulating past participles ; as *able-bodi-ed, three-corner-ed.* The abstract noun would appear to have been originally distinguished from the participle, or participial adjective, by some additional affix, as in lec-t-io. In Greek and Latin this additional affix very often consisted in a reduplication of the formative element *t*, as if for the purpose of denoting multitude, generality ; as in Greek (νεό-τητ-ος), Latin *juven-tut-is, sani-tat-is.* It is not impossible that Goth. *diupi-tha,* O.H.G. *heili-da* are abbreviations of *diupi-tha-th, heili-da-d,* just as Lat. *sani-tat* has dwindled down in modern Ital. to *sani-tà.*

In a great many words essentially belonging to the same class both in meaning and in mode of formation, the *-th* has, for the sake of euphony or from other causes, given place to *t* or *d.* Thus *mood* corresponds to Goth. *mo-th,* and means a motion (Lat. *motus*) or affection (of the mind) ; *blood,* to Goth. *blo-th; theft,* is in Ang. Sax. *theof-th.* *Mur-ther,* from a root akin to Lat. *mori ; burthen,* from the root of to *bear*, are of similar formation, with additional affixes.

All these considerations would seem to put Horne Tooke's proposed derivation of these abstracts from the third person singular of the present indicative of the verb, completely out

verbs ; and this ought to be done ; but for the present inquiry it would be an operation misplaced. The nature of the words, and the mode of their signification, is all which here is necessary to be understood.

One grand class of connotative terms is composed of such words as the following : walking, running, flying, reading, striking ; and we have seen that, for a very obvious utility, a generical name was invented, the word ACTING, which includes the whole of these specific names ; and to which the non-connotative, or abstract term ACTION corresponds.. There was equal occasion for a generical name to include all the specific names belonging to the other class of connotative terms ; such as coloured, sapid, hard, soft, hot, cold, and so on. But language has by no means been so happy in a general name for this, as for the other class. The word SUCH, is a connotative term, which includes them all, and indeed the other class along with them ; for when we apply the word SUCH to anything, we comprehend under it all the ideas of which the cluster

---

of court. The famous case of *truth* from *troweth* is especially absurd. For one thing the Ang. Sax. verb *treowan* does not mean " to think," but " to trust," " rely on," " believe." This implies a ground for the trust, and that ground lies in the quality expressed by the adjective, true. *Truth* has the same relation, logically and etymologically, to *true*, that *dearth* has to *dear*, *health* to *hale*. Remarking on the identity in form between the Ang. Sax. *treow*, " trust," " a treaty," and *treow*, " a tree," Jacob Grimm suggests that they are radically related, and that the idea common to *tree* and *true* is firmness, fixedness. Thus the " true" would be the " firm" the " fixed"—what may be relied on. This view is supported by the analogy of the Lat. *robur*, which means both an oak and strength.—*F*.

is composed. But this is not all which is included under the word such. It is a relative term, and always connotes so much of the meaning of some other term. When we call a thing *such*, it is always understood that it is such *as* some other thing. Thus we say, John is such as James. Corresponding with our "such as," the Latins had *talis qualis*. If we could suppose *qualis* to have been used without any connotation of *talis*, *qualis* would have been such a word as the occasion which we are now considering would have required. The Latins did not use *qualis*, in this sense, as a general concrete, including all the other names of the properties of objects other than actions. But they made from it, as if used in that very sense, a non-connotative or abstract term, the word QUALITY, which answers the same purpose with regard to both classes, as action does to one of them. That is to say; it is a very general non-connotative term, including under it the non-connotatives or abstracts of hot, cold, hard, soft, long, short; and not only of all other words of that description, but of acting, and its subordinates also.

Quantus, is another concrete which has a double connotation like *qualis*. It connotes not only the substantive with which it agrees, but also, being a relative, the term *tantus*, which is its correlate. By dropping both connotations, the abstract QUANTITY is made; a general term, including under it the abstracts of all the names by which the modifications of greater and less are denominated; as large, small, a mile long, an inch thick, a handful, a ton, and so on.

Much remains, beside what is here stated, of the full explanation of the mode in which *talis qualis*,

tantus quantus, are made conducive to the great purposes of marking. But this must be reserved till we
come to treat of RELATIVE TERMS, in general.

We have previously observed, that one of the purposes for which we abstract, or sunder the parts of a
complex idea, marked by a general name, is, to form
those adjectives, or connotative terms, which, denoting
differences, enable us to form, and to name, subordinate classes. We now come to the next of the great
purposes to which abstraction is subservient, and it is
one to which the whole of our attention is due.

Of all the things in which we are interested, that is,
on which our happiness and misery depend, meaning
here by things, both objects and events, the most important by far are the successions of objects ; in other
words, the effects which they produce. In reality,
objects are interesting to us, solely on account of the
effects which they produce, either on ourselves, or on
other objects.

But an observation of the greatest importance
readily occurs ; that of any cluster, composing our
idea of an object, the effects or consequents depend, in
general, more upon one part of it than another. If
a stone is *hot*, it has certain effects or consequences ;
if *heavy*, it has others, and so on. It is of great importance to us, in respect to those successions, to be
able to mark discriminately the real antecedent ; not
the antecedent combined with a number of things
with which the consequent has nothing to do. I observe, that other objects, as iron, lead, gold, produce
similar effects with stone ; as often as the name *hot*
can, in like manner, be predicated of them. In the
several clusters therefore, hot stone, hot iron, hot gold,

hot lead, there is a portion, the same in all, with which, and not with the rest, the effects which I am contemplating are connected. This part is marked by the word *hot;* which word, however, in the case of each cluster, connotes also the other parts of the cluster. It appears at once, how much convenience there must be in dropping the connotation, and obtaining a word which, in each of those cases, shall mark exclusively that part of the cluster on which the effect depends. This is accomplished by the abstract or non-connotative terms, heat, and weight.

Certain alterations, also, are observed in those parts of clusters on which such and such effects depend ; which alterations make corresponding alterations in the effects, though no other alteration is observable, in the cluster, to which such parts belong. Thus, if a stone is more or less hot, the effects or successions are not the same ; so of iron, so of lead ; but the same alteration in the same part of each of those clusters, is followed by the same effects. It is true, that we know nothing of the alteration in the cause, but by the alteration in the effects ; for we only say that a stone is hotter, because it produces such other effects, either in our sensations immediately, or in the sensations we receive from other objects. It is, however, obvious that we have urgent use for the means of marking, not only the alterations in the effects, but the alterations in the antecedents. This we do, by supposing the alterations to be those of increase and diminution, and marking them by the distinction of lower and higher degrees. But, for this purpose, it is obvious that we must have a term which is not connotative ; because we suppose no alteration in any part of the cluster but that which is not connoted; thus we can say, with sufficient precision, that a greater or less degree of heat produces such and such effects; but we cannot say, that a greater or less degree of hot stone, of hot iron, of hot any thing else, produces these effects.

This then, is another use, and evidently a most important use, of abstract, non-connotative terms. They enable us to mark, with more precision, those successions, in which our good and evil is wholly contained.

This also enables us to understand, what it is which recommends such and such aggregates, and not others, for classification. Those successions of objects, in which we are interested, determine the classifications which we form of them.

Some successions are found to depend upon the clusters, called objects, all taken together. Thus a tree, a man, a stone, are the antecedents of certain consequents, as such; and not on account of any particular part of the cluster.

Other consequents depend not upon the whole of the cluster, but upon some particular part: thus a tall tree, produces certain effects, which a tree not tall, cannot produce; a strong man, produces certain effects, which a man not strong cannot produce. When these consequents are so important, as to deserve particular attention, they and their antecedents must be marked. For this purpose, are employed the connotative terms marking differences. These terms enable us to group the clusters containing those antecedents into a sub-class; and NON-CONNOTATIVE or ABSTRACT terms, derived from them, enable us to speak separately of that part of the cluster which we have to mark as the precise antecedent of the consequent which is engaging our attention.

It is presumed, that these illustrations will suffice, to enable the reader to discern the real marking power of abstract terms, and also to perceive the mode of their formation.

CHAPTER X.

MEMORY.

" The science of metaphysics, as it regards the mind, is, in its most important respects, a science of analysis ; and we carry on our analysis, only when we suspect that what is regarded by others as an ultimate principle, admits of still finer evolution into principles still more elementary."—*Inquiry into the Relation of Cause and Effect, by Thomas Brown, M.D.* P. iv. s. i. p. 331.

It has been already observed that if we had no other state of consciousness than sensation, we never could have any knowledge, excepting that of the present instant.   The moment each of our sensations ceased, it would be gone for ever ; and we should be as if we had never been.

The same would be the case if we had only ideas in addition to sensations.   The sensation would be one state of consciousness, the idea another state of consciousness.   But if they were perfectly insulated ; the one having no connexion with the other ; the idea, after the sensation, would give me no more information, than one sensation after another.   We should still have the consciousness of the present instant, and nothing more.   We should be wholly incapable of acquiring experience, and accommodating our actions to the laws of nature.   Of course we could not continue to exist.

Even if our ideas were associated in trains, but only as they are in Imagination, we should still be without the capacity of acquiring knowledge.   One idea, upon this supposition, would follow another.   But that would be all.   Each of our successive states of consciousness, the moment it ceased, would be gone for ever.   Each of those momentary states would be our whole being.

Such, however, is not the nature of man.   We have states of consciousness, which are connected with past states.   I hear a musical air ; I recognise it as the air which was sung to me in my infancy.   I have an idea of a ghost ; I recognise the terror with which, when I was alone in the dark, that idea, in my childish years, was accompanied.   Uniting in this manner the present with the past, and not otherwise, I am susceptible of knowledge ; I am capable of ascertaining the qualities of things ; that is, their power of affecting me ; and of knowing in what circumstances what other circumstances will take place.   Suppose that my present state of consciousness is the idea of putting my finger in the flame of the candle.   I recognise the act as a former act ;[87] and this recognition is followed

---

[87] The recognition of an act as a former act, or of a present sensation as having formerly occurred, is a phrase of the intellectual power named consciousness of Agreement, or Similarity, which is both an essential of our Knowledge, and a means of mental Reproduction.   The defectiveness of the author's view of this function of the intellect has been elsewhere commented on. — B.

by another, namely, that of the pain which I felt immediately after. This part of my constitution, which is of so much importance to me, I find it useful to name. And the name I give to it is MEMORY. When the memory of the past is transferred into an anticipation of the future, by a process which will be explained hereafter, it gets the name of experience; and all our power of avoiding evil, and obtaining good, is derived from it. Unless I remembered that my finger had been in the flame of the candle; and unless I anticipated a similar consequent, from a similar antecedent, I should touch the flame of the candle, after being burned by it a hundred times, just as I should have done, if neither burning nor any of its causes had ever formed part of my consciousness.

Our inquiry is, what this part of our constitution, so highly important to us, is composed of. All inquirers are agreed, that it is complex; but what the elements are into which it may be resolved, has not been very successfully made out.

It is proper to begin with the elements which are universally acknowledged. Among them, it is certain, that IDEAS are the fundamental part. Nothing is remembered but through its IDEA. The memory, however, of a thing, and the idea of it, are not the same. The idea may be without the memory; but the memory cannot be without the idea. The idea of an elephant may occur to me, without the thought of its having been an object of my senses. But I cannot have the thought of its having been an object of my senses, without having the idea of the animal at the same time. The consciousness, therefore, which I call memory, is an idea, but not an idea alone ; it is an idea and something more. So far is our inquiry narrowed. What is that which, combined with an idea, constitutes memory ?

That memory may be, the idea must be. In what manner is the idea produced ?

We have already seen in what manner an idea is called into existence by association. It is easy to prove that the idea which forms part of memory is called up in the same way, and no other. If I think of any case of memory, I shall always find that the idea, or the sensation which preceded the memory, was one of those which are calculated, according to the laws of association, to call up the idea involved in that case of memory; and that it was by the preceding idea, or sensation, that the idea of memory was in reality brought into the mind. I have not seen a person with whom I was formerly intimate for a number of years ; nor have I, during all that interval, had occasion to think of him. Some object which had been frequently presented to my senses along with him, or the idea of something with which I have strongly associated the idea of him, occurs to me ; instantly the memory of him exists. The friend with whom I had often seen him in company, accidentally meets me ; a letter of his which had been long unobserved, falls under my eye ; or an observation which he was fond of producing, is repeated in my hearing; these are circumstances all associated with the idea of the individual in question ; the idea of him is excited by them, and with the mere idea of the

man, all the other circumstances which constitute
memory.

The necessary dependence of memory upon association, may be proved still more rigidly in this way. It
has been already observed, that we cannot call up any
idea by willing it. When we are said to will, there
must be in the mind, the idea of what is willed.
"Will, without an idea," are incongruous terms; as
if one should say, "I can will, and will nothing."
But if the idea of the thing willed, must be in the
mind, as a condition of willing, to will to have an
idea in the mind, is to will to have that in it, which,
by the supposition, is in it already.

There is a state of mind familiar to all men, in which
we are said to try to remember. In this state, it is
certain that we have not in the mind the idea which
we are trying to have in it. How then is it, that we
proceed in the course of our endeavour to procure its
introduction into the mind? If we have not the idea
itself, we have certain ideas connected with it. We run
over those ideas, one after another, in hopes that some
one of them will suggest the idea we are in quest of;
and if any of them does, it is always one so connected
with it, as to call it up in the way of association. I
meet an old acquaintance, whose name I do not
remember, and wish to recollect. I run over a number of names, in hopes that some of them may be
associated with the idea of the individual. I think of
all the circumstances in which I have seen him engaged; the time when I knew him, the place in which
I knew him, the persons along with whom I knew
him, the things he did, or the things he suffered; and,
if I chance upon any idea with which the name is

associated, then immediately I have the recollection ; if not, my pursuit of it is in vain.[88]

There is another set of cases, very familiar, but affording very important evidence on the subject. It frequently happens, that there are matters which we desire not to forget. What is the contrivance to which we have recourse for preserving the memory ; that is, for making sure that it will be called into existence, when it is our wish that it should. All men, invariably employ the same expedient. They endeavour to form an association between the idea of the thing to be remembered, and some sensation, or some idea, which they know beforehand will occur at or near the time when they wish the remembrance to be in their minds. If this association is formed, and the sensation or the idea, with which it has been formed, occurs ; the sensation, or idea, calls up the remembrance ; and the object of him who formed the association is attained. To use a vulgar instance ; a man receives a commission from his friend, and, that he may not forget it, ties a knot on his handkerchief. How is this fact to be explained ? First of all, the idea of the commission is associated with the making of the knot. Next, the handkerchief is a thing which it is known beforehand will be frequently seen, and of

---

[88] This process seems best expressed by laying down a law of Compound or Composite Association ; under which a plurality of feeble links of connexion may be a substitute for one powerful and self-sufficing link.—*B.*

[The laws of compound association are the subject of one of the most original and profound chapters of Mr. Bain's treatise (The Senses and the Intellect. Part ii. Chap. 3.).—*Ed.*]

course at no great distance of time from the occasion on which the memory is desired. The handkerchief being seen, the knot is seen, and this sensation recalls the idea of the commission, between which and itself, the association had been purposely formed.

What is thus effected through association with a sensation, may be effected through association with an idea. If there is any idea, which I know will occur to me at a particular time, I may render myself as sure of recalling any thing which I wish to remember at that time, by associating it with this idea, as if I associated it with a sensation. Suppose I know that the idea of Socrates will be present to my mind at twelve o'clock this day week : if I wish to remember at that time something which I have to do, my purpose will be gained, if I establish between the idea of Socrates, and the circumstance which I wish to remember, such an association that the one will call up the other.

A very remarkable application of this principle offers itself to our contemplation, in the artificial memory which was invented by the ancient orators and rhetoricians. The orator made choice of a set of objects, sufficient in number to answer his purpose. The ideas of those objects he taught himself, by frequent repetition, to pass through his mind in one constant order. The objects which he chose were commonly such as aided him in fixing them according to a certain order in his memory; the parts, for example, of some public building, or other remarkable assemblage. Having so prepared himself, the mode in which he made use of his machinery was as follows. The topics or sentiments of his speech were

to follow in a certain order.   The parts of the building he had chosen as his instrument had previously
been taught to follow by association, in a certain
order.   With the first of these, then, he associated
the first topic of his discourse ; with the second, the
second, and so on.   The first part of the building
suggested the first topic ; the second, the second ; and
each another, to the end of his discourse.[89]

We not only have ideas of memory, individually
taken ; that is, separately, each by itself ; as in the
instances which we have just been considering : we
have also trains of such ideas.   All narratives of
events which ourselves have witnessed are composed
of such trains.   The ideas forming those trains do
not follow one another in a fortuitous manner.   Each
succeeding idea is called up by the one which pre-

---

[89] The conditions of the success of this expedient are interesting to study as illustrations of the working of association.
The supposition is that the parts of the building are perfectly
coherent in the mind, that they can recall each other easily
and rapidly.   The advantage gained will depend entirely upon
the superior facility of attaching a head of discourse to the
visible appearance of a room, as compared with the facility of
attaching it to a previous head.   If we can form an enduring
bond between a topic and the picture of an interior, by a smaller
mental effort than is necessary to conjoin two successive topics,
there is a gain by the employment of the device ; the difference
of the two efforts is the measure of the gain.   Probably the
result would depend upon the relative force of the pictorial
and the verbal memory in the individual mind.   In minds
where the pictorial element prevails, there might be a positive
advantage ; in cases where the pictorial power is feeble and the
verbal power strong, there would almost certainly be a dead
loss.—*B.*

cedes it ; and every one of these successions takes
place according to a law of association. After a lapse
of many years, I see the house in which my father
died. Instantly a long train of the circumstances
connected with him rise in my mind : the sight of
him on his death-bed ; his pale and emaciated countenance ; the calm contentment with which he looked
forward to his end ; his strong solicitude, terminating
only with life, for the happiness of his son ; my own
sympathetic emotions when I saw him expire ; the
mode and guiding principles of his life ; the thread
of his history; and so on. In this succession of ideas,
each of which is an idea of memory, there is not a
single link which is not formed by association ; not
an idea which is not brought into existence by that
which precedes it.

Whensoever there is a desire to fix any train in
the memory, all men have recourse to one and the
same expedient. They practise what is calculated to
create a strong association. The grand cause of strong
associations is repetition. This, accordingly, is the
common resource. If any man, for example, wishes
to remember a passage of a book, he repeats it a sufficient number of times. To the man practised in applying the principle of association to the phenomena
in which it is concerned, the explication of this process presents itself immediately. The repetition of
one word after another, and of one idea after another,
gives the antecedent the power of calling up the consequent from the beginning to the end of that portion
of discourse, which it is the purpose of the learner to
remember.

That the remembrance is produced in no other way,

is proved by a decisive experiment. For, after a passage has been committed to memory in the most perfect manner, if the learner attempts to repeat it in any other order than that, according to which the association was formed, he will fail. A man who has been accustomed to repeat the Lord's Prayer, for example, from his infancy, will, if he has never tried it, find the impossibility of repeating it backwards, small as the number is of the words of which it consists.

That words alone, without ideas, suggest one another in a train, is proved by our power of repeating a number of words of an unknown language.[90] And, it is worth observing, that the power of arithmetical computation is dependent upon the same process. Thus, for example, when a child learns the multiplication table, and says, 11 times 11 is 121, or 12 times 12 is 144, he annexes no ideas to those words; but, by force of repetition, the expression 12 times 12 instantly calls up the expression 144, or 11 times 11 the expression 121, and so upwards from twice 2, with which he begins. In illustrating the mode in which repetition makes association more and more easy, I used the process of arithmetical addition as a striking example. Persons little accustomed to the process perform it with great difficulty; persons

---

[90] There is here a lapse, of mere expression. The meaning is not that words suggest one another without ideas; words do not suggest words, but the ideas of words. The author intended to say that words, or the ideas of them, often suggest the ideas of other words (forming a series) without suggesting along with them any ideas of the things which those words signify.—*Ed.*

much accustomed to it, with astonishing facility. In men of the first class, the association is imperfectly formed, and the several antecedent expressions slowly suggest the proper consequent ones ; in those of the latter class the association is very perfectly formed, and the expressions suggest one another with the greatest expedition and ease.

Thus far we have proceeded with facility. In Memory there are ideas, and those ideas both rise up singly, and are connected in trains by association. The same occurs in Imagination. Imagination consists of ideas, both suggested singly, and connected in trains, by association. This is the whole account of Imagination. But Memory is not the same with Imagination. We all know, when we say, we imagine a thing, that we have not the same meaning, as when we say, we remember it. Memory, therefore, has in it all that Imagination has ; but it must also have something more. We are now, then, to inquire what that additional something is.

There are two cases of Memory. One is, when we remember sensations. The other is, when we remember ideas. The first is, when we remember what we have seen, felt, heard, tasted, or smelt. The second is, when we remember what we have thought, without the intervention of the senses. I remember to have seen and heard George III., when making a speech at the opening of his Parliament. This is a case of sensation. I remember my conceptions of the Emperor Napoleon and his audience, when I read the account of his first address to the French Chambers. This is a case of ideas.

We shall consider the case of sensations first. What is it to remember any thing I have seen ?

First, there is the idea of it ; and that idea brought into existence by association.

But, in Memory, there is not only the idea of the thing remembered ; there is also the idea of my having seen it.　Now .these two, 1, the idea of the thing, 2, the idea of my having seen it, combined, make up, it will not be doubted, the whole of that state of consciousness which we call memory.[91]

But what is it we are to understand by what I have called " the idea of my having seen the object ?" This is a very complex idea ; and, in expounding, clearly, to the comprehension of persons, not familiar with these solutions, the import and force of a very complex idea, lies all the difficulty of the case.

It will be necessary for such persons to call to mind the illustrations they have already contemplated of the remarkable case of association, in which a long train of ideas is called up so rapidly as to appear but one idea ; and also the other remarkable case, in which one idea is so strongly associated with another, that it is out of our power to separate them.　Thus, when we use the word battle, the mind runs over the

---

[91] The doctrine which the author thinks " will not be doubted" is more than doubted by most people, and in my judgment rightly.　To complete the memory of seeing the thing, I must have not only the idea of the thing, and the idea of my having seen it, but the belief of my having seen it ; and even this is not always enough ; for I may believe on the authority of others that I have seen a thing which I have no remembrance of seeing.—*Ed.*

train of countless acts, from the beginning of that
operation to the end ; and it does this so rapidly, that
the ideas are all clustered into one, which it calls a
battle.   In like manner, it clusters a series of battles,
and all the intermediate operations, into one idea, and
calls it a campaign ; also several campaigns into one
idea, and calls it a war.   Of the same nature is the
compound idea, which we denote by the word year ;
and the still more compound idea, which we denote
by the word century.   The mind runs over a long
train of ideas, and combines them so closely together, that they assume the appearance of a single
idea ; to which, in the one case, we assign the name
year, in the other, the name century.

In my remembrance of George III., addressing
the two Houses of Parliament, there is, first of all,
the mere idea, or simple apprehension ; the conception
as it is sometimes called, of the objects.   There is
combined with this, to make it memory, my idea of
my having seen and heard those objects.   And this
combination is so close, that it is not in my power to
separate them.   I cannot have the idea of George
III. ; his person and attitude, the paper he held in his
hand, the sound of his voice while reading from it,
the throne, the apartment, the audience ; without
having the other idea along with it, that of my
having been a witness of the scene.

Now, in this last-mentioned part of the compound,
it is easy to perceive two important elements ; *the
idea of my present self*, the remembering self ; and *the
idea of my past self*, the remembered or witnessing
self.   These two ideas stand at the two ends of a
portion of my being ; that is, of a series of my states

of consciousness. That series consists of the successive states of my consciousness, intervening between the moment of perception, or the past moment, and the moment of memory, or the present moment. What happens at the moment of memory? The mind runs back from that moment to the moment of perception. That is to say, it runs over the intervening states of consciousness, called up by association. But " to run over a number of states of consciousness, called up by association," is but another mode of saying, that " we associate them ;" and in this case we associate them so rapidly and closely, that they run, as it were, into a single point of consciousness, to which the name MEMORY is assigned.

If this explanation of the case in which we remember sensations is understood, the explanation of the case in which we remember ideas cannot occasion much of difficulty. I have a lively recollection of Polyphemus's cave, and the actions of Ulysses and the Cyclops, as described by Homer. In this recollection there is, first of all, the ideas, or simple conceptions of the objects and acts ; and along with these ideas, and so closely combined as not to be separable, the idea of my having formerly had those same ideas. And this idea of my having formerly had those ideas, is a very complicated idea ; including the idea of myself of the present moment remembering, and that of myself of the past moment conceiving ; and the whole series of the states of consciousness, which intervened between myself remembering, and myself conceiving.

If we contemplate forgetfulness, not memory, we shall see how completely the account of it confirms the account we have just rendered of memory. Every case of forgetfulness, is a case of weakened, or extinct, association. Some years ago, I could repeat a certain discourse with accuracy and ease, from beginning to end; attempting it, the other day, I was unable to repeat more than a few sentences. The reason is obvious. The last of the words and ideas which occurred to me failed to suggest the following; that is to say, the association which formerly existed between them was dissolved.

A remarkable piece of natural scenery, composed of mountains, woods, rivers, lakes, ocean, flocks, herds, cultivated fields, gay cottages, and splendid palaces, of which I had a lively recollection many years ago, presents itself to me now very much faded : in other words, a great variety of the circumstances, which make up the detail and minute features of the scene, were formerly remembered by me, but are now forgotten. And how forgotten ? The manner is obvious. The greater features, which I still remember, had formerly the power of calling up the smaller along with them, and the whole scene was revived; the association gradually declining, the great objects have no longer the power to excite the idea of the small; and they are therefore gone from me for ever.

There are things of which I have so entirely lost the recollection, that it never can be revived. The meaning is, that the associations which were formed between the ideas of them, and other ideas, are so completely dissolved, that none of my present ideas has the power of exciting them.

It is observable, that sensations have a stronger power to excite recollections than is possessed by ideas.[92] A man, after an absence of many years, revisits the scenes of his infancy : a variety of circumstances crowd into his memory, which, but for the scene before him, would never have been remembered again. These are the circumstances between which, and the perception of the pristine objects, the association is not yet dissolved. There are other circumstances, without number, which (the association being completely dissolved) not even that perception can revive, and which never can be remembered more.

We have seen that there are two cases of memory ; that in which sensations are remembered, and that in which ideas.

It is said, that there are men, who, by often telling a mendacious story as true, come at last to believe it to be true. When this happens, the fact is, that a case of the memory of *ideas*, comes to be mistaken for a case of the memory of *sensations*.

How did the man know at first that it was a fictitious story ; and how did he afterwards lose that knowledge ?

He knew, at first, by certain associations ; he lost his knowledge, by losing those associations, and ac-

---

[92] This is for no other reason than the superior intensity or impressiveness of the actual as compared with the ideal. Although as a rule, the sensation has a greater hold of the mind, than the corresponding idea, there are exceptions. An idea may sometimes be accompanied with an intensity of mental occupation and excitement, surpassing the reality : what we have looked at with indifference when it occurred, may take on an extraordinary importance in the retrospect ; in which case its power of resuscitating collateral circumstances will be far greater than the power of the original sensation.—*B.*

quiring others in their stead. When he first told the
story, the circumstances related called up to him the
idea of himself fabricating the story. This was the
memory of the fabrication. In repeating the story as
real, the idea of himself fabricating the story is hurried
over rapidly ; the idea of himself as actor in the story
is dwelt upon with great emphasis. In continued repetitions, the first circumstance being attended to as
little as possible, the association of it grows weaker
and weaker ; the other circumstance engrossing the
attention, the association of it grows stronger and
stronger ; till the weaker is at last wholly overpowered
by the stronger, and ceases to have any effect.

In delirium, madness, and dreams, men believe that
what they only imagine, they hear, see, and do. This
so far agrees with the case of forgetfulness, just explained, that, in both, there is a mistake of ideas for
sensations ; but, in the case of memory, it is a mistake
of past ideas for past sensations ; in delirium, madness,
and dreaming, it is a mistake of present ideas for
present sensations.

How men in sound memory distinguish the ideas
remembered, from sensations remembered, and know
that the one is not the other, seems to be accounted
for by the difference of the things themselves. A
sensation is different from an idea, only because it is
felt to be different ; and being felt to be different, and
known to be different, are not two things, but one
and the same thing. I have a sensation ; I have an
idea : if these two are distinguishable in the having,
it is likely that the copy of the sensation should be
distinguishable from the revival of the idea, when they
are both brought up by association ; just as when I

have two distinguishable sensations, one, for example, of red, and another of black, the copies of them, when brought up by association, are distinguishable. Besides, the accompaniments of a sensation are always generically different from those of an idea; of course, the associations are generically different. The accompaniments of a sensation, are all the simultaneous *objects of sensation*, together with all those which, to a certain extent, both preceded and followed it. The accompaniments of an idea are not the simultaneous objects of sensation, but *other ideas;* namely, the neighbouring parts, antecedent and consequent, of the mental train. A sensation, therefore, called up by association, and an idea called up by association, are distinguished both by the difference of the two feelings, and the difference of the associated circumstances.

It is observable, that the idea of a *sensation* called up by association, and recognised as the idea of a sensation, is of course a remembrance. The recognition consists in that highly complex idea, consisting of three principal ingredients : 1, the point of consciousness called the remembering self; 2, the point of consciousness called the percipient self; 3, the successive states of consciousness which filled up the interval between these two points.

An *idea* called up by association is not necessarily a remembrance; it is only a remembrance when recognised as having been an idea before. And it is recognised as having been an idea before, by the association of that idea, which connects the self of the present moment with the self of the past moment, the remembering self with the conceiving self : in other

words, the complex idea is made up of those two selfs
and the intermediate states of consciousness.

Another distinction is here suggested between the
memory of a sensation and the memory of an idea.
The complex idea, which needs to be associated with
a mere simple idea, to make it memory, is not the
same in the two cases. There is a specific difference.
The self which is at the antecedent end of the associated train, in the case of sensation, is the sentient
self; that is, seeing or hearing; the self at the antecedent end of the associated train, in the case of
ideas, is not the sentient self, but the conceptive self,
self having an idea. But myself percipient, and myself imagining or conceiving, are two very different
states of consciousness : of course the ideas of these
states of consciousness, or these states revived by
association, are very different ideas.

The simplest of all cases of memory is that of a
sensation immediately past. I have one sensation,
and another sensation ; call them A and B ; and I
recognise them as successive. Every man has experience of the fact, and is familiar with it. But not
every man can tell what it involves.

When a sensation ceases, it is as completely gone,
as if it had never existed.[93] It is, in a certain sense,

---

[93] This is a statement that should be qualified. Looking to
the change of outward situation, we may say that the difference
between the present reality, and the idea of it when past, is
total and vast : the wide prospect before the eyes at one
moment is gone, annihilated, non-existent. But looking at
the mental process, we must use more moderate language.
The mind does not adapt itself to the new situation with the
same rapidity. If one is very much impressed with a picture,

revived again in its idea. But that idea must be
called into existence by something with which it is
associated. In my two sensations, supposed above,
the one antecedent, the other consequent, how do I
recognise the succession; if the first is gone, before
the coming of the second ? It is evident that it
must be by memory. And how by memory ? The
preceding developments seem to make the process
clear. The consciousness of the present moment calls
up the idea of the consciousness of the preceding
moment. The consciousness of the present moment
is not absolutely simple ; for, whether I have a sensation or idea, the idea of what I call Myself is always
inseparably combined with it. The consciousness,
then, of the second of the two moments in the case
supposed, is the sensation combined with the idea of
Myself, which compound I call " Myself Sentient."
This "Self Sentient," in other words sensation B, combined with the idea of self, calls up the idea of
sensation A combined with the idea of self. This we
call MEMORY ; and, there being no intermediate link,
immediate MEMORY. Suppose that, instead of two
sensations, there had been three, A, B, C. In order

---

one maintains the rapt attitude for a little time, after the picture is withdrawn, and only by degrees loses the hold in
favour of the next thing presented to the view. It is possible
for us to resist the solicitation of the actual scene, and to be
absorbed to the full measure of actuality by something no
longer actual. The immediate past may still divide the empire
with the present. The psychological transition follows a
different law from the objective transition : a circumstance in
no small degree involved in the subtle question of our mental
continuity or personal identity.—*B.*

to remember A, it is necessary to step over B. The consciousness of the third moment, namely, "sensation C, united with the idea of self," calls up the idea of "sensation A, united with the idea of self," and along with this the intermediate state of consciousness, "B, with the constant concomitant self." If the intermediate state, B, were not included, the sensation A would appear to have immediately preceded sensation C, and the memory would be inaccurate.

We have thus carried the analysis of Memory to a certain point. We have found the association to consist of three parts ; the remembering self ; the remembered self ; and the train which intervened. Of these three parts, the last has been fully expounded. The recalling of the successive states of consciousness, which composed the intervening train, is an ordinary case of association. The other parts, *the two selfs*, at the two extremities of this train, require further consideration. The self, at the first end, is the remembered self ; the *self which had a sensation, or an idea.* The idea of this self, therefore, consists of two parts : of self, and a sensation, or an idea. The last-mentioned part of this combination, the sensation or idea, needs no explanation ; the first, that which is called self, does. The self at the other extremity of the chain of consciousness, is the *remembering self.* Remembering is associating. The idea of this self, then, is the combination of self with the idea of associating. And here, too, associating needs no explanation ; it is the other part of the combination that does. The analysis, then, of SELF, or the account of what is included in that state of consciousness commonly

called the *idea of personal identity*, is still wanting
to the complete developement of Memory.

Philosophers tell us also, that the idea of *Time* is
included in every act of MEMORY ; and again, that it
is from MEMORY we obtain our idea of *Time*: thus
asserting that the idea of *Time* must precede MEMORY,
and that MEMORY must precede the idea of *Time*.
These contradicting propositions imply that the idea
of Time in the minds of those who make them, is a
very confused idea. Nevertheless, as there can be no
memory without the idea called Time, the exposition
of that idea, likewise, is necessary to the full understanding of Memory.

The idea of personal IDENTITY, and the idea of
TIME, two very remarkable states of consciousness,
will be very carefully examined hereafter. But for
the more ready understanding of what is necessary to
be adduced in expounding those complicated cases of
association, some other phenomena of the mind will
first be explained.

What is to be understood by that BELIEF which is
said to accompany MEMORY, will be seen in the next
chapter, where all the different cases of belief will be
resolved into their elements.[94]

---

[94] The only difficulty about Memory, when once the laws of
Association are understood, is the difference between it and
Imagination ; but this is a difference which will probably long
continue to perplex philosophers. The author finds in Memory,
besides the idea of the fact remembered, two other ideas: "the
idea of my present self, the remembering self, and the idea of
my past self, the remembered or witnessing self :" and a supposed rapid repetition in thought, of the whole of the impressions which I received between the time remembered and the

time of remembering. But (apart from the question whether we really do repeat in thought, however summarily, all this series) explaining memory by Self seems very like explaining a thing by the thing. For what notion of Self can we have, apart from Memory? The fact of remembering, i.e. of having an idea combined with the belief that the corresponding sensation was actually felt *by me*, seems to be the very elementary fact of Self, the origin and foundation of the idea; presupposed in our having the very complex notion of a Self, which is here introduced to explain it. As, however, the author admits that the phenomenon of Belief, and the notions of Time and of Personal Identity, must be taken into account in order to give a complete explanation of Memory, any further remarks had better be deferred until these subjects have been regularly brought under our consideration.—*Ed.*

CHAPTER XI.

BELIEF.

" Cette recherche peut infiniment contribuer aux progrès de l'art de raisonner ; elle le peut seule développer jusques dans ses premiers principes.   En effet, nous ne découvrirons pas une manière sûre de conduire constamment nos pensées ; si nous ne savons pas comment elles se sont formées."—*Condillac, Traité des Sensations*, p. 460.

IT is not easy to treat of MEMORY, BELIEF, and JUDGMENT, separately.   For, in the rude and unskilful manner in which naming has been performed, the states of consciousness, marked by those terms, are not separate and distinct.

Part of that which is named by MEMORY is included under the term BELIEF ; and part of that which is named by JUDGMENT, is also included under the name BELIEF.   BELIEF, therefore, instead of having a distinct province to itself, encroaches on the provinces both of MEMORY, and JUDGMENT ; from which great confusion has arisen.

I take MEMORY first, and JUDGMENT last, from no other principle of arrangement, than facility of exposition ; and I have in this way found it convenient to treat of JUDGMENT as a case of BELIEF.[95]

We begin as usual with the simplest cases. These are, the case of a simple sensation, and the case of a simple idea. When we have a sensation, we BELIEVE that we have it ; when we have an idea, we BELIEVE that we have it.

But, *to have a sensation, and to believe that we have it*, are not distinguishable things. When I say " I have a sensation," and say, " I believe that I have it," I do not express two states of consciousness, but one and the same state. A sensation is a feeling ; but a feeling, and the belief of it are the same thing. The observation applies equally to ideas. When I say I have the idea of the sun, I express the same thing exactly, as when I say, that I believe I have it. The feeling is one, the names, only, are two.[96] [97]

---

[95] How is it possible to treat of Belief without including in it Memory and Judgment ? Memory is a case of belief. In what does Memory differ from Imagination, except in the belief that what it represents did really take place ? Judgment, in its popular acceptation, is Belief resulting from deliberate examination, in other words, Belief grounded on evidence : while in its philosophical sense it is coextensive, if not synonymous, with Belief itself. I do not know how it is possible to distinguish a judgment from any other process of the mind, except by its being an act of belief.—*Ed.*

[96] In the case of a present reality, belief has no place ; it can be introduced only by a fiction or a figure. The believing state comes into operation when something thought of is still remote, and attainable by an intermediate exertion. The fact " I see the sun" is full fruition : the fact that I can see the

It may be alleged that, when I say "I have a sensation," I express the simple feeling, as derived from the outward sense ; but that when I say "I believe I have a sensation," I express two things, the simple sensation, and the association with it, of that remarkable idea, the idea of myself. The association, however, is the same in both cases. As I never have the *sensation* of an object, the sight, for example, of a rose, without associating with it, the idea of position, and also that of unity ; nor the *idea* of such an object, without the same association ; so I never have a sensation, nor the idea of that sensation, without associating with it, the idea of myself. And in both cases, the associations are of that remarkable class, which we have denominated inseparable. It is not in our power to prevent them. Whensoever the perception of the object exists, the idea of its position is sure to exist along with it ; whensoever one of my *sensations* exists, the idea of myself exists along with

---

sun by going out of doors affords scope for belief or disbelief.—*B*.

[97] The difference between Mr. Bain and the author is but in language and classification. It is necessary for the reader of the Analysis to remember, that the author uses the word Belief as the most general term for every species of conviction or assurance ; the assurance of what is before our eyes, as well as of that which we only remember or expect ; of what we know by direct perception, as well as of what we accept on the evidence of testimony or of reasoning : all this we are convinced or persuaded of ; all this, in the author's language, we believe. Mr. Bain, on the other hand, like Sir William Hamilton and many others, restricts the term to those cases of conviction which are short of direct intuition.—*Ed*.

it ; whensoever one of my *ideas* exists, the idea of myself is sure to exist along with it.

In the case, then, of a present sensation, and that of a present idea ; the sensation, and the belief of the sensation ; the idea, and the belief of the idea, are not two things ; they are, in each case, one and the same thing ; a single thing, with a double name.

The several cases of Belief may be considered under three heads : I., Belief in events, real existences; II., Belief in testimony; and III., Belief in the truth of propositions. We shall consider them in their order ; and first, Belief in events, real existences.

I. This is subdivided into three distinct cases : 1, Belief in present events ; 2, Belief in past events ; 3, Belief in future events.

1. Belief in present events, again, is divided into two cases : 1, Belief in immediate existences present to my senses ; 2, Belief in immediate existences not present to my senses.

Belief in existences present to my senses, includes, for one element, belief in my sensations ; and belief in my sensations, as we have just observed, is only another name for having the sensations.

But belief in the external objects, is not simply belief in my present sensations ; it is this, and something more. The something more, is now the object of our inquiry. I see, for example, a rose : my sensation is a sensation of sight ; that of a certain modification of light ; but my belief of the rose is not this ; it is this, and much more.

Besides the sensation of colour, I have, for one thing, the belief of a certain distance, at which I see the rose ; and that of a certain figure, consisting of leaves disposed in a certain form.   I believe that I see this distance and form ; in other words, perceive it by the eye, as immediately as I perceive the colour. Now this last part of the process has been explained by various philosophers.   There is no dispute, or uncertainty, about the matter.   All men admit, that this, one of the most remarkable of all cases of belief, is wholly resolvable into association.[93]   It is acknowledged, that, by the sense of sight, we receive no sensation but that of a certain modification of light. It is equally proved, that the sensations from which our ideas of distance and figure are derived, are sensations of the muscular actions and touch.   How, then, is the Belief generated, that we see extension and figure, as well as colour ?   After the experience the learner has now had in tracing the rapid combinations of the mind, this presents but little difficulty. He knows, that when we are receiving through the muscles and the touch, the sensations which yield us the idea of extension and figure, we are receiving the sensations of sight at the same time, from the same objects.   The sensations of sight, therefore, are asso-

---

[98] "All men admit."   Certainly not all men ; though, at the time when the author wrote, it might be said, with some plausibility, all psychologists.   Unfortunately this can no longer be said : Mr. Samuel Bailey has demanded a rehearing of the question, and has pronounced a strong and reasoned opinion on the contrary side ; and his example has been followed by several other writers: but without, in my opinion, at all weakening the position which since the publication of Berkeley's Essay on Vision, had been almost unanimously maintained by philosophers.—*Ed.*

ciated with the ideas of these tactile and muscular
sensations; and associated in the most perfect possible
manner; because the conjunction is almost invariable,
and of incessant occurrence, during the whole period
of life.   We are perpetually feeling, and seeing, the
same objects, at the same time ; so much so, that our
lives may be said to consist of those sensations in
union ; to consist, at least to a far greater degree, of
this, than of any one other state of consciousness.

This intensity of association, we know, produces
two effects.   One, is to blend the associated feelings
so intimately together, that they no longer appear
many, but one feeling.   The other is, to render
the combination inseparable ; so that if one of the
feelings exist, the others necessarily exist along
with it.

The case of association which we are now considering, brings to view another circumstance, of some
importance in tracing the effects of this great law of
our nature.   It is this: that in any associated cluster,
the idea of sight is almost always the prevalent part.
The visible idea is that which takes the lead, as it
were ; and serves as the suggesting principle to the
rest.   So it happens in the combination of the sensations of colour, with those of extension and figure :
the visible idea stands foremost ; and calls up the rest.
It calls them up also with such intensity, that both
the remarkable cases of association are exemplified.
Whenever we have the sensation of colour, we cannot avoid having the ideas of distance, of extension,
and figure, along with it ; nor can we avoid having
them in such intimate union with the ocular sensation, that they appear to be that sensation itself.

This is the whole of what is ever supposed to be in the case. Of no phenomenon of the human mind is the developement more complete or more important. Our belief that we *see* the shape, and size, and distance of the object we look at, is as perfect as belief in any instance can be. But this belief is nothing more than a case of very close association.

The case of belief by association, any one may illustrate further, for himself, by recollecting some of the commonest cases of optical deception. If we look at a landscape with the naked eye, we believe the several objects before us, the men, the animals, the trees, the houses, the hills, to be at certain distances. If we next look at them through a telescope, they seem as if they were brought near; we have the distinct belief of their proximity, and though a belief immediately corrected by accompanying reflection, it is not only belief, but a belief that we can by no means shake off. We can, after this, invert the telescope, and then we cannot help believing, that the nearest objects are removed to a distance. Now what is it that the telescope performs in these two instances ? It modifies in a certain manner the rays of light to the eye. The rays, proceeding from the objects, are so distributed on the eye, as they would be if the distance of the objects was less, or greater. Instantly we have the belief that it is less or greater; because, the sensation of the eye, by means of the glass, is made to resemble that which it receives, when objects are seen at a smaller or greater distance ; and each of the sensations calls up that idea of distance which is habitually associated with it.

We have thus far proceeded, with some certainty,

in detecting the component parts of that which we call our "belief in the existence of external objects." We have taken account of the sensation from which is derived the visible idea, of the sensations from which are derived the ideas of position, extension, and figure; and we have explained the intimate combination of those two sets of ideas by association. But these, though the leading sensations and ideas, are not the only ones. There are, besides, the sensations from which we derive the idea of resistance, in all its modifications, from that of air, to that of adamant. There are also sensations which are not common to all objects, but peculiar to some; as smell, peculiar to odorous bodies; taste, to sapid; and sound, to sonorous ones.

Now, though the most remarkable case of the associations among those feelings, is that between colour, and extension and figure, they are all blended by association into one idea; which, though in reality a cluster of ideas, affects us in the same manner as if it were a single idea; an idea, the parts of which we detect by an analysis, which it requires some training to be able to make.

With the colour of the rose, the size and figure of the rose,—which are the predominant ideas,—I associate the idea of that modification of hardness and softness, which belongs to the rose; its degree of resistance, in short; also its smell, and its taste. These associations have been formed, as other associations are, by repetition. I have had so uniformly the sight, along with the handling, these, along with the smell, and the taste—of the rose, that they are always called up together, and in the closest combination.

Now then let us ask, what we mean, when we affirm, that the rose exists. In this meaning are undoubtedly included the above sensations, in a certain order. I see the rose on the garden wall, and I affirm that it exists : that is, along with my present sensation, the sight of the rose, I have the ideas of a certain order of other sensations. These are, first, the idea of distance, that is, the idea of the feelings involved in the act of going to the rose : after this, the idea of the feelings in handling it ; then in smelling, then in tasting it ; all springing up by association with the sight of the rose. It is said, we believe we should have these sensations. That is, we have the idea of these sensations inseparably united one with the other, and inseparably united with the idea of ourselves as having them. That this alone constitutes belief, in the remarkable case of the association of extension and figure with the sensations of sight, has already been seen ; that this alone constitutes it, in many other remarkable cases, will be seen as we proceed ; and in no case can it be shewn, that any thing more is included in it.

In my belief, then, of the existence of an object, there is included the belief, that, in such and such circumstances, I should have such and such sensations. Is there any thing more ? It will be answered immediately, yes : for that, along with belief in my sensations as the *effect*, there is belief of something as the *cause ;* and that to the *cause*, not to the *effect*, the name object is appropriated.

This is a case of Belief, which deserves the greatest possible attention. It is acknowledged, on all hands, that we know nothing of objects ; but the sensations we have from them. There is a cause, however, of those sensations, and to that we give the name object : or, rather, there is a cluster of causes, corresponding with the cluster of sensations. Thus, when I see, and handle, and smell, and taste the rose, there is a cause of the sensation red, a cause of the sensation soft, a cause of the sensation round, a cause of the smell, and a cause of the taste ; and all these causes are united in the rose. But what is the rose, beside the colour, the form, and so on ? Not knowing what it is, but supposing it to be something, we invent a name to stand for it. We call it a *substratum*. This substratum, when closely examined, is not distinguishable from Cause. It is the cause of the qualities ; that is, the cause of the causes of our sensations. The association, then, is this. To each of the sensations we have from a particular object, we annex in our imagination, a cause ; and to these several causes we annex a cause, common to all, and mark it with the name substratum.

This curious case of association we now proceed to develop. The word cause, means the antecedent of a consequent, where the connection is constant. This has been established on such perfect evidence, that it is a received principle of philosophy. More of the evidence of this important principle will appear as we go on. Here we shall take the proposition for granted.

Not only are we, during the whole period of our lives, witnesses of an incessant train of events ; that is, of antecedents and consequents, between which, for the greater part, the order is constant; but these constant conjunctions are, of all things in the world, what we are the most deeply interested in observing; for, on the knowledge of them, all our power of obtaining good and avoiding evil depends. From this, it necessarily follows, that between none of our ideas is the association more intimate and intense, than between antecedent and consequent, in the order of events. Whenever we perceive an event, the mind instantly flies to its antecedent. I hear words in the street; *event:* some one, of course, is making them; *antecedent.* My house is broken, and my goods are gone; *event:* a thief has taken them; *antecedent.* This is that remarkable case of association, in which the combination is *inseparable;* a case of so much importance in explaining some of the more mysterious phenomena of thought. Other instances of this remarkable phenomenon, to which we have already had occasion to advert, are, the sight of an object, and the ideas of its distance, its extension, and figure; the idea of colour, and the idea of extension; the idea of an object, and the idea of position and unity; the idea of one of my sensations, and the idea of myself. In no instance is this inseparable association more perfect, or its consequences more important, than in that between an event, and its antecedent. We cannot think of the one without thinking of the other. The two ideas are forced upon us at the same time; and by no effort of ours can they be disjoined. So necessarily, from the first moment of experience, are we employed in observing the constant conjunctions of events; and so deeply are we interested, in looking out for, and knowing the constant antecedent of every event, that the association becomes part of our being. The perception, or the idea, of an event, instantly brings up the idea of its constant antecedent ; definite and clear, if the antecedent is known; and indefinite and obscure, if it is unknown. Still, the idea of an event, of a change, without the idea of its cause, is impossible. That a cause means, and can mean nothing to the human mind, but constant antecedent, is no longer a point in dispute.[99]

Of this remarkable case of association, that which we call " Our Belief in External Objects" is one of the most remarkable instances. Of the sensations, of sight, of handling, of smell, of taste, which I have from a rose, each is an event ; with each of those events, I associate the idea of a constant antecedent, a cause ; that cause unknown, but furnished with a name, by which it may be spoken of, namely, quality ; the quality of red, the cause of the sensation red ; the qualities of consistence, extension and figure, the causes of the sensations of handling ; the qualities of smell and taste, the causes of the sensations of smell and taste. Such is one part of the process of association in this case. Another is that by which the ideas of those sensations are so intimately united, as to appear not several ideas, but one idea, the idea of a rose. We have now two steps of association ; that

---

[99] Here again the author takes too sanguine a view of the amount of agreement hitherto attained among metaphysical philosophers. " That a cause means, and can mean, nothing to the human mind but constant antecedent" is so far from being " no longer a point in dispute" that it is denied with vehemence by a large numerical majority of philosophers ; and its denial is perhaps the principal badge of one of the two schools which at this, as at most other times, bisect the philosophical world—the intuitional school and the experiential—*Ed.*

of the several sensations into one idea; that of the several sensations each with a separate cause. But we do not stop here; for, as in a train of events, consisting of several links, A, B, C, D, and so on, though C is the antecedent or cause of D, it is itself the consequent or effect of B ; and in all cases, when we have found the cause of any particular event, we have still to find out what was the cause of that cause. In this manner, when our habit of association has carried us from our sensations to the causes of them, the same habit carries us still farther.

As each of our sensations must have a cause, to which, as unknown, we give the name quality; so each of those qualities must have a cause. And as the ideas of a number of sensations, concomitant in a certain way, are combined into a single idea; as that of rose, that of apple ; the unity, which is thus given to the effects, is of course transferred to the supposed causes, called qualities : they are referred to a common cause. To this supposed cause of supposed causes, we give a name; and that name is the word *Substratum*.

It is obvious, that there is no reason for stopping at this *Substratum ;* for, as the sensation suggested the quality, the quality the substratum, the substratum as properly leads to another antecedent, another substratum, and so on, from substratum to substratum, without end. These inseparable associations, however, rarely go beyond a single step, hardly ever beyond two. The Barbarian, in accounting for the support of the earth, placed it on the back of a great elephant, and the great elephant on the back of a great tortoise ; but neither himself, nor those whom he instructed, were carried by their habits of association any farther.[100]

Such appear to be the elements included in our belief of the existence of objects acting on our senses. We have next to unfold the case of belief in the present existence of objects not acting on our senses.

Of this Belief, there are two cases : 1, Belief in the existence of objects, which we have not perceived ; 2, Belief in the existence of objects, which we have perceived.

The first of these, is a case of the Belief in testimony ; which is to be explained hereafter. What we are to examine at the present moment, then, is, our Belief in the existence of objects, which, though not

---

[100] It is a question worth considering, why that demand for a cause of everything, which has led to the invention of so many fabulous or fictitious causes, so generally stops short at the first step, without going on to imagine a cause of the cause. But this is quite in the ordinary course of human proceedings. It is no more than we should expect, that these frivolous speculations should be subject to the same limitations as reasonable ones. Even in the region of positive facts—in the explaining of phenomena by real, not imaginary, causes— the first semblance of an explanation generally suffices to satisfy the curiosity which prompts the inquiry. The things men first care to inquire about are those which meet their senses, and among which they live ; of these they feel curious as to the origin, and look out for a cause, even if it be but an abstraction. But the cause once found, or imagined, and the familiar fact no longer perplexing them with the feeling of an unsolved enigma, they do not, unless unusually possessed by the speculative spirit, occupy their minds with the unfamiliar antecedent sufficiently to be troubled respecting it with any of the corresponding perplexity.—*Ed.*

now present to our senses, have been so at a previous time. Thus, I believe in the present existence of St. Paul's, which I saw this morning.

In tracing the elements of this Belief, it is obvious, in the first place, that in so far as it is founded on my past sensations, memory is concerned in it. But Memory relates to *past* events, Belief in which, is to be considered under a following head. This part of the development, therefore, we postpone.

But, beside Memory, what other element is concerned in it? There is evidently an anticipation of the future. In believing that St. Paul's exists, I believe, that whenever I am in the same situation, in which I had perception of it before, I shall have perception of it again. But this Belief in future events, is also a case, which remains to be considered under a subsequent head. This, therefore, is another part of the development, which must be postponed.

I not only believe, that I shall see St. Paul's, when I am again in St. Paul's Churchyard; but I believe, I should see it if I were in St. Paul's Churchyard this instant. This, too, is also a case, of the anticipation of the future from the past, and will come to be considered under the subsequent head already referred to.

Besides these cases, the only one which remains to be considered, is, my Belief that, if any creature whose senses are analogous to my own, is now in St. Paul's Churchyard, it has the present sensation of that edifice.

My belief in the sensations of other creatures, is wholly derived from my experience of my own sensations. The question is, How it is derived. That it is an inference from similitude, will not be denied. But what is an inference from similitude ?

I have no direct knowledge of any feelings but my own. How is it, then, that I proceed ?

There are certain things which I consider as marks or signs of sensations in other creatures. The Belief follows the signs, and with a force, not exceeded in any other instance. But the interpretation of signs is wholly a case of association, as the extraordinary phenomena of language abundantly testify.[101] And whenever the association, between the sign and the

---

[101] This is true in by far the greater number of instances. Nevertheless, there are some of the signs of feeling that have an intrinsic efficacy, on very manifest grounds. While the meanings of the smile and the frown could have been reversed, if the association had been the other way, there is an obvious suitability in the harsh stunning tones of the voice to signify anger and to inspire dread, and a like suitability in the gentle tones to convey affection and kindly feeling. We might have contracted the opposing associations, had the facts been so arranged, just as in times of peace, we associate joy with deafening salvos of artillery; and as loud, sharp-pealing laughter serves in the expression of agreeable feeling. But there is a gain of effect when the signs employed are such as to chime in, by intrinsic efficacy, with the associated meanings. On this coincidence depend the refinements of elocution, oratory, and stage display.—B.

[The fact here brought to notice by Mr. Bain is, that certain of the natural expressions of emotion have a kind of analogy to the emotions they express, which makes an opening for an instinctive interpretation of them, independently of experience. But if this be so (and there can be little doubt that it is so) the suggestion takes place by resemblance, and therefore still by association.—Ed.]

thing signified, is sufficiently strong to become inseparable, it is belief. Thus, rude and ignorant people, to whom the existence of but one language is known, believe the name by which they have always called an object to belong to it naturally, as much as its shape, its colour, or its smell.* Thus the perceptions of sight, mere signs of distance, magnitude, and figure, are followed by belief of the sight of them. And it is remarked, with philosophical accuracy, by Condillac, that if our constitution had been such, as to give us, instead of a different modification of sight, a different modification of smell, with each variety of distance, extension, and figure, we should have smelt distance, extension and figure, in the same manner as, by the actual conformation of our organs, we see them. Nor can we doubt the truth of the ingenious observation of Diderot, that if we had seen, and heard, and tasted, and smelt, at the ends of our fingers, in the same manner as we feel, we should have believed our mind to be in the fingers, as we now believe it to be in the head.

The process of our Belief in this case, then, is evidently, as follows. Our sensations are inseparably associated with the idea of our bodies. A man cannot think of his body without thinking of it as sensitive. As he cannot think of his own body without thinking of it as sensitive, so he cannot think of another man's

---

* " It has been very justly remarked, that if all men had uniformly spoken the same language, in every part of the world, it would be difficult for us not to think [believe] that there is a natural connexion of our ideas, and the words which we use to denote them."—*Brown, Lectures*, ii. p. 80. 2d ed.

body, which is like it, without thinking of it as sensitive. It is evident that the association of sensitiveness, is more close with certain parts of the complex idea, our bodies, than with other parts ; because the association equally follows the idea of horse, of dog, of fowl, and even of fish, and insect : and it will be found, I think, that there is nothing with which it is so peculiarly united as the idea of spontaneous motion. What is the reason we do not believe there is any sensation in the most curiously-organized vegetable ; while we uniformly believe there is in the polypus, and the microscopic insect ? Nothing whatsoever can be discovered, but a strong association which exists in the one case, and is wanting in the other. And this is one of the most decisive of all experiments to prove the real nature of Belief.

As, then, our belief in the sensations of other creatures is derived wholly from the inseparable association between our own sensations and the idea of our own bodies, it is apparent that the case in which I believe other creatures to be immediately percipient of objects, of which I believe that I myself should be percipient if I were so situated as they are, resolves itself ultimately into this particular case of my belief in certain conditional sensations of my own. This, again, as we have seen above, resolves itself into that other important law of Belief, which we are shortly to consider, the anticipation of the future from the past.

2. It comes next in order, that we notice our Belief in past existences ; that is, our present belief, that something had a present existence at a previous time.

Much of the development of this case is included in the expositions already afforded. Our present belief, means, for one thing, a present idea ; our pre-sent belief of an existence, the idea of something existing. Of what associations the idea of something existing consists, we have just ascertained. Our pre-sent belief of a past existence, then, consists of our present idea of something existing, and the assign-ment of it to a previous time.

There are two cases of this assignment ; one, in which the thing in question had been the object of our senses ; another, in which it had not been the object of our senses.

When the thing, the existence of which we assign to a previous time, had been the object of our senses, and when the time to which we assign it is the time when it had so been the object of our senses, the whole is Memory. In this case, Memory, and Belief, are but two names for the same thing. Memory is, in fact, a case of Belief. Belief is a general word. Memory is one of the species included under it. Memory is the belief of a past existence, as Sensation is the belief of a present existence. When I say, that I remember the burning of Drury-Lane Theatre ; the *remembering* the event, and *believing* the event, are not distinguish-able feelings, they are one and the same feeling, which we have two ways of naming. The associa-tions included in Memory we have already endeavoured to trace. It is a case of that indissoluble connexion of ideas which we have found in the preceding article to constitute belief in present existences. When I remember the burning of Drury-Lane Theatre, what happens ? We can mark the following parts of the process. First, the idea of that event is called up by association ; in other words, the copies of the sensations I then had, closely combined by association. Next, the idea of the sensations calls up the idea of myself as sentient ; and that, so instantly and forcibly, that it is altogether out of my power to separate them. But when the idea of a sensation forces upon me, whether I will or no, the idea of myself as that of which it was the sensation, I remember the sensation. It is in this process that memory consists ; and the memory is the Belief. No obscurity rests on any part of this process, except the idea of *self*, which is reserved for future analysis. The fact, in the mean time, is indisputable ; that, when the idea of a sensation, which I have formerly had, is revived in me by association, if it calls up in close association the idea of myself, there is memory; if it does not call up that idea, there is not memory ; if it calls up the idea of myself, it calls up the idea of that train of states of consciousness which constitutes the thread of my existence ; if it does not call up the idea of myself, it does not call up the idea of that train, but some other idea. A sensation remembered, then, is a sensation placed, by association, as the consequent of one feeling and the antecedent of another, in that train of feelings which constitute the existence of a conscious being. All this will be more evident, when what is included in the notion of Personal Identity is fully evolved.

The case of Belief in past existences which have not been the object of our senses, resolves itself into the belief, either of testimony, or of the uniformity of the laws of nature ; both of which will, after a few intervening expositions, be fully explained.

3. The process which we denote by the words,

" Belief in future events," deserves, on account of its importance, to be very carefully considered. That it is a complex process, will very speedily appear. Our endeavour shall be to resolve it into its elements ; in doing which, we shall see whether it consists wholly of the elements with which we have now become familiar, or whether it is necessary to admit the existence of something else.

I believe that, to-morrow, the light of day will be spread over England ; that the tide will ebb and flow at London-bridge; that men, and houses, and waggons, and carriages, will be seen in the streets of this metropolis ; that ships will sail, and coaches arrive ; that shops will be opened for their customers, manufactories for their workmen, and that the Exchange will, at a certain hour, be crowded with merchants. Now, in all this, what is involved ?

First of all, in the Belief of any future event, there is, of course, involved the idea of the event. It will be immediately understood, from what has been already adduced, that there can be no Belief in any existence, without an idea of that existence. If I believe in the light of day to-morrow, I must have an, idea of it ; if I believe in the flux and reflux of the water at London-bridge, I must have ideas of those several objects ; and so of all other things.

In the next place ; as it has already been shewn, that we cannot call up any idea by willing it ; and that none of our ideas comes into existence but by association ; the idea which forms the fundamental part of Belief, is produced by association. Ideas and association, then, are necessary parts of belief.

But there can be no idea of the future ; because, strictly speaking, the future is a nonentity. Of nothing there can be no idea. It is true we can have an idea of that which never existed, and which we do not suppose ever will exist, as of a centaur ; but this is a composition of the ideas of things which have existed. We can conceive a sea of milk, because we have seen a sea, and milk ; a mountain of gold, because we have seen a mountain, and gold. In the same manner we proceed with what we call the future. The ideas which I have recently enumerated as parts of my belief of to-morrow ; the light of day, the throng in the streets, the motion of the tide at London-bridge, are all ideas of the past. The general fact, indeed, is not a matter of dispute. Our idea of the future, and our idea of the past, is the same ; with this difference, that it is accompanied with retrospection in the one case, anticipation in the other. What retrospection is, we have already examined. It is Memory. What Anticipation is, we are now to inquire ; and to that end it is necessary to recall, distinctly, some important facts which we have already established.

The fundamental law of association is, that when two things have been frequently found together, we never perceive or think of the one without thinking of the other. If the visible idea of a rose occurs to me, the idea of its smell occurs along with it ; if the idea of the sound of a drum occurs to me, the visible idea of that instrument occurs along with it.

Of these habitual conjunctions, there is none with which we are more incessantly occupied, from the first moment of our existence to the last, and in which we are more deeply interested, than that of antecedent and consequent.   Of course there is none between the ideas of which the association is more intimate and intense.

In fact, our whole lives are but a series of changes ; that is, of antecedents and consequents.   The conjunction, therefore, is incessant ; and, of course, the union of the ideas perfectly inseparable.   We can no more have the idea of an event without having the ideas of its antecedent and it consequents, than we can have the idea and not have it at the same time. It is utterly impossible for me to have the visible idea of a rose, without the idea of its having grown from the ground, which is its antecedent ; it is utterly impossible for me to have the idea of it without the ideas of its consistence, its smell, its gravity, and so on, which are its consequents.

Of the numerous antecedents and consequents, forming the matter of our experience, some are constant, some are not.   Of course the strength of the association follows the frequency.   The crow is seen flying as frequently from east to west, as from west to east ; from north to south, as from south to north ; there is, therefore, no association between the flight of the crow and any particular direction.   Not so with the motion of a stone let go in the air : that takes one direction constantly.   The order of antecedent and consequent is here invariable.   The association of the ideas, therefore, is fixed and inseparable. I can no more have the idea of a stone let go in the air, and not have the idea of its dropping to the ground, than I can have the idea of the stone, and not have it, at the same time.[102]

Where the sequence of two events is merely casual, it passes speedily away from the mind; because it is not associated with the idea of any thing in which we are interested. The things in which we are interested, are the immediate antecedents of our pleasures and pains, and the ideas of them are all inseparably associated with constant conjunctions. The association of the ideas of a constant antecedent and consequent, therefore, has both causes of strength, the interesting nature of the ideas, and the frequency of conjunction, both at their greatest height. It follows, that it should be the most potent and inseparable of all the combinations in the mind of man.

As we are thus incessantly, and thus intensely, occupied with cases of constant conjunction, while cases of casual conjunction pass slightly over the mind, and

---

[102] The theory maintained so powerfully and with such high intellectual resources by the author, that Belief is but an inseparable association, will be examined at length in a note at the end of the chapter. Meanwhile let it be remarked, that the case of supposed inseparable association given in this passage, requires to be qualified in the statement. We cannot, indeed, think of a stone let go in the air, without having the idea of its falling; but this association is not so strictly inseparable as to disable us from having the contrary idea. There are analogies in our experience which enable us without difficulty to form the imagination of a stone suspended in the air. The case appears to be one in which we can conceive both opposites, falling and not falling; the incompatible images not, of course, combining, but alternating in the mind. Which of the two carries belief with it, depends on what is termed Evidence.—*Ed.*

quickly vanish from our consciousness, every event calls up the idea of a constant antecedent. The association is so strong, that the combination is necessary and irresistible. It often enough, indeed, happens, that we do not know the constant antecedent of an event. But never does it fail to call up the idea of such an antecedent; and so inseparably, that we can as little have and not have the idea of an event, as we can have the idea of it, and not have the idea of an inseparable antecedent along with it.—Ignorant, sometimes, of the constant antecedents of such and such events, we find them out by subsequent inquiry. Those cases of successful investigation still further strengthen the association. All that we call good, and all that we call evil, depend so entirely upon those constant conjunctions, that we are necessarily under the strongest stimulus to find them out, and to trace them with greater and greater accuracy. Thus we very often find a constancy of sequence, in which we acquiesce for a while; but after a time discover, that though constant, indeed, it is not immediate; for, that between the event and supposed antecedent, several antecedents intervene. At first we regard the ignition of the gunpowder, as the immediate antecedent of the motion of the ball. Better instructed, we find that a curious process intervenes. The constancy of the sequence is always more certain, the more nearly immediate the antecedent is. And so frequent is our detection of antecedents, more immediate than those which we have just observed, that an association is formed between the idea of every antecedent, and that of another antecedent, as yet unknown, intermediate between it and the consequent which we know.   In no sequence do we ever feel satisfied that we have discovered all.   We see a spark ignite the gunpowder, we see one billiard-ball impel another. Though we consider these as constant antecedents and consequents, the idea of something intermediate is irresistibly conjoined.   To this, though wholly unknown, we annex a name, that we may be able to speak of it.   The name we have invented for this purpose is POWER.   Thus, we conceive that it is not the spark which ignites the gunpowder, but the *power* of the spark; it is not one billiard-ball that moves the other, but the *power* of the ball.   The Power, in this case, is a *supposed* consequent of the moving ball, and antecedent of the moved; and so in all other cases.

But the idea of an event does not call up the idea of its constant antecedent in closer and more intense association, than it calls up that of its consequent or consequents.   I cannot have the idea of water, without the idea of its mobility, its weight, and other obvious properties.   I cannot have the idea of rhubarb, without the idea of its nauseous taste, and other familiar properties.   I cannot have the idea of the stroke of a sword upon the head of a man, without the idea of a wound inflicted on his head.   I cannot have the idea of my falling from a ship into the middle of the sea, without the idea of my being drowned.   I cannot have the idea of my falling from the top of a high tower, without having the idea of my being killed by the fall.   If I have the first idea, the second forces itself upon me.   The union has in it all that I mark by the word necessity; a sequence, constant, immediate, and inevitable.

This great law of our nature shews to us immediately in what manner our idea of the future is generated. Night has regularly been followed by morning. The idea of night is followed by that of morning; the idea of morning is followed by that of the events of the morning, the gradual increase of light, the occupations of men, the movements of animals and objects, and all their several successions from morning till night. This is the idea of to-morrow; to this succeeds another to-morrow; and an indefinite number of these to-morrows makes up the complex idea of futurity.

But I am told, that we have not only the idea of to-morrow, but the belief of to-morrow; and I am asked what that belief is. I answer, that you have not only the idea of to-morrow, but have it *inseparably.* It will also appear, that wherever the name belief is applied, there is a case of the indissoluble association of ideas. It will further appear, that, in instances without number, the name belief is applied to a mere case of indissoluble association; and no instance can be adduced in which any thing besides an indissoluble association can be shewn in belief.[103] It would seem

---

[103] The case that is most thoroughly opposed to the theory of indissoluble association is our belief in the Uniformity of Nature. Our overweening tendency to anticipate the future from the past is shown prior to all association; the first effect of experience is to abridge and modify a strong primitive urgency. There is, no doubt, a certain stage when association co-operates to justify the believing state. After our headlong instinct has, by a series of reverses, been humbled and toned down, and after we have discovered that the uniformity, at first imposed by the mind upon everything, applies to some things and not to others, we are confirmed by our experience

to follow from this, with abundant evidence, that the whole of my notion of to-morrow, belief included, is nothing but a case of the inevitable sequence of ideas.

This, however, is a part of our constitution, of so much importance, that it must be scrutinized with more than ordinary minuteness.

Our first assertion was, that in every instance of belief, there is indissoluble association of the ideas. We shall confine our examples, for the present, to that case of belief which is more immediately under our examination; belief in the future.   I believe, that if I put my finger in the flame of the candle, I shall feel the pain of burning.   I believe, that if a stone is dropped in the air, it will fall to the ground.   It is evident that in these cases, the belief consists in uniting two events, the antecedent, and the consequent.   There are in it, therefore, two ideas, that of the antecedent, and that of the consequent, and the union of those ideas.   The previous illustrations have abundantly shewn us, in what manner the two ideas are united by association, and *indissolubly* united.   *These* ingredients in the belief are all indisputable.   That there is any *other* cannot be shewn.

---

in the cases where the uniformity prevails; and the intellectual growth of association counts for a small part of the believing impetus.   Still, the efficacy of experience is perhaps negative rather than positive; it saves, in certain cases, the primitive force of anticipation from the attacks made upon it in the other cases where it is contradicted by the facts.   It does not make belief, it conserves a pre-existing belief. (See Note at the end of the chapter.)—*B*.

Our second assertion was, that cases of indissoluble association, admitted by all men to be this, and nothing more, are acknowledged as Belief. The facts (which any one may call to recollection), in proof of this assertion, deserve the greatest attention ; they shew the mode of investigating some of the most latent combinations of the human mind.

No fact is more instructive, in this respect, than one, which more than once we have had occasion to make use of; the association of the ideas of distance, extension, and figure, with the sensations of sight. I open my eyes; I see the tables, and chairs, the floor, the door, the walls of my room, and the books ranged upon the walls; some of these things at one distance, some at another; some of one shape and size, some of another. My belief is, that I see all those particulars. Yet the fact is, that I see nothing but certain modifications of light ;[104] and that all my belief of seeing the distance, the size, and figure of those several objects, is nothing but the close and *inseparable* association of the ideas of other senses. There is no room for even a surmise that there is any thing in this case but the immediate blending of the ideas of one sense with the sensations of another, derived from the constant concomitance of the sensations themselves.

The case of hearing is perfectly analogous, though

---

[104] More guardedly—' I am affected by certain modifications of light.' The word ' see' carries with it too much meaning for the case put. There is also the omission, previously remarked on, to take into account the mental elements due to the movements of the eye—visible forms, magnitudes, and movements.—*B.*

not so exact. I am in the dark; I hear the voice of
one man, and say he is behind me; of another, and
say he is before me; of another, he is on my right
hand; another, on my left. I hear the sound of a
carriage, and say, it is at one distance; the sound of a
trumpet, and say, it is at another. In these cases I
believe, not only that I hear a sound, but the sound
of a man's voice, the sound of a carriage, the sound of
a trumpet. Yet no one imagines that my belief is
any thing, in these cases, but the close association of
the sounds with the ideas of the objects. I believe,
not only that I hear the sound of a man's voice, but
that I hear it behind me, or before me; on my right
hand, or on my left; at this distance, or at that. The
indisputable fact, in the mean time, is, that I hear
only a modification of sound, and that the position
and distance, which I believe I hear, are nothing but
ideas of other senses, closely associated with those
modifications of sound. That this state of consciousness, the result of an immediate irresistible association,
is identical with the state which we name belief, is
proved by a very remarkable experiment, the deception produced by ventriloquism. A man acquires the
art of forming that peculiar modification of sound,
which would come from this or that position, different
from the position he is in; in other words, the sound
which is associated, not with the idea of the position
he is in, but that of another position. The sound is
heard; the association takes place; we cannot help
believing that the sound proceeds from a certain place,
though we know, that is, immediately recognize, that
it proceeds from another.

We must not be afraid of tediousness, while we

adduce instances in superabundance, to prove that indissoluble association (in one remarkable class of its cases, which, on account of their vast importance, it is found expedient to distinguish by a particular name) is that state of consciousness, to which we have given the name of BELIEF.

We are all of us familiar with that particular feeling, which is produced, when we have turned ourselves round with velocity several times. We BELIEVE that the world is turning round.

The sound of bells, opposed by the wind, appears to be farther off. A person speaking through a trumpet appears to be nearer. Our experience is, that sounds decrease by distance. A sound is decreased by opposition of the wind ; the idea of distance is associated ; and the association being inseparable, it is belief. A sound is increased by issuing from a trumpet, the idea of proximity is associated, and the association being indissoluble, it is belief.

In passing, on board of ship, another ship at sea, we believe that she has all the motion, we none : though we may be sailing rapidly before the wind, she making hardly any progress against it.

When we have been making a journey in a stage coach, or a voyage in a ship, we believe, for some time after leaving the vehicle, that still we are feeling its motion; more especially just as we are falling asleep.

Nobody doubts, that these, and similar cases of belief, which are very numerous, are all to be resolved into pure association. What the associations are, we leave to be traced by the learner ; so many repetitions of the same process, though a useful exercise to him, would be very tedious here.

The Belief which takes place in Dreaming merits
great attention in this part of our inquiry. No belief
is stronger than that which we experience in dreaming. Our belief of some of the frightful objects,
which occur to us, is such, as to extort from us loud
cries ; and to throw us into such tremors and bodily
agitations, as the greatest real dangers would fail in
producing. Not less intense is our belief in the
pleasurable objects which occur to us in dreams ; nor
are the agitations which they produce in our bodies
much less surprising. Yet there is hardly any difference of opinion about the real nature of the phenomena which occur in dreaming. That our dreams
are mere currents of ideas, following one another by
association ; not controlled, as in our waking hours,
by sensations and will ; is the substance of every
theory of dreaming. The belief, therefore, which
occurs in dreaming, is merely a case of association ;
and hence it follows that nothing more is necessary to
account for Belief.

There is not a more decisive instance of the identity
of Belief and Association, than the dread of ghosts,
felt in the dark, by persons who possess, in its greatest
strength, the habitual disbelief of their existence.
That dread implies belief, and an uncontrollable belief,
we need not stay to prove. When the persons of
whom we speak feel the dread of ghosts in the dark,
the meaning is, that the idea of ghost is irresistibly
called up by the sensation of darkness. There is here,
indisputably, a case of indissoluble association ; nor
can it be shewn that there is anything else. In the
dark, when this strong association is produced, there

is the belief; not in the dark, when the association is not produced, there is no belief.[105]

Few men, except those who are accustomed to it, could walk on the ridge of a high house without falling down. Yet the same men could walk with perfect security, on similar footing, placed on the ground. What is the interpretation of this contrariety? Fear, we are told, is that which makes the

---

[105] The efficacy of association is not correctly explained in this instance. The influence of Terror on belief is unquestionably great; but the operation is more complicated than the description given of it in the text. Terror, in the first place, is a depressing passion, and as such impairs the tone of mind suited to the anticipation of coming good, or in the obverse, increases the tendency to anticipate coming evil. In the next place, it is the state most liable to a morbid fixed idea of evil, calamity, or danger. Thirdly, we have learned in the course of our lives to expect numerous possible calamities; and are maintained in serenity only by seeing clearly a good way before us, so as to be sure that none of these possible evils are approaching. Darkness extinguishes for the time our assuring fore-sight, and thus, by removing a counteractive, leaves us a prey to all the demons of mischief. Fourthly, the emotion of Terror has its corresponding imaginations, into which are taken up with avidity all the suggestions of danger that have ever been made to us, including ghosts, hobgoblins, and other agents of calamity, when we have not natural vigour or express training to set them at nought.

The mere fact communicated to us, on a few occasions, that ghosts appear in the dark, and sometimes perform dreadful deeds, would not by force of association alone produce all that un-nerving effect which children and weak or superstitious persons are liable to when, at night, exposed in a lonely place, or passing a churchyard.—B.

inexperienced person fall. But fear implies belief. There is nothing, however, in the case, but the intense association of the idea of his falling, with his sight of the position in which he is placed. In some persons this idea is so easily excited, that they cannot look down from even a very moderate height, without feeling giddy, as they call it ; that is, without having the apprehension ; in other words, the belief, of falling.*

---

* The same account, in substance, of some of the last of these phenomena, is given by Dr. Brown ; and it may aid the conceptions of the learner, to observe the different modes of exposition used by two different writers.

"There can be no question, that he who travels in the same carriage, with the same external appearances of every kind by which a robber could be tempted or terrified, will be in equal danger of attack, whether he carry with him little of which he can be plundered, or such a booty as would impoverish him if it were lost. But there can be no question also, that though the probabilities of danger be the same, the fear of attack would, in these two cases, be very different; that, in the one case, he would laugh at the ridiculous terror of any one who journeyed with him, and expressed much alarm at the approach of evening ; and that, in the other case, his own eye would watch suspiciously every horseman who approached, and would feel a sort of relief when he observed him pass carelessly and quietly along at a considerable distance behind.

"That the fear, as a mere emotion, should be more intense, according to the greatness of the object, might indeed be expected ; and if this were all, there would be nothing wonderful in the state of mind which I have now described. But there is not merely a greater intensity of fear, there is, in spite of reflection, a greater belief of probability of attack. There is fear, in short, and fear to which we readily yield, when otherwise all fear would have seemed absurd. The reason of this it will

From these illustrations, then, it does not appear that the anticipation of the future from the past, contains in it any thing peculiar. So far from standing by itself, a phenomenon *sui generis;* it is included in one of the most general of the laws of the human mind. When Professor Stewart, therefore, and other writers, erect it into an object of wonder, a prodigy, a thing falling within no general rule; and tell us they can refer it to nothing but instinct; which is as much

---

perhaps not be difficult for you to discover, if you remember the explanations formerly given by me, of some analogous phenomena. The loss of what is valuable in itself, is of course a great affliction. The slightest possibility of such an evil makes the evil itself occur to us, as an object of conception, though not at first, perhaps, as an object of what can be termed fear. Its very greatness, however, makes it, when thus conceived, dwell longer in the mind; and it cannot dwell long, even as a mere conception, without exciting, by the common influence of suggestion, the different states of mind, associated with the conception of any great evil; of which associate or resulting states, in such circumstances, fear is one of the most constant and prominent. The fear is thus readily excited as an associate feeling; and when the fear has once been excited, as a mere associate feeling, it continues to be still more readily suggested again, at every moment, by the objects that suggested it, and with the perception or conception of which it has recently co-existed. There is a remarkable analogy to this process, in the phenomena of giddiness, to which I have before more than once alluded. Whether the height on which we stand, be elevated only a few feet, or have beneath it a precipitous abyss of a thousand fathoms, our footing, if all other circumstances be the same, is in itself equally sure. Yet though we look down, without any fear, on the gentle slope, in the one case, we shrink back in the other case with painful dismay. The lively conception of the evil which we should

as to say, to nothing at all ; the term instinct, in all
cases, being a name for nothing but our own ignorance ; they only confess their failure in tracing the
phenomena of the mind to the grand comprehensive
law of association ; to the admission of which, in its
full extent, they seem to have had a most unaccount-
able, and a most unphilosophical aversion ;—as if
that simplicity, according to which one law is found

---

suffer in a fall down the dreadful descent, which is very naturally suggested by the mere sight of the precipice, suggests and
keeps before us the images of horror in such a fall, and thus
indirectly the emotions of fear, that are the natural accompaniments of such images, and that but for those images never
would have arisen. We know well, on reflection, that it is a
footing of the firmest rock, perhaps, on which we stand, but in
spite of reflection, we feel, at least, at every other moment, as
if this very rock itself were crumbling or sinking beneath us.
In this case, as in the case of the traveller, the liveliness of the
mere conception of evil that may be suffered, gives a sort of
temporary probability to that which would seem to have little
likelihood in itself, and which derives thus from mere imagination all the terror that is falsely embodied by the mind in
things that exist around.

"It is not, then, any simple ratio of probabilities which
regulates the rise of our hopes and fears, but of these combined with the magnitude or insignificance of the objects."—
Lectures on the Philosophy of the Human Mind. Lecture
LXV., vol. iii., p. 345—347. 2d ed.

Notwithstanding this, the ideas of Dr. Brown were so far
from being clear and settled on the subject, that in the same
work, Lecture VI., v. i., p. 115, he *seems* to affirm, that belief
cannot be accounted for by association, but must be referred
to instinct; though it is necessary to use the word *seems*,
for it is not absolutely certain that he does not by *instinct*
mean association.—(*Author's Note.*)

included in a higher, and that in a yet higher, till we arrive at a few which seem to include the whole, were not as much to be expected in the world of mind, as in the world of matter.*

We have now then explored those states of Consciousness which we call Belief in existences;—Belief in present existences; Belief in past existences; and Belief in future existences. We have seen that, in the most simple cases, Belief consists in sensation alone, or ideas alone; in the more complicated cases, in sensation, ideas, and association, combined; and in no case of belief has any other ingredient been found.

In accounting for belief in present objects not acting on the senses,—it appeared, that a certain anticipation of the future entered, for so much, into this compound phenomenon; the explanation of which part we were obliged to leave, till the anticipa-

---

* Locke, at a period subsequent to the publication of his Essay, seems to have become more sensible of the importance of association. These are his words :—" I think I shall make some other additions to be put into your Latin translation, and particularly concerning the connexion of ideas, which has not, that I know, been hitherto considered, and has, I guess, a greater influence upon our minds, than is usually taken notice of."—*Locke, Lett. to Molineux, April 26th,* 1695.—(*Author's Note.*)

[When Locke wrote the letter here quoted, he had not yet written the chapter of his Essay which treats of the Association of Ideas. That chapter did not appear in the original edition, but was first inserted in the fourth, published in 1690. The intention, therefore, which he expressed to Molineux, has received its fulfilment; and the passage quoted further on in the text, is part of the " addition" which he contemplated.—*Ed.*]

tion of the future had undergone investigation. We
have now seen that this part, as well as the rest,
consists of association. The whole, therefore, of this
case of belief, is now resolved into association.

Mr. Locke, whose expositions of any of our mental
phenomena are almost always instructive, even when
they stop short of being complete, has given the above
account of belief precisely, in one remarkable and very
extensive class of cases ; those in which the belief is
unfounded ; which he denominates prejudices.

" There is," he says,* " scarce any one that does not
observe something that seems odd to him, and is in
itself really extravagant in the opinions, reasonings,
and actions, of other men.

" This sort of unreasonableness is usually imputed
to education and prejudice ; and for the most part
truly enough ; though that reaches not the bottom of
the disease, nor shews distinctly enough whence it
rises, or wherein it lies.

" Education is often rightly assigned for the cause ;
and prejudice is a good general name for the thing
itself ; but yet, I think, he ought to look a little
farther, who would trace this sort of madness to the
root it springs from, and so explain it, as to shew
whence this flaw has its original in very sober and
rational minds, and wherein it consists."

Mr. Locke affords the explanation, which he
thought necessary to be given, and proceeds as
follows.

" Some of our ideas have a natural correspondence
and connexion one with another. It is the office, and

---

* Essay on the Human Understanding, B. II., Ch. 33.

excellence, of our reason, to trace these; and hold them together in that union and correspondence, which is founded in their peculiar beings.

" Besides this, there is another connexion of ideas, wholly owing to chance or custom.   Ideas, that in themselves are not at all of kin, come to be so united in some men's minds, that it is very hard to separate them.   They always keep in company ; and the one no sooner at any time comes into the understanding, but its associate appears with it.   And if they are more than two which are thus united, the whole gang, always inseparable, shew themselves together.

" This wrong connexion, in our minds, of ideas in themselves loose and independent of one another, has such an influence, and is of so great force, to set us awry in our actions, as well moral as natural, passions, reasonings, and notions themselves ; that perhaps there is not any one thing that deserves more to be looked after.

" The ideas of goblins and sprights have really no more to do with darkness than light.   Yet let but a foolish maid inculcate these often in the mind of a child, and raise them there together, possibly he shall never be able to separate them again so long as he lives; but darkness shall ever afterwards bring with it those frightful ideas, and they shall be so joined, that he can no more bear the one than the other.

" A man receives a sensible injury from another ; thinks on the man and that action over and over ; and by ruminating on them strongly, or much in his mind, so cements those two ideas together, that he makes them almost one."

" When this combination is settled, and while it

lasts, it is not in the power of reason to help us and relieve us from the effects of it. Ideas in our minds, when they are there, will operate according to their nature and circumstances. And, here, we see the cause why Time cures certain affections, which reason, though in the right, has not power over, nor is able, against them, to prevail with those who are apt to hearken to it in other cases."

After adducing various examples, to illustrate the effect of these associations, in producing both vicious affections, and absurd opinions, he thus concludes :

" That which thus captivates our reasons, and leads men blindfold from common sense, will, when examined, be found to be what we are speaking of. Some independent ideas of no alliance to one another, are, by education, custom, and the constant din of their party, so coupled in their minds, that they always appear there together ; and they can no more separate them in their thoughts, than if there were but one idea ; and they operate as if they were so. This gives sense to jargon, demonstration to absurdity, and consistency to nonsense ; and is the foundation of the greatest, I had almost said, of all, the errors in the world."

Such is Mr. Locke's account of wrong belief, or error. But wrong belief is belief, no less than right belief. Wrong belief, according to Locke, arises from a bad association of ideas. Right belief, then, arises from a right association of ideas ; and this also was evidently Locke's opinion. It is, thus, association, in both cases ; only, in the case of wrong belief, the association is between ideas which ought not to be associated; in the case of right belief, it is between ideas which ought to be associated. In the case of right belief, the association is between ideas which, in the language of Locke, "have a natural correspondence and connexion one with another:" in the case of wrong belief, it is between ideas, which "in themselves are not at all of kin, and are joined only by chance or custom." The ideas of the colour, shape, and smell of the rose; the ideas of the spark falling on the gunpowder, and the explosion,—are the sorts of ideas which are understood, by Mr. Locke, as having "a natural correspondence and connexion." Ideas, such as those of darkness, with those of ghosts; of the miseries suffered at school, with the reading of books,—are the kind which he describes as "not of kin, and united in the mind only by chance or custom." This, put into accurate language, means, that when the ideas are connected in conformity with the connexions of things, the belief is right belief; when the ideas are connected not in conformity with the connexions of things, the belief is wrong belief. The ideas, however, which are connected in conformity with the connexions among things, are connected by custom, as much as those which are connected not in conformity with those connexions. And the custom which unites them in conformity, is by far the most common of the two. It is, in fact, the regular, the ordinary, the standard custom, the other only constitutes the exceptions.

II. We have divided Belief into, 1, Belief in events, real existences; 2, Belief in testimony; 3, Belief in the truth of propositions.

Though this division, suggested by the ordinary

forms of language, appeared to me didactically convenient, it is not logically correct. The expression,
"Belief in testimony," is elliptical. When completed, it becomes "Belief in events upon the evidence of testimony." There are then, in reality, only
two kinds of Belief; 1. Belief in events or real existences; and 2. Belief in the truth of Propositions.
But Belief in events or real existences has two foundations; 1. our own experience; 2. the testimony of
others. The first of these we have examined, the
consideration of the second remains.

When we begin, however, to look at the second of
these foundations more closely, it soon appears, that
it is not in reality distinct from the first. For what
is testimony? It is itself an event. When we believe any thing, therefore, in consequence of testimony,
we only believe one event in consequence of another.
But this is the general account of our belief in events.
It is the union of the ideas, of an antecedent, and a
consequent, by a strong association. I believe it is
one o'clock. Why? I have just heard the clock
strike. *Striking of the clock*, antecedent; *one o'clock*,
consequent; the *second* closely associated with the
first. The striking of the clock is in fact a species of
testimony. What does it testify? Not one event,
but an infinite number of events, of which the term
"one o'clock" is the name. At every instant in the
course of the day, a number of events are taking
place, some known to us, some unknown. The term
one o'clock, is the name of those which take place at
a particular point of the diurnal revolution. I believe
in them all upon the testimony of the clock. Why?
From experience;—every one would directly and

truly reply. I have found the events constantly, or at least very regularly, conjoined. From junction of the events, junction of the ideas; in other words, belief.

If proof, only, were wanted, this would suffice. For the purpose, however, of instruction, tuition, training,—a more minute developement of this important case of belief seems too useful to be dispensed with, notwithstanding the tediousness which so many repetitions of the same process are too likely to produce.

The watchman calling the hour, is a case of human testimony. That the account of our belief, in this case, is precisely the same as that in the case of the striking of the clock, it is wholly unnecessary to prove. But if our reliance on testimony in one case is pure experience, it may reasonably be inferred that it is so in all.

The forms of expression, which we apply to this case of belief, are very misleading. We say, "we believe a man," or, "we believe his testimony." "We attach belief to the man," or, "to his testimony." In these expressions, the name belief is applied to the wrong event; to the antecedent, instead of the consequent. What we mean to say is, that we believe the consequent, the thing testified, not the antecedent, the speaking of the words. The words the man uses, are, to us, sensations : belief that he uses the words, is not what is meant by belief in his testimony. The same form of expression is perfectly absurd, when applied to other cases. We never say that we believe the flame of the candle, or we attach belief to the flame of the candle, when we mean to state the belief, that a finger will be burnt if it is put into the flame ;

we never say we believe the spark, when we mean to express our belief of an explosion when the spark falls upon the gunpowder.

The only question, then, is, in what manner the words of the testifier, the antecedent, come to be so united with the idea of the thing testified, as to constitute belief. And surely there is no difficulty here, either in conceiving, or admitting the process. Words call up ideas by association, solely. There is no natural connexion between them. The manner in which words are applied to events, I know most intimately by my own experience. I am constantly, and, from the first moment I could use them, have constantly been, employing words in exact conformity with events. Cases occur in which I do not, but they are few in comparison with those in which I do. It has been justly remarked, that the greatest of liars speak truth a thousand times for once that they utter falsehood. The connexion between the use of words, and the idea of conformable existence, is, of course, established into one of the strongest associations of the human mind. In other words, belief, in consequence of testimony, is, strictly, a case of association. That we interpret other men's actions by our own, no one doubts ; and that we do so entirely by association has already been proved.

In accounting for belief in past existences where it is not memory, we have found that it is resolvable into belief in testimony, and in the uniformity of the laws of nature ; and the explanation of this we postponed till the cases of belief in testimony, and in the uniformity of the laws of nature, should be expounded. A few words will now suffice to connect the explanations formerly given with those which have now been presented.

The two cases, as we have seen, resolve themselves into one ; as belief in testimony is but a case of the anticipation of the future from the past ; and belief in the uniformity of the laws of nature is but another name for the same thing.

I believe the event called the fire of London, upon testimony. I believe that the stranger who now passes before my window, had a father and mother, was once an infant, then a boy, next a youth, then a man, and that he has been nourished by food from his birth ; all this, from my belief in the uniformity of the laws of nature.

After the preceding developments, it is surely unnecessary to be minute in the analysis of these instances. I have had experience, of a constant series of antecedents and consequents, in the life of man ; generation, birth, childhood, and so on ; as I have had of pain from putting my finger in the flame. A corresponding association is formed. If the sight of a stranger calls up the idea of his origin and progress to manhood, the ordinary train of antecedents and consequents is called up ; nor is it possible for me to prevent it. The association is indissoluble, and is one of the cases classed under the name of Belief.

The explanation is still more simple of my belief in the fire of London. The testimony in this case is of that sort which I have always experienced to be conformable to the event. Between such testimony, and the idea of the event testified, I have, therefore, an indissoluble association. The testimony uniformly calls up the idea of the reality of the event, so closely, that I cannot disjoin them. But the idea, irresistibly forced upon me, of a real event, is Belief.[106]

It is in this way that belief in History is to be explained. It is because I cannot resist the evidence; in other words, because the testimony calls up irresistibly the idea, that I believe in the battle of Marathon, in the existence of the Thirty Tyrants of Athens, in that of Socrates, Plato, and so on.

III. We come now to what we set out with stating as the third case of Belief; but which, as there are in reality but two kinds of belief, is, strictly speaking, the second,—I mean Belief in the Truth of Propositions; in other words, verbal truths.

The process by which this Belief is generated, or rather the combination wherein it consists, has, by the writers on Logic, at least those in the Latin and modern languages, been called JUDGMENT. This, however, is a restricted sense. In general, the word Judgment is used with more latitude. Sometimes it is nearly co-extensive with Belief, excluding hardly

---

[106] The belief in Testimony is derived from the primary credulity of the mind, in certain instances left intact under the wear and tear of adverse experience. Hardly any fact of the human mind is better attested than the primitive disposition to receive all testimony with unflinching credence. It never occurs to the child to question any statement made to it, until some positive force on the side of scepticism has been developed. Gradually we find that certain testimonies are inconsistent with fact; we have, therefore, to go through a long education in discriminating the good testimonies from the bad. To the one class, we adhere with the primitive force of conviction that in the other class has been shaken and worn away by the shocks of repeated contradictions.—*B.*

any but the sudden and momentary cases. We should hardly say, A man *judges* there are ghosts, who is afraid of them in the dark, but firmly believes his fear is unfounded; or *judges* the surgeon to be noxious, whom he shudders at the sight of, from recollection of the terrible operation which he underwent at his hands. In all cases, however, either of deliberate or well-founded belief, we seem to apply the word judgment without impropriety. I judge that I see the light, that I hear the drum, that my friend speaks the truth, that water is flowing in the Ganges.

All Belief of events, except that of our present sensations, and ideas, consists, as we have seen, in the combination of the ideas of an antecedent and a consequent. The antecedent is sometimes simple, sometimes compound, being not one event, but various events taken together. These varieties in the antecedent constitute two distinguishable cases of belief. The last of them, that in which the antecedent is complex, is that in which the term judgment is most commonly applied. Again, there are two cases of complex antecedent, one, in which all the events are concordant; another, in which they are not all concordant. It is to this last case that the term judgment is most peculiarly applied. Thus, it is not usual to say, that we judge we shall feel pain if we put a finger in the flame of the candle. But if we saw two armies ready to engage, one of which had considerable superiority, both in numbers and discipline, we should say we judge that it would gain the victory. This case, however, of belief, where the antecedent is complex, will receive additional illustration farther on.

We have now to consider the case of Belief in the truth of propositions.

PROPOSITION is a name for that form of words which makes a predication. What Predication is, of what parts it consists, what end it serves, and into how many kinds it is divided, we have already explained. It remains to inquire what is meant by the TRUTH of a Predication, and what state of consciousness it is which is called the recognition or BELIEF of that truth.

Predication consists essentially in the application of two marks to the same thing. Of this there are two remarkable cases; one, That in which two names of equal extent are applied to the same thing; another, That in which two names, one of less, another of greater extent, are applied to the same thing. The questions we have to resolve are, What is meant by truth in these cases; and, What is the process, or complex state of consciousness, which is called assent to the proposition, or belief of it.

And, first, as to the case of two names of equal extent, as when we say, "Man is a rational animal;" here the two names are, "Man," and "Rational animal," exactly equivalent; so that "man" is the name of whatever "rational animal" is the name of; and "rational animal" is the name of whatever "man" is the name of. This coincidence of the names is all that is meant by the truth of the proposition; and my recognition of that coincidence is another name for my belief in its truth.

Now, how is it that I recognise two names as equivalent? About this, there will not be any dispute. I recognise the meaning of names solely by association. I recognise that such a name is of such a meaning, by association. I recognise that another name is of the same signification, by the same means. That I recognise the meaning of the last, whatever it is, by association, cannot be doubted, because it is by this that the meaning of every word is established. There is, however, another fact ; that I recognise the meaning in the second case, as the same with the meaning in the first case. What is the process of this recognition ? The word " Man " is the mark or name of a certain cluster of ideas. A certain cluster of ideas I know to be what it is, by having it. Having it, and knowing it, are two names for the same thing. Having it, and having it again, is knowing it, and knowing it again ; and that is the recognition of its sameness. It is a single name for the two states of consciousness. This, then, is all that is meant by our belief in the truth of a proposition, the terms of which are convertible, or of equal extent.

When of two names, applied to the same thing, one is of less, another of greater extent, the association is more complex ; but in that is all the difference. Thus, when I believe the truth of the proposition, " Man is an animal," the meaning of the name " man" is called up by association, and the meaning of the name "animal" is called up by association. Thus far is certain. But there is something further. I recognise, that "animal" is a name of whatever " man" is a name of, and also of more. In having the meaning of the name " man" called up by association, that is, in having the ideas, I recognise that " man" is a name of James, and John, and Homer, and Socrates, and all the individuals of the class.

This is pure association. In having the meaning of the name "animal" called up by association, I recognise that it is a name of James, and John, and all the individuals of the same class, as well as of all the individuals of other classes; and this is all that is meant by my Belief in the truth of the proposition. Man is the name of one cluster of ideas; animal is the name of a cluster, including both this and other clusters. The latter cluster is partly the same with, and partly different from, the former. But having two clusters, and knowing them to be two, is not two things, but one and the same thing; knowing them in the case in which I call them same, and knowing them in the case in which I call them different, is still having them, having them such as they are, and nothing besides. In this second case also, of the belief of a proposition, there is, therefore, nothing but ideas, and association.

We have already shewn, under the head NAMING, when explaining the purpose to which Predication is subservient, that all Predication may be strictly considered as of one kind, the application to the same thing of another name of greater extent; in other words, that Predication by what Logicians call the Difference, Property, or Accident of a thing, may be reduced to Predication by the Genus or Species; but as there is a seeming difference in these latter cases, a short illustration of them will probably be useful.

Thus, suppose I say, "Man is rational," and that I choose to expound it, without the aid of the word animal, understood; what is there in the case? The word "man," marks a certain cluster of ideas. "Rational" marks a portion of that cluster. In the cluster marked "man," the cluster marked "rational" is included. To recognise this, is also called believing the proposition. But to have one cluster of ideas, and know what it is ; then another, and know what it is, is merely to have the two clusters. To have a second cluster, part of a first, and to know that it is a part of the first, is the same thing.

The peculiar property of that class of words to which "Rational" belongs, must here be recollected. They are the *connotative* class. Beside marking something peculiarly, they mark something else in conjunction ; and this last, they are said to *connote.* Thus the word "rational," beside the part of the cluster, man, which it peculiarly marks, connotes, or marks in conjunction with it, the part included under the word animal.

It will be easy to apply the same explanation to all other cases. I say, the rose is red. Red is a connotative term, distinctively marking the idea of red. The idea of red is part of the cluster I mark by the word rose.

Take a more obscure expression ; Fire burns. It is very obvious, that in the cluster of ideas I mark by the word fire, the idea of burning is included. To have the idea, "fire," therefore, and the idea "burning," called up by the names standing in predication,—is to believe the proposition.

The Predications, "Virtue is lovely," "Vice is hateful," and the like, all admit of a similar exposition. In the cluster "virtue," the idea of loveliness is included; in the cluster "vice," that of hatefulness is included. Such propositions, therefore, merely say, that what is a part of a thing, is a part of it. The two words call up the two ideas; and to have two ideas, one a part of another, and know that one is part of another, is not two things, but one and the same thing. To have the idea of rose, and the idea of red, and to know that red makes part of rose, is not two things, but one and the same thing.

Little more is necessary to explain this case of Belief in the truth of Propositions. Propositions are formed, either of general names, or particular names, that is, names of individuals. Propositions consisting of general names are by far the most numerous class, and by far the most important. The preceding exposition embraces them all. They are all merely verbal; and the Belief is nothing more than recognition of the coincidence, entire or partial, of two general names.

The case of Propositions formed of particular names, is different, and yet remains to be explained. " Mr. Brougham made a speech in the House of Commons on such a day." The Predicate, " making a speech in the House of Commons," is neither general, so as to include the subject, " Mr. Brougham," as in a species ; nor is the cluster of ideas, marked by the predicate, included in the cluster marked by the subject, as a part in its whole. The proposition marks a case either of experience, or of testimony. If I heard the speech, the proposition is an expression of the Memory of an event; Mr. Brougham, antecedent, and making a speech, consequent ; and the Belief of the Proposition, is another name for the Memory of the Event. If I did not hear it, Belief of the proposition, is belief in the testimony of those who say they heard it.

As all propositions relating to individual objects are, after this manner, marks either of other men's testimony, or of our own experience, what belief, in these cases, is, has already been explained.

Propositions relating to individuals may be expressions either of past, or of future events. Belief in past events, upon our own experience, is memory; upon other men's experience, is Belief in testimony; both of them resolved into association. Belief in future events, is the inseparable association of like consequents with like antecedents.

It is not deemed necessary to unfold these associations. It has been already done. It seems enough, if they are indicated here.[107] [108]

---

[107] The author has treated in different places several questions intimately allied. These are:—

1. The essential nature of the state of mind called Belief, the mental region whence it springs, or the phenomena that it is to be classed with—whether Intellect, Feeling, or Will.

2. The belief in the Past, and the belief in the Future; in what respect they differ from belief in the present. Inseparably implicated with this, if not prior to it and preparatory to it, is the difference between ideas of Memory and ideas of Imagination.

3. The nature of our continuous Mental Life, or Identity; or what is meant by the Permanent Existence of Mind.

The chapters on Memory, and on Belief, and the section on Identity (Chap. XIV.), all treat of these questions, and contain profound original views on them all.

As regards the nature of Belief, he errs (in common with philosophers generally) in calling it a purely intellectual state. The consequence is to mar the explanations of the other points.

He displays a remarkably just and penetrating insight into the differences between Memory and Imagination, and between our own self or Personality, and the personality of others; whereby he fully accounts for what is involved in Personal Identity.

To resolve the difficult phenomenon of Belief in Memory, of which the belief in the Permanent Existence of Mind is merely another expression, we must clear up the foundations of the state of Belief in general.

The prevailing error on this subject consists in regarding Belief as mainly a fact of the Intellect, with a certain participation of the feelings. The usual assumption is, that if a thing is conceived in a sufficiently vivid manner, or if two things are strongly associated in the mind, the state of belief is thereby induced.

A better clue to the real character of belief is found in the connexion between faith and works. The practical test applied to a man's belief in a certain matter, is his acting upon it. A capitalist's trust in the soundness of a project, is shown by his investing his money.

In its essential character, Belief is a phase of our active nature,—otherwise called the Will. Our tendency to action, under special circumstances, assumes the aspect called belief; as in other circumstances, it takes the form of Desire, and in a third situation, appears as Intention; none of all which are essential to voluntary action in its typical form.

The state of belief or of disbelief is manifested when we are pursuing an Intermediate End. In masticating something sweet, the fruition of the sweetness sustains the energy of the will; there is no case for the believing function properly so called, any more than there is for Desire, Deliberation, or Resolution. In going to a shop to purchase sweets, there is wanting this immediate support of the voluntary energies; the support grows out of an ideal state, the anticipation of the pleasure of sweetness; this state is called Belief. We are said to believe that what we are going to purchase will impart an agreeable sensation. The state is one of degree; we may have a strong belief or a weak belief; the strength having no other measure than the energy of pursuit inspired by it. If we follow the intermediate end with all the avidity shown when we are realizing the full actuality, we have the perfect belief that what we aim at will bring the actuality. If, as often happens, we are less strongly moved than this, our belief is said to be so much weaker. Or, the comparison may be expressed in a different form. If two things are connected together as means and end ; and, if on attaining the means, we feel as much elated (the end being something good) as if we had attained the end, then our belief is at the maximum ; if less so, our belief is less. The promise made to us by one man gives all the satisfaction of the performance ; the promise of another man gives a very inferior satisfaction ; the comparison measures our comparative trust in the two men.

So far the matter seems plain. The real difficulty lies in assigning the mental origin or seat of the believing attitude. The view to be maintained in this note is, that the state of belief is identical with the activity or active disposition of the system, at the moment, and with reference to the thing believed. Now as there are various sources of activity, so there are various sources of belief. These are :—First, Spontaneous Activity, or the mere overflow of energy growing out of the nourishment of the system. Secondly, Voluntary Action, in the strictest signification, or the pursuit of pleasure and the avoidance of pain, under the stimulus of one or other of those states. Thirdly, the tendency of an Idea to become an Actuality, the degree of which tendency accords with the mental excitement attending the idea. Fourthly, the addition of Habit to all the others. Under every one of these four influences, we are prompted to act, and in the same degree disposed to believe. Not one of the tendencies is any guarantee for the truth of the thing believed ; which is a somewhat grave consequence of the theory contended for.

It will now be asked, in what acceptation, or under what circumstances, does mere activity, no matter how arising, constitute, or amount to, the state of belief. There are certain situations where the two states are on the surface the same ; the fact of going along a certain road implicates the belief that a certain destination will be reached. Nay, farther, a great amount of natural energy would sustain a vigorous pace, irrespective of the certainty of the goal ; while physical feebleness would make one languid, however strong the evidence of the distant good. All this shows that the mental state called believing is of little use without the active power, and that the active power readily simulates the believing state, and makes it seem greater or less than it really is.

Let us now look at the question in another light. Having a natural fund of activity, with or without the addition of proper volitional impulses, we commence moving in a certain direction, no matter what. We are not necessarily urged to move by any prospect of what we are to find. We act somehow, because action comes upon us ; and we take the consequences. Suppose, however, that we encounter a check, in the form of obstruction or pain : this stops our activity in that direction, but does not prevent it from taking another direction. Now, not only does the actual pain arrest our steps, but also the memory of it (if the circumstances are such as to give it a certain degree of strength) is deterring. We avoid that track in the future. With reference to it there is generated a voluntary activity and determination, containing the whole essence of belief; namely, the avoidance of a certain course, *before* the point of actual pain. This is, to all intents, belief on the side of prospective harm. Equally important is it to remark, that wherever we have not experienced any positive harm, check, or obstruction, we go on as readily and as energetically as ever. Our natural state of mind, our primitive start is tantamount to full confidence or belief; which is broken in upon, only after hostile experiences ; by these, the original condition of implicit confidence is impaired ; and in certain directions, a positive anticipation or determining volition and belief of evil is substituted. An animal born on a summer morning, and able to move about from the first, would not anticipate darkness ; it would behave exactly as if light were never intermitted. A few days' experience makes an inroad on this primitive confidence, and modifies it to suit the facts.

Let us add another circumstance to the foregoing example. Instead of the individual moving blindly on, by mere exuberance or spontaneity, let the movement be favoured by bringing pleasure at every step.   In this situation, the whole force of the spontaneity at the time, and the whole force of the will (proportioned to the stimulating pleasure), sustain the movements at a more energetic pace ; and there is nothing to counter-work them.   The mental disposition is now equivalent to the highest confidence ; there is no hesitation, no distrust, nothing but exuberant unrestrained activity. Neither scepticism as to the unknown future, nor a demand for assurance that the present condition is to last, is entertained by the mind.   The individual does not inquire whether a precipice, or the lair of a devouring beast be on the track.   The ignorance is at once bliss and belief.

Here, then, we may discern the original tendency of the mind as regards belief.   To have gone a certain way with safety and with fruition, is an ample inducement to continue in that particular path.   The situation contains all that is meant by full and unbounded confidence that the future and the distant will be exactly what the present is.   The primary impulse of every creature is at the farthest remove from a procedure according to Logic.   In the beginning, confidence is at its maximum ; the course of education is towards abating, and narrowing it, so as to adapt it to the fact of things.   Every check is a lesson, destroying to a certain extent the over-vaulting assurance of the natural mind, and planting a belief in evil, at points where originally flourished only the illimitable belief in good.

There is thus wrapped up, in the active impulses of our nature, a power of credulity leading us habitually to overstep the experience of the present.   We believe in the uniformity of nature with a vengeance.   We have to be schooled by adverse encounters, before we are brought within the limits of the real uniformity. Our natural credulity is equally excessive on the side of evil and on the side of good ; where we have once suffered we expect always to suffer. In short, whereas to the logician, there is a great gulf between the present and future, the known and the unknown, to the natural man there is not even a break. The early mind laughs the logician's gulf to scorn. All that science or logic has been able to do is to show that at certain points the assumed uniformity is broken in upon ; tractable and docile minds learn to respect these exceptions ; but wherever an outlet exists, with no barrier, or express prohibition, not only is that outlet followed, it is followed with all the pristine impetuosity of our active nature. The ordinary logician, over-awed by this force of determination, seldom asserts the principle that the present can by no logical implication contain the future, that a present reality holds in itself no warrant for the unknown past, the distant or the future. The barrier that this principle would interpose to our inferences has been carried by assault ; the gordian knot is always cut with the sword.

From the point of view of the logician, a serious difficulty attaches to our belief in the Memory of the Past ; the psychologist can refer it to the incontinence of the mind, in moving freely away from the present in any direction, in accounting the step next to be entered upon in the absence of impediment, as secure as the one actually taken.

Let us consider the process first by reverting to the antici-- pation of the Future. That a state of things now begun will continue indefinitely is what the mind not only assumes but proceeds upon with a vehemence proportioned to its active endowments and dispositions, until admonished to the contrary by the experience of being checked. All instruction, or corroborating information, is dispensed with at the outset : the burden is always laid upon the denier. Of this tendency of the mind the examples are innumerable, and need only to be indicated. In the default of evidence, on one side, and against what ought to be considered evidence on the other side, we believe that, as we feel now, so we shall feel always. And our belief is not simply giving the benefit of any doubt there may be to the opinion we incline to; it is a powerful impulse, counteracted only by a severe and protracted discipline. Also, we believe that our own feelings exactly measure and correspond to the feelings of every one else. Very few are ever brought within the limits of the actual truth on this point; the primitive tendency is not met by a sufficient force of the requisite education.

It is the belief in the future that offers the simplest and clearest example of the mind's tendency to overleap the actual, to see no hard line between the present and the remote. The belief in nature's continuance and uniformity has always been in excess. From the very same tendency springs whatever belief we have of our own continued existence and identity. We make light of the difference between the conceived future and the real present.

Much more subtlety attends the Belief in Memory: the meaning of which is, that, whereas certain ideas recalled by memory are, *de facto*, ideas, or mental elements of a kind that imagination might furnish, they yet carry with them the belief that they represent what was once actuality, like any sensation of the present moment.

Let us first apply to the case the overweening instinct now fully set forth. To the logician, the past, however recent, is divided by a deep gulf from the present: the idea and the actuality can never be interchanged. It is not so with the mind following its native disposition. I have a present sensation of thirst; in that present consciousness, I have the highest attainable assurance; my action upon it is unhesitating and complete. Let that sensation, however, pass away for one minute, and there remains only the idea which, as a mere idea, by virtue of its recency, may be at its maximum strength. The point now to be explained is, why I believe not merely that I have the idea, which as a fact of present consciousness I am entitled to believe to the utmost, but that the idea was lately a full actuality as much as is my present state of satisfied sensation. The explanation seems to be, that we really make no radical difference between a present and a proximate past;

the march of the mind is to and fro, into the past and the
future, with the same tendency to act out both, as to act out
the present, assuming always the absence of a positive check or
break. Such is the inveterate persistence of the natural
activity, that the belief in the thirst when present (shown by
action in accordance therewith) has a continuing efficacy
second only to the belief in a still present state. At the
moment of actual thirst, I, in the absence of corrective influences, (and to some degree in spite of these), would be disposed to believe that I always was, and always would be thirsty.
The satisfaction that has followed reduces that belief to a fraction of its former state ; and my utmost licence of assumption
would be, (in the absence of contradictory beliefs) that all my
past has been one thirst. The fact is, that, in these moments,
when I give full licence to the sway of the idea, by voluntarily
remitting attention to my new experience, that idea may swell
out into a pitch of mental occupation hardly distinguishable
from the real presence ; in which case, my past self and my
present self are, as it were, one and indivisible ; they are freely
interchanged ; the actual consciousness compounds and contains them both.

Going another step backward, let us consider the state prior
to the thirst ; say a consciousness of heat and muscular
fatigue. What proof have I that these penultimate states were
present in continuity of time and in immediate precedence to
the thirst, and are not vagaries of imagination, nor drawn from
a remote past, accidentally revived ? There seems no other
evidence than that already given regarding the proximate
state. In surrendering our mind to the idea still remaining,
and so imparting a momentary quasi-reality to the state, we
have an experience possessing the characteristic features of
present reality.

Another consideration has to be mentioned. The state of
transition from reality to reality is a distinct and unmistakeable
experience. The transition from a present sensation of thirst
to a present sensation of satisfied thirst is a march of its own
kind—unique and explicit. There are in it attendant circum-

stances, not to be confounded with the transition from a present to a past across a break. The recent and proximate state of thirst has a mode of continuity, a setting in contact with the present, such as did not belong to the thirst of yesterday, and still less belongs to the idea of the narrated thirst of another person. No sensation ever comes to us alone, or without a group of collaterals; and the collaterals of the formerly actual, and of the ideal never an actual, are wholly different. (This point has been well illustrated in the text, Chap. X. on Memory). The peculiar link whereby a present actual passes out of actuality into proximate actuality, when it is barely deprived of existence in the real, is a fact that remains and attaches to everything that has been actual; and the unbroken sequence of these is our past life of actuality, clearly marked out from every aggregate of ideas indiscriminately culled and united in a whole of imagination. This last process has its own distinctive collaterals; it is accompanied by numerous shocks of agreement in difference, under the law of similarity; but we do not confound these or other accompaniments with the gliding movement of the mind over the chronological past. Thus to take the extreme instance. We can assume another person's mental state (to a certain degree); and yet we do not fuse that with our own identity. There is a broad line of demarcation between each one's experience that they term their actual, and the assumption of a second person's experience, say of thirst, of fear, of curiosity. Our own past has continuity and fusion, in itself, and a peculiar set of circumstantial surroundings; in general, too, it is easy to remember. The other person's experience is received through a machinery of objective signs, laboriously interpreted, and not realized with the collaterals of an experience of our own; it is shorn of all the beams of our own personality, whether in the present or in the recollected past.

The distinction now drawn, (substantially what is exemplified at length in the chapter referred to,) is confirmed by what happens on occasions when memory and imagination are confounded. When a fact is long past, and all but forgotten, the oblivion overtakes the evidentiary collaterals, the marks of continuity that link together what has been one actual state to what has been another actual state. I remember having had the idea or purpose to say or to do something on a certain occasion ; but I do not remember whether I actually did or said the thing. The memory of the occasion is incomplete ; the links are snapped that connect that idea with my remembered acting at the time referred to ; it is not in its place in that authenticated series ; and it is not associated with the collateral circumstances that always attend an actual transaction. On the other hand, as is well remarked in the chapter quoted, imagination may simulate remembered reality, when there is wanting the real memory that would people the occasion with authentic circumstances, and when the imagination has been excited and exercised so as to include in its compass the collaterals that go with an experience in the actual.—*B.*

[108] The analysis of Belief presented in this chapter, brings out the conclusion that all cases of Belief are simply cases of indissoluble association : that there is no generic distinction, but only a difference in the strength of the association, between a case of belief and a case of mere imagination : that to believe a succession or coexistence between two facts is only to have the ideas of the two facts so strongly and closely associated, that we cannot help having the one idea when we have the other.

If this can be proved, it is the greatest of all the triumphs of the Association Psychology. To first appearance, no two things can be more distinct than thinking of two things together, and believing that they are joined together in the outward world. Nevertheless, that the latter state of mind is only an extreme case of the former, is, as we see, the deliberate doctrine of the author of the Analysis ; and it has also in its favour the high psychological authority of Mr. Herbert Spencer. Mr. Bain, in the preceding note, as well as in his systematic work, looks at the phenomenon from another side, and pronounces that what constitutes Belief is the power which an

idea has obtained over the Will. It is well known and understood that a mere idea may take such possession of the mind
as to exercise an irresistible control over the active faculties,
even independently of Volition, and sometimes in opposition
to it. This, which Mr. Bain calls the power of a Fixed Idea,
is exemplified in the cases of what is called fascination: the
impulse which a person looking from a precipice sometimes
feels to throw himself down it; and the cases of crimes said to
have been committed by persons who abhor them, because
that very horror has filled their minds with an intense and
irrepressible idea of the act. Since an idea is sometimes able
to overpower volition, it is no wonder that an idea should determine volition; as it does whenever we, under the influence
of the idea of a pleasure or of a pain, will that which obtains
for us the pleasure or averts the pain. In this voluntary
action, our conduct is grounded upon a relation between means
and an end; (that is, upon a constant conjunction of facts in
the way of causation, ultimately resolvable into a case of resemblance and contiguity): in common and unanalytical language, upon certain laws of nature on which we rely. Our
reliance is the consequence of an association formed in our
minds between the supposed cause and its effect, resulting
either from personal experience of their conjunction, from the
teachings of other people, or from accidental appearances.
Now, according to Mr. Bain, when this association between
the means and the end, the end calling up the idea of the
means, arrives at the point of giving to the idea thus called up
a command over the Will, it constitutes Belief. We believe a
thing, when we are ready to act on the faith of it; to face the
practical consequences of taking it for granted: and therein
lies the distinction between believing two facts to be conjoined,
and merely thinking of them together. Thus far Mr. Bain:
and with this I fully agree. But something is still wanting to
the completeness of the analysis. The theory as stated, distinguishes two antecedents, by a difference not between themselves,
but between their consequents. But when the consequents
differ, the antecedents cannot be the same. An association

of ideas is or is not a Belief, according as it has or has not the power of leading us to voluntary action : this is undeniable : but when there is a difference in the effects there must be a difference in the cause : the association which leads to action must be, in some respect or other, different from that which stops at thought. The question, therefore, raised, and, as they think, resolved, by the author of the Analysis and by Mr. Spencer, still demands an answer.   Does the difference between the two cases consist in this, that in the one case the association is dissoluble, in the other it is so much more closely riveted, by repetition, or by the intensity of the associated feelings, as to be no longer dissoluble ?   This is the question we are compelled to face.

I.

In the first place, then, it may be said—If Belief consisted in an indissoluble association, Belief itself would be indissoluble.   An opinion once formed could never afterwards be destroyed or changed.   This objection is good against the *word* indissoluble.   But those who maintain the theory do not mean by an indissoluble association, one which nothing that can be conceived to happen could possibly dissolve.   All our associations of ideas would probably be dissoluble, if experience presented to us the associated facts separate from one another.   If we have any associations which are, in practice, indissoluble, it can only be because the conditions of our existence deny to us the experiences which would be capable of dissolving them.   What the author of the Analysis means by indissoluble associations, are those which we cannot, by any mental effort, at ·present overcome.   If two ideas are, at the present time, so closely associated in our minds, that neither any effort of our own, nor anything else which can happen, can enable us now to have the one without its instantly raising up the other, the association is, in the author's sense of the term, indissoluble.   There would be less risk of misunderstanding if we were to discard the word indissoluble, and confine ourselves to the expression which the author employs as its equivalent, inseparable.   This I will henceforth do, and we will now enquire whether Belief is nothing but an inseparable association.

In favour of this supposition there is the striking fact, that an inseparable association very often suffices to command belief. There are innumerable cases of Belief for which no cause can be assigned, except that something has created so strong an association between two ideas that the person cannot separate them in thought. The author has given a large assortment of such cases, and has made them tell with great force in support of his theory. Locke, as the author mentions, had already seen, that this is one of the commonest and most fertile sources of erroneous thought; deserving to be placed high in any enumeration of Fallacies. When two things have long been habitually thought of together, and never apart, until the association between the ideas has become so strong that we have great difficulty, or cannot succeed at all, in separating them, there is a strong tendency to believe that the facts are conjoined in reality; and when the association is closer still, that their conjunction is what is called Necessary. Most of the schools of philosophy, both past and present, are so much under the influence of this tendency, as not only to justify it in principle, but to elect it into a Law of Things. The majority of metaphysicians have maintained, and even now maintain, that there are things which, by the laws of intelligence, cannot be separated in thought, and that these things are not only always united in fact, but united by necessity: and, again, other things, which cannot be united in thought—which cannot be thought of together, and that these not only never do, but it is impossible they ever should, coexist in fact. These supposed necessities are the very foundation of the Transcendental schools of metaphysics, of the Common Sense school, and many others which have not received distinctive names. These are facts in human nature and human history very favourable to the supposition that Belief is but an inseparable association, or at all events that an inseparable association suffices to create Belief.

On the contrary side of the question it may be urged, that

the inseparable associations which are so often found to generate Beliefs, do not generate them in everybody. Analytical
and philosophical minds often escape from them, and resist the
tendency to believe in an objective conjunction between facts
merely because they are unable to separate the ideas. The
author's typical example of an inseparable association, (and
there can be none more suited to the purpose,) is the association between sensations of colour and the tangible magnitudes,
figures, and distances, of which they are signs, and which are
so completely merged with them into one single impression,
that we believe we see distance, extension, and figure, though
all we really see is the optical effects which accompany them,
all the rest being a rapid interpretation of natural signs. The
generality of mankind, no doubt, and all men before they have
studied the subject, believe what the author says they do ; but
a great majority of those who have studied the subject believe
otherwise : they believe that a large portion of the facts which
we seem to see, we do not really see, but instantaneously infer.
Yet the association remains inseparable in these scientific
thinkers as in others : the retinal picture suggests to them the
real magnitude, in the same irresistible manner as it does to
other people. To take another of the author's examples :
when we look at a distant terrestrial object through a telescope,
it appears nearer; if we reverse the telescope it appears further
off. The signs by which we judge of distance from us, here
mislead, because those signs are found in conjunction with real
distances widely different from those with which they coexist in
our ordinary experience. The association, however, persists,
and is irresistible, in one person as much as in another ; for
every one recognises that the object, thus looked at, *seems*
nearer, or farther off, than we know it to be. But does this
ever make any of us, except perhaps an inexperienced child,
believe that the object is at the distance at which we seem to
see it ? The inseparable association, though so persistent and
powerful as to create in everybody an optical illusion, creates
no *de*lusion, but leaves our belief as conformable to the
realities of fact as if no such illusive appearance had presented

itself. Cases similar to this are so frequent, that cautious and thoughtful minds, enlightened by experience on the misleading character of inseparable associations, learn to distrust them, and do not, even by a first impulse, believe a connexion in fact because there is one in thought, but wait for evidence.

Following up the same objection, it may be said that if belief is only an inseparable association, belief is a matter of habit and accident, and not of reason. Assuredly an association, however close, between two ideas, is not a sufficient *ground* of belief; is not *evidence* that the corresponding facts are united in external nature. The theory seems to annihilate all distinction between the belief of the wise, which is regulated by evidence, and conforms to the real successions and coexistences of the facts of the universe, and the belief of fools, which is mechanically produced by any accidental association that suggests the idea of a succession or coexistence to the mind: a belief aptly characterized by the popular expression, believing a thing because they have taken it into their heads.

Indeed, the author of the Analysis is compelled by his theory to affirm that we actually believe in accordance with the misleading associations which generate what are commonly called illusions of sense. He not only says that we believe we see figure and distance—which the great majority of psychologists since Berkeley do not believe; but he says, that in the case of ventriloquy "we cannot help believing" that the sound proceeds from the place, of which the ventriloquist imitates the effect; that the sound of bells opposed by the wind, not only appears farther off, but is believed to come from farther off, although we may know the exact distance from which it comes; that "in passing on board ship, another ship at sea, we *believe* that she has all the motion, we none:" nay even, that when we have turned ourselves round with velocity several times, "we believe that the world is turning round." Surely it is more true to say, as people generally do say, "the world *seems* to us to turn round." To me these cases appear so many experimental proofs, that the tendency of an inseparable association to generate belief, even when that

tendency is fully effectual in creating the irresistible appearance of a state of things that does not really exist, may yet be
impotent against reason, that is, against preponderant evidence.
In defence of these paradoxes, let us now consider what the
author of the Analysis might say. One thing he would certainly say : that the belief he affirms to exist in these cases of
illusion, is but a momentary one ; with which the belief entertained at all other times may be at variance. In the case, for
instance, of those who, from an early association formed
between darkness and ghosts, feel terror in the dark though
they have a confirmed disbelief in ghosts, the author's
opinion is that there is a temporary belief, at the moment
when the terror is felt. This was also the opinion of Dugald
Stewart : and the agreement (by no means a solitary one)
between two thinkers of such opposite tendencies, reminds one
of the saying " Quand un Français et un Anglais sont d'accord,
il faut bien qu'ils aient raison." Yet the author seems to
adopt this notion not from observation of the case, but from
an antecedent opinion that " dread implies belief, and an uncontrollable belief," which, he says, " we need not stay to
prove." It is to be wished, in this case, that he had stayed to
prove it : for it is harder to prove than he thought. The emotion of fear, the physical effect on the nervous system known
by that name, may be excited, and I believe often is excited,
simply by terrific imaginations. That these imaginations are,
even for a moment, mistaken for menacing realities, may be true,
but ought not to be assumed without proof. The circumstance
most in its favour (one not forgotten by the author) is that in
dreams, to which may be added hallucinations, frightful ideas
are really mistaken for terrible facts. But dreams are states in
which all other sensible ideas are mistaken for outward facts.
Yet sensations and ideas are intrinsically different, and it is not
the normal state of the human mind to confound the one
with the other.

Besides, this supposition of a momentary belief in ghosts
breaking in upon and interrupting an habitual and permanent
belief that there are no ghosts, jars considerably with the doc-

trine it is brought to support, that belief is an inseparable association.   According to that doctrine, here are two inseparable
associations, which yet are so far from exclusively possessing
the mind, that they alternate with one another, each Inseparable implying the separation of the other Inseparable.   The
association of darkness with the absence of ghosts must be
anything but inseparable, if there only needs the presence of
darkness to revive the contrary association.   Yet an association so very much short of inseparable, is accompanied, at least
in the absence of darkness, by a full belief.   Darkness is in
this case associated with two incompatible ideas, the idea of
ghosts and that of their absence, but with neither of them inseparably, and in consequence the two associations alternately
prevail, as the surrounding circumstances favour the one or
the other ; agreeably to the laws of Compound Association
laid down with great perspicuity and reach of thought by Mr.
Bain in his systematic treatise.

To the argument, that the inseparable associations which
create optical and other illusions, do not, when opposed by
reason, generate the false belief, the author's answer would probably be some such as the following.   When the rational thinker
succeeds in resisting the belief, he does so by more or less
completely overcoming the inseparableness of the association.
Associations may be conquered by the formation of counter-
associations.   Mankind had formerly an inseparable association between sunset and the motion of the sun, and this inseparable association compelled them to believe that in the
phenomenon of sunset the sun moves and the earth is at rest.
But Copernicus, Galileo, and after them, all astronomers,
found evidence, that the earth moves and the sun is at rest :
in other words, certain experiences, and certain reasonings
from those experiences, took place in their minds, the tendency
of which was to associate sunset with the ideas of the earth in
motion and the sun at rest.   This was a counter-association,
which could not coexist, at least at the same instant, with the
previous association connecting sunset with the sun in motion
and the earth at rest.   But for a long time the new associa-

ting influences could not be powerful enough to get the better of the old association, and change the belief which it implied. A belief which has become habitual, is seldom overcome but by a slow process. However, the experiences and mental processes that tended to form the new association still went on; there was a conflict between the old association and the causes which tended to produce a new one; until, by the long continuance and frequent repetition of those causes, the old association, gradually undermined, ceased to be inseparable, and it became possible to associate the idea of sunset with that of the earth moving and the sun at rest; whereby the previous idea of the sun moving and the earth at rest was excluded for the time, and as the new association grew in strength, was at last thrown out altogether. The argument should go on to say that after a still further prolongation of the new experiences and reasonings, the old association became impossible and the new one inseparable; for, until it became inseparable, there could, according to the theory, be no belief. And this, in truth, does sometimes happen. There are instances in the history of science, even down to the present day, in which something which was once believed to be impossible, and its opposite to be necessary, was first seen to be possible, next to be true, and finally came to be considered as necessarily true, and its opposite (once deemed necessary) as impossible, and even inconceivable; insomuch that it is thought by some that what was reputed an impossibility, might have been known to be a necessity. In such cases, the quality of inseparableness has passed, in those minds at least, from the old association to the new one. But in much the greatest number of cases the change does not proceed so far, and both associations remain equally possible. The case which furnished our last instance is an example. Astronomers, and all educated persons, now associate sunset with motion confined to the earth, and firmly believe this to be what really takes place; but they have not formed this association with such exclusiveness and intensity as to have become unable to associate sunset with motion of the sun. On the contrary, the visible appearance still suggests

motion of the sun, and many people, though aware of the
truth, find that they cannot by any effort make themselves
see sunset any otherwise than as the sinking of the sun below
the earth.　My own experience is different : I find that I can
represent the phenomenon to myself in either light ; I can,
according to the manner in which I direct my thoughts, see
sunset either as the earth tilting above the sun, or as the sun
dipping below the earth : in the same manner as when a rail-
way train in motion passes another at rest, we are able, if we
prevent our eyes from resting on any third object, to imagine
the motion as being either in the one train or in the other. How,
then, can it be said that there is an inseparable association of
sunset with the one mode of representation, and a consequent
inability to associate it with the other ?　It is associated with
both, and the one of the two associations which is nearest to
being inseparable is that which belief does not accompany.
The difference between different people in the ability to represent to themselves the phenomenon under either aspect, depends
rather on the degree of exercise which they have given to their
imagination in trying to frame mental pictures conformable to
the two hypotheses, than upon those considerations of reason
and evidence which yet may determine their belief.

The question still remains, what is there which exists in the
hypothesis believed, and does not exist in the hypothesis rejected, when we have associations which enable our imagination to represent the facts agreeably to either hypothesis ? In
other words, what is Belief ?

I think it must be admitted, that when we can represent to
ourselves in imagination either of two conflicting suppositions,
one of which we believe, and disbelieve the other, neither of
the associations can be inseparable ; and there must therefore
be in the fact of Belief, which exists in only one of the two
cases, something for which inseparable association does not
account. We seem to have again come up, on a different side,
to the difficulty which we felt in the discussion of Memory, in
accounting for the distinction between a fact remembered, and
the same fact imagined. There is a close parallelism between

the two problems. In both, we have the difference between a fact and a representation in imagination ; between a sensation, or combination of sensations, and an idea, or combination of ideas. This difference we all accept as an ultimate fact. But the difficulty is this. Let me first state it as it presents itself in the case of Memory. Having in our mind a certain combination of ideas, in a group or a train, accompanying or succeeding one another ; what is it which, in one case, makes us recognize this group or train as representing a group or train of the corresponding sensations, remembered as having been actually felt by us, while in another case we are aware that the sensations have never occurred to us in a group or train corresponding to that in which we are now having the ideas? This is the problem of Memory. Let me now state the problem of Belief, when the belief is not a case of memory. Here also we have ideas connected in a certain order in our own mind, which makes us think of a corresponding order among the sensations, and we believe that this similar combination of the sensations is a real fact : *i.e.*, whether we ever felt it or not, we confidently expect that we should feel it under certain given conditions. In Memory, we believe that the realities in Nature, the sensations and combinations of sensations presented to us from without, *have* occurred to us in an order which agrees with that in which we are representing them to ourselves in thought : in those cases of Belief which are not cases of Memory, we believe, not that they have occurred, but that they would have occurred, or would occur, in that order.

What is it that takes place in us, when we recognize that there is this agreement between the order of our ideas and the order in which we either had or might have had the sensations which correspond to them—that the order of the ideas represents a similar order either in our actual sensations, or in those which, under some given circumstances, we should have reason to expect ? What, in short, is the difference *to our minds* between thinking of a reality, and representing to ourselves an imaginary picture ? I confess that I can perceive no escape from the opinion that the distinction is ultimate and primordial.

There is no more difficulty in holding it to be so, than in holding the difference between a sensation and an idea to be primordial. It seems almost another aspect of the same difference. The author himself says, in the chapter on Memory, that, a sensation and an idea being different, it is to be expected that the remembrance of having had a sensation should be different from the remembrance of having had an idea, and that this is a sufficient explanation of our distinguishing them. If this, then, is an original distinction, why should not the distinction be original between the remembrance of having had a sensation, and the actually having an idea (which is the difference between Memory and Imagination); and between the expectation of having a sensation, and the actually having an idea (which is the difference between Belief and Imagination)? Grant these differences, and there is nothing further to explain in the phenomenon of Belief. For every belief is either the memory of having had a sensation (or other feeling), or the expectation that we should have the sensation or feeling in some given state of circumstances, if that state of circumstances could come to be realized.

II.

That all belief is either Memory or Expectation, will be clearly seen if we run over all the different objects of Belief. The author has already done so, in order to establish his theory ; and it is now necessary that we should do the same.

The objects of Belief are enumerated by the author in the following terms :—1. Events, real existences. 2. Testimony. 3. The truth of propositions. He intended this merely as a rough grouping, sufficient for the purpose if it includes everything : for it is evident that the divisions overlap one another, and it will be seen presently that the last two are but cases of the first.

Belief in events he further divides into belief in present events, in past events, and in future events. Belief in present events he subdivides into belief in immediate existences present to my senses, and belief in immediate existences not present to my senses. We see by this that he recognises no difference, in a metaphysical sense, between existences and events, because he regards, with reason, objects as merely the supposed antecedents of events. The distinction, however, requires to be kept up, being no other than the fundamental difference between simultaneousness, and succession or change.

Belief in immediate existences present to my senses, is either belief in my sensations, or belief in external objects. Believing that I feel what I am at this moment feeling, is, as the author says, only another name for having the feeling ; with the idea, however, of Myself, associated with it ; of which hereafter.

The author goes on to analyse Belief in external objects present to our senses ; and he resolves it into a present sensation, united by an irresistible association with the numerous other sensations which we are accustomed to receive in conjunction with it. The Object is thus to be understood as a complex idea, compounded of the ideas of various sensations which we have, and of a far greater number of sensations which we should expect to have if certain contingencies were realized. In other words, our idea of an object is an idea of a group of possibilities of sensation, some of which we believe we can realize at pleasure, while the remainder would be realized if certain conditions took place, on which, by the laws of nature, they are dependent. As thus explained, belief in the existence of a physical object, is belief in the occurrence of certain sensations, contingently on certain previous conditions. This is a state of mind closely allied to Expectation of sensations. For—though we use the name Expectation only with reference to the future, and even to the probable future—our state of mind in respect to what *may* be future, and even to what *might have been* future, is of the same general nature, and depends on the same principles, as Expectation. I believe that a certain event will positively happen, because the known conditions which always accompany it in experience have already taken place. I believe that another event will certainly happen *if* the known conditions which always accompany it take place, and those conditions I can produce when I please. I believe that a third event will happen if its conditions take place, but I must wait for those conditions; I cannot realize them at pleasure, and may never realize them at all. The first of these three cases is positive expectation, the other two are conditional expectation. A fourth case is my belief that the event would have happened at any former time if the conditions had taken place at that time. It is not consonant to usage to call this Expectation, but, considered as a case of belief, there is no essential difference between it and the third case. My belief that I should have heard Cicero had I been present in the Forum, and my belief that I shall hear Mr. Gladstone if I am present in the House of Commons, can nowise be regarded as essentially different phenomena. The one we call Expectation, the other not, but the mental principle operative in both these cases of belief is the same.

The author goes on to say, that the belief that we should have the sensations if certain conditions were realized, that is, if we had certain other sensations, is merely an inseparable association of the two sets of sensations with one another, and their inseparable union with the idea of ourselves as having them. But I confess it seems to me that all this may exist in a case of simple imagination. The author would himself admit that the complex idea of the object, in all its fulness, may be in the mind without belief. What remains is its association with the idea of ourselves as percipients. But this also, I cannot but think, we may have in the case of an imaginary scene, when we by no means believe that any corresponding reality exists. Does the idea of our own personality never enter into the pictures in our imagination? Are we not ourselves present in the scenes which we conjure up in our minds? I apprehend we are as constantly present in them, and as conscious of our presence, as we are in contemplating a real prospect. In either case the vivacity of the other impressions eclipses, for the most part, the thought of ourselves as spectators, but not more so in the imaginary, than in the real, spectacle.

It appears to me, then, that to account for belief in external

objects, we must postulate Expectation ; and since all our expectations, whether positive or contingent, are a consequence
of our Memory of the past (as distinguished from a representation in fancy), we must also postulate Memory. The
distinction between a mere combination of ideas in thought,
and one which recals to us a combination of sensations as
actually experienced, always returns on our hands as an ultimate postulate.

The author proceeds to shew how this idea of a mere group
of sensations, actual or contingent, becomes knit up with an
idea of a permanent Something, lying, as it were, under these
sensations, and causing them ; this further enlargement of the
complex idea taking place through the intimate, or, as he
calls it, inseparable association, generated by experience, which
makes us unable to imagine any phenomenon as beginning to
exist without something anterior to it which causes it. This
explanation, seems to me quite correct as far as it goes ; but,
while it accounts for the difficulty we have in not ascribing our
sensations to some cause or other, it does not explain why we
accept, as in fact we do, the group itself as the cause. I have
endeavoured to clear up this difficulty elsewhere (Examination
of Sir William Hamilton's Philosophy), and in preference to
going over the ground a second time, I subjoin, at the end of
the volume, the chapter containing the explanation. That
chapter supplies all that appears to me to be further necessary
on the subject of belief in outward objects ; which is thus
shewn to be a case of Conditional Expectation.

It is unnecessary to follow the author into the minute consideration of Belief in the existence of objects not present,
since the explanation already given equally applies to them.
My belief in the present existence of St. Paul's is correctly
set forth by the author as consisting of the following elements :
I believe that I have seen St. Paul's : I believe that I shall see
St. Paul's, when I am again in St. Paul's Churchyard : I
believe that I should see St. Paul's, if I were in St. Paul's
Churchyard at this instant. All this, as he justly remarks, is
Memory or Expectation. And this, or some part of this, is

the whole of what is in any case meant by belief in the real existence of an external object. The author adds, I also believe that if any creature whose senses are analogous to my own, is now in St. Paul's Churchyard, it has the present sensation of that edifice. But this belief is not necessary to my belief in the continued existence of St. Paul's. For that, it suffices that I believe I should myself see it. My belief that other creatures would do so, is part of my belief in the real existence of other creatures like myself; which is no more mysterious, than our belief in the real existence of any other objects some of whose properties rest not on direct sensation, but on inference.

Belief in past existences, when those existences have been perceived by ourselves, is Memory. When the past existences are inferred from evidence, the belief of them is not Memory, but a fact of the same nature as Expectation ; being a belief that we *should have had* the sensations if we had been cotemporary with the objects, and had been in the local position necessary for receiving sensible impressions from them.

We now come to the case of Belief in testimony. But testimony is not itself an object of belief. The object of belief is what the testimony asserts. And so in the last of the author's three cases, that of assent to a proposition. The object of belief, in both these cases, is an assertion. But an assertion is something asserted, and what is asserted must be a fact, similar to some of those of which we have already treated. According to the author, belief in an assertion is belief that two names are both of them names of the same thing : but this we have felt ourselves obliged to discard, as an inadequate explanation of the import of any assertions, except those which are classed as merely verbal. Every assertion concerning Things, whether in concrete or in abstract language, is an assertion that some fact, or group of facts, has been, is, or may be expected to be, found, wherever a certain other fact, or group of facts, is found. Belief in this, is therefore either remembrance that we did have, or expectation that we shall have, or a belief of the same nature with expectation that in some given circumstances we should have, or should have had, direct perception of a particular fact. Belief, therefore, is always a case either of Memory or of Expectation; including under the latter name conditional as well as positive expectation, and the state of mind similar to expectation which affects us in regard to what *would* have been a subject of expectation, if the conditions of its realization had still been possible.

It may be objected, that we may believe in the real existence of things which are not objects of sense at all. We may. But we cannot believe in the real existence of anything which we do not conceive as capable of acting in some way upon our own or some other being's consciousness; though the state of consciousness it produces may not be called a sensation. The existence of a thing means, to us, merely its capacity of producing an impression of some sort upon some mind, that is, of producing some state of consciousness. The belief, therefore, in its existence, is still a conditional expectation of something which we should, under some supposed circumstances, be capable of feeling.

To resume : Belief, as I conceive, is more than an inseparable association, for inseparable associations do not always generate belief, nor does belief always require, as one of its conditions, an inseparable association : we can believe that to be true which we are capable of conceiving or representing to ourselves as false, and false what we are capable of representing to ourselves as true. The difference between belief and mere imagination, is the difference between recognising something as a reality in nature, and regarding it as a mere thought of our own. This is the difference which presents itself when Memory has to be distinguished from Imagination; and again when Expectation, whether positive or contingent (i.e. whether it be expectation that we shall, or only persuasion that in certain definable circumstances we should, have a certain experience) has to be distinguished from the mere mental conception of that experience.

III.

Let us examine, once more, whether the speculations in the text afford us any means of further analysing this difference.

The difference presents itself in its most elementary form in the distinction between a sensation and an idea. The author admits this distinction to be ultimate and primordial. " A " sensation is different from an idea, only because it is felt to be " different." But, after having admitted that these two states of consciousness are distinguishable from each other in and by themselves, he adds, that they are also distinguishable by their accompaniments. " The accompaniments of a sensation " are always generically different from those of an idea. . . . . " The accompaniments of a sensation, are all the simultaneous " *objects of sensation,* together with all those which, to a cer- " tain extent, both preceded and followed it. The accompani- " ments of an idea are not the simultaneous objects of sensation, " but *other ideas ;* namely, the neighbouring facts, antecedent " and consequent, of the mental train." There can be no doubt that in those individual cases in which ideas and sensa- tions might be confounded, namely, when an idea reaches or approaches the vivacity of a sensation, the indication here pointed out helps to assure us that what we are conscious of is, nevertheless, only an idea. When, for instance, we awake from a dream, and open our eyes to the outward world, what makes us so promptly recognise that this and not the other is the real world, is that we find its phenomena connected in the accustomed order of our objects of sensation. But though this circumstance enables us, in particular instances, to refer our impression more instantaneously to one or the other class, it cannot be by this that we distinguish ideas at first from sensations ; for the criterion supposes the distinc- tion to be already made. If we judge a sensation to be a sensa- tion because its accompaniments are other sensations, and an idea to be an idea because its accompaniments are other ideas, we must already be able to distinguish those other sensations from those other ideas.

A similar remark is applicable to a criterion between sensa- tions and ideas, incidentally laid down by Mr. Bain in the First Part of his systematic treatise. " A mere picture or " *idea* remains the same whatever be our bodily position or

" bodily exertions ; the sensation that we call the *actual* is
" entirely at the mercy of our movements, shifting in every
" possible way according to the varieties of action that we go
" through." (*The Senses and the Intellect*, 2nd ed. p. 381.)
This test, like the author's, may serve in cases of momentary
doubt ; but sensations in general must have been already distinguished from ideas, before we could have hit upon this
criterion between them. If we had not already known the
difference between a sensation and an idea, we never could
have discovered that one of them is " at the mercy of our
movements," and that the other is not.

It being granted that a sensation and an idea are *ipso facto*
distinguishable, the author thinks it no more than natural that
" the copy of the sensation should be distinguishable from the
" revival of the idea, when they are both brought up by asso-
" ciation." But he adds, that there is another distinction between the memory of a sensation, and the memory of an idea,
and it is this. In all Memory the idea of self forms part of
the complex idea ; but in the memory of sensation, the self
which enters into the remembrance is " the sentient self, that
" is, seeing and hearing :" in the memory of an idea, it is " not
" the sentient self, but the conceptive self, self having an idea.
" But" (he adds) " myself percipient, and myself imagining, or
" conceiving, are two very different states of consciousness : of
" course the ideas of these states of consciousness, or these
" states revived by association, are very different ideas."

Concerning the fact there is no dispute. Myself percipient,
and myself imagining or conceiving, are different states,
because perceiving is a different thing from imagining; and
being different states, the remembrance of them is, as might be
expected, different. But the question is, in what does the difference between the remembrances consist ? The author calls
one of them the *idea* of myself perceiving, and the other the
idea of myself imagining, and thinks there is no other difference.
But how do the *idea* of myself having a sensation, and the
idea of myself having an idea of that sensation, differ from
one another ? since in either case an idea of the sensation is all

that I am having now.   The thought of myself perceiving a
thing at a former time, and the thought of myself imagining
the thing at that former time, are both at the present moment
facts of imagination—are now merely ideas.   In each case I
have an ideal representation of myself, as conscious in a manner very similar in the two cases ; though not exactly the same,
since in the one case I remember to have been conscious of a
sensation, in the other, to have been conscious only of an idea
of that sensation : but, in either case, that past consciousness
enters only as an idea, into the consciousness I now have by
recollection.   In what, then, as far as mere ideas are concerned,
do my present mental representations of the two cases differ ?
Will it be said, that the idea of the sensation is one thing,
the idea of the idea of the sensation another thing ?   Or are
they both the same idea, namely, the idea of the sensation; and
is the element that is present in the one case, but absent in
the other, not an idea but something else ?   A difference there
is admitted to be between the remembrance of having had a
sensation, and the remembrance of having merely thought of
the sensation, i.e. had the idea of it : is this difference a difference in the ideas I have in the two cases, or is the idea the
same, but accompanied in the one case by something not an
idea, which does not exist in the other ? for if so, this something is a Belief.

I have touched upon this question in a former note, and
expressed my inability to recognise, in the idea of an idea,
anything but the idea itself ; in the thought of a thought,
anything but a repetition of the thought.   My thought of Falstaff, as far as I can perceive, is not a copy but a repetition of
the thought I had of him when I first read Shakespeare : not
indeed an exact repetition, because all complex ideas undergo
modification by time, some elements fading away, and new
ones being added by reverting to the original sources or by
subsequent associations ; but my first mental image of Falstaff,
and my present one, do not differ as the thought of a rose
differs from the sight of one ; as an idea of sensation differs
from the sensation.   On this point the author was perhaps of

the same opinion, since we find him contrasting the "copy"
of the sensation with the "revival" of the idea, as if the
latter was a case of simple repetition, the former not.   It
would have been well if he had made this point a subject of
express discussion ; for if his opinion upon it was what, from
this passage, we may suppose it to have been, it involves a
serious difficulty. If (he says) a sensation and an idea "are
"distinguishable in the having, it is likely that the copy of
"the sensation should be distinguishable from the revival of
"the idea." But the copy of the sensation is the idea ; so that,
on this shewing, the idea is distinguishable from its own revival, that is, from the same idea when it occurs again.   The
author's theory would thus require him to maintain that an
idea revived is a specifically different idea, and not the same idea
repeated : since otherwise the two states of mind, so far as regards the ideas contained in them, are undistinguishable, and
it is necessary to admit the presence in Memory of some other
element.

Let us put another case.   Instead of Falstaff, suppose a
real person whom I have seen : for example General Lafayette.
My idea of Lafayette is almost wholly, what my idea of Falstaff is entirely, a creation of thought : only a very small portion of it is derived from my brief experience of seeing and
conversing with him.   But I have a remembrance of having
seen Lafayette, and no remembrance of having seen Falstaff,
but only of having thought of him.   Is it a sufficient explanation of this difference to say, that I have an idea of myself
seeing and hearing Lafayette, and only an idea of myself
thinking of Falstaff ?   But I can form a vivid idea of myself
seeing and hearing Falstaff.   I can without difficulty imagine
myself in the field of Shrewsbury, listening to his characteristic soliloquy over the body of Hotspur ; or in the tavern
in the midst of his associates, hearing his story of his encounter
with the men in buckram.   When I recal the scene, I can as
little detach it from the idea of myself as present, as I can in
the case of most things of which I was really an eye-witness.
The spontaneous presence of the idea of Myself in the con-

ception, is always that of myself as percipient. The idea of myself as in a state of mere imagination, only substitutes itself for the other when something reminds me that the scene is merely imaginary.

I cannot help thinking, therefore, that there is in the remembrance of a real fact, as distinguished from that of a thought, an element which does not consist, as the author supposes, in a difference between the mere ideas which are present to the mind in the two cases. This element, howsoever we define it, constitutes Belief, and is the difference between Memory and Imagination. From whatever direction we approach, this difference seems to close our path. When we arrive at it, we seem to have reached, as it were, the central point of our intellectual nature, presupposed and built upon in every attempt we make to explain the more recondite phenomena of our mental being.—*Ed.*

CHAPTER XII.

RATIOCINATION.

"It would afford great light and clearness to the art of Logic, to determine the precise nature and composition of the ideas affixed to those words which have complex ideas; *i.e.*, which excite any combinations of simple ideas, united intimately by association."—*Hartley.* *Prop.* 12, *Corol.* 3.

RATIOCINATION is one of the most complicated of all the mental phenomena. And it is worthy of notice, that more was accomplished towards the analysis of it, at an early period in the history of intellectual improvement, than of any other of the complex cases of human consciousness.

It was fully explained by Aristotle, that the simplest case of Ratiocination consists of three propositions, which he called a syllogism. A piece of ratiocination may consist of one, or more syllogisms, to any extent; but every single step is a syllogism.

A ratiocination, then, or syllogism, is first resolved into three propositions. The following may be taken as one of the simplest of all examples. "All men are animals : kings are men : therefore kings are animals."

Next, the Proposition is resolved into its proximate elements. These are three; two Terms, one called the Subject, the other the Predicate, and the Copula.

What is the particular nature of each of these elements we have already seen, and here, therefore, need not stay to inquire.

The ancient writers on Logic proceeded in their analysis, no farther than Terms. After this, they only endeavoured to enumerate and classify terms; to enumerate and classify propositions; to enumerate and classify syllogisms; and to give the rules for making correct syllogisms, and detecting incorrect ones. And this, as taught by them, constituted the whole science and art of Logic.

What, under this head, we propose to explain, is— the process of association involved in the syllogism, and in the belief which is part of it.

That part of the process which is involved in the two antecedent propositions, called the premises, has been already explained. It is only, therefore, the third proposition, called the conclusion, which further requires exposition.

We have seen, that in the proposition, "All men are animals," Belief is merely the recognition that the meaning of the term, "all men," is included in that of the term "animals," and that the recognition is a case of association. In the proposition also, "kings are men," the belief is merely the recognition, that the individuals named "kings," are part of the many, of whom "men," is the common name. This has already been more than once explained. And now, therefore, remains only to be shewn what further is involved in the third proposition, or conclusion, "kings are animals."

In each of the two preceding propositions, two terms or names are compared. In the last proposition, a third name is compared with both the other two ; immediately with the one, and, through that, with the other ; the whole, obviously, a complicated case of association.

In the first proposition, " all men are animals," the term, " all men," is compared with the term animals ; in other words, a certain association, already expounded, takes place. In the second proposition, " kings are men," the term " kings," is compared with the term " all men ;" comparison here, again, being only a name for a particular case of association. In the third proposition, " kings are animals," the name " kings," is compared with the name " animals," but mediately through the name, " all men." Thus, " kings," is associated with " all men," " all men," with " animals ;" " kings," therefore, with " animals," by a complicated, and, at the same time, a rapid, and almost imperceptible process. It would be easy to mark the steps of the association. But this would be tedious, and after so much practice, the reader will be at no loss to set them down for himself.[109]

---

[109] This chapter, which is of a very summary character, is a prolongation of the portion of the chapter on Belief, which examines the case of belief in the truth of a proposition ; and must stand or fall with it. The question considered is, how, from belief in the truth of the two premises of a syllogism, we pass into belief in the conclusion. The exposition proceeds on the untenable theory of the import of propositions, on which I have so often had occasion to comment. That theory, however, was not necessary to the author for shewing how two ideas may become inseparably associated through the inseparable association of each of them with a third idea : and inasmuch as an inseparable association between the subject and

predicate, in the author's opinion, constitutes belief, an explanation of ratiocination conformable to that given of belief follows as a matter of course.

Although I am unable to admit that there is nothing in belief but an inseparable association, and although I maintain that there may be belief without an inseparable association, I can still accept this explanation of the formation of an association between the subject and predicate of the conclusion, which, when close and intense, has, as we have seen, a strong tendency to generate belief. But to shew what it is that gives the belief its validity, we must fall back on logical laws, the laws of evidence. And independently of the question of validity, we shall find in the reliance on those laws, so far as they are understood, the source and origin of all beliefs, whether well or ill-founded, which are not the almost mechanical or automatic products of a strong association—of the lively suggestion of an idea. We may therefore pass at once to the nature of Evidence, which is the subject of the next chapter.

I venture to refer, in passing, to those chapters in my System of Logic, in which I have maintained, contrary to what is laid down in this chapter, that Ratiocination does not *consist* of Syllogisms ; that the Syllogism is not the analysis of what the mind does in reasoning, but merely a useful formula into which it can translate its reasonings, gaining thereby a great increase in the security for their correctness.—*Ed.*

CHAPTER XIII.

EVIDENCE.

" In consequence of some very wonderful laws, which regulate
the successions of our mental phenomena, the science of mind is,
in all its most important respects, a science of analysis."—
Brown's Lect., i., 108.

BEFORE leaving the subject of Belief, it will be
proper to shew, in a few words, what is included,
under the name Evidence.   Evidence, is either the
same thing with Belief, or it is the antecedent, of
which Belief is the consequent.

Belief we have seen to be of two sorts : Belief of
events ; Belief of propositions.

Of events, believed on our own experience, the
evidence of the present is sense ; of the past, memory ;
and in these cases, the evidence and the belief are not
two things, but one and the same thing.   The lamp,
which at this moment lights me, I say that I see
burning, and that I believe it burning.   These are
two names of one and the same state of consciousness.
—" I remember it was burning at the same hour last
night," and " I believe it was burning at the same
hour last night," are also two expressions for the
same thing.—In the simple anticipation of the future,
from the past, also, the evidence, and the belief, are

not two things, but one and the same thing. There is a close and inseparable association of the idea of a like antecedent, with the idea of a like consequent. This has not a single name, like memory; but, like memory, it is both evidence and belief.

The case of testimony is different. The Testimony is one thing, the Belief is another. The name Evidence is given to the testimony. The association of the testimony, with the event testified, is the belief.

Beside the belief of events which are the immediate objects of sense, of memory, and of anticipation (the consequence of sense and memory), and of those which are the immediate objects of testimony; there is a belief of events which are not the immediate objects of any of those operations. The sailor, who is shipwrecked on an unknown coast, sees the prints of a man's foot on the sand. The print of the foot is here called the evidence; the association of the print, as consequent, with a man, as antecedent, is called the belief. In this case, the sensation of one event, the print of a foot on the sand, induces the belief of another event, the existence of a man. The sailor who has seen the mark, reports it to his companions who have not quitted the wreck. Instantly they have the same belief; but it is a remove farther off, and there is an additional link of evidence. The first event to them, is the affirmation of their companion; the second, the existence of the print; the third, that of the man. There is here evidence of evidence; the testimony, evidence of the print; the print, evidence of the man.

The companions of the sailor, having themselves gone on shore, perceive, indeed, no man, but see a large monkey, which leaves prints on the sand very much resembling those which had first been perceived by their companion. What is now the state of their minds ? Doubt. But doubt is a name ; what do we call by that name ? A phenomenon of some complexity, but of which the elements are not very difficult to trace. There is, here, a double association with the print of the foot. There is the association of a man, and there is the association of a monkey. First, the print raises the idea of a man, but the instant it does so, it raises also the idea of a monkey. The idea of the monkey, displacing that of the man, hinders the first association from the fixity which makes it belief; and the idea of man, displacing that of monkey, hinders the second association from that fixity which constitutes belief.

When evidence is complex; that is, consists of more than one event ; the events may be all on the same side, or not all on the same side; that is, they may all tend to prove the same event ; or some of them may tend to prove it, some may have an opposite tendency.

Thus, if after discovering the print on the sand, the sailors had seen near it a stick, which had any appearance of having been fashioned into a club, or a spear,—this would have been another event, tending, as well as the print on the sand, to the belief of the presence of men. The evidence would have been complex, but all on one side. The process is easy to trace. There is now a double association with the existence of men. The print of the foot excites that idea, the existence of the club excites that idea. This double excitement gives greater permanence to the idea. By repetition, the two exciting causes coalesce, and, by their united strength, call up the associated idea with greater force.

In the case of the appearance of the monkey, in which one of the events tended to one belief, the other to another, we have just seen that the effect is precisely contrary; to lessen the strength of the association with the existence of a man, and to hinder its becoming belief.

These expositions may be applied with ease to the other cases of complex evidence, which can only consist of a greater or less number of events, either all tending to the belief of the same event, or some tending that way, some another; but all operating in the manner which has just been pointed out. Thus we may complicate the present case still further, by the supposition of additional events. After the appearance of the monkey, the sailors may discover, in the neighbourhood, the vestiges of a recent fire, and of the victuals which had been cooked by it. The association of human beings with these appearances is so strong, that, combined with the association between the print and the same idea, it quite obscures the association between the print and the monkey; and the belief that the place has inhabitants becomes complete. But suppose, further; that after a little observation, they discover an English knife, and fork, and a piece of English earthenware near the same place. The idea of an English ship having touched at the place, is immediately excited, and all the evidence of local inhabitants, derived from the marks of fire and cookery, is immediately destroyed. In other words, a new association, that with an English ship,

is created, which completely supersedes the idea,
formerly associated, that of inhabitants existing on
the spot.

The whole of the events, which go in this manner
to form a case of belief, or of doubt, or of disbelief,
are called Evidence.   And the association, which
binds them together into a sort of whole, as antecedent, and connects with them the event to which they
apply as consequent, and which constitutes the belief,
doubt, or disbelief, very often goes by the names of
"judgment," "judging of the evidence," "weighing
the evidence," and so on.

In these cases of the belief of Events upon complicated evidence, there is an antecedent and a consequent; the antecedent consisting of all the events
which are called evidence, the consequent of the event,
or events evidenced; and lastly, there is that close
association of the antecedent and the consequent,
which we have seen already, in so many instances,
co. stitutes belief.

We have now to consider, what we call evidence in
the case of the Belief of Propositions.

There are two cases of the Belief of propositions.
There is belief in the case of the single proposition;
and there is belief of the conclusion of a syllogism,
which is the result of a combination of Propositions.

We have seen what the process of belief in Propositions is.   The subject and predicate, two names for
the same thing, of which the predicate is either of the
same extent with the subject, or of a greater extent,
suggests, each of them, its meaning; that is, call up,
by association, each of them, its peculiar cluster of
ideas.   Two clusters of ideas are called up in con-

nexion, and that a peculiar connexion, marked by the copula. To have two clusters of ideas, to know that they are two, and to believe that they are two, this is nothing more than three expressions for the same thing. To know that two clusters are two clusters, and to know that they are either the same, or different, is the same with having them. In this case, then, as in that of the belief of events, in sense and memory, the belief and the evidence are the same thing.

Belief of the conclusion of a syllogism, is preceded by two other beliefs There is belief of the major proposition ; belief of the minor proposition ; by the process immediately above explained, in which the evidence and the belief are the same thing. These are the antecedent. There is, thirdly, belief of the conclusion, this is the consequent. The process of this belief has been so recently explained, that I do not think we need to repeat it. In this case, it is sometimes said, that the two premises are the evidence ; sometimes it is said, that the ratiocination is the evidence ; in the former of these applications of the word evidence, the belief of the concluding proposition of the syllogism is not included ; in the last, it is. The ratiocination is the belief of all the three propositions ; and, in this acceptation of the word, the evidence and the belief are not considered as two things, but one and the same thing. This, however, is only a difference of naming. About the particulars named, there is no room for dispute.[110]

---

[110] This chapter on Evidence is supplementary to the chapter on Belief, and is intended to analyse the process of weighing and balancing opposing grounds for believing.

Evidence is either of individual facts (not actually perceived by oneself), or of general truths. The former is the only case to which much attention is paid in the present chapter; which very happily illustrates it, by the case of navigators having to decide on the existence or non-existence of inhabitants in a newly discovered island. The process of balancing the evidence for and against, is depicted in a very lively manner. Let us see whether the mental facts set down in the exposition, are precisely those which take place.

When the sailors have seen prints of a foot, resembling those of a man, the idea is raised of a man making the print. When they afterwards see a monkey, whose feet leave traces almost similar, the idea is also raised of a monkey making the print, and the state of their minds, the author says, is doubt. Of this state he gives the following analysis: " There is here a " double association with the print of the foot. There is the " association of a man, and there is the association of a " monkey. First, the print raises the idea of a man, but the " instant it does so, it raises also the idea of a monkey. The " idea of the monkey, displacing that of the man, hinders the " first association from the fixity which makes it belief; and " the idea of man, displacing that of monkey, hinders the " second association from that fixity which constitutes belief."

This passage deserves to be studied; for without having carefully weighed it, we cannot be certain that we are in complete possession of the author's theory of Belief.

There are two conflicting·associations with the print of the foot. The picture of a man making it, cannot co-exist with that of a monkey making it. But the two may alternate with one another. Had the association with a man been the only association, it would, or might (for on this point the author is not explicit) have amounted to belief. But the idea of the monkey and that of the man alternately displacing one another, hinder either association from having the fixity which would make it belief.

This alternation, however, between the two ideas, of a monkey making the footprint and of a man making it, may very well take place without hindering one of the two from being accompanied by belief. Suppose the sailors to obtain conclusive evidence, testimonial or circumstantial, that the prints were made by a monkey. It may happen, nevertheless, that the remarkable resemblance of the foot prints to those of a man, does not cease to force itself upon their notice : in other words, they continue to associate the idea of a man with the footsteps ; they are reminded of a man, and of a man making the footsteps, every time they see or think of them. The double association, therefore, may subsist, and the one which does not correspond with the fact may even be the most obtrusive of the two, while yet the other conception may be the one with which the men believe the real facts to have corresponded.

All the rest of the exposition is open to the same criticism. The author accounts very accurately for the presence of all the ideas which the successive appearance of the various articles of evidence arouses in the mind. But he does not shew that the belief, which is ultimately arrived at, is constituted by the expulsion from the mind of one set of these ideas, and the exclusive possession of it by the other set. It is quite possible that neither of the associations may acquire the "fixity" which, according to the apparent meaning of the author, would defeat the other association altogether, and drive away the conception which it suggests ; and yet, one of the suppositions may be believed and the other disbelieved, according to the balance of evidence, as estimated by the investigator. Belief, then, which has been already shewn not to require an inseparable association, appears not to require even "fixity"— such fixity as to exclude the idea of the conflicting supposition, as it does exclude the belief.

The problem of Evidence divides itself into two distinguishable enquiries: what effect evidence ought to produce, and what determines the effect that it does produce : how our belief ought to be regulated, and how, in point of fact, it is regulated. The first enquiry—that into the nature and probative force of evidence : the discussion of what proves what, and of the precautions needed in admitting one thing as proof of another—are the province of Logic, understood in its widest sense : and for its treatment we must refer to treatises on Logic, either inductive or ratiocinative. All that would be in place here, reduces itself to a single principle : In all cases, except the case of what we are directly conscious of (in which case, as the author justly observes, the evidence and the belief are one and the same thing)—in all cases, therefore, in which belief is really grounded on evidence, it is grounded, in the ultimate result, on the constancy of the course of nature. Whether the belief be of facts or of laws, and whether of past facts or of those which are present or future, this is the basis on which it rests. Whatever it is that we believe, the justification of the belief must be, that unless it were true, the uniformity of the course of nature would not be maintained. A cause would have occurred, not followed by its invariable effect ; an effect would have occurred, not preceded by any of its invariable causes ; witnesses would have lied, who have always been known to speak the truth ; signs would have proved deceptive, which in human experience have always given true indication. This is obvious, whatever case of belief on evidence we examine. Belief in testimony is grounded on previous experience that testimony is usually conformable to fact : testimony in general (for even this may with truth be affirmed) ; or the testimony of the particular witness, or the testimony of persons similar to him. Belief that the sun will rise and set to-morrow, or that a stone thrown up into the air will fall back, rests on experience that this has been invariably the case, and reliance that what has hitherto occurred will continue to occur hereafter. Belief in a fact vouched for by circumstantial evidence, rests on experience that such circumstances as are ascertained to exist in the case, never exist unaccompanied by the given fact. What we call evidence, whether complete or incomplete, always consists of facts or events tending to convince us that some ascertained general truths or laws of nature must have proved false, if the conclusion which the evidence points to is not true.

Belief on evidence is therefore always a case of the generalizing process; of the assumption that what we have not
directly experienced resembles, or will resemble, our experience.
And, properly understood, this assumption is true; for the
whole course of nature consists of a concurrence of causes, producing their effects in a uniform manner; but the uniformity
which exists is often not that which our first impressions lead
us to expect.   Mr. Bain has well pointed out, that the generalizing propensity, in a mind not disciplined by thought, nor
as yet warned by its own failures, far outruns the evidence, or
rather, precedes any conscious consideration of evidence; and
that what the consideration of evidence has to do when it
comes, is not so much to make us generalize, as to limit our
spontaneous impulse of generalization, and restrain within just
bounds our readiness to believe that the unknown will resemble
the known.   When Mr. Bain occasionally speaks of this propensity as if it were instinctive, I understand him to mean, that
by an original law of our nature, the mere suggestion of an
idea, so long as the idea keeps possession of the mind, suffices
to give it a command over our active energies.   It is to this
primitive mental state that the author's theory of Belief most
nearly applies.   In a mind which is as yet untutored, either by
the teachings of others or by its own mistakes, an idea so
strongly excited as for the time to keep out all ideas by which
it would itself be excluded, possesses that power over the
voluntary activities which is Mr. Bain's criterion of Belief;
and any association that compels the person to have the idea
of a certain consequence as following his act, generates, or
becomes, a real expectation of that consequence.   But these expectations often turning out to have been ill grounded, the unduly
prompt suggestion comes to be associated, by repetition, with
the shock of disappointed expectation; and the idea of the
desired consequent is now raised together with the idea not of
its realization, but of its frustration : thus neutralizing the
effect of the first association on the belief and on the active
impulses.   It is in this stage that the mind learns the habit of
looking out for, and weighing, evidence.   It presently discovers

that the expectations which are least often disappointed are those which correspond to the greatest and most varied amount of antecedent experience. It gradually comes to associate the feeling of disappointed expectation with all those promptings to expect, which, being the result of accidental associations, have no, or but little, previous experience conformable to them : and by degrees the expectation only arises when memory represents a considerable amount of such previous experience; and is strong in proportion to the quantity of the experience. At a still later period, as disappointment nevertheless not unfrequently happens notwithstanding a considerable amount of past experience on the side of the expectation, the mind is put upon making distinctions in the kind of past experiences, and finding out what qualities, besides mere frequency, experience must have, in order not to be followed by disappointment. In other words, it considers the conditions of right inference from experience ; and by degrees arrives at principles or rules, more or less accurate, for inductive reasoning. This is substantially the doctrine of the author of the Analysis. It must be conceded to him, that an association, sufficiently strong to exclude all ideas that would exclude itself, produces a kind of mechanical belief; and that the processes by which this belief is corrected, or reduced to rational bounds, all consist in the growth of a counter-association, tending to raise the idea of a disappointment of the first expectation : and as the one or the other prevails in the particular case, the belief, or expectation, exists or does not exist, exactly as if the belief were the same thing with the association. It must also be admitted that the process by which the belief is overcome, takes effect by weakening the association ; which can only be effected by raising up another association that conflicts with it. There are two ways in which this counter-association may be generated. One is, by counter-evidence ; by contrary experience in the specific case, which, by associating the circumstances of the case with a contrary belief, destroys their association with the original belief. But there is also another mode of weakening, or altogether destroying, the belief, without adducing contrary experience : namely, by merely recognising the insufficiency of the existing experience ; by reflecting on other instances in which the same amount and kind of experience have existed, but were not followed by the expected result.   In the one mode as in the other, the process of dissolving a belief is identical with that of dissolving an association ; and to this extent—and it is a very large extent—the author's theory of Belief must be received as true.

I cannot, however, go beyond this, and maintain with the author that Belief is identical with a strong association ; on account of the reason already stated, viz. that in many cases— indeed in almost all cases in which the evidence has been such as required to be investigated and weighed—a final belief is arrived at without any such clinging together of ideas as the author supposes to constitute it ; and we remain able to represent to ourselves in imagination, often with perfect facility, both the conflicting suppositions, of which we nevertheless believe one and reject the other.—*Ed.*

APPENDIX.

*(From "An Examination of Sir William Hamilton's
Philosophy.")*

THE PSYCHOLOGICAL THEORY OF THE BELIEF
IN AN EXTERNAL WORLD.

WE have seen Sir. W. Hamilton at work on the question of
the reality of Matter, by the introspective method, and, as it
seems, with little result.   Let us now approach the same subject by the psychological.   I proceed, therefore, to state the
case of those who hold that the belief in an external world is
not intuitive, but an acquired product.

This theory postulates the following psychological truths,
all of which are proved by experience, and are not contested,
though their force is seldom adequately felt, by Sir W.
Hamilton and the other thinkers of the introspective school.

It postulates, first, that the human mind is capable of Expectation.   In other words, that after having had actual
sensations, we are capable of forming the conception of Possible
sensations ; sensations which we are not feeling at the present
moment, but which we might feel, and should feel if certain
conditions were present, the nature of which conditions we
have, in many cases, learnt by experience.

It postulates, secondly, the laws of the Association of Ideas.
So far as we are here concerned, these laws are the following :
1st. Similar phænomena tend to be thought of together. 2nd.
Phænomena which have either been experienced or conceived

in close contiguity to one another, tend to be thought of
together. The contiguity is of two kinds; simultaneity, and
immediate succession. Facts which have been experienced or
thought of simultaneously, recall the thought of one another.
Of facts which have been experienced or thought of in immediate succession, the antecedent, or the thought of it, recalls
the thought of the consequent, but not conversely.   3rd. Associations produced by contiguity become more certain and
rapid by repetition.   When two phænomena have been very
often experienced in conjunction, and have not, in any single
instance, occurred separately either in experience or in thought,
there is produced between them what has been called Inseparable, or less correctly, Indissoluble Association : by which is
not meant that the association must inevitably last to the end
of life—that no subsequent experience or process of thought
can possibly avail to dissolve it ; but only that as long as no
such experience or process of thought has taken place, the
association is irresistible ; it is impossible for us to think the
one thing disjoined from the other.   4th. When an association
has acquired this character of inseparability—when the bond
between the two ideas has been thus firmly riveted, not only
does the idea called up by association become, in our consciousness, inseparable from the idea which suggested it, but the
facts or phænomena answering to those ideas come at last to
seem inseparable in existence : things which we are unable to
conceive apart, appear incapable of existing apart ; and the
belief we have in their coexistence, though really a product
of experience, seems intuitive.   Innumerable examples might
be given of this law.   One of the most familiar, as well as the
most striking, is that of our acquired perceptions of sight.
Even those who, with Mr. Bailey, consider the perception of
distance by the eye as not acquired, but intuitive, admit that
there are many perceptions of sight which, though instantaneous and unhesitating, are not intuitive.   What we see is a
very minute fragment of what we think we see.   We see artificially that one thing is hard, another soft.   We see artificially
that one thing is hot, another cold.   We see artificially that

what we see is a book, or a stone, each of these being not merely an inference, but a heap of inferences, from the signs which we see, to things not visible. We see, and cannot help seeing, what we have learnt to infer, even when we know that the inference is erroneous, and that the apparent perception is deceptive. We cannot help seeing the moon larger when near the horizon, though we know that she is of precisely her usual size. We cannot help seeing a mountain as nearer to us and of less height, when we see it through a more than ordinarily transparent atmosphere.

Setting out from these premises, the Psychological Theory maintains, that there are associations naturally and even necessarily generated by the order of our sensations and of our reminiscences of sensation, which, supposing no intuition of an external world to have existed in consciousness, would inevitably generate the belief, and would cause it to be regarded as an intuition.

What is it we mean, or what is it which leads us to say, that the objects we perceive are external to us, and not a part of our own thoughts? We mean, that there is concerned in our perceptions something which exists when we are not thinking of it ; which existed before we had ever thought of it, and would exist if we were annihilated ; and further, that there exist things which we never saw, touched, or otherwise perceived, and things which never have been perceived by man. This idea of something which is distinguished from our fleeting impressions by what, in Kantian language, is called Perdurability ; something which is fixed and the same, while our impressions vary ; something which exists whether we are aware of it or not, and which is always square (or of some other given figure) whether it appears to us square or round—constitutes altogether our idea of external substance.   Whoever can assign an origin to this complex conception, has accounted or what we mean by the belief in matter. Now all this, according to the Psychological Theory, is but the form impressed by the known laws of association, upon the conception or notion, obtained by experience, of Contingent Sensations ;

by which are meant, sensations that are not in our present consciousness, and individually never were in our consciousness at all, but which in virtue of the laws to which we have learnt by experience that our sensations are subject, we know that we should have felt under given supposable circumstances, and under these same circumstances, might still feel.

I see a piece of white paper on a table. I go into another room. If the phænomenon always followed me, or if, when it did not follow me, I believed it to disappear *è rerum naturâ*, I should not believe it to be an external object. I should consider it as a phantom—a mere affection of my senses: I should not believe that there had been any Body there. But, though I have ceased to see it, I am persuaded that the paper is still there. I no longer have the sensations which it gave me ; but I believe that when I again place myself in the circumstances in which I had those sensations, that is, when I go again into the room, I shall again have them ; and further, that there has been no intervening moment at which this would not have been the case. Owing to this property of my mind, my conception of the world at any given instant consists, in only a small proportion, of present sensations. Of these I may at the time have none at all, and they are in any case a most insignificant portion of the whole which I apprehend. The conception I form of the world existing at any moment, comprises, along with the sensations I am feeling, a countless variety of possibilities of sensation : namely, the whole of those which past observation tells me that I could, under any supposable circumstances, experience at this moment, together with an indefinite and illimitable multitude of others which though I do not know that I could, yet it is possible that I might, experience in circumstances not known to me. These various possibilities are the important thing to me in the world. My present sensations are generally of little importance, and are moreover fugitive : the possibilities, on the contrary, are permanent, which is the character that mainly distinguishes our idea of Substance or Matter from our notion of sensation. These possibilities, which are conditional certainties, need a special name to distinguish them from mere vague possibilities, which experience gives no warrant for reckoning upon. Now, as soon as a distinguishing name is given, though it be only to the same thing regarded in a different aspect, one of the most familiar experiences of our mental nature teaches us, that the different name comes to be considered as the name of a different thing.

There is another important peculiarity of these certified or guaranteed possibilities of sensation ; namely, that they have reference, not to single sensations, but to sensations joined together in groups. When we think of anything as a material substance, or body, we either have had, or we think that on some given supposition we should have, not some *one* sensation, but a great and even an indefinite number and variety of sensations, generally belonging to different senses, but so linked together, that the presence of one announces the possible presence at the very same instant of any or all of the rest. In our mind, therefore, not only is this particular Possibility of sensation invested with the quality of permanence when we are not actually feeling any of the sensations at all ; but when we are feeling some of them, the remaining sensations of the group are conceived by us in the form of Present Possibilities, which might be realized at the very moment. And as this happens in turn to all of them, the group as a whole presents itself to the mind as permanent, in contrast not solely with the temporariness of my bodily presence, but also with the temporary character of each of the sensations composing the group ; in other words, as a kind of permanent substratum, under a set of passing experiences or manifestations : which is another leading character of our idea of substance or matter, as distinguished from sensation.

Let us now take into consideration another of the general characters of our experience, namely, that in addition to fixed groups, we also recognise a fixed Order in our sensations ; an Order of succession, which, when ascertained by observation, gives rise to the ideas of Cause and Effect, according to what I hold to be the true theory of that relation, and is on any theory the source of all our knowledge what causes produce what effects. Now, of what nature is this fixed order among our sensations? It is a constancy of antecedence and sequence. But the constant antecedence and sequence do not generally exist between one actual sensation and another. Very few such sequences are presented to us by experience. In almost all the constant sequences which occur in Nature, the antecedence and consequence do not obtain between sensations, but between the groups we have been speaking about, of which a very small portion is actual sensation, the greater part being permanent possibilities of sensation, evidenced to us by a small and variable number of sensations actually present. Hence, our ideas of causation, power, activity, do not become connected in thought with our sensations as *actual* at all, save in the few physiological cases where these figure by themselves as the antecedents in some uniform sequence. Those ideas become connected, not with sensations, but with groups of possibilities of sensation. The sensations conceived do not, to our habitual thoughts, present themselves as sensations actually experienced, inasmuch as not only any one or any number of them may be supposed absent, but none of them need be present. We find that the modifications which are taking place more or less regularly in our possibilities of sensation, are mostly quite independent of our consciousness, and of our presence or absence. Whether we are asleep or awake the fire goes out, and puts an end to one particular possibility of warmth and light. Whether we are present or absent the corn ripens, and brings a new possibility of food. Hence we speedily learn to think of Nature as made up solely of these groups of possibilities, and the active force in Nature as manifested in the modification of some of these by others. The sensations, though the original foundation of the whole, come to be looked upon as a sort of accident depending on us, and the possibilities as much more real than the actual sensations, nay, as the very realities of which these are only the representations, appearances, or effects. When this state of mind has been arrived at, then, and from that time forward, we are never conscious of a present sensation without instantaneously referring it to some one of the groups of possibilities into which a sensation of that particular description enters; and if we do not yet know to what group to refer it, we at least feel an irresistible conviction that it must belong to some group or other; *i.e.* that its presence proves the existence, here and now, of a great number and variety of possibilities of sensation, without which it would not have been. The whole set of sensations as possible, form a permanent background to any one or more of them that are, at a given moment, actual; and the possibilities are conceived as standing to the actual sensations in the relation of a cause to its effects, or of canvas to the figures painted on it, or of a root to the trunk, leaves, and flowers, or of a substratum to that which is spread over it, or, in transcendental language, of Matter to Form.

When this point has been reached, the Permanent Possibilities in question have assumed such unlikeness of aspect, and such difference of apparent relation to us, from any sensations, that it would be contrary to all we know of the constitution of human nature that they should not be conceived as, and believed to be, at least as different from sensations as sensations are from one another. Their groundwork in sensation is forgotten, and they are supposed to be something intrinsically distinct from it. We can withdraw ourselves from any of our (external) sensations, or we can be withdrawn from them by some other agency. But though the sensations cease, the possibilities remain in existence; they are independent of our will, our presence, and everything which belongs to us. We find, too, that they belong as much to other human or sentient beings as to ourselves. We find other people grounding their expectations and conduct upon the same permanent possibilities on which we ground ours. But we do not find them experiencing the same actual sensations. Other people do not have our sensations exactly when and as we have them: but they have our possibilities of sensation; whatever indicates a present possibility of sensations to ourselves, indicates a present possibility of similar sensations to them, except so far as their organs of sensation may vary from the type of ours. This puts the final seal to our conception of the groups of possibilities as the fundamental reality in Nature. The permanent possibilities are common to us and to our fellow-creatures; the actual sensations are not. That which other people become aware of when, and on the same grounds, as I do, seems more real to me than that which they do not know of unless I tell them. The world of Possible Sensations succeeding one another according to laws, is as much in other beings as it is in me; it has therefore an existence outside me; it is an External World.

If this explanation of the origin and growth of the idea of Matter, or External Nature, contains nothing at variance with natural laws, it is at least an admissible supposition, that the element of Non-ego which Sir W. Hamilton regards as an original datum of consciousness, and which we certainly do find in our present consciousness, may not be one of its primitive elements—may not have existed at all in its first manifestations. But if this supposition be admissible, it ought, on Sir W. Hamilton's principles, to be received as true. The first of the laws laid down by him for the interpretation of Consciousness, the law (as he terms it) of Parcimony, forbids to suppose an original principle of our nature in order to account for phænomena which admit of possible explanation from known causes. If the supposed ingredient of consciousness be one which might grow up (though we cannot prove that it did grow up) through later experience; and if, when it had so grown up, it would, by known laws of our nature, appear as completely intuitive as our sensations themselves; we are bound, according to Sir W. Hamilton's and all sound philosophy, to assign to it that origin. Where there is a known cause adequate to account for a phænomenon, there is no justification for ascribing it to an unknown one. And what evidence does Consciousness furnish of the intuitiveness of an impression, except instantaneousness, apparent simplicity, and unconciousness on our part of how the impression came into our minds? These features can only prove the impression to be intuitive, on the hypothesis that there are no means of accounting for them otherwise. If they not only might, but naturally would, exist, even on the supposition that it is not intuitive, we must accept the conclusion to which we are led by the Psychological Method, and which the Introspective Method furnishes absolutely nothing to contradict.

Matter, then, may be defined, a Permanent Possibility of Sensation. If I am asked, whether I believe in matter, I ask whether the questioner accepts this definition of it. If he does, I believe in matter : and so do all Berkeleians. In any other sense than this, I do not. But I affirm with confidence, that this conception of Matter includes the whole meaning attached to it by the common world, apart from philosophical, and sometimes from theological, theories. The reliance of mankind on the real existence of visible and tangible objects, means reliance on the reality and permanence of Possibilities of visual and tactual sensations, when no such sensations are actually experienced. We are warranted in believing that this is the meaning of Matter in the minds of many of its most esteemed metaphysical champions, though they themselves would not admit as much : for example, of Reid, Stewart, and Brown. For these three philosophers alleged that all mankind, including Berkeley and Hume, really believed in Matter, inasmuch as unless they did, they would not have turned aside to save themselves from running against a post. Now all which this manœuvre really proved is, that they believed in Permanent Possibilities of Sensation. We have therefore the unintentional sanction of these three eminent defenders of the existence of matter, for affirming, that to believe in Permanent Possibilities of Sensation is believing in Matter. It is hardly necessary, after such authorities, to mention Dr. Johnson, or any one else who resorts to the *argumentum baculinum* of knocking a stick against the ground. Sir W. Hamilton, a far subtler thinker than any of these, never reasons in this manner. He never supposes that a disbeliever in what he means by Matter, ought in consistency to act in any different mode from those who believe in it. He knew that the belief on which all the practical consequences depend, is the belief in Permanent Possibilities of Sensation, and that if nobody believed in a material universe in any other sense, life would go on exactly as it now does. He, however, did believe in more than this, but, I think, only because it had never occurred to him that mere Possibilities of Sensation could, to our artificialized consciousness, present the character of objectivity which, as we have now shown, they not only can, but unless the known laws of the human mind were suspended, must necessarily, present.

Perhaps it may be objected, that the very possibility of framing such a notion of Matter as Sir W. Hamilton's—the capacity in the human mind of imagining an external world which is anything more than what the Psychological Theory makes it—amounts to a disproof of the theory. If (it may be said) we had no revelation in consciousness, of a world which is not in some way or other identified with sensation, we should be unable to have the notion of such a world. If the only ideas we had of external objects were ideas of our sensations, supplemented by an acquired notion of permanent possibilities of sensation, we must (it is thought) be incapable of conceiving, and therefore still more incapable of fancying that we perceive, things which are not sensations at all. It being evident however that some philosophers believe this, and it being maintainable that the mass of mankind do so, the existence of a perdurable basis of sensations, distinct from sensations themselves, is proved, it might be said, by the possibility of believing it.

Let me first restate what I apprehend the belief to be. We believe that we perceive a something closely related to all our sensations, but different from those which we are feeling at any particular minute; and distinguished from sensations altogether, by being permanent and always the same, while these are fugitive, variable, and alternately displace one another. But these attributes of the object of perception are properties belonging to all the possibilities of sensation which experience guarantees. The belief in such permanent possibilities seems to me to include all that is essential or characteristic in the belief in substance. I believe that Calcutta exists, though I do not perceive it, and that it would still exist if every percipient inhabitant were suddenly to leave the place, or be struck dead. But when I analyse the belief, all I find in it is, that were these events to take place, the Permanent Possibility of Sensation which I call Calcutta would still remain; that if I were suddenly transported to the banks of the Hoogly, I should still have the sensations which, if now present, would lead me to affirm that Calcutta exists here and now. We may infer, therefore, that both philosophers and the world at large, when they think of matter, conceive it really as a Permanent Possibility of Sensation. But the majority of philosophers fancy that it is something more; and the world at large, though they have really, as I conceive, nothing in their minds but a Permanent Possibility of Sensation, would, if asked the question, undoubtedly agree with the philosophers: and though this is sufficiently explained by the tendency of the human mind to infer difference of things from difference of names, I acknowledge the obligation of showing how it can be possible to believe in an existence transcending all possibilities of sensation, unless on the hypothesis that such an existence actually is, and that we actually perceive it.

The explanation, however, is not difficult. It is an admitted fact, that we are capable of all conceptions which can be formed by generalizing from the observed laws of our sensations. Whatever relation we find to exist between any one of our sensations and something different from *it*, that same relation we have no difficulty in conceiving to exist between the sum of all our sensations and something different from *them*. The differences which our consciousness recognises between one sensation and another, give us the general notion of difference, and inseparably associate with every sensation we have, the feeling of its being different from other things: and when once this association has been formed, we can no longer conceive anything, without being able, and even being compelled, to form also the conception of something different from it.

This familiarity with the idea of something different from *each* thing we know, makes it natural and easy to form the notion of something different from *all* things that we know, collectively as well as individually. It is true we can form no conception of what such a thing can be; our notion of it is merely negative; but the idea of a substance, apart from its relation to the impressions which we conceive it as making on our senses, *is* a merely negative one. There is thus no psychological obstacle to our forming the notion of a something which is neither a sensation nor a possibility of sensation, even if our consciousness does not testify to it; and nothing is more likely than that the Permanent Possibilities of sensation, to which our consciousness does testify, should be confounded in our minds with this imaginary conception. All experience attests the strength of the tendency to mistake mental abstractions, even negative ones, for substantive realities; and the Permanent Possibilities of sensation which experience guarantees, are so extremely unlike in many of their properties to actual sensations, that since we are capable of imagining something which transcends sensations, there is a great natural probability that we should suppose these to be it.

But this natural probability is converted into certainty, when we take into consideration that universal law of our experience which is termed the law of Causation, and which makes us mentally connect with the beginning of everything, some antecedent condition, or Cause. The case of Causation is one of the most marked of all the cases in which we extend to the sum total of our consciousness, a notion derived from its parts. It is a striking example of our power to conceive, and our tendency to believe, that a relation which subsists between every individual item of our experience and some other item, subsists also between our experience as a whole, and something not within the sphere of experience. By this extension to the sum of all our experiences, of the internal relations obtaining between its several parts, we are led to consider sensation itself—the aggregate whole of our sensations—as deriving its origin from antecedent existences transcending sensation. That we should do this, is a consequence of the particular character of the uniform sequences, which experience discloses to us among our sensations. As already remarked, the constant antecedent of a sensation is seldom another sensation, or set of sensations, actually felt. It is much oftener the existence of a group of possibilities, not necessarily including any actual sensations, except such as are required to show that the possibilities are really present. Nor are actual sensations indispensable even for this purpose ; for the presence of the object (which is nothing more than the immediate presence of the possibilities) may be made known to us by the very sensation which we refer to as its effect. Thus, the real antecedent of an effect—the only antecedent which, being invariable and unconditional, we consider to be the cause—may be, not any sensation really felt, but solely the presence, at that or the immediately preceding moment, of a group of possibilities of sensation. Hence it is not with sensations as actually experienced, but with their Permanent Possibilities, that the idea of Cause comes to be identified : and we, by one and the same process, acquire the habit of regarding Sensation in general, like all our individual sensations, as an Effect, and also that of conceiving as the causes of most of our individual sensations, not other sensations, but general possibilities of sensation. If all these considerations put together do not completely explain and account for our conceiving these Possibilities as a class of independent and substantive entities, I know not what psychological analysis can be conclusive.

It may perhaps be said, that the preceding theory gives, indeed, some account of the idea of Permanent Existence which forms part of our conception of matter, but gives no explanation of our believing these permanent objects to be external, or out of ourselves. I apprehend, on the contrary, that the very idea of anything out of ourselves is derived solely from the knowledge experience gives us of the Permanent Possibilities. Our sensations we carry with us wherever we go, and they never exist where we are not; but when we change our place we do not carry away with us the Permanent Possibilities of Sensation : they remain until we return, or arise and cease under conditions with which our presence has in general nothing to do. And more than all—they are, and will be after we have ceased to feel, Permanent Possibilities of sensation to other beings than ourselves. Thus our actual sensations, and the Permanent Possibilities of sensation, stand out in obtrusive contrast to one another : and when the idea of Cause has been acquired, and extended by generalization from the parts of our experience to its aggregate whole, nothing can be more natural than that the Permanent Possibilities should be classed by us as existences generically distinct from our sensations, but of which our sensations are the effect.

The same theory which accounts for our ascribing to an aggregate of possibilities of sensation, a permanent existence which our sensations themselves do not possess, and consequently a greater reality than belongs to our sensations, also explains our attributing greater objectivity to the Primary Qualities of bodies than to the Secondary. For the sensations which correspond to what are called the Primary Qualities (as soon at least as we come to apprehend them by two senses, the eye as well as the touch) are always present when any part of the group is so. But colours, tastes, smells, and the like, being, in comparison, fugacious, are not, in the same degree, conceived as being always there, even when nobody is present to perceive them. The sensations answering to the Secondary Qualities are only occasional, those to the Primary, constant. The Secondary, moreover, vary with different persons, and with the temporary sensibility of our organs ; the Primary, when perceived at all, are, as far as we know, the same to all persons and at all times.

END OF VOL. I.